THE I TATTI
RENAISSANCE LIBRARY

James Hankins, General Editor

Gianfrancesco Pico della Mirandola
LIFE OF
GIOVANNI PICO DELLA MIRANDOLA

Giovanni Pico della Mirandola
ORATION

ITRL 93

Gianfrancesco Pico della Mirandola
✦ ✦ ✦
LIFE OF
GIOVANNI PICO DELLA MIRANDOLA

Giovanni Pico della Mirandola
✦ ✦ ✦
ORATION

EDITED AND TRANSLATED BY
BRIAN P. COPENHAVER
in consultation with Michael J. B. Allen

THE I TATTI RENAISSANCE LIBRARY
HARVARD UNIVERSITY PRESS
CAMBRIDGE, MASSACHUSETTS
LONDON, ENGLAND
2022

Series design by Dean Bornstein

First printing

Library of Congress Cataloging-in-Publication Data

Names: Pico della Mirandola, Giovanni Francesco, 1470–1533, author. |
Pico della Mirandola, Giovanni, 1463–1494, author. | Copenhaver, Brian P.,
editor, translator. | Allen, Michael J. B., editor, translator. | Pico della
Mirandola, Giovanni, 1463–1494. De hominis dignitate. | Pico della
Mirandola, Giovanni, 1463–1494. De hominis dignitate. English.
Title: Life of Giovanni Pico della Mirandola / Gianfrancesco Pico della
Mirandola. Oration / Giovanni Pico della Mirandola ; edited and translated
by Brian P. Copenhaver in consultation with Michael J. B. Allen.
Other titles: I Tatti Renaissance library ; 93.
Description: Cambridge, Massachusetts : Harvard University Press, 2022. |
Series: I Tatti Renaissance library; 93 | Includes bibliographical references
and index. | Editorial matter in English; text in Latin and English.
Identifiers: LCCN 2020057341 | ISBN 9780674023420 (cloth)
Subjects: LCSH: Pico della Mirandola, Giovanni, 1463–1494. |
Philosophical anthropology—Early works to 1800. |
Philosophy, Renaissance—Early works to 1800.
Classification: LCC B785.P54 P52613 2022 | DDC 195—dc23
LC record available at https://lccn.loc.gov/2020057341

Contents

❦❦❦

Introduction

ཨོཾ

Two Picos

Giovanni Pico, Count of Mirandola and Concordia, became an international celebrity not long ago — after World War II. He was already well known and had been, with ups and downs, for centuries. In the second half of the twentieth century, textbooks written for college students in North America enlarged his fame and amplified it into stardom, complete with pictures, personality, and a stunning résumé. Cascades of exuberant adjectives — "brilliant," "dazzling," "gargantuan," and so on — flooded the pages about him and about a speech on human dignity. Some praised him as a philosophical visionary — a Christian of the fifteenth century who peered across the ages through veils of creed and custom to foresee a movement whose founder, when he launched it in 1945, named it "existentialism" and called it "a humanism."[1] This was the atheist humanism of Jean-Paul Sartre.

Pico's path to celebrity was crooked, however. Before existentialist humanism there was an episode with actual idealism, the court philosophy of the Italian Leader who led his nation to disgrace in World War II. Before that, some commentators were bored or baffled or both by the prince's writings. Until after World War I, few detected any praise of human dignity in them. Jacob Burckhardt, in the middle of the nineteenth century, was the transformative exception — transformative in the fullness of time. While he lived, however, many critics stuck with the verdict handed down by Voltaire in the middle of the previous century: he had written Pico off as a dupe of medieval Svengalis. Along the same lines, also dismissive but with more heat, other Enlightened judges found Pico guilty of *Schwärmerei*: 'enthusiasm' is too mild to render this word for delirious religiosity. A diagnosis of cankered piety all but erased earlier sketches of the prince — as maudlin as the pictures on holy cards that nuns used to give to children.[2]

For many years Pico was a plaster saint who never quite lost his halo. Archaeologists of culture will find one pious image made as recently as 1842, but Pico hagiography goes back to 1496, when Gianfrancesco Pico — Giovanni's nephew but not much younger — published a *Life* of his uncle. This short biography was the first substantial piece of prose about him, and its contents informed later authors, who used the information in quite varied ways. This was Gianfrancesco's main contribution to his uncle's celebrity: he supplied a template for fame that others could bend to their own purposes and distort.[3]

Gianfrancesco had his own projects, of course, often compatible with Giovanni's though not identical: the nephew and the uncle were close, but they were different people. Like many Christians of their day, both disliked Jews and hoped to convert them. But the elder Pico's attitudes were stronger and stranger. In his notorious *900 Conclusions*, he wrote that

> any Hebrew Kabbalist, following principles and statements of the knowledge of Kabbalah, is forced inevitably to grant precisely — without addition, subtraction or variation — what the Catholic faith of Christians declares about the Trinity and each divine person, Father, Son and Holy Spirit.[4]

What was a "Hebrew Kabbalist"? And why would a Kabbalist be compelled to accept doctrines that were not just denied by Jews but repugnant to them? When the *Conclusions* were printed in the last weeks of 1486, Gianfrancesco — still in his teens — could have had no idea. Ten years later, as he finished his *Life*, his grasp of Kabbalah was not much better — though by that time he had seen the Latin word *Cabala* in his uncle's papers and printed works.[5]

When Gianfrancesco used his *Life* to introduce two volumes of his uncle's writings, he left the *Conclusions* out. For a loyal son of the Church, this was a reasonable choice: Pope Innocent VIII had condemned the whole book in 1487, and more than thirty years passed before Leo X allowed all of Giovanni's works to be published. Leo gave his consent personally to Gianfrancesco in 1519, along with the right to print books in Mirandola. The new press started operations right away, but its first product was Gianfrancesco's own work *On the Real Causes of Calamities in Our Times*. Also in 1519, however, Giovanni's *Opera omnia* appeared elsewhere—in Venice. Despite the title, the *Conclusions* were still missing from this and other editions, and until 1532 there was no replacement for the two original printings of the theses, few of which survived the heresy hunters.[6]

Although Leo gave permission to publish all of Giovanni's works, neither Gianfrancesco nor anyone else at the time ventured to print the *Conclusions*. If they were published, how would the Vatican react? Innocent had forbidden "the book that contained the conclusions," as Gianfrancesco acknowledged. But he also insisted that the contents were "freed of criminal stain" by his uncle's *Apology*. He said this in 1496, in an evasive account of the scandal. Twenty years later, the pot was still boiling. Johann Reuchlin's *Art of Kabbalah* came out in 1517, and by 1520 he too was condemned: Pope Leo had deserted him. But one of Reuchlin's supporters in the Curia was an expert Hebraist and a powerful cardinal, Egidio da Viterbo. During the same years, when Martin Luther was also causing trouble, Egidio urged his own weird Kabbalah on Leo as papal policy. The situation was fluid.[7]

One thesis of every seven in the *Conclusions*, 119 out of 900, comes under the heading of "Kabbalah"—not counting dozens of mentions or allusions in propositions about other topics. The book has two major divisions, and Kabbalah comes last in both — in the place of honor, like a bishop at the end of a procession. Did Gianfrancesco leave the *Conclusions* out because Kabbalah was so conspicuous in it? He knew Kabbalah was a high-value target because Innocent's condemnation had singled out a thesis about it — though this was not Giovanni's only provocation. And if the Kabbalah in the *Conclusions* was Gianfrancesco's motive for excluding it, was he afraid or bewildered or both? Maybe he thought that his uncle's propositions gave comfort to Judaizers, or maybe he just concluded that no one could understand such obscure theses.[8]

In any case, Gianfrancesco's *Life* opens a collection that omits the *Conclusions* but includes the speech that we — unlike Pico — know as an *Oration on the Dignity of Man*. He wrote the *Oration* to introduce the *Conclusions*, but his nephew's editorial decision cut the theses off from the speech that their author had connected with them. Several times in the *Oration*, the orator mentions "theorems" to be proposed in the *Conclusions*: he clearly saw the book and the speech as tools for the same task. Either Gianfrancesco missed his uncle's intentions, which seems unlikely, or he meant to seal off his other writings — including the *Oration* — from a book that he found embarrassing for himself and his relative and too risky to make public.[9]

This is the fact of the matter: Gianfrancesco left the *Conclusions* unpublished while publishing the *Oration* in a collection introduced by his *Life*. Both the speech and the biography are presented here, in this edition, in the same way — apart from the *Conclusions*: this reflects the situation in 1496 and respects Gianfrancesco's choice, even though his decision blocked understanding of the speech for many years. Today, with access to all the relevant texts in many versions, readers can move from one work to another as needed.

The Silence of the Frogs

On the day after Christmas of 1476, Galeazzo Maria Sforza, fifth Duke of Milan, was murdered in church, leaving his sickly son in charge—Gian Galeazzo. The boy's uncle Ludovico, called the Moor, needed only three years to take control. But Gian Galeazzo lived until 1494, weakened by intermittent fever, reckless eating, and too much wine, as court physicians and astrologers tried to lighten his diet and restore his health. While the patient lingered, the Moor was duke in all but name. Like his Sforza ancestors, he consulted astrologers about personal problems and affairs of state, asking the diviners when to travel, when to stay home, when and whom to marry, when to consummate a marriage, when and whom to fight, and when to make peace. When Gian Galeazzo finally wasted away, and Ludovico was supreme in Milan, some assumed that he had his nephew poisoned or bewitched and that all the fuss about astrology was just another dodge.

Science and technology were state business in Ludovico's Milan: Leonardo da Vinci, who painted his mistress, also designed war machines. But the great engineer was contemptuous of alchemy and astrology—merely "a way to make a living from fools." Although Ludovico was no fool, his judgment was erratic, and he kept experts on the payroll to cover his faults by pointing at the skies. Even astrologers were not always mistaken: sometimes they got lucky and made the right predictions. And when they were wrong, the intricate celestial geometry in their charts provided calculations to hide under. Ambrogio Varesi da Rosate was Ludovico's top consultant on the heavens. Leonardo showed him designs for new weapons, and Ambrogio foretold the strategies of his enemies.

By the time Ludovico's nephew died and he ruled alone in Milan, the duke had encouraged foreigners—Charles VIII of France and the (soon-to-be) emperor Maximilian I — to meddle in Italian affairs. He hoped to gain by the threat of intervention, but the French actually invaded. In November 1494, just a month after Gian Galeazzo succumbed, they entered Florence, disrupting Italian politics and undermining Milan's power. Ludovico took astrological advice from Ambrogio before making his moves, even though the adviser warned that political outcomes were hard to predict in enough detail to be reliable.[10]

A few months after Florence fell to the French, Marsilio Ficino remembered "the day when great King Charles of France entered our city." The day was November 17, also when "our Mirandola left us, afflicting the learned with grief nearly as great as the joy that the King meanwhile provided." Writing to a subject of the king about their mutual friend — the deceased Giovanni Pico — Ficino was polite about the new realities as he listed

> what Pico had written already or what he was writing then. He wrote a *Hexameron*, an *Apology* and a work *On Being and the One* as well as some letters. When still young and passionate, he wrote something about love, but he condemned it when his judgment ripened. . . . Every day he would labor at three things — concord between Aristotle and Plato, commentaries on sacred scripture and refutations of the astrologers.[11]

Ficino probably knew that these texts were being edited by Pico's nephew, Gianfrancesco. In March 1496, a year after Ficino sent his letter to France, Gianfrancesco named the same writings by his uncle in the same order, "a *Heptaplus*, an *Apology*, a treatise *On Being and the One* and several others, never given the praise they deserve but now made public." After this description of the first volume of his edition, he promised a second where "the rest of his writings will be published, . . . especially proofs against the plague of astrology."

Gianfrancesco made this promise to Ludovico Sforza on March 1, 1496, in a letter dedicating his two volumes to the duke. Ludovico was offered books by Giovanni Pico with titles — we still use the same ones — that may have been meaningless to the duke. He could not have seen Ficino's similar statement nor would he have missed what neither list includes — the text now known as an *Oration on the Dignity of Man*. Otherwise, without giving a title, Ficino declared his disapproval of "something about love" that his friend had written, probably the unpublished *Commento*. Likewise, Gianfrancesco supplied no title for Pico's "proofs against the plague of astrology" — a topic sure to get the duke's attention.[12]

Ludovico and Gianfrancesco had already discussed astrology, perhaps as early as January 1491 at festivities for Ludovico's marriage to Beatrice d'Este, from the powerful family of Gianfrancesco's mother. The wedding day was selected to align with favorable stars and planets. But five years later, in his letter of dedication, Gianfrancesco insisted that the "theories of astrologers are the purest nonsense," and he remembered joking with the duke about stargazers and frogs. Astrologers were liars, he complained, always croaking like the noisy frogs heard in Italy. Elsewhere these beasts were mute, however, as in Macedonia, and astrologers ought to be silenced in the same way by Giovanni Pico's proofs. Despising astrologers as fake prophets was a lesson that Gianfrancesco also learned from Girolamo Savonarola, the preacher who inspired him even more than his uncle. Early in 1494 the friar warned that "divination and that branch of astrology that seems to predict future contingents are utterly false and . . . the cause of much superstition and heresy."[13]

Gianfrancesco married two months after attending the duke's wedding. When Giovanni died three years later, this new alliance supplied resources that enabled his nephew to acquire family lands and alienate his own younger brothers: new real estate would expand their tiny principality, not too far from mighty Milan.

Within a few years, their father died, the brothers went to war, and in 1502 they drove Gianfrancesco out of Mirandola. A few months earlier, he had dedicated a treatise *On Imagination* to the emperor Maximilian. This short philosophical study—about a faculty of the soul—was the first of many with implications for religion. His most famous book appeared in 1520, the *Weighing of False Pagan Learning against True Christian Teaching*, which turned skepticism into fideism at the outbreak of the Reformation.[14]

In 1533 a nephew, while assaulting the family castle, killed Gianfrancesco and his son. At the time of the murder, the pious philosopher was working on a *Compendium of Amazing Things Done by the Venerable Servant of God, Caterina da Racconigi*, a charismatic nun who had been exchanging letters with him for six years. Her gift of prophecy impressed him, just as Savonarola's predictions had won him over in the 1490s with sermons that mesmerized and agitated Florence. For the lords of Mirandola, the friar was a celebrity with local roots—born in Ferrara and briefly active there, only thirty miles from the family estates. In 1497 Gianfrancesco began to publish in his defense, and neither the preacher's arrest in 1498 nor his execution halted the propaganda. Through the rest of his career, Gianfrancesco kept revising a *Life of Savonarola* that remained unpublished for more than a century after the author's death. This *Life* was hagiography, the story of a saint—as Gianfrancesco saw it close up.[15]

Gianfrancesco was a 'weeper' (*piagnone*) moved to repent by the friar's apocalyptic lamentations. But by the spring of 1494, politics had put Savonarola and the Duke of Milan at odds. Although Ludovico was pleased when the French threatened Italy, he changed his mind when they marched from Genoa through Florence and entered Naples. Turning against the French also turned the Moor against Savonarola. The friar saw his prophecies vindicated when Florence fell: just as he promised, God's scourge came down on the Florentines when armies descended on their city from France. In this moment of disaster on the Arno and shame for Italy, Gianfrancesco commended the "extraordinary goodwill of this magnanimous monarch" because the French king sent physicians to care for his dying uncle.

In the year after Pico's death, Ficino was politic about the French triumph, but a year later Gianfrancesco was effusive. And his remarks to the Duke of Milan were impolitic in two ways. First, in a letter meant to please, he denounced astrology to a prince and distant relative whose astrological obsession was notorious. Then, in the biography of his uncle introduced by the letter — while producing other writings to fortify Savonarola's Francophile jeremiads — he praised the king of France, who had caused the duke so much trouble, for "courtesy and generosity" to a closer relative.[16]

The biography of Giovanni Pico came first in the book that Gianfrancesco dedicated to Ludovico — a collection of writings (*Commentationes*) by his uncle. The dedication to the duke was printed after this table of contents:

Writings by Giovanni Pico della Mirandola contained in this volume and preceded by a Life composed by Gianfrancesco, son of the Illustrious Prince Galeozzo Pico.

A heptaplus on the work of the six days of Genesis.

An apology in thirteen questions.

A treatise on being and the one with various objections and replies.

A very elegant oration.

Several letters.

On a prayer to God in elegiac verse.

Testimonies of his life and teaching.

In the next days disputations against astrology will come out with several other things pertaining both to sacred scripture and to philosophy.

In his first volume, Gianfrancesco sent the duke all these items except the last. But he focused his dedicatory letter on his own *Life* of his uncle and named the models that he followed. Since Giovanni was remarkably learned and a master of ancient wisdom, his nephew thought about imitating a pagan biography, like the *Life of Plotinus* by Porphyry that Ficino had translated and published in 1492. As in the *Life of Savonarola*, however, a secular story was not Gianfrancesco's project. He honored his uncle with a hagiography — a family hagiography — where commemoration took second place to edification. He told Ludovico that his examples were patristic lives of saints, like Ambrose, Anthony, and Martin. Just to memorialize these holy men was right and useful, but not as valuable as supplying ideal types of penitent piety for the faithful to emulate.[17]

Gianfrancesco wrote to make his uncle an example of saintliness. His *Life*, a text of 8,200 words, uses only ten or so to describe an "oration of the utmost elegance" printed in the *Commentationes* — the first collection of Pico's works. Virtues that Gianfrancesco saw in the speech were "penetrating intelligence," "abundant learning," and "very fruitful eloquence," but he said nothing about its content. Elsewhere in the same volume, in a headnote to the *Oration* and letters, he said only a little more. The orator

> very cleverly unlocked many recondite teachings of the ancients previously shrouded in fables and riddles. He strove mightily and with charms of oratory to show how the poetic theology of ancient sages was handmaid to the mysteries of

our theology, and he tried to attract people to intellectual combat by unraveling various tangles of both.

Later he abandoned such conflicts as "trivial squabbles and preliminaries to serious study." The speech written to set the stage for them had come from "the eagerness of youth," though scholars often admired it as "the pinnacle of learning and eloquence." To explain his errors away, Pico had to publish an *Apology*, but he always kept the speech "private and shared it with no one but his friends." Gianfrancesco—perhaps the first person besides the orator himself to see a complete text of the *Oration*—thought that Giovanni was ashamed of this juvenile mistake that he had kept out of print, and the nephew said nothing to downplay his uncle's regrets. He was proud, however, that his relative was "especially fierce against devotees of divinatory astrology." Unlike those false prophets, Savonarola—in Gianfrancesco's eyes—was an authentic visionary.[18]

A Saint for Weepers

The sanctimonious *Life* by Pico's nephew that barely mentions the *Oration* shaped his uncle's story for centuries—or rather the many stories about him. They changed over time, often condensed in works of reference or contained in books on other subjects. The *Life* was especially attractive to Anglophone readers in an abridged translation by Thomas More. A later English writer compressed More's version again in 1723 in order to compare Pico with Pascal—another saint of the intellect. In those early days of the Enlightenment, hagiography still prevailed in tales about the prince. But an eminent historian of philosophy, Jacob Brucker, eventually revoked his sainthood, and Brucker was seconded by Voltaire: both mocked him for religious delirium and passed their derision on to other enlightened critics. Accordingly, in 1824, another British writer called Pico's theories "humbug" while reviewing a biography from 1805: the author of this earlier work could find no "regular account of his life, if we except the brief and unsatisfactory production of his nephew." Nonetheless, Walter Pater used More's rendering of the *Life* to meditate on Pico after 1866. In 1890 a deluxe edition of the same English *Life* expected that most readers would "owe such interest as he [Pico] excites in them to Mr. Pater's charming sketch."

Talking about Pico, the editor concluded that "few will ever care to follow his eager spirit through the labyrinths of recondite speculation." This assessment was still common just before World War I when a new edition of the *Encyclopedia Britannica* snubbed the prince: his books were no longer "read with much interest, but the man himself is still interesting" — the man whose story had been told by Gianfrancesco and retold by Thomas More.[19]

A new-model Pico was in production, however, renovated for a twentieth-century audience by talented writers with many readers — Burckhardt, Pater, and John Addington Symonds. They said little about Pico, but they said it forcefully. And Burckhardt added a durable theme to the usual stories: human dignity. This idea, as derived from Kant's moral philosophy, was less than a century old, but post-Kantian historians of philosophy had been debating it while discussing Pico. Then Burckhardt linked the prince with dignity again in unforgettable prose, eventually inspiring philosophers — Ernst Cassirer, Eugenio Garin, Giovanni Gentile, and Paul Kristeller — to embroider the connection.[20]

Since Gianfrancesco Pico, his uncle's first biographer and the first editor of his writings, knew Giovanni so well, the nephew's silence about the idea of dignity in those writings is stunning — from our perspective. But our Pico was created by Cassirer, Garin, Gentile, and Kristeller, and Gianfrancesco's Pico was not that personage. His *Life* of his uncle barely mentions the *Oration* and pays no attention at all to the idea of dignity. Was the younger Pico obtuse about the elder Pico's achievement? Was he blinded by *piagnone* zeal? One approach to these questions starts with the *Life* that Gianfrancesco wrote.[21]

Thinking of his uncle, who imitated the "deeds of the greatest saints," Gianfrancesco took his bearings from hagiographers, singling out the *Life of Ambrose* by Paulinus of Milan. He mentions the same work in his dedication to Ludovico, though it was a good fit for his purposes only at the start and the finish of his biography. This early example of its genre, written shortly after Ambrose died in 397, has little structure. The main events are contests with Arians and demons against a backdrop of Imperial intrigue — a long way from Pico's world.

Born into privilege — just as the prince would be in his day — Ambrose set an example by shunning ecclesiastical office. His family was Christian, so he needed no conversion — the axial event in the *Life* of Pico. The two stories converge at birth and after death. Strange signs were seen when both were infants. The later *Life* opens with an omen, a hagiographical motif, like the bees that buzzed around baby Ambrose in his cradle — a *topos* borrowed from pagan biography. Paulinus "made much of this portent," according to Gianfrancesco, because the saint's writings were like honey for the saved. To close his biography, the nephew reported other marvels at the time of his uncle's death — no surprise, considering the genre. Less expected is that Pico's passing — with the grief it caused and lessons to be learned — does not end the tale. Gianfrancesco added a coda — about a seventh of his text — to rationalize Savonarola's harsh response to the prince's death and attack the friar's opponents. The story by Paulinus also ends with complaints about detractors. But they were enemies of Ambrose, not critics of his critics.[22]

Gianfrancesco concluded by praising a preacher who had just announced to Florence that his uncle was a sinner who deserved to burn in Purgatory. This cold ending aside, the rest of the *Life* is a predictable expression of piety, both familial and religious. The narrative can be divided into seven parts, though what outline the author had in mind is unknown: organization is not strongly marked in this *Life*. After a few preliminaries, the nephew proceeds through (1) Pico's birth and early life, (2) his failed plan to debate nine hundred theses in Rome, (3) the resulting crisis and conversion, (4) his writings and unfinished projects, (5) his way of thinking, speaking and writing, (6) his character and conduct, and (7) his final illness and death.[23]

The *Life* is unbalanced by the bookishness of both Picos — more talk and less action than might be expected in a biography. Except for the hero's birth and death and some remarks by Savonarola, not much is dated, even roughly or implicitly. Some events datable by other sources — like the papal condemnation of thirteen of Pico's theses in March 1487 — were too shameful to record in detail. At least one scandal was not reported at all: Giovanni's botched escapade with Margherita, a married woman and a Medici cousin, in May 1486. Other events not assigned a time by Gianfrancesco, such as a meeting with Dominicans at Ferrara in May 1492, made for happier memories.[24]

Gianfrancesco's account supplied a foundation and a framework for later legends about Pico, while leaving room for slippage. The nephew's three comments on his uncle's appearance, for example, were the first of many. Near the beginning of the story, he calls the prince "striking and aristocratic — tall and proud in stature, with smooth skin, generally good looks, complexion on the pale side with a nice mix of ruddiness, eyes blue-gray and alert, blond hair left natural, teeth white and even." Later, from a passage about sins of the flesh, we learn that "because of his handsome body and good looks . . . many women fell passionately in love with him." (Was one of them the unmentioned Margherita?) The descriptions are enthusiastic, and the details suggest eyewitness experience. Yet "generally good looks" was understated by later norms. Paolo Giovio printed an ugly picture of Pico while crediting him with "all the very rarest gifts of body and mind." Walter Pater's word portrait, citing no evidence at all, was even more splendid — "not unlike the archangel Raphael, as the Florentines of that age depicted him."[25]

Another part of the legend was the prince's amazing memory. Gianfrancesco supported this piece of his story with anecdotal information: "once he heard any verses recited, he would astonish everyone by repeating them both forward and backward." Since all educated people in those days knew poems by heart, the biographer's recollection was recognizable and communicable — effective testimony about an "unfailingly retentive memory."[26]

Pico showed his genius early in poetry and oratory, before trying canon law in Bologna at the age of fourteen — a roughly datable milestone. After two years he left the law for other "learned schools not only in Italy but also in France," and he stayed "with those teachers for seven years." The dating is only annual, however, and Pico was born late in the year, so the chronology is shaky, though the main sequence holds up. The narrative puts Pico in Rome, with doom impending, in 1486. But nothing is said about which "learned schools" he had attended or who taught him. Although Gianfrancesco knew that Giovanni was an expert on "modern theologians" — medieval masters like Aquinas and Scotus — all we learn about his university career is that it happened. In Padua he made a formative contact with a Jewish teacher, Elia del Medigo. Elia was still in touch with Pico in 1486, but his nephew, seventeen at the time, may not have known about him and would not have trusted Elia's Averroism — a position later called "ungodly" in Gianfrancesco's *Life*.[27]

Pico's biographer whitewashed the catastrophe in Rome. The thugs who poisoned his uncle's well were jealous, he charged, furious to be shown up by a rich young aristocrat who went to the "world's leading city to test his genius . . . in many subjects untouched by our people for many centuries." An objective observer might have called this adventuring rash. Although Gianfrancesco claimed to have "quite a few" endorsements of Giovanni's theses, he cited only one, by the bishop of Reggio, Bonfrancesco Arlotti, who was a client of his Este relatives. And he never acknowledged that Pope Innocent VIII condemned some of the propositions, only that the pope was pressured to forbid "the book that contained the conclusions" even though some had been "misrepresented" and their "Catholic meaning" was "freed of criminal stain" by the *Apology*.[28]

Pico proved his innocence in that book, according to Gianfrancesco, who called it a "many-sided and refined work . . . loaded with information about things worth knowing." The biographer looked carefully at it, citing his uncle's plea to "friends and enemies, learned and unlearned, to read the *Apology* but to leave his little book of undeveloped conclusions unread." Belittling the theses as a "school exercise for academic purposes" was technically correct.[29]

But another remark about the theses was false: that their author aimed "not to spread them around everywhere on street corners but to debate them in a private meeting with a small number of experts." Gianfrancesco simply repeated what Giovanni said in the *Apology*. But the last item printed on the last page of the *Conclusions* was an advertisement. Pico told his readers that the theses would be "disputed only after Epiphany," but in the meantime they were to be sent to "all the universities of Italy. And if any philosopher or theologian, even from distant parts of Italy, wishes to come to Rome and debate, the same Lord who intends to dispute also promises to cover the costs of travel." Gianfrancesco confirmed that Giovanni "posted all of this at the same time in public places as a quick way to make it known." Yet he also claimed that his uncle disliked debates "held in public to make a show of learning, capture popular attention or get applause from the ignorant." In fact, Pico's speech was meant to do exactly that: his plans were extravagant and noisy, and the braying surely provoked the Vatican.[30]

Despite special pleading about his uncle's failure in Rome, Gianfrancesco understood its devastating force, which let the young genius

> see how far he had strayed from the true path. Until then, in fact, he longed for glory while false love fueled his fires and the wiles of women stirred them up. . . . But when dissension woke him up, he pulled his spirit back from dissolute indulgence and turned to Christ. . . . Ceasing to care for the trifling, glittering glory that he had desired, he began seeking God's glory and the welfare of the Church with his whole mind.

Pico's turnabout was total, in other words, and for this effect the biographer could point to a proportionate cause.[31]

Less convincing is Gianfrancesco's framing of the next part of the biography. After a few paragraphs on the penitent Pico comes a long section on his finished writings and unfinished projects. "During his twenty-eighth year," says Gianfrancesco, he "offered up his first fruits in God's temple—a *Heptaplus*." The chronology is about right, once again. But why "first fruits"? Roberto Salviati, who was close to both Picos, said the same when he wrote a letter of dedication for the book to Lorenzo de' Medici. Yet not only the *Conclusions*, which Gianfrancesco disliked and left out of his collection, but also the *Apology*, which he liked and reprinted, were already in print before the *Heptaplus*.

Maybe the biographer saw the later book as his hero's first offering to God *after* he had changed his life and abandoned the "Hebrew mysteries that he had dug up." Although Gianfrancesco praised the *Apology*, much of it would have been closed to him without help from the *Conclusions*, whose Jewish secrets were entirely beyond his reach. By not putting the *Conclusions* in his 1496

collection, he authorized the practice — long continued — of insu-
lating Pico's other writings from them. With the *Oration* isolated
from the theses that it introduced, its account of magic and Kabbalah was exotic and inscrutable. Bewildered readers could have
been helped by the *Conclusions*, but Gianfrancesco's decision not to
publish kept the book out of circulation for nearly half a century.[32]

Gianfrancesco also left the *Commento* out of his Latin collection, perhaps because it was a vernacular text or because it was
linked with a genre — love poetry — renounced by his saintly uncle.
The nephew's attitude to this little work is hard to divine from his
vague description: "Platonic materials condensed by Pico in the
volgare, . . . untangling the theology of the ancients, . . . unlocking
ideas concealed . . . in allegories and riddles." The *Commento* (if
this was the work in question) inspired Gianfrancesco to consider
making a Latin version "so that the towering teaching on such
matters of so great a mind will not be readily available for any ordinary person to look at." He thought about Latinizing the *Commento* so that *fewer* people would understand it — in striking agreement with his uncle's belief, proclaimed in the *Oration*, that genuine
wisdom must be kept secret.[33]

As reviewed in the *Life*, the works produced after the *Conclusions*
had a purpose in common: "seeking God's glory and the welfare of
the Church." Since Holy Scripture sparked this intention in Pico,
his *Heptaplus* was clearly valuable: it was a book about the Bible.
But the ancient theology studied by the *Commento* also foreshad-
owed Christian doctrine, according to Gianfrancesco, and even
Pico's most abstract work, a metaphysical treatise *On Being and the
One*, taught "how to live and correct one's behavior." Since reform-
ing souls and saving them promoted God's glory in this abysmal
world, Pico's publicizing of his own talent was also righteous,
meant to teach "rules of good conduct" to his admirers.[34]

Pico's unfinished projects, as Gianfrancesco described them,
dwarfed the finished products. The central item was apologetic,

attacking "seven enemies of the Church." The only surviving part is Pico's longest work by far, the *Disputations Against Divinatory Astrology*, which filled the whole second volume of Gianfrancesco's 1496 collection. Since this was just one of seven parts, the complete undertaking would have been immense. The seven enemies to be defeated were infidels, idolaters, and Muslims, also Christians who Judaized or disobeyed the Church or defiled the faith with superstition or had "faith but no works." Others had counted fewer than a hundred heresies propagated by such reprobates, but Pico detected twice as many, and Jews were prime targets.[35]

What Pico left unfinished was hard for his editor to handle. He had "written all over the page and blotted out old comments while adding new ones, so that I found some discarded and erased, others put down piecemeal in patches, everything mixed up, disorganized and a tangled mess." Out of thirteen books against the astrologers planned by Giovanni, Gianfrancesco thought he had salvaged only twelve that were finished. Maybe everything else about the seven enemies was unreadable, or maybe the editor's own zeal focused him on the astrological part of the enterprise. In his house and his uncle's, he also came across "various small pieces," including prayers, devotional works, and comments on the Psalms. "About fifty letters turned up as well . . . together with a speech that he would have given in Rome if the debate had happened." Gianfrancesco called the speech thoughtful, elegant, and rich, but its message made no discernible impression on him.[36]

Turning from particular works and projects to ideas, attitudes, and style, Gianfrancesco claimed that Pico's eloquence was "free of affectation." Yet in diction, syntax, and structure—from an age that loved artifice in Latin—it would be hard to find any piece of prose more artful than the *Oration*. True, Pico could write in the simpler way of medieval philosophers, and the Latin of his devotional fragments is sometimes plain, in keeping with his aims and audience. But when Gianfrancesco claimed that he favored "prose

by writers who did not stuff their Latin with flowers of eloquence,"
his point, only half-true, was more moral than aesthetic—to corroborate his uncle's pious simplicity. One use of language that
stirred Gianfrancesco was Savonarola's preaching—fiery, repeti-
tive, incantatory, carefully structured, sometimes intellectualized
yet straight from a burning heart.[37]

Although Gianfrancesco worried that "those who love antiquity" would balk at his comments on Pico's style, he acknowledged the prince's experience with texts written in unclassical Latin. Of
all those "said to write disputatiously, in the French manner, he
usually praised Thomas Aquinas more than the others." When
pressed on this choice, according to the nephew, the uncle confirmed that Aquinas was the best of the scholastics because the
"foundation of truth that Thomas relied on was firmer." Traces of
Albert the Great, Scotus, and other scholastics also showed up in
the papers that Gianfrancesco read, from which he reported that
his uncle despised the "swill for the Pigheaded called 'calculations.'"
But these *Suiseticae quisquiliae* were specialties of only one school—
Richard and Roger Swynshead, William Heytesbury, and the
other 'Calculators' at Oxford's Merton College—and the younger Pico understood that the elder was "well-informed in these
matters."[38]

Gianfrancesco's philosophical information, at the time he wrote
the *Life*, is harder to gauge. Later, as the mature author of a *Weighing of False Pagan Learning*, his reliance on Aquinas—a supernatu-
ralist Aristotelian—was subtle and sophisticated. But the biographer, when he was younger by almost twenty-five years, seems
simply to have sheltered under Thomas's name to guarantee his
uncle's orthodoxy. To defend the *Conclusions*, he insisted that "only
three or four propositions out of a thousand disagree with
Thomas." His defense was specious, however.

Some of Pico's theses aim to resolve disagreements between
philosophers—Thomas and Scotus, for example—and a doctri-

naire Thomist might see such applications of concordism as disloyal, though Gianfrancesco, evidently, did not. But he should have worried about two other theses described as "disagreeing with the usual philosophy." According to one of them, "If Thomas says that, according to Aristotle, the Intelligences are in a genus, he will oppose himself no less than Aristotle." The other thesis is parallel: "If Thomas says that, according to Aristotle, there are accidents in the Intelligences, he will contradict not only Aristotle but himself." If these two propositions were Gianfrancesco's only concerns, he could rest assured that only a careful reader of a nearly unobtainable book, the *Conclusions*, would ever spot them.

But every spectator of his uncle's Roman scandal would recognize other deviations from the Thomist line. One was the first thesis condemned in 1487: "Christ did not truly, and as far as real presence is concerned, descend to Hell, as proposed by Thomas and on the shared approach, but only in regard to the effect." Another statement, also called "quite different from the usual way of talking about theology," was the third condemned thesis: "Neither the cross of Christ nor any image should be adored with the adoration of worship, even in the way that Thomas proposes." Pico's public disagreements with Thomas may have been few, just as Gianfrancesco said. But these two theses — on notoriously sensitive points of dogma — helped make him a heretic by papal declaration.[39]

Pico's expertise in scholastic philosophy was a problem for Gianfrancesco because friends of his uncle, like Ermolao Barbaro and Poliziano, were renowned lovers of antiquity who might see such expertise as shameful. When Barbaro — the prince's opponent in a genteel debate about philosophical language — jeered with his own name at "modern barbarian philosophers" and called them "enemies of eloquence," he implied that Latinity was the only serious issue, that proper diction, grammar, and syntax could solve the merely philosophical problems.

Like Barbaro, Gianfrancesco knew better. But cheap shots at the Merton Calculators were irresistible — exploiting a tradition of invective started by Petrarch and sustained by Salutati, Bruni, and their many imitators. The "sophistical fallacies" that they railed against "may not have been widely known in Italy," according to Gianfrancesco. But he was mistaken. By the time his uncle began touring the universities, Swineshead and his colleagues had been famous names in Italy as philosophical 'moderns' for most of a century — despite Bruni's swooning at the very sound of them: "even their names horrify me!" Even so, Gaetano da Thiene, Paul of Venice, and other distinguished teachers saw great promise — for theology as well as natural philosophy — in the efforts at Merton to quantify quality.

One label for their theory was 'intension and remission' of forms, and the forms in question were like the valor of a knight or the red on his shield: by intension, the color and the virtue would become stronger, by remission weaker. Philosophers at Merton applied arithmetic and geometry to such changes in order to measure them. But a thesis by Pico challenged the Calculators, declaring that "moderns who use mathematics to discuss natural problems have destroyed the foundations of natural philosophy." He registered his objection, however, in a long section (eighty-five theses) of the *Conclusions* "about mathematics," which lists seventy-four "questions that he promises to answer with numbers." Plainly, Pico did not oppose the Calculators in order to exclude mathematics from philosophy: he wanted to replace their modernism with his own mathematical novelties, displayed at length in the *Conclusions*, where he also placed theses throughout the book to challenge the Calculators from Merton.[40]

How well Gianfrancesco understood Giovanni's response to these British thinkers is unclear from his few sentences on the topic, before offering a general assessment of his uncle's intellectual achievement. Pico had mastered "every branch of knowledge," he maintained, as if each were "his own specialty," and he attributed this universal mastery to superlative gifts of mind, memory, energy, detachment, and wealth. As for riches, he saw no conflict between "contempt for worldly things" and the money spent to buy so many books. Concluding that the prince was a "divine man," he then turned from his "mental powers" to the "splendid faculties of soul" that guided his actions. And he followed up with a catalog of virtues — generosity, humility, kindness, serenity, and simplicity — presented in anecdotes about saintly asceticism.

Gianfrancesco knew that Giovanni did penance by punishing himself, and he described what he witnessed. A disciple of Savonarola would have had no qualms about a sinner giving "alms from his own body." The friar had been warning the Florentines for years that God would scourge them for their sins. Pico "beat his own flesh, especially on those days that mark Christ's suffering and death. . . . I have often seen the lash with my own eyes," said Gianfrancesco, and he prayed that it would "all be for the glory of God."[41]

This prince who went so hard on himself was generous to others — to the point of irresponsibility: sometimes he seemed not to care whether he was a good steward of the riches that God gave him. When Gianfrancesco wrote that his uncle transferred "all his inherited property" to him, he could not say "whether this was a sale or a gift." It was a sale, in fact, for thirty thousand ducats. Such sums and such distinctions about real estate had consequences — prosperity or poverty for future generations. When Pico sold his lands, some of the proceeds went to the poor, but the rest went "to improve lands that would support him and his household." No longer tied to property but still assured of an income, he could live in learned detachment like a prince of the intellect. And it seems that he did, eating little but maintaining "some of his former luxury in silver plate and the dishes served." He made these arrangements "three years before he died" — hence in 1491.[42]

Giovanni had changed his ways some years earlier, according to Gianfrancesco, after a "dazzling illumination." In the nephew's narrative, this visitation came around the time of the *Apology*, which was probably printed late in the spring of 1487. Pico's defense was truculent, however, and within months the Vatican multiplied the charges against him. The accused thought it best to leave for France, and he was arrested there (politely) in January 1488. Gianfrancesco made none of this clear. After calling the pertinacious *Apology* submissive to Church and pope, he went on to praise the *Heptaplus*, probably published in the fall of 1489.[43]

This too was a book that Pico "perfected by his genius." Its contents were "mysteries of our Christian theology" and "lofty teachings by philosophers." If Gianfrancesco saw anything Jewish in them, he failed to say so. Discussing Pico's other projects, he noticed "stipulations from Jewish scholarship" as well as "slanders" by "utterly unredeemable Jews." He also described "Hebrew mysteries" in the *Conclusions*, even identifying them as "Kabbalah — a secret tradition of Hebrew doctrines": there was simply too much Kabbalah in the *Conclusions* to ignore. And even though the *Heptaplus* never mentions the word 'Kabbalah,' its method reflects the Kabbalist *Conclusions* that Gianfrancesco chose not to publish. Jewish arcana may have mystified him, but he could not have missed the exegesis at the end of the *Heptaplus*, where the Hebrew letters in the Bible's first word — *bereshit*, "in-the-beginning" — conceal sacred meanings.

By Gianfrancesco's reckoning, the *Heptaplus* had to be a good book because it came two years after Pico's conversion. And yet a book about Kabbalah could not be good for Christians. A way out was silence about Hebrew hermeneutics — the route taken by Gianfrancesco's hagiography, whose pivotal moment is Pico's conversion. The *Heptaplus* is certainly quieter about Kabbalah than the *Oration* and *Conclusions*: but this was prudence, not a conversion. Maybe the prince had grown up a little, learning better judgment from humiliation and acquiring discretion with age — without any sudden transformation. In worldly matters, such as what to do with his wealth, he was still changing in 1491 while holding on to "some of his former luxury."[44]

In these years, as Savonarola entranced Giovanni's friends and Gianfrancesco, Giovanni himself was also captivated. Did he ever experience conversion, however? As far as we know, no holy lightning ever struck his *piagnone* nephew, who kept battling his family to protect his patrimony after Savonarola was gone. He enraged his mother by not sharing it with his brothers. But uncle Giovanni's deeds and misdeeds far surpassed his own. The prince's short life was so grand a spectacle that only drama — hagiographic drama — could do it justice. His sins were so grave that only the hand of God could turn the sinner around. Accordingly, the great turning — as recounted by Gianfrancesco — came swiftly, like a "beam of light." But the illumination, in all likelihood, was pious family fiction.[45]

The narrative seems more grounded where secondary characters, not just the protagonist, were well known to the author. The mother angered by Gianfrancesco was the (illegitimate) sister of the Duke of Ferrara, Ercole I d'Este, who intervened with the reluctant Giovanni when the Dominicans wanted him to perform in the duke's (and Savonarola's) city. Since the biographer knew the actors in this scene, he was well placed to comment on Pico's state of mind when he "finally complied with the many entreaties from this prince" — Ercole, also Gianfrancesco's uncle — "in order to humor someone who had no small regard for him."[46]

Savonarola was another celebrity from Ferrara watched closely by Gianfrancesco. Otherwise, in the turbulent fall of 1494, he might not have reported what the friar said to a crowd in the Duomo shortly after Giovanni died. Pico's last day was a Monday, November 17. On the following Sunday, November 23, Savonarola added remarks about the prince to his sermon in the Duomo.

Gianfrancesco used more than three hundred words to record these comments in Latin, in a version three times longer than the surviving *volgare* text, which may be just a sketch of a longer performance. Since Gianfrancesco was traveling when Pico died, he missed the deathbed events that he reported in detail, but he claimed to have heard the friar talk about his uncle "with my own ears."

Savonarola's statement about Pico, in Gianfrancesco's telling, is by far the longest attributed or attributable to anyone in the *Life*—including Pico himself. His death and its sequel take up more than a fifth of the story, and the finale is all about the friar, who ended his sermon by revealing a secret to the Florentines,

> which before now I had not wanted to tell you because until ten hours ago I was not sure enough. I believe that each of you knew Count Giovanni of Mirandola, who was staying here in Florence and died a few days ago. I tell you that his soul—because of prayers from the friars, also some good works that he did in this life and other prayers as well—is in Purgatory: pray for him. He was slow and did not enter religion while he lived, as had been hoped, and so he is in Purgatory.

Although the core of the *volgare* text matches Gianfrancesco's version, the biographer's Latin report is longer and harsher. He confirmed that his uncle was burning in Purgatory for ingratitude to the Savior who had called him to enter a religious order. He agreed that Giovanni lived most of his life in sin among sinners, that he "kept company with those who dwell in Kedar"—banished from the Promised Land—and that he was still suffering in their company. This was the nephew's closing statement about a beloved relative.[47]

Gianfrancesco's main purpose at the end of the *Life* was to defend Savonarola's verdict—that Pico deserved to be in torment temporarily because he ignored God's summons for too long. At the last, in the fog of fever that killed him, he had seen the Virgin and heard her promise salvation — eventually. Savonarola too was a visionary, who spoke as God's prophet to confirm Mary's message but also the prince's suffering. The preacher had enemies, however, and some laughed at his threats. Gianfrancesco watched them "straining to hold back their jokes," but he believed the friar and endorsed his severity. He agreed that miscreants like his uncle, even if their sins were venial, should be "tortured with fire for failing to keep a vow to enter the religious life." He was unbending and unfeeling about the obligation to love God above all, though he loved his family too and wrote to defend its good name. In the end, however, Savonarola's reputation and harsh faith meant more to him.[48]

If you were the Duke of Milan and no friend of the friar in 1496, when the younger Pico sent you his *Life*, what would you think of his treatment of the elder Pico? In human terms — and at the time when Ludovico (or an adviser) could have read the *Life* — surprise at the biographer's attitude would have been natural. A different problem about the *Life* — no mention of an *Oration on the Dignity of Man* — looks obvious to us but would have raised no questions in Milan because Gianfrancesco sent the duke nothing that would alert him to Pico's previously unpublished speech or link it with human dignity.

Chameleons Are Not What They Seem

Put yourself in Ludovico's place. Would you care about a nameless oration that Gianfrancesco treated as he did? If you or an adviser read it, would either of you think it was about human dignity? If your expert was a lover of Latin literature, he might have known Giannozzo Manetti's book on *dignitas* and earlier discussions of the topic, from Lotario dei Segni's medieval polemic to Bartolomeo Fazio's more recent treatment. But the *Oration* says nothing about Fazio, Lotario, Manetti and their debates. What message was Pico not sending?[49]

Looking at the speech on the Latin pages of Gianfrancesco's edition, a reader would see a few words in Greek—also pages where the printer left empty spaces. Since Greek letters could be printed, a different script or scripts must have required the blanks. Maybe the missing words were Hebrew, or maybe Aramaic or Syriac, both known at the time as 'Chaldean.' One passage with blanks mentions Chaldean, which comes up several times in the *Oration*—also in the *Conclusions* at the head of theses on "Zoroaster and his Chaldean Expositors."[50]

To the learned in Gianfrancesco's Italy, Zoroaster and the Chaldeans were well known—unlike Euanthes, or Evantes, an unidentified Persian cited on human variability by Giovanni's speech. What the Persian says—that human appearances are many and fleeting—is a gloss on a saying "of the Chaldeans," but this is only an empty space in the printed Latin. Pico supplied a translation, however: "man is a living thing whose nature is variable, manifold and inconstant." For the exotic words, what should fill the blanks? If Pico (or a scribe) wrote in Hebrew letters, the words (reading right to left) could have been

ברנש הוא חי מטבע משתנה ונדד ומחלפת גרמה כה וכה

But a partial manuscript of the speech (*F* in this edition) uses an even more exotic script—Ethiopic.

በረናሠ ሀ ሐየ ሚጠበዐ ሚሠታኔ ዌናዷዷ ሚመሐለጸተ ጋረማሀ
ከ ወከ

Reading the manuscript from left to right, after *chaldaeorum* in the center of the top line, the first four characters (in a modern typeface) are በ ረ ና ሠ, corresponding to ב ר נ ש in Hebrew script, also

MS Florence, Biblioteca Nazionale Centrale, Palatino 885, fol. 147r

from left to right, and to B R N SH in the Roman alphabet — translated near the end of the third line as *homo* or 'human being.'[51]

The *Oration* printed in Gianfrancesco's collection displayed no Ethiopic or Hebrew writing. And while Ludovico ruled in Milan, readers of the published *Conclusions* (not many, given the book's fate) would have seen only Roman script: all they had were the crude original printings. Besides "Chaldean expositors," however, they would also have found "Hebrew sages" and "Kabbalist conclusions" in the same part of the book. On the next page there were blanks again. Context would suggest filling them with Hebrew names of God. Further reconnaissance of the *Oration*, starting with the empty places, would locate Hebrew wisdom, including Kabbalah, in the speech as well. Gianfrancesco acknowledged the Kabbalah in the *Conclusions*, but he excluded the book from his 1496 collection. He included the *Oration* but gave no hint that it discusses — at some length — the same Jewish secrets. Did he want to suppress them, or did he just not care about the speech? He certainly saw nothing noteworthy in it about human dignity.[52]

Gianfrancesco's silence echoes the whispers of *dignitas* in Giovanni's speech. The Latin word occurs there only twice, once for *rank* — angelic, not human — and once for the *value* of philosophy. It corresponds in neither place to 'dignity' in English, the Italian *dignità*, the German *Würde*, or their cousins in other vernaculars:

these usages are modern, grown from Immanuel Kant's Enlightenment philosophy.[53]

Pico had been dead for ten years when an editor, Jerome Emser, first used *dignitas* to title the *Oration*. A theologian with a classical education, Emser was teaching at Erfurt in 1504 when he finished a new edition of Pico's works — the third since Gianfrancesco's collection of 1496. In a letter to the printer, Johann Prüs of Strasbourg, he explained that he had emended the 1496 text — "the first and authentic original from Mirandola's hand." Jacob Wimpfeling, also a learned theologian and employed at the time by a bishop in Strasbourg, contributed a letter to readers, printed on the same page with Gianfrancesco's commendation of the *Disputations*. Since Wimpfeling and Gianfrancesco had met in 1502, the younger Pico may have encouraged the Strasbourg edition. Wimpfeling's *ad lectorem* mentions the *Disputations* and the elder Pico's letters but not his speech.[54]

The index (*regestum*) that Emser made for his edition fills six leaves with more than seven hundred entries. This detailed record of what seemed noteworthy in Pico's *Opera* is the first such response by any reader to the prince's writings and the first comprehensive treatment since Gianfrancesco's. Emser's nineteen entries for astrology and astronomy and eleven for planets reflect both the large size of the *Disputations* and the strong attractions of its polemic against stargazing for readers like himself and Wimpfeling. *Philosophia*, given eleven entries, also caught his attention, but he was less curious about *magia* and *magus* (four entries) or *Cabala* (three entries), and there is no sign at all of *dignitas* in his *regestum*.[55]

The title page of Emser's edition, like the front of Gianfrancesco's collection, lists an *Oratio quaedam elegantissima* with no *dignitas*. But inside his book — after reprinting Gianfrancesco's headnote to the speech, the letters, and the minor works — Emser gave this text a new and persistent title: *Oratio Ioannis Pici Mirandulae*

Abdala saracenus
Mercurius   **1**

Hois dignitas

Persæ
Dauid

Homo vltimo creatus
Moses
Timæus

Hoi cōia q̃ alijs ꝓpria

Oratio Ioānis Pici Mirandulæ cōcordiæ Comitis. De hoīs dignitate.
Egi patres Colendissimi in Arabū monumētis interrogatū Abdalam saracenū: quod in hac quasi Mūdana scæna: admirandū maxime spectaretur. Nihil spectari hoīe admirabilius respōdisse. Cui sentētiæ illud Mercurij adstipulat. Magnū o asclepi miraculū est homo. Horū dictorū rōne cogitāti mihi nō satis illa faciebant: quæ multa de humanæ naturæ præstātia afferunt a multis: esse hominē creaturarū internuntiū superis familiarē: regē inferiorū sensuū per spicacia rōnis indagine: intelligētiæ lumine: naturæ interpretē. Stabilis æui & fluxi tēporis interstitiū: &(quod Persæ dicūt)mūdi copulam: immo hymenæū: ab angelis. Te ste Dauide paulo deminutū. Magna hæc quidē/ sed nō principalia. i. quæ summæ ad mirationis priuilegiū sibi iure vendicēt. Cur eni nō ipsos angelos & beatissimos cæli choros magis admiremur? Tandē intellexisse mihi sum visus cur foelicissimū; ꝓindeq; dignū omni admiratione aial sit homo. Et quæ sit demū illa cōditio quā in vniuersi serie sortitus sit: nō brutis modo/ sed astris: sed vltramūdanis mētibus iuidiosam. Res supra fidē & mira. Quidni? Nā & ꝓpterea magnū miraculū & admirādū ꝑfecto aial iure homo & dici & existimat. Sed quænā ea sit audite patres: & benignis auribus ꝑ vestra humanitate hāc mihi operā cōdonate. Iam sūmus Pater architectus deus: hanc quā vīdemus mūdanā domū diuinitatis tēplū augustissimū archanæ legibus sapiētiæ fabrefecerat. Supercælestē regionē mētibus decorarat: æthereos globos æternis animis vegetarat: excremētarias ac feculentas inferioris mūdi partes omnigena aialium turba cōplerat. Sed ope cōsumato: desiderabat artifex esse aliquē qui tanti operis rōne ppenderet: pulchritudinē amaret: magnitudinē admiraret. Iccirco iam rebus oibus(ut Moses Timæusq; testant absolutis)de ꝓducendo hoīe postremo cogitauit. Verū nec erat in archytypis unde noua sobolem effingeret: nec in thesauris: quod nouo filio hæreditariū largiret: nec in subsellijs totius orbis: vbi vniuersi cōtēplator iste sederet. Iam plena oīa: oīa summis: medijs: infimisq; ordinibus fuerāt distributa. Sed nō erat paternæ potestatis in extrema fœtura: quasi effœtā defecisse: nō erat sapiētiæ. Consilij inopia in re necessaria fluctuasse. Non erat beneficij amoris: ut qui in alijs esset diuinæ liberalitatē laudaturus in se illam damnare cogeret. Statuit tandē optimus opifex: ut cui dari nihil propriū poterat cōmune esset quicqd priuatū singulis fuerat. Igit hominē accepit indiscretæ opus imaginis: atq; in mūdi positū meditullio:sic est alloquutus. Nec certam se

Jacob Emser Gives Pico's Speech a Title: Strasbourg, 1504

Concordiae Comitis de hominis dignitate. He repeated only part of it at the end of the speech: *Ioannis Mirandulae orationis de homine.*[56]

After 1517, Emser's attacks on Luther and Zwingli made him a prominent champion of Rome. Wimpfeling, who tolerated the classics while defending scholastic theology, also stayed with Rome and intervened on Emser's behalf with the Reformers. Centuries later, other German scholars made Pico a doctrinal football in squabbles about Zwingli. They had no way to know that the prince's celebrity would soon peak, in the twentieth century, because of a work given its false title by Emser, a forgotten ancestor of their craft. Italians who dismissed this fuss about Zwingli and Pico as Teutonic *campanilismo* might also have been chastened.[57]

How much thought Emser gave to the new title is unclear. *Dignitas* never occurs in the most original part of his edition, the *regestum*, which was also the most laborious for him. But someone also made additions to words and phrases printed in the margins of his base text, Gianfrancesco's collection, where the first three marginal notes are *Abdala sarracenus*, *Mercurius*, and *hominis dignitas*, probably supplied by Benedetto Faelli, Gianfrancesco's printer in Bologna. Since there is no *dignitas* in any of the places where Gianfrancesco himself names the speech—just *oratio quaedam elegantissima* on the first page of the book, *oratio elegantissima* in the headnote, and *oratio* in the *Life*—nothing that he wrote, including the biography, indicates that he thought of his uncle's *Oration* as a discussion of human dignity.

While preparing the speech for the press in 1504, Emser's publisher, Johann Prüs—or maybe Emser himself, following up his work on the *regestum*—was thinking about the human condition. Toward the end of the fourth paragraph, "man created last" is a new marginal note; then, "for man things are shared that belong to others" toward the end of the next paragraph; for the eighth paragraph, "man can change himself into any nature whatever"; and for the twentieth, "nature in man is double." The rest of the notes either repeat what was there in the 1496 edition or add no more anthropology.[58]

Preachers constantly discussed the human condition, however, whether as God's glorious creation or as corrupted by sin. On All Saints Day 1497, when Alexander VI heard Tommaso Inghirami preach joyfully in the Vatican, some of the preacher's words and ideas came from Pico's speech. Other papal orators serving Julius II and Leo X used bits of the same oratory in Lent for penitential sermons. Curial officials may have known about the speech, with or without reading it, before it was printed: some took part in Pico's inquest; others surely gossiped about it. Since borrowings happened as late as 1531, the *Oration* and its anthropology had at least a few powerful readers in Rome for more than thirty years. But no preacher who used the speech mentioned it or its author — probably because both were unmentionable in the Vatican. Outside those walls, the sermons — some unpublished — had little effect, and they did nothing to promote a speech that they could not name.[59]

The only Latin text of the *Oration* separately published in the pre-modern era appeared in Basel in 1530, expanding the title in a different direction than Emser indicated — referring not to *dignitas* but to "loftier mysteries of sacred and human philosophy." Meanwhile, the front-matter of the other five collected editions or reprints between 1498 and 1521 stayed with a bare *Oratio* or with Gianfrancesco's formulation: *Oratio quaedam elegantissima*. In 1557 the title at the front of a book finally became *De hominis dignitate* in a Basel collection and, in a Venice edition of the same year, *Oratio quam elegantissima de hominis celsitudine et dignitate*. In 1572 and 1601, two other early modern collections took the speech off the marquee: they no longer listed contents by title at the front.[60]

Emser's *de hominis dignitate* had already borne fruit, however: a *Very Elegant Oration on the High Nobility and Rank of Man* was advertised in 1557 at the front of the Venice edition. But the facts behind the flamboyant vocabulary were different: the first paragraphs of the speech — glossed in the Strasbourg edition with "man can change himself into any nature whatever" — are about freedom and change, not the dignity so prized in modern times. To be sure, two centuries after Pico died, Kant linked freedom inseparably with dignity in a theory of human personhood. Kant's ethics and metaphysics — enormously influential in his time and afterward — still color our conceptions of dignity. But the prince knew nothing about them. Moreover, no loyal Catholic — had such ideas been available at the time — could have accepted the moral autonomy and self-legislating freedom theorized by Kant, or even religious freedom from the Law as Luther would proclaim it.[61]

But in an audacious passage of the *Oration*, not repeated in the *Apology*, Pico put words in the Creator's mouth. God's insistent speaking in the first two chapters of Genesis — fifteen uses of *dicere* and *vocare* — was not enough for the prince. So he fictionalized his own divine address to Adam that promised liberation from any "definite nature confined within laws." Pico's fabricated God spoke his extra-biblical lines to an Adam who had not yet transgressed. But when he disobeyed, he became a "slave of sin" — in the plain words of Scripture. For himself and his children, he forfeited God's promise; otherwise, they all would have been free, though only from natural constraints. As things turned out, Adam's heirs were "enslaved by the senses," in Pico's words, because their fallen nature was bodily as well as spiritual. Pico loathed the body: he called it a "noose round the soul's neck."

Once the first parents sinned, the body's fetters bound mankind with laws of nature. Had Adam and Eve been obedient, the freedom guaranteed by God would have held humanity harmless from those natural laws. But laws of nature are not the Law. In fact, humans are bound by a double Law, according to the *Oration*, "not just the Law that he [Moses] recorded for posterity in five books but also a true and more secret reading of the Law." This unwritten Law, as Pico explained, was disclosed later in books of Kabbalah.[62]

Like Burckhardt, Pater, and Symonds, many intelligent and well-informed readers have been misled by Pico's speech, mistaking it for a declaration of freedom that entailed the dignity treasured in modern times. What deceived the experts? One possibility — often rejected by experts — is that the flashy rhetoric in the *Oration* is just that: exquisite form without much content. Pico never had the occasion to re-think the part of his speech — the part not repeated by the *Apology* — where rhetoric rules. Throughout the speech, the orator's native wit was enough to make the oratory sparkle but not enough to make his short-order philosophy coherent.[63]

Character and circumstance made it hard for Pico to use rhetoric prudently: cleverness came easier to him. A principle or rule of method was also at work, though he left it unstated until near the end of the speech: it was a "divine command, not human judgment," he proclaimed, "to keep secret from the populace what should be told to the perfect." Jesus himself warned against "giving something holy to dogs and casting pearls before swine," a Gospel maxim that governs Pico's speech—and not just near the end of it on the origins of Kabbalah. His procedure in the *Oration*, emphatic and explicit, was esoteric from start to finish: the language of mystery and secrecy (*arcana, mysteria, secreta*) pervades the speech. This haughty young nobleman—speaking to the few and unconcerned that questions about his insights might deserve answers—aimed to mystify the many, and he succeeded.[64]

Mystification begins at the beginning, with a Saracen named Abdala and a few words from a Hermetic treatise. The quotation about a human miracle from the *Asclepius*—plainly labeled—has distracted readers looking for dignity in the speech. A little later, Pico quotes silently from the same text to express disgust about humans because they have bodies. Read together in their original context, the two Hermetic passages disparage the human condition: only mortals who abandon their bodies and rise to divinity—not a human state at all—are praiseworthy. Pico, while diverting his readers with exotic erudition, lets them in on none of these complications. And he says nothing more about the Muslim known as Abdala, as anonymous as any Christian named John. The Saracen has never been identified. Maybe Pico planted a red herring—not the last diversion, intended or unintended—in the speech.[65]

A little later, as the *Oration* confronts the fact that people change, the orator says that human nature (after the Fall) became "variable, manifold and inconstant," citing another unidentified authority, Euanthes the Persian. A Kantian, thinking in such terms about autonomy, freedom, and spontaneity, might be building a case for human dignity. But Pico's concern was a sinful human creature, given "no image of his own" by the Creator, who has nonetheless acquired images, which are "many, alien and accidental." For human nature embodied in the way of all flesh, inconstancy follows from mortality and the body's corruption. If remedies of self-fashioning are merely human, the results will be dismal — not dignified. Even if mutability were a gain — which Pico never claimed — contingency and inconstancy would be losses.[66]

Exploring possibilities for change, Pico startles his audience with a (rhetorical) question: "Who would not be astonished (*admiretur*) at this chameleon of ours?" Abdala has just said that "there was nothing to see more astonishing (*admirabilius*) than man," and this amazement might be joyous. Wonder is a theme in this part of the speech: *admiror* and its cognates appear repeatedly in the first ten paragraphs. And the homely chameleon is indeed an amazing sight. If humans too could change how they look, they might seem adaptable, flexible, versatile, and so on — all good (in a Kantian way) as signs of freedom. But some surprises are shocks, as the ancient comedian and moralist Terence warned: "Watch out for what has astonished you (*admiratus*)." And the imagery? Man's images are "many, alien and accidental." Pico's friend and rival Ficino linked the chameleon with the mutable Proteus as emblems of the sensory imagination and its phantasms. Could a shifty lizard be a trustworthy icon for mortals?[67]

Pico was a wizard with classical allusions and loved to put his magic on stage. He packed the *Oration* with nuggets of erudition that surely pleased him more than his audience: much of the treasure was buried too deep to find. His remark about the chameleon addressed those learned enough to know the ancient literature on the lizard — not just Greek and Latin but biblical and rabbinic. One way to judge this dossier is to check the *Adages* for what Erasmus would say, not much later, about chameleons. To see pictures of the lizard, look at Alciato's *Emblems*. The little beast in his images is ugly, and the ancients called it harmless, timid, and torpid—an icon for toadies, turncoats, and the unchaste. Erasmus reported Aristotle's "use of the word 'chameleon' to express the vice of inconstancy." If the lizard's coat of many colors was a garment of vice, why would Pico want a human miracle to wear it? Maybe he kept his vision of that miracle unfocused by design.[68]

Pico continues with a sketch of Proteus, the slimy—yet divine—Old Man of the Sea. Like the seals that he herds, Proteus is a smelly, slippery god—elusive and indeterminate. He can "change blessed matter into many forms," according to the *Orphic Hymns*, which were among Pico's favorites. Matter is "blessed" in this line from the *Hymns*, but the prince calls it "worthless" elsewhere in his speech, like "the dirt of the ground." Are we to trust the orator or the sacred verses? After Proteus, Pico moves on to Pythagoreans who "transmute wicked people into beasts and, if Empedocles is to be believed, even into plants." Empedocles was a sage. Why not believe him? Perhaps because such changes—alluding to metempsychosis without mentioning it—slip down the slope of biology and morality into a "vegetating life," as Pico warned in the *Conclusions*. After toying with his audience in the *Oration*, the orator would surely not welcome such transmigrations: they could not be good in any way, and the Church regarded belief in them as heresy. They were not progressive changes, no more inspiring than sabbath-breakers turned into apes or infidels into sheep, according to the Koran that Pico also cited.[69]

The only glorious change in this part of Pico's speech is Enoch becoming Metatron. But who or what is Metatron? The *Oration* has said nothing yet about Kabbalah when the orator announces that "with their more secret theology, Hebrews too sometimes transform the blessed Enoch into an angel of divinity, whom they call מטטרון." The Hebrew letters of Metatron's name are missing in Gianfrancesco's 1496 edition, but manuscript *F* fills the blank. Unlike Proteus and the chameleon, Enoch and the angel stand for change that Pico could advocate — change that is disembodying, divinizing, and therefore dehumanizing. A miracle produced in this way would no longer be human at all. Angelic rank (*dignitas*) was a step toward the utmost heights, up to the Godhead, where everything human would have fallen away.[70]

Pico's Ladder

Sinners hoping to be one with God must first "aspire to the angelic life." Even on earth, they must live like Cherubs in heaven. Somewhere beneath the rhetoric, Pico reasoned like this: (1) God made (the unfallen) Adam free to change; (2) the change that Adam's (fallen) children must make is to live like angels. Whether the orator sensed the bumps in his road — after less than a fifth of his speech — we cannot know. He moved quickly to the next section — more than a fourth of his address. There (3) he counsels the wicked to mount a ladder of grace. Since sin defiled them, they could not touch the holy ladder. Before they could be purified, they needed lessons in purification, and Pico turned to "ancient Fathers" to teach them.[71]

Half the speech — the half not repeated in the *Apology* — was over before these instructions were complete. Pico used the other half to (4) defend his philosophical ambitions, (5) present a new theory of magic, (6) introduce Kabbalah through its origins, and (7) close by asking his judges for gratitude after taunting them.[72]

The orator let the armature of his oratory show through in transitions. "Let us go to the ancient Fathers," he wrote, while announcing the third part of his speech. He addressed these Fathers in order to ask their advice: "let us consult the apostle Paul," "let us consult the patriarch Jacob," and "let us also consult the very wise Pythagoras." Repetitions punctuate his conversations with other biblical heroes and ancient theologians, including Job, Moses, and Zoroaster. They all answer the same question—how to be purified and climb the ladder—which is asked seven times, just as the whole speech seems to have seven parts. But none of this architecture is obvious, of course: explicit signposting was not the prince's way. He was attuned to numerical resonance, however, and wrote about a "method of number"—numerology—in the *Conclusions*. He would also use a hebdomadal word, a seven, to title the *Heptaplus*, whose structure is sevenfold, and the *Oration's* architecture may be the same.[7]

1 (1–10)	Adam is free to change.
2 (11–15)	Adam's children must change into angels.
3 (16–35)	Ancient sages teach them how to change.
4 (36–55)	Pico defines and defends his philosophical ambitions.
5 (56–62)	As part of philosophy, he proposes a new theory of magic.
6 (63–68)	He also gives a brief history of Kabbalah.
7 (69–72)	He asks for thanks and closes.

The ladder in the speech is both theory and praxis, both words and deeds, a staged curriculum and a graded regimen. Pico learned it from Greek philosophers like Iamblichus and Proclus, from Christian theologians like Dionysius the Areopagite, and from Kabbalists like Abraham Abulafia, whose Kabbalist polemics against philosophy had been circulating in Italy since the late thirteenth century.[74]

At that time, Abulafia wrote an introduction to Kabbalah, and the prince later commissioned a Latin version. "All the prophets," according to the Kabbalist, and also learned gentiles "wished to know the level and height of the ladder of the soul, from the lowest to the very top." Abulafia's personal experience of the ladder was mystical and ecstatic. Iamblichus had been more professorial about climbing "from low to high, as by a bridge or ladder," and he counted the rungs in several different ways. One pattern examined by him and other Platonists was curricular, starting with ethics and then advancing through dialectic and natural science before rising to theology. But when the Areopagite described what awaited "beyond the summit of every holy ascent to . . . the One beyond all," he traced the path that Moses followed from action up to contemplation through three moments — not four — of purgation, illumination, and divinizing union.[75]

Traditionally, the ascent could have three, four, or even five levels, and Pico's response was also variable. Mostly he treated ethics, dialectic, natural philosophy, and theology as the first four theoretical or curricular rungs of the ladder. After theology, the final three stages were more regimen than curriculum, more practical than theoretical, not so much instructional as experiential, until the journey was over and all experience disappeared. To prepare for the trip, Pico devised a theory of magic, but his magic was also the "practical part of natural knowledge." He also knew a "practical part of Kabbalah [that] puts into practice all formal metaphysics and lower theology." Gathering the pieces together, he assembled a ladder in seven stages at two levels:[76]

7 mystical union
6 Kabbalah
5 magic

   (mainly regimen)

4 theology
3 natural philosophy
2 dialectic
1 ethics

   (mostly curriculum)

Up Pico's ladder the wise "climb for the heights" because they "scorn things of earth." Beyond the last rung and "above the ladder" initiates are "consumed in theological bliss." After the ascent, "we shall be ourselves no longer, but shall be Him, the very One who made us." Past the top of the ladder, all the climbers leave it "as absolutely one." Meanwhile, on the way up, they will have been "made into angels." Pico's words are bold, but the outcome is unclear. If, as he says, the goal is becoming "one with God . . . in the Father's darkness," the Areopagite's exclusion applies: in total unification, there is "neither oneself nor anyone else." Selves, persons, individuals—they all vanish. But angelic rank is not divine unity. There are many angels—"hundreds of thousands"— some known by name as individuals, like Gabriel, Michael, Raphael, and Metatron. The elect who turn into angels, as Enoch became Metatron, have not yet passed the top of the ladder to melt into the One.[77]

This may be Pico's response—or one of his responses—to a problem of plurality. Nearing the peak of the climb (at steps 5 and 6), pilgrims already instructed in theology and its philosophical preliminaries (steps 1 through 4) experience the power of magic and Kabbalah combined in angelic transformation, a holy theurgy or god-work (*theourgeia*) as a last step before *theôsis*—becoming God. Another solution, also known to Pico, treats Metatron not as an angel but as the Agent Intellect, the face of the Creator closest to creation but—unlike angels—not a creature at all. If Metatron is the Agent Intellect, humans who imitate Enoch and become Metatron are divinized: sons of God become the Son of the Christian Trinity, called the Boy and the Intellect by Pico in one of his conclusions. But for Muslims and Jews who devised theologies of the Agent Intellect, there was no plurality in God. Apotheosis as the Agent Intellect was absolute *henôsis*—pure mystical union beyond any manifold.[78]

Pico may have wanted it both ways, as elsewhere in his speech, where evocation and suggestion override clarity and definition. He was well informed about the Agent Intellect, especially from his contacts with Elia del Medigo, an Averroist Aristotelian. Averroes — like other Muslims as well as Jews — made the Intellect the dynamo of two processes, one cognitive, the other ecstatic, both overcoming plurality. As a philosopher, Averroes taught that the Intellect is absolutely one, that humans have no intellects — strictly speaking — only lower faculties clouded by the manifold of human cognitions. Many Christian thinkers rejected this metaphysical psychology, but Averroists like Elia mastered every syllable of it and taught it to their students.

Since Pico studied with Elia, he will have known the most important study of cognition by Averroes, an examination of Aristotle's books *On the Soul*. He summarized its most troubling teaching in the *Conclusions*: "in all humans there is a single intellective soul." He thought it possible, nonetheless, "while holding the unity of the Intellect," that "after death my soul remains particularly mine." Yet Pico stated this canon of faith as merely "possible" — up for discussion. He listed it with debating points not claimed as his own, perhaps because he disagreed, writing in the *Oration* about many souls becoming "absolutely one." In the same part of the *Conclusions* he also wrote that "supreme human happiness comes when the Agent Intellect connects with a potential intellect as its form." He was alluding to a different issue, parallel to the problem of cognition, about conjunction. Averroes discussed it in several places; one was his *Letter on the Possibility of Conjunction with the Agent Intellect*.[79]

Like Averroes, other Muslim and Jewish thinkers debated whether and how human souls — seen by Aristotelians as formal components of matter/form composites — could conjoin with the Intellect, despite their reliance on bodies and their plurality. Since conjunction was an intellectualized version of going to heaven, of being saved or not, the problem was consequential. As in cognition, so also in conjunction: a human soul, once conjoined, would be identical with the Intellect. The price of this reward was to eliminate anything distinctly individual and human.

When Pico urged his readers to be "consumed in theological bliss," he understood the cost, which to him was trivial. A year before he died, well after the alleged conversion, he was studying a treatise by Ibn Tufayl, a Muslim philosopher, who was emphatic about extinction in the Godhead. The perfect mystic must seek "his own obliteration. . . . His essence receded along with the rest of the essences; all vanished and faded away. . . . Only the one true permanent Existent remained, . . . leaving nothing in existence but the One, the Living, the Everlasting." For Pico in the fifteenth century, as for Ibn Tufayl in the twelfth, self-annihilation was glorious: the 'I' was baggage dropped in the ascent. Seeing no absolute value in human individuals, why would Pico worry about their dignity — as we worry now? Our dignity was never his concern.[80]

Pico, in his short time on earth, dreamed of a staircase to heaven, like Jacob's ladder in the Bible. Retelling this familiar story, he described a figure "whose gleaming image is carved in the Glory Seat." This was God's Throne, or Chariot, seen with a human face on it by Ezekiel in his visions; the rabbis described the face as carved into it. The face was Jacob's, they said, and the angels in his dream saw his image on the Throne. Moving up and down the ladder, they came upon Jacob sleeping — lazy and careless. Snoozing in the dirt, soiled by sin, the patriarch needed purification — Pico's topic where Jacob enters his speech.

Jacob's ladder was a powerful symbol for Jews and Christians. Before and after Pico offered his views, Christians saw the ladder as Christ bridging the human and the divine; or as foreshadowing Paul's trip to the third heaven; or as a promise that humans would turn into angels in paradise; or as an allegory of mystical ascent or monastic progress through humility toward perfect charity. Two years after the prince died, Savonarola preached in darker tones about Jacob. He had his dream "where the temple was built, where Abraham attempted to sacrifice Isaac and where Christ was crucified. . . . The ladder signifies the cross of Christ, a ladder leading to Paradise . . . by seven steps," including the need to suffer, accept God's will and endure every tribulation. To others the ladder gave hope of spiritual growth. But Pico was apprehensive—like Savonarola. Fixed on sin and its filth, he feared being "turned away from the ladder, desecrated and defiled."[81]

Extraordinary knowledge—previously unavailable to Christians—of rabbinic and other Jewish responses to Jacob's dream enabled the prince to move beyond traditional gentile exegesis of the ladder. But the excursion left his readers in the dark. Learning that Jacob's face was carved in God's wheeled Throne, the Chariot of Ezekiel's vision, how could they—lacking Pico's privileged information—know where this lesson might lead? A mystical Account of the Chariot, *Ma'aseh Merkabah*, was basic in Jewish hermeneutics but for Pico's audience a secret under seal. A thesis on Kabbalah in the *Conclusions* mentions a "threefold *Merkabah*"—*Merchiava* in Latin—as like a "threefold particularizing philosophy." This was sacred wisdom for the prince but gibberish to his judges in Rome.[82]

Throughout the long third section of the *Oration*, the brash young orator dazzled his readers and left them blinded. He spoke to them in ciphers whose keys were hidden in Targums, Talmud, Midrash, and Kabbalah. These were at his disposal because Jews—especially the convert who called himself Flavius Mithridates—translated and explained Hebrew and Aramaic books for him. He called on this exotic lore not only to interpret Jacob's dream but also to decode words and deeds of Abraham, Apollo, Bacchus, Dionysius the Areopagite, Empedocles, Job, Moses, Orpheus, Paul, Pythagoras, Zoroaster, and other keepers of mysteries—divine and human, biblical and mythical, Christian, Jewish, and pagan.[83]

Pico's Philosophical Vocation

In the third part of the *Oration*, in seven visions of the angelic life, Pico describes the reasons that "have not just excited me to study philosophy but have forced me to it." He needed philosophy because theology required it before he could ascend to God through magic and Kabbalah. Once he chose the life of angels, philosophy was a necessity, obliging him to refute critics who attacked his pledge to study it. The refutation in the fourth section of the speech is its plainest part.

Philosophy thrilled the prince, and the wise advised him to learn it—never mind the abuse from opponents who called it useless. Philosophy itself, not money or power, was his motive, but some still found his project offensive. They complained about argumentative disputing in public and about him as a disputant: he was too young; his propositions were too unsettling, too many, and too hard; and the capital of Christendom was the wrong place to debate them. He treated these charges as merely envious yet could not resist rebutting them, first by pointing out that philosophers had always disputed. Modesty tempered his self-defense—he crowed—and such limitations were no reason to avoid a contest of minds where losers win by learning. As for debating too many theses, the burden was on him, and if some of his claims proved true, why assume that others were false just because there were many of them? He insisted that the number was exactly right for the issues at hand.[84]

Pico's program was large because of its goal and rule: to know every school of philosophy while defending no one's dogma. Christian, Muslim, and Greek thinkers all have their admirable qualities. Even sects that attack the truth make it stronger. This abundance of wisdom moved Pico to study all the schools, both barbarian and Greek, Arab as well as Latin, Aristotelians along with Platonists: he claimed (though Ficino was older and a friend) to be the first to dispute Platonism in public. Inspired by ancient theologies, he also had something of his own to offer. Most of all, he could prove that Plato's ideas agree with Aristotle's and that Christian thinkers only appear to clash with Muslims. These harmonious insights also led him to breakthroughs — so he said — in mathematics, metaphysics, and natural philosophy.[85]

At first sight Pico's method looks eclectic: having read all the philosophers, he has "picked out what truly suits him." While disclaiming sectarian commitments and deploring "squabbles and scraps," he nonetheless arranged his theses by "nations and heads of sects, though without distinction for parts of philosophy." The usual parts of philosophy were metaphysics, natural philosophy, ethics, logic, and so on, which was how Aristotle divided his works. The prince bypassed this taxonomy, which mapped the university curriculum, in order to organize his thinking by the schools and masters whose conflicts he aimed to resolve. Philosophers combine "strife and friendship" in their earthly debates in order to seek the "peace that God makes on high."[86]

To reveal what philosophy can achieve in this way, he proposed a "concord between Plato and Aristotle" that was long sought, something "no one has managed to prove," to demonstrate that their philosophies "are the same." Even where the two "seem to disagree in words," they "agree in meaning and substance." The claim could not be stronger, and Gianfrancesco, like Ficino, repeatedly stressed its importance for his uncle, who insisted that this single proposition about Plato and Aristotle would justify adding "hundreds of theses, not to say more," to his nine hundred.[87]

Others have disagreed, seeing harmony as a mixed blessing in philosophy — or a curse. By raising the issue, Pico anticipated the wars between eclectics and their enemies that broke out later, starting in the seventeenth century. In this respect he was prescient. But when enlightened eclectics attacked their opponents, they marked the prince down with the enemy. His 'concord' was their 'syncretism'—the muddle-headed error of ignoring distinctions needed for clear thinking.

Concord, from this perspective, was also a religious blunder, and eclectics made Pico a parody of confusion that was not just foolish but ungodly as well. Jacob Brucker, in the first modern history of philosophy, denounced him as an "author of philosophy's corruption and debasement, . . . clumsily mixing everything together—Kabbalist, Pythagorean, Platonic, Aristotelian, Jewish and Christian—and sadly confusing them all." Brucker made this "bizarre syncretism" a target for other progressive critics, like Voltaire, who wrote Pico off as a "blind man guided by blind masters, . . . masters of lies who base their power on human stupidity."[88]

Poor Pico: it was hard for a Prince of Concord to govern in philosophy's quarrelsome domain. Voltaire's acid phrases were still eating his reputation away in the twentieth century. In a field that thrived on dispute, Pico wanted to muffle it—strange to say about an author of hundreds of disputatious theses. Once again, he may not have thought his project through. As Gianfrancesco pointed out, the *Oration* was "written in the eagerness of youth" before the orator withdrew from "trivial squabbles" and "intellectual combat"—the whole purpose of the *Conclusions*. Neither in that book nor in the shorter speech—both constrained by their genres—could he expect to demonstrate what he claimed about concord. He could only brag: "where others find discord, . . . I find harmony," while conceding that he had not "worked point by point through those issues."[89]

An orator can praise or blame philosophy in an oration, but a speech is a bad setting for philosophical deliberation, which proceeds by minute questioning. Pico, who acknowledged these limitations, attempted no philosophical demonstrations—as distinct from assertions—in his *Conclusions* or his *Oration*. In works like these, he could make no principled case for the harmony that he advertised, though cases there were to be made.

For example: among scholastic philosophers, according to Gianfrancesco's *Life*, Giovanni liked Aquinas best. An epistemic doctrine cherished by Thomas and other Aristotelians could have inspired an argument for concord. In its classic formulation, the doctrine denies that there is anything "in the intellect that is not (*non sit*) previously in a sense." Pico might have reasoned from this maxim to a middle ground where idealists stand with empiricists. What could there be "in the intellect"? Immaterial forms, perhaps? And "in a sense"? Maybe something more empirical, like sensory forms resembling things made of matter. There you have it: idealists find concord with empiricists when formal ideas harmonize with material forms.

A real test would take longer, of course, with no happy outcome assured. For one thing, there might be a problem about the *non sit* in the statement—a subjunctive in the present tense. Why not *non erat* for 'was not' instead? Would a shift in time clarify the situation? What would it take to handle all the unclear situations? Addressing such questions and meta-questions could fill a very long book, like the younger Pico's *Weighing of False Pagan Learning*, which on this very point weighed Aquinas—allegedly the elder's favorite scholastic—in the balance. But there was little room for careful judgment and orderly analysis in the *Oration*. Pico said he was a philosopher in a speech where he could not philosophize much.[90]

Two greater princes of philosophy—Plato and Aristotle—were Pico's top candidates for harmonizing. The first four hundred of the *900 Conclusions* include a few dozen theses about their disciples, interpreters, and opponents where Pico questions both masters—though not in separate sets of conclusions about their ideas. The proposition that declares concord between them comes first in the second batch of five hundred. Then nine of the seventeen theses that open this group aim to dissolve conflicts between Thomas and Scotus; three do the same for Avicenna and Averroes. While

Plato and Platonists star throughout the *Conclusions*, Aristotle and Aristotelians also shine: the light of truth blazes everywhere, so Pico thought. He began with Albert the Great, Thomas Aquinas, Francis of Meyronnes, John Duns Scotus, Henry of Ghent, and Giles of Rome. Albert, Thomas, and Scotus were famous; specialists studied the others; all wrote before 1328, in the great age of scholasticism.

Pico listed the same "Latin philosophers and theologians" in the *Oration* because recent scholastic debates were on his mind when he wrote the speech. Even though he put Plato and Aristotle at the center of the problem of concord, he could solve it only on his own terms and in his own time. In one sense, this is obvious: the Academy and Lyceum were long gone, and almost all philosophers qualified to judge Pico's effort were teaching at Bologna, Padua, Paris, and other universities founded since the twelfth century.[91]

The only part of Pico's project about concord that survives is the little treatise *On Being and the One*, whose environment was as much the late scholasticism of Antonio Cittadini — a conventional professor of arts, logic, and medicine at Ferrara and Pisa — as the new classicism of Poliziano, to whom Pico dedicated the work. What we have is the short text that he left in the spring of 1491. Six months later he was still debating its metaphysical conundrums with Cittadini. By 1492, the prince was bored with the fight, but Antonio was relentless. He kept objecting and piled up a disputatious debt of honor for Gianfrancesco to settle after his uncle died. Two years before his death, Pico was not yet ready to put these "trivial squabbles" behind him. This battle of objections and replies was scholastic combat in the grand style.

In his original text, trying to close a gap in ontology between Plato and Aristotle, Pico engaged Anselm, Aquinas, Averroes, Avicenna, and unnamed Peripatetics alongside Iamblichus, Olympiodorus, Pletho, Simplicius, and anonymous Platonists. He revered the ancients, but he also relied on the moderns: likewise for Antonio, his opponent. Thomas was the scholastic most often enlisted in their exchange of proofs and refutations, but they also called on Albert the Great, Henry of Ghent, Swineshead, and other "British philosophers" as well. And Pico added a living Italian to his roster — Nicoletto Vernia. In the eyes of his peers in philosophy (where Ficino was a brilliant anomaly), medieval thought, as received in the late Quattrocento, was where the prince had to take his stand if he wanted to prove, not just boast, that he was right about concord.[92]

Philosophizing about Magic

Time ran out, causing Pico to fail in an enterprise headlined by the *Oration*. More durable than his vision of concord was his theory of magic — perhaps because it had already been theorized by others. He summed it up (without proving it) in the fifth part of the speech, after outlining his efforts "to put forward a new philosophy." At this point, he moved on from sketching his whole project (part 4) to describing one piece of it (part 5). Like the whole, this magical part of the speech was meant to be philosophical. Pico's intention is hard to credit now because magic has long since lost its academic standing as a science underwriting a technology — likewise its respectability in the high culture. But the prince, having observed the culture of his own day from its summit, would have been dismayed to see magic banished from the world of learning. Magic in his view could be a "higher and holier philosophy" and the "final realization of natural philosophy."[93]

This was not oratorical bluster. Pico knew that many people scorned magic as the "most dishonest of arts," fearing it as something "monstrous and accursed" and under the "authority of demons," so he proposed a theory to salvage its benefits by mitigating the damage it might do. The risks were great: magic gone wrong could attract unclean spirits. Accordingly, his *Conclusions* included a minatory thesis about magic, that a fearsome demon named Azazel might devour an inept practitioner.

As surely as Pico believed in angels, he also feared demons. But he thought that magic—a natural magic, not demonic—could do without them. In the *Oration*, this was his main idea about magic, which was not new: philosophers and theologians of high standing had made similar proposals. Pico knew that Alkindi, Roger Bacon, and William of Auvergne were "more recent authorities"—in the scholastic tradition—who promoted natural magic. William's position was a step toward Pico's: "certain marvelous effects are actually produced naturally; . . . [they] should not be called enchantments (*incantationes*), . . . and are in fact natural actions, the knowledge of which is one of the eleven parts of natural knowledge (*scientia*), where nothing is done with help from demons."

Ficino, the prince's advocate, also supported this distinction. He was more cautious than the younger philosopher, however, knowing that the natural magic promoted by the ancients was compromised by their own theology, where "all things are full of gods." How could gods and demons be detached from magic if they were everywhere, wherever a wizard might wave a wand? Facing such questions, Ficino was evasive, but Pico never hesitated: his quick solution was a naturalized magic, which is what the fifth part of his speech endorses.

Within limits accepted by William of Auvergne and others, magic could be supernaturalized only by unclean spirits. But Kabbalah—as unknown to Pico's judges as it had been to William—convinced the prince to look beyond nature to higher powers that could strengthen magic without defiling it. In a thesis stating that any effective magic requires an "act of Kabbalah," he made this novelty public. But in the speech he only hinted that a supernatural magic could be licit if Kabbalah was its gateway to transcendence. He implied the need for such an opening when he said that good magic acts *quasi ipsa sit Artifex*—not *as* the divine Artificer and Workman but *as if* such wonders were possible, acquiring the Creator's powers from his creations. But if magic were somehow divine, would God be somehow magical? The question is vague and blasphemous, but if the orator's judges had seen his *Oration*, they might well have asked it. And he might have turned to philosophy for answers.[94]

In six paragraphs on magic, however, partly used up by a capsule history, Pico had little room to philosophize—while making bold assertions. The magic he preferred was "as divine and helpful as the other is dreadful and harmful." Bad magic enslaves its users to demons—"God's enemies." The good kind excites "astonishment at God's works" and leads to "contemplating God's marvels." The marvels are natural, "concealed in the world's secret parts" by the Creator but discoverable by magicians who could never really make them. Likewise for scholastic theologians: they too could only observe the wonders that God had put into the world and then reason from them to God's existence and perfections. This was the dialectic of medieval natural theology, made famous by Aquinas in his Five Ways. Pico's case for natural magic—in its broad structure, if not in its depths—reflects this scholastic paradigm.[95]

In a short speech, however, the prince could not even state his case completely and explicitly, much less solve every puzzle about natural magic. The debate continued—along with Pico's contribution to it—for the better part of two centuries after he died. During this period natural magic got more attention than philosophical concord from thinkers of the first rank—Boyle, Campanella, Descartes, Newton, and others—as they battled their way to philosophies suited to a new age of science.[96]

Ancient Mysteries and Trinities

The Boyle who discovered Boyle's Law was an alchemist, like the Newton of Newton's physics. Campanella published a *Defense of*

Galileo but also wrote *On Magic and the Sense in Things*. Descartes, who denied reading Campanella's books, demolished the philo- sophical foundations of the magic in them. To do so, he had to investigate theories developed by eminent predecessors — Plotinus, Proclus, Albertus, Aquinas, and others — whom he ignored in his published writings. But his main target was the physics and meta- physics of scholastic philosophy, where natural magic was part of natural philosophy — what we now call 'science.' Although this was also Pico's position, no one would call his speech 'scientific' in the way of the *Principia* or *The Sceptical Chymist*. Those texts are hon- ored now because they shaped a part of our past that was their proximate future. But no earthly future is on the *Oration*'s horizon: the setting is God's eternal now, and the remote past is the orator's locus of authority. The future at stake is an otherworldly and de- personalized eternity.[97]

"Ancient mysteries of the Jews" are the topic of the sixth and last part of the speech before it concludes. Having claimed that magic underwrites Christian doctrine, Pico next declares that Kabbalah also confirms the faith, though others might deride its mysteries as frauds. Consulting wise men of antiquity — both Jew- ish and Christian — and looking closer at secrets kept by Jews, he saw great value in them despite their obscurity: he was convinced that the Church needed them to protect itself against attacks by Jews. He believed that early Christian authorities approved of Hebrew sages who traced Kabbalah to Moses on Sinai, where God gave him not only a public Law but also a private interpreta- tion and ordered him not to reveal it. Greeks and Egyptians, pa- gans and Christians, had kept such rules of secrecy.[98]

The word *Kabbalah* means 'reception,' Pico explained, and the priest Ezra described the receiving and recording. Ezra's words hint at secrets of natural philosophy, metaphysics, and theology preserved in Latin translations of Hebrew and Aramaic books commissioned by a pope, Sixtus IV. When Pico bought such books for himself at great cost, he found—in texts revered and protected by Jews—the same wisdom taught by Paul and the Church Fathers, along with Pythagorean and Platonic philosophy. In these secret books he discovered not just the Trinity but a triad of Trinities, holy learning to confound the Jews in any contest—contests that the prince himself witnessed.[99]

The last seventy-two theses in the *Conclusions* are about Kabbalah. The heading that introduces them claims "powerful confirmation of the Christian religion from the very principles of Hebrew sages," and the *Oration* says the same: books of Kabbalah support "a religion not so much Mosaic as Christian." How could that possibly be? Kabbalah is a Jewish tradition, and Jews deny fundamentals of the Christian creed: the one God incarnate as Christ, his coming as a Messianic King, and his eternal reign as a divine Son in a Trinity alongside a Father and a Holy Spirit.[100]

The *Conclusions* claim that this "mystery of the Trinity along with the possibility of the Incarnation is revealed to us through a method of Kabbalah." The method is distinctly Kabbalist, scrutinizing Hebrew names of God and other sacred words in order to extract theology from them. The *Oration* never explains the method, however. The speech says almost nothing about Kabbalah except to stress its secrecy and trace its origins—back to Moses on Sinai through the prophet Ezra from clues in Hebrew and Aramaic books. Who wrote the arcane books that Pico read? He never named their authors, even the two most important to him: Abulafia and Menahem Recanati. He realized how valuable they were, however, and also understood that their Kabbalah had not only a "method" but also "mysteries" of its own. He said so in the *Conclusions*, but in the *Oration* he revealed nothing on either point, staying silent about Kabbalah's most conspicuous method, alphabetic numerology, and never disclosing its most memorable content, sefirotic theosophy.

By the time Pico wrote the speech, he had thought a great deal about Christianizing this alien system: the thinking enabled him to put more than a hundred explicit statements about his project in the *Conclusions*. One of the final theses on Kabbalah, for example, adapts a conventional psychology of mental faculties and passions to the hierarchy of ten *Sefirot*—features of divinity itself. The general point was a familiar one, famously explored by Augustine in *De Trinitate*: human psychology mirrors the structure of the Godhead. But this is how Pico described it.

> I relate our soul to the ten *Sefirot* in this way: through her unity she goes with the first, through intellect with the second, with the third through reason, the fourth through higher desire, the fifth through higher wrath, the sixth through free will, as she turns back through all of this to those above with the seventh and with the eighth toward those below, then with the ninth mixing both, through indifference or cleaving to each in turn rather than holding back from both, and she goes with the tenth by her power to dwell in the first Dwelling.

Christian readers of the *Conclusions* would easily recognize one pole of the analogy: intellect, reason, will, and desire as the usual furniture of mind and soul. Even at this point, however, after seeing almost all nine hundred theses, they would still be puzzled about what these commonplace notions were meant to illuminate—the *Sefirot*. Nonetheless, by supplying just a little guidance, Pico's theses made a start on educating Christians about Kabbalah.[101]

Pico gave no such help in his speech, however, and his decision to keep its audience uninformed was overdetermined. Just as a practical matter, Kabbalist exegesis and theosophy were complicated, utterly unknown at the time except to a few learned Jews and likely to offend Christians who might be told about them. There was also an obstacle in principle because Pico not only adopted Kabbalah's rule of secrecy but also internalized it.

By the time he wrote the speech, Pico had read many books of Kabbalah. One work by Abulafia was particularly useful because it was brief and introductory—though hard to understand. It starts with fifteen propositions from assorted texts, biblical and Talmudic, presented as acrostic verse in the Hebrew original. If Pico relied only on the Latin translation, the poetry would have been invisible. And to eyes less practiced than his, the string of sentences would have looked incoherent. "Until the Lord looks down from heaven and sees" is the sixth statement. The seventh says that "my eye has done more harm to my soul than the daughters of my city." The statements seem disconnected. But Abulafia took them from the same part of the Book of Lamentations, expecting readers of his treatise to recognize them instantly, remember their context, and connect them thematically.[102]

Growing up in a world of Torah and Talmud taught Abulafia's readers conventions of communication that were strange to Christians of Pico's day. Another book of Kabbalah known to Pico was Recanati's commentary on the Pentateuch, which condensed and adapted material from the *Zohar*, the magnum opus of Kabbalah that Pico probably never read directly, though he knew its name. What follows is a typical page of the *Zohar*, where words and phrases from the Bible and other sacred texts are italicized in the standard English translation. The topic is *bereshit*, the first word of the Bible:

> *Because of beginning*, which is awe, *God created heaven and earth.* Whoever violates this violates the commandments, and his punishment is the evil lash. This is *the earth was chaos and void with darkness over the face of the abyss.* These are four types

of punishment. . . . *Chaos* is strangulation, as is written, *a line of chaos, a measuring rope.* Void is stoning, stones sunk in the immense abyss for punishing the wicked. *Darkness* is burning, as is written, *when you heard the voice from the midst of the darkness,* and *the mountain was ablaze with fire to the heart of heaven,* darkness. . . . And the wind is death by sword, *a stormy wind.*

The italicized phrases from Genesis and longer quotations from other biblical books would be easier for Christians to spot than the "line of chaos" from Isaiah and the "measuring rope" from Zechariah. But experienced readers of rabbinic literature would recognize these fragments right away.[103]

Pico, for all his brilliance, was less well equipped by experience. But the Kabbalah that he read so closely and in such quantities immersed him in this cryptic style, visible throughout the *Oration,* as in this passage near the beginning of the speech, with key words and phrases italicized:

I was not satisfied — *thinking over* the basis for these statements — with claims often made for man's outstanding nature: that among creatures man . . . is an *interval* between fixed eternity and flowing time and (as the Persians say) the *bond* — no, the *wedding knot* — of the world, *a little lower than the angels,* according to David.

Pico went easy on his readers by naming David when he quoted a Psalm. He connected less familiar "Persians" with a "bond" or *copula,* which is also a *hymenaeum* — the world's "wedding knot." Such a bond, or *desmos,* was well known from Plato's *Timaeus.* And maybe a close friend — like Angelo Poliziano, also a friend of Ficino's — would have remembered what Ficino had written about such a link, or *vinculum,* in the world. But what would take less learned readers from these clues to the *humên* in the Greek text of the *Chaldean Oracles*, recondite even by Poliziano's standards? Whatever Pico had in mind, some readers would remember *hymen hymenaee* from the famous wedding song by Catullus. Experienced readers and writers of Latin had been drilled and drilled themselves in such lines by canonical authors, none more renowned than Cicero. To describe what he was "thinking over," Pico signaled the Roman's presence with just two words: *cogitanti mihi*. Only their placement at the start of Cicero's work *On the Orator* marked them as also Pico's where the prince put them—near the start of his own *Oration*.[104]

This flourish of classical usage would have been wasted on some Christian readers, even among the learned clergy in Rome. Had the cardinals in Pico's notional audience been learned Jews, allusions of the same fragmented type in texts of Kabbalah would have been transparent. Esoteric writing—deliberately evasive, not just telegraphic and cryptic—was common in their tradition, approved even by a paragon of reason like Maimonides. Pico believed that ancient pagans and Christians did the same—including the Apostles: "Christ revealed much to his disciples that they decided not to write down in order to keep it from becoming common knowledge." Kabbalah's esoteric habits were additional evidence of the Christian wisdom in it.[105]

Only about eight hundred words of the *Oration* describe Kabbalah—three hundred of them to make a case for secrecy. The rest of the speech applies this principle, especially the first half that leads Pico's audience up his ladder to mystical extinction. The fourth and fifth parts, on his philosophical project and his theory of magic, are less arcane. But secrecy comes back in the sixth part of the *Oration*, where mysteries of Kabbalah remain mystifying because the orator leaves them unexplained.[106]

Before introducing Kabbalah, the speech describes numbering as the "supreme and preeminently divine science." The exposition of Kabbalah also mentions two numbers—forty and seventy—because Ezra and his scribes took forty days to produce seventy books. The minimum age for studying Kabbalah was also forty. Otherwise, there is nothing numerical in this part of the speech, except that the books of Kabbalah commissioned by Pope Sixtus IV were three. After finishing with Kabbalah, however, Pico attributed a "secret doctrine of numbers" to the *Orphic Hymns*, even though he placed his Orphic theses before Kabbalah in the *Conclusions*. Numbering comes up again at the close of the speech to insist that a total of nine hundred was exactly right for the *Conclusions* and that the author was not "piling the numbers up." As he completed his *Oration*, the orator was thinking about numbers, after saying nothing about numerology as a method in Kabbalah.[107]

In a speech so loaded with unsolved puzzles, why not reveal this method? Pico could have said more, as he did in the *Conclusions*. Three theses show mystical numbers at work in the *Orphic Hymns*, and one of them applies this theological arithmetic to Hebrew secrets; another conclusion identifies an Orphic avatar of Athena with Metatron. One of these propositions says that in Kabbalah the "purest wine" signifies what nine Bacchi mean "according to Orpheus": the nine manifestations of Bacchus are Kabbalah's Muses, nine of the *Sefirot*. On the *Sefirot*, more to come soon: the biblical text that led Pico to them by way of Bacchus and Orpheus was a Psalm by David, the Jewish Orpheus, named in an Orphic thesis:

> Just as David's hymns are wonderfully useful for an act of Kabbalah, so are the hymns of Orpheus useful for an act of true, licit and natural magic.

Pico had precedent for hiding secrets in the number of his theses because Orpheus, a sacred singer like David, had done this with his own songs, as revealed by the next thesis:

Numbered under the figure of the Pythagorean tetractys, the number of the *Orphic Hymns* is the same as the number by which the threefold God created the world.

The number of the Psalms, exactly 150, was read as a signal of hidden meaning: the placement of each Psalm in this sequence convinced the Church Fathers that counting them revealed their power, which Pico called magical in his *Apology*. Likewise, just as the *Hymns* hid a secret in their total count, mysteries also lurked in smaller numbers of songs, like the "eightfold number of maritime hymns" in the twelfth Orphic thesis or the "septet of hymns attributed to the Father's Mind" by the twentieth. Speaking of those seven, another thesis about Orpheus declares that

> the effect of the preceding hymns is nothing without an act of Kabbalah, whose special result is to put every figural, continuous and discrete quantity into practice.

"Discrete quantity" is material for arithmetic with integers. "Continuous" quantity is geometry, which needs other operations, like taking a root, which integers and their ratios cannot always manage. Between geometry and arithmetic come figural or formal shapes that combine geometry's pictorial force with the precision of arithmetic, as seen in the tetractys, a triangular amulet of ten unities hallowed in Pythagorean lore:

*

*   *

*   *   *

*   *   *   *

The *Hymns* show by their number — Pico thought it was eighty-six — that Pythagorean arithmetic is figural, according to the fifth Orphic thesis, and that God created the world with the same

number. In the Torah that Moses made public, in the story of the
first day, the Creator's name is Elohim, whose letters add up to
eighty-six. Is this sum correct? To provide a check, Pico could
have explained that letters of the Hebrew alphabet are also numer-
als standing for numbers. Since the same is true of Greek letters
(also a few Latin letters), the point was familiar from other con-
texts and need not have taken long to make.[108]

The Creator in the fifth Orphic thesis is a "threefold God," and
a thesis about Kabbalah unveils a triad of his fourfold names:

> Someone with a deep knowledge of Kabbalah can under-
> stand that the three great fourfold names of God contained
> in secrets of Kabbalists ought to be assigned to the three
> persons of the Trinity through a wondrous allocation so that
> the name אהיה belongs to the Father, the name יהוה to the
> Son, the name אדני to the Holy Spirit.

In 1486 the printer of the *Conclusions* left blank spaces for the Hebrew. Reconstructed by Chaim Wirszubski, they are אהיה (Ehyeh),
יהוה (YHWH) and אדני (Adonai). All three are "fourfold" because
each has four letters, whereas אלהים (Elohim) has five, adding up
to eighty-six — which Pico thought to be the number of the *Orphic
Hymns*. This number, like the name Elohim and its number, was
public, unlike the trinitarian mystery of the "three great fourfold
names." Since one of their secrets was the number seventy-two,
they revealed — as figural numbers — what Pico would not disclose
to his audience in Rome: that just as the number of all his theses
was a "mystical number," as he told a friend in private, so was the
number of his final theses on Kabbalah — the culminating part of
the nine hundred *Conclusions*.[109]

If Pico had revealed a little more about Kabbalah in his speech,
his hearers could have learned that God's holiest Name, YHWH,

has four letters — *yod* (י), *he* (ה), *waw* (ו), *he* (ה), which are 10, 5, 6 and 5 again. By repeated addition,

10 is *yod*;
15 is 10 + 5, *yod* + *he*;
21 is 10 + 5 + 6, *yod* + *he* + *waw*;
26 is 10 + 5 + 6 + 5, *yod* + *he* + *waw* + *he*.

The sum of the subtotals is 72: 10 + 15 + 21 + 26. Displayed in Hebrew as a Pythagorean tetractys, an analogous figural number is

י
ה + י
ו + ה + י
ה + ו + ה + י

One reason for Pico to keep his mathematics secret was practical: laying out techniques of numerology in an unfamiliar script would have made his speech too long and too hard. But he was also following his own rule of secrecy. Obviously, since his theses revealed more than a few Kabbalist secrets, the rule was not inviolable. Some mysteries were more threatening than others, however, like the angelic seventy-two.

A person who understood this mystical number would know that three verses from the book of Exodus, each with exactly seventy-two letters, add up to God's own Name and also conceal names of seventy-two angels. Angels who can help humans can also harm them. Pico could ask Metatron, the mightiest angel of all, to protect him against such dangers, and an amulet inscribed with a figural 72 might summon such kindly spirits. Metatron was the angel prince identified by Abulafia with the Agent Intellect. Mystical union with the Intellect, or Metatron, would eradicate the self — a happy result for a Kabbalist. As Pico disclosed in two theses, this was the "death of the kiss" that Kabbalists called "precious in the sight of the Lord." But making an amulet to invoke the right angel would need just the right Kabbalah, and a mistake might summon a destroying demon. There were good reasons to keep quiet about seventy-two.[110]

Pico planned to use Jewish secrets against Jews. There is "hardly any point of contention," according to the *Oration*, "on which these books by Kabbalists cannot defeat and rebut them." Arrogance grew out of experience: Jews trapped in debate with Christians had little chance, especially against grandees like the prince. He recalled one such demonstration hosted by a powerful Venetian: "At his house, with his own ears he heard Dattilo, a Jew skilled in this science, accept a thoroughly Christian position on the Trinity from top to toe." Who this Dattilo was—Joab in Hebrew—is unknown. Since the ritual shaming was probably staged in 1482 or earlier, Pico may not have remembered much when he claimed that Joab had conceded the truth of the Trinity.[111]

A Jewish foundation for this central Christian dogma is the main message of the last seventy-two propositions of the *Conclusions*, where Kabbalah is the medium. The *Oration* says that the orator read in books of Kabbalah "about the mystery of the Trinity, about the incarnation of the Word, about the divinity of the Messiah," but he left the evidence hidden in his Kabbalist theses. There, in 119 propositions on Kabbalah, the word *numeratio* appears eight times—often enough to catch a reader's attention. If the reader was a student of Hebraica, like Reuchlin or Egidio da Viterbo, he would know that *numeratio* translates *sefirah* (plural *sefirot*), 'numbering' or 'counting' in Hebrew. But in a theosophical setting, a *Sefirah* is more than that—a feature of God to inform Pico's quest for Jews to confess the Trinity. *Numeratio* never occurs in the *Oration*, where *numerus*, *numerare*, and their derivatives come up sixteen times.[112]

Pico knew that Kabbalists treated God's sacred speech, the Hebrew text of the Bible, as infinite in meaning and power. "In the whole Law," he explained, "there are no letters whose forms, ligatures, separations, twisting, direction, defect, excess, smallness, greatness, crowning, closing, opening and order do not reveal secrets of the ten Numerations." The Law's mightiest words were God's own names: the holiest name, YHWH, could not be uttered; by proxy it was pronounced *Adonai*, speakable like other divine names in the Bible. Names of *Sefirot*, unknown as such in Scripture, were also words of great power. They were names not of God but of God's aspects or actions or manifestations. Since the Creator stays concealed in his highest essence, creatures could know the Infinite only as it descends from its hidden heights. The last moments of descent make up the world of human awareness. The first moments, far beyond human perception, are the *Sefirot*.

The *Sefirot* were often shown in a 'tree' with a central trunk and branches to the right and the left. Their number is ten, but the highest has two aspects: the Crown or No-End, hidden at $S1a$, also shows itself as Knowledge at $S1b$, with Wisdom ($S2$) on the viewer's right, and Intelligence ($S3$) on the left. Each *Sefirah* has many such names, some used more than others. Familiar designations of $S4$, for example, are Greatness and Love or Piety. The divine name usually associated with $S4$ is El, but Pico knew that other words and names (Abraham, Michael, the South, Water) belonged there as well. He was the first Christian to uncover these enigmas and value them, but no contemporary except a learned Jew could have seen how they shaped his *Oration*.[113]

$$S1a$$
$$S3 \quad S1b \quad S2$$
$$S5 \qquad S4$$
$$S6$$
$$S8 \qquad S7$$
$$S9$$
$$S10$$

Jewish proof of the Trinity was Pico's great hope for the Christianized Kabbalah promised by the *Oration*. Although he provided no such proof, he gestured at it in the *Conclusions*, but even the gestures are missing from the speech. Either because he lacked time or because a wave of prudence washed over him or because of his commitment to secrecy, he omitted a teaching of Kabbalah—sefirotic theosophy—that was absolutely crucial for his esoteric trinitarian theology.

In one thesis he wrote that the hidden God—the No-End beyond the summit of the *Sefirot* at S_1—was "not to be numbered along with other Numerations because it is the unity of those Numerations, removed and uncommunicated." This was one of the "principles and statements of the knowledge of Kabbalah," according to another thesis, that compelled Kabbalists to accept "precisely . . . what the Catholic faith of Christians declares about the Trinity." A corollary maintains that "those who deny the Trinity . . . can plainly be refuted if principles of Kabbalah are accepted." Then comes another thesis claiming that "no Hebrew Kabbalist can deny that the name Jesus . . . signifies . . . God, the Son of God and the Wisdom of the Father united through the third person of the Deity (who is the hottest fire of Love) to human nature."

Sefirotic theosophy conceals the Trinity—or Trinities—in Pico's Kabbalah. Some Hebrew names assigned by him to its persons put the Father at S_1, the Son at S_6, and the Holy Spirit at S_{10}. There are ten *Sefirot*, however, not three. But there was room in the ten for more Trinities: S_1, S_2, and S_3, a first triad, absolutely undescended into creation and transcending it; S_1, S_6, and S_{10}, a second triad, reaching through the Godhead from top to bottom and starting a descent toward immanence; then a third triad, S_1, S_9, and S_{10}, as far descended as a *Sefirah* could be. The Father is S_1 in all three of these "groups" or "groupings" (or-

dines, coordinationes) — Pico's terms for configurations of the *Sefirot*. But the Son, S2 in the undescended Trinity, becomes S6 when descending or S9 when descended, and when the Holy Spirit is S10 rather than S3. This trinitarian Kabbalah was Pico's main doctrinal goal in the final seventy-two propositions of his *Conclusions*.[114]

Pico knew where to find the metaphysical infrastructure for a triplet of trinities grouped in a matrix of ten — three times three persons within a unity beyond naming, from a Christian mystic's perspective, but also attributes or emanations or names of God learned from Jews and pagans. Pico's explorations of Neoplatonic philosophy revealed a pattern of Remaining, Procession, and Reversion to frame such trinities — as in his unusually detailed thesis on a sefirotic soul that 'dwells,' 'goes,' and 'turns back.' In that proposition, by relating "our soul to the ten *Sefirot*," he leaped from a Christianized pagan theology that was traditional and merely recondite to a Christianized Jewish theosophy that was outlandish and entirely inscrutable — unless the prince could unriddle it, starting with the easier puzzles.

A related thesis on Plotinus confronts a paradox: "not all the soul descends when it descends." How could that be? Because Soul, like the One and Mind, the other two hypostases, also always remains. In a sequence of propositions on Proclus, the dynamics are more intricate but also more forthcoming.

> Every middle order abides, stable in the order before, and in itself supports the one that follows.

> Just as the first Trinity after Unity is everything as intelligible, commensurate and bounded in form, so the second Trinity is everything as living, true and unbounded in form, and the third is all of this as belonging properly to the mixture and beautiful in form.

The first Trinity only abides, the second abides and processes, the third turns back after processing.

Proclus—in his *Elements of Theology*, his *Platonic Theology*, and his commentaries on Plato—left a blueprint for a Neoplatonic architecture of divine triads; Ficino explicated it; and Pico responded enthusiastically. Proclus got so much attention in the *Conclusions*—fifty-five theses—because he said so much about trinities.

Similar insights convinced Pico that books of Kabbalah also confirmed Christian dogma and, therefore, that such books were priceless. They revealed a new and arcane creed "revered by Jews" that he could turn against them to "do battle for religion." But first he had to win a preliminary fight: he had a speech to give and an audience to excite. To conclude his *Oration*, after saying so much and so little about Kabbalah, he injected a few words about Orpheus and his *Hymns* as a pagan voice for numerical mysteries. He added these final enigmas to show how hard he was working to clarify philosophy's mysteries.

Yet sniping critics still complained that he talked too much about nothing. He replied that just one thesis—about Plato and Aristotle agreeing—could have justified many more propositions. Nonetheless, even a prince had to set a limit to his statements. The real problem was that others were ignorant, not that he was ambitious. The Fathers should call for the dispute to begin with a trumpet blast.[115]

NOTES

1. Jean-Paul Sartre, *L'Existentialisme est un humanisme* (Paris: Nagel, 1946), pp. 12, 21; Eugenio Garin, "Mezzo secolo dopo in Cina," *Belfagor* 53 (1998): 153–54; Margaret King, *Renaissance Humanism: An Anthology of Sources* (Indianapolis: Hackett, 2014), pp. 52–55; Brian Copenhaver,

"Contro 'l'umanesimo': L'Autocoscienza di Pico e la sua fama," *Rinascimento* 56 (2016): p. 361 n. 5.

2. How Pico's fame waxed and waned is discussed at length, with full documentation, in Copenhaver, *Magic and the Dignity of Man*: some mileposts are works by Jacob Brucker, Voltaire, Wilhelm Tennemann, August Ritter, Georg Dreydorff, Jacob Burckhardt, Giovanni Gentile, and Eugenio Garin; also other works mentioned in this Introduction, nn. 19 and 20. (Secondary literature is cited by short title in the notes to this Introduction and in the Notes to the Translations; full citations appear in the Bibliography. Works by Giovanni and Gianfrancesco Pico are cited by short title and date; full details are given in the Bibliography. References to Introduction notes refer to the note number in the Introduction text itself.)

3. *Vit.*; for Gianfrancesco's own biography, see Schmitt, *Gianfrancesco Pico*, pp. 11–30; and Elisabetta Scapparone, "Giovan Francesco Pico," *DBI* (2015). Also, for a strange painting by Paul Delaroche of the infant Pico as the baby Jesus, see Stephen Bann, *Paul Delaroche: History Painted* (Princeton: Princeton University Press, 1997), pp. 216, 239–41; pl. 131 reproduces the painting, called *The Childhood of Pico della Mirandola*, 1842, now in the Musée des Beaux Arts of Nantes. References to the *Oration* (*Orat.*) and Life (*Vit.*) in this Introduction refer also to materials cited in the notes to the English translations.

4. *Orat.* 63, 68; *Vit.* 28–30; *Concl.* p. 61; *App.* 1.33.5; *Apol.* pp. 53, 55–58.

5. *Orat.* 68; *Vit.* 38; *Concl.* pp. 24–28, 60–69; *App.* 1.21, 33. ISTC ip00639300, also rare, was a second edition, not a reprint, of the *Conclusions*, around the same time; since it was probably printed in Ingolstadt, perhaps by Bartholomew Golsch, involvement by Pico is unlikely.

6. Gianfrancesco Pico, *Liber de veris calamitatum causis nostrorum temporum* (1519); Schmitt, *Gianfrancesco Pico*, 26–27, 192, 206; Paolo Fornaciari, "Introduzione," in Giovanni Pico, *Apologia: L'Autodifesa di Pico di fronte al tribunale dell'Inquisizione*, (Florence: Galluzzo, 2010), xiv–xxii; Quaquarelli and Zanardi, *Pichiana*, no. 8 (pp. 144–47), 21 (pp. 180–82), 25 (pp. 1901–2); no. 9 is a reprint of 8. See the previous note for the second edition of the *Conclusions*.

7. *Vit.* 15; Erika Rummel, *The Case Against Johann Reuchlin: Religious and Social Controversy in Sixteenth-Century Germany* (Toronto: University of Toronto Press, 2003), pp. 3–25; Copenhaver and Kokin, "Egidio da Viterbo's Book on Hebrew Letters."

8. *Concl.* pp. 24–28, 60–69; *App.* 1.5, 21, 33; *Apol.* pp. 47–60; *B*, fol. [1^r].

9. *Orat.* 52–56; *Vit.* 16–17, 41, 47; Copenhaver, "Studied as an Oration," pp. 154–56.

10. Martin Kemp, *Leonardo da Vinci: The Marvellous Works of Nature and Man* (Cambridge, MA: Harvard University Press, 1981), pp. 152–59, 199–210; Gino Benzoni, "Ludovico Sforza, detto il Moro, duca di Milano," *DBI* (2006); Azzolini, *The Duke and the Stars*, pp. 126–209; Copenhaver, *Magic in Western Culture*, pp. 291–99.

11. *B*, sig. YYiv^r; Paul Oskar Kristeller, ed., *Supplementum Ficinianum: Marsilii Ficini florentini philosophi Platonici opuscula inedita et dispersa . . .* (Florence: Olschki, 1937), 2.91–93; Copenhaver, "Studied as an Oration," p. 173.

12. *Vit. ep.* 4–5; note 10 in this Introduction; and for another disagreement between Pico and Ficino, see Allen, "The Second Ficino-Pico Controversy," pp. 417–55; on the *Commento* and Pico's disparagement of Ficino's grasp of Platonism, Allen, "The Birth Day of Venus," pp. 81–117; Copenhaver, "Giovanni Pico della Mirandola on Virtue, Happiness and Magic," in *Plotinus' Legacy: The Transformation of Platonism from the Renaissance to the Modern Era*, ed. Stephen Gersh (Cambridge: Cambridge University Press, 2019), pp. 44–70.

13. *Vit.* 92; *Vit. ep.* 6: Gianfrancesco wrote against astrology and illicit divination in *De rerum praenotione* (1507); Savonarola, "Renovation Sermon," January 13, 1495, in *Selected Writings of Girolamo Savonarola: Religion and Politics, 1490–1498*, ed. and trans. Anne Borelli et al. (New Haven: Yale University Press, 2006), p. 60; Schmitt, *Gianfrancesco Pico*, pp. 11–12, 192; Weinstein, *Savonarola and Florence*, pp. 86–91, 191–92; Azzolini, *The Duke and the Stars*, pp. 170–81; Intro., nn. 15, 22, and 23.

14. Gianfrancesco Pico, *Liber de imaginatione* (1501); *Examen vanitatis doctrinae gentium* (1520); Schmitt, *Gianfrancesco Pico*, pp. 12–18, 43–54, 191.

15. Gianfrancesco Pico, *Compendio delle cose mirabili* (1681); *Vita fratris Hieronymi Savonarolae* (1674), and for a modern edition, *Vita Hieronymi Savonarolae* (1999); Schmitt, *Gianfrancesco Pico*, pp. 15–18, 26–30, 34–37, 193–96; Weinstein, *Savonarola and Florence*, pp. 83–84, 100–101; Lorenzo Polizzotto, *The Elect Nation: The Savonarolan Movement in Florence* (Oxford: Clarendon Press, 1994), pp. 98–118, 163–68; Martines, *Scourge and Fire*, pp. 8–18.

16. *Vit.* 79; Weinstein, *Savonarola and Florence*, pp. 107–8, 126–28, 136–37; Martines, *Scourge and Fire*, pp. 94–95, 104–10, 156; Azzolini, *The Duke and the Stars*, pp. 199–209; Intro., n. 11.

17. *Vit. ep.* 1; B, fol. [1ʳ]; Francesco Bausi, "Giovanni Pico della Mirandola: Filosofia, teologia, religione," *Interpres: Rivista di Studi Quattrocenteschi* 18 (1999): 74–75, 88–90.

18. *Vit.* 31, 41, 47; B, fol. [1ʳ], sigs. QQᵛ–RRiiiʳ; the full text of the headnote is edited with a translation in App. V; Copenhaver, "Studied as an Oration," pp. 154–57, 166–67.

19. Full documentation for these works by Thomas More and others, especially Edward Jesup, William Parr Greswell, Walter Pater, and James Rigg, can be found in Copenhaver, *Magic and the Dignity of Man*.

20. Full documentation on this later generation of Pico experts can be found in Copenhaver, *Magic and the Dignity of Man*; on the idea of dignity, see also Brian Copenhaver, "Dignity, Vile Bodies and Nakedness: Giovanni Pico and Giannozzo Manetti" in *Dignity: A History*, ed. Remy Debes (Oxford: Oxford University Press, 2017), pp. 127–79; Intro., nn. 2 and 19.

21. *Vit.* 41; Intro., n. 9.

22. *Vit.* 5, 41, 77, 85, 88, with remarks by and about Savonarola from 80 through 93; *Vit. ep.* 1; Paulinus of Nola, *Vita di S. Ambrogio*, ed. M. Pellegrino (Rome: Editrice Studium, 1961); Hippolyte Delehaye, *The Legends of the Saints* (Notre Dame: University of Notre Dame Press, 1961), pp. 33–34, 51–52; Thomas Heffernan, *Sacred Biography: Saints and Their Biographers in the Middle Ages* (Oxford: Oxford University Press, 1988), pp. 28–32, 66–71, 265–67.

23. *Vit.* 84; cf. Savonarola, *Prediche sopra Aggeo con il trattato circa il reggimento e governo della città di Firenze*, ed. Luigi Firpo (Rome: Belardetti, 1965), pp. 104, 506, which may be a digest of the longer sermon described by Gianfrancesco's report. Before the section on Savonarola, the biography covers Pico's birth and early life in paragraphs 1–9; the Roman disaster in 10–15; crisis and conversion, 16–20; writings and unfinished projects, 21–41; thinking, speaking, and writing, 42–51; character and conduct, 52–73; illness and death, 74–79.

24. *Vit.* 3, 15, 49, 74, 79–80: for the chronology, see Garin, *Pico: Vita e dottrina*, pp. 3–48; Bacchelli, "Giovanni Pico," *DBI*; and for Pico and Margherita, see Bori and Marchignoli, *Pluralità delle vie*, pp. 11–15.

25. *Vit.* 6, 18, 59; Paolo Giovio, *Elogia virorum literis illustrium, quotquot vel nostra vel avorum momoria vixere; ex eiusdem musaeo (cuius descriptionem una exhibemus) ad vivum expressis imaginibus exornata* (Basel: Petrus Perna, 1577), pp. 50–51; Walter Pater, *The Renaissance: Studies in Art and Poetry, the 1893 Text*, ed. D. Hill (Berkeley: University of California Press), p. 29.

26. *Vit.* 7.

27. *Vit.* 8–10, 27, 45; Bacchelli, "Giovanni Pico," *DBI*; Kalman Bland, "Elijah del Medigo's Averroist Response to the Kabbalahs of Fifteenth-Century Jewry and Pico Della Mirandola," *Journal of Jewish Thought and Philosophy* 1 (1991): 23–63; Bland, "Elijah Del Medigo, Unicity of Intellect, and Immortality of Soul," *Proceedings of the American Academy for Jewish Research* 61 (1995): 1–22; Edward P. Mahoney, "Giovanni Pico della Mirandola and Elia del Medigo, Nicoletto Vernia and Agostino Nifo," in *L'Opera e il pensiero di Giovanni Pico della Mirandola*, 1: 127–38; Michael Engel, *Elijah del Medigo and Paduan Aristotelianism: Investigating the Human Intellect* (London: Bloomsbury, 2017).

28. *Vit.* 12–13, 15; Nicola Raoni, "Bonfrancesco Arlotti," *DBI* (1962).

29. *Vit.* 14, 16–17, quoting *Apol.* p. III.

30. *Vit.* 11, 16, 50; *Concl.* p. 70; *App.* 1.34.

31. *Vit.* 18–19.

32. *Vit.* 10, 21–41, esp. 21; Salviati to Lorenzo, in *Hept.* sig. a^v; Quaquarelli and Zanardi, *Pichiana*, pp. 413–14; Black, *Pico's* Heptaplus, p. 26; Intro,

n. 29. For a modern text of the *Heptaplus*, see Pico, *De hominis dignitate, Heptaplus, De ente et uno e scritti vari* (1942); English versions are *Heptaplus*, trans. Douglas Carmichael, in *Pico della Mirandola, On the Dignity of Man; On Being and the One; Heptaplus*, ed. Paul J. W. Miller (Indianapolis: Hackett, 1965), pp. 63–174; *Heptaplus or Discourse on the Seven Days of Creation*, trans. Jesse Brewer McGaw (New York: Philosophical Library, 1977).

33. *Vit.* 26; *Orat.* 64; B, fol. [1ʳ]; for a modern text of the *Commento*, see Pico, *Kommentar zu einem Lied der Liebe, italienisch-deutsch*, ed. and trans. Thorsten Bürklin (Hamburg: Meiner, 2001), and for analysis, Allen, "The Birth Day of Venus."

34. *Vit.* 19, 20–21, 24, 26, 40, 91–92; for a modern text of *De ente et uno*, see Pico, *Dell'Ente e dell'uno con le obiezioni di Giovanni Pico della Mirandola*, ed. and trans. Franco Bacchelli and Raphael Ebgi (Milan: Bompiani, 2010).

35. *Vit.* 29–34; Intro, n. 17. For a text of the *Disputations*, see Pico, *Disputationes adversus astrologiam divinatricem* (1946–52).

36. *Vit.* 31, 38, 41; above, n. 18.

37. *Vit.* 44; Weinstein, *Savonarola and Florence*, pp. 99–101, 126–29; Martines, *Scourge and Fire*, pp. 93–101.

38. *Vit.* 44, 47–48, 51; Breen, "Conflict of Philosophy and Rhetoric"; Carlo Dionisotti, "Ermolao Barbaro e la fortuna di Suiseth," *Medioevo e Rinascimento* 1 (1955): 218–53; Eugenio Garin, "La Cultura fiorentina nella seconda metà del Trecento e i *barbari Britanni*," *Rassegna della letteratura Italiana* 64 (1960): 181–95; John Marenbon, *Medieval Philosophy: An Historical and Philosophical Introduction* (London: Routledge, 2007), pp. 311–15; Cesare Vasoli, *La Dialettica e la retorica dell'umanesimo: 'Invenzione' e 'Metodo' nella cultura del XV e XVI secolo* (Naples: La Città del Sole, 2007), pp. 41–53.

39. *Vit.* 47; *Concl.* pp. 28–30, 33–34, 42; *App.* 1.24.44, 53; 26.8, 14; Schmitt, *Gianfrancesco Pico*, pp. 86, 103, 110–12, 122–23; Edelheit, *Ficino, Pico and Savonarola*, pp. 305–22.

40. *Vit.* 44; *Concl.* pp. 1, 3, 9–11, 30, 51; App. 1.3.1, 5; 7.35; 8.9; 9.9–10; 24.1–3, 6; 25.1; 28.5; 29.12–14; Petrarch, *Epist. fam.* 1.2 (18–19, trans. Bernardo), 1.7 (37–40, trans. Bernardo); Leonardo Bruni, *Dialogi ad Petrum Paulam Histrum*, ed. S. Baldassarri (Florence: Olschki, 1994), p. 247; Breen, "Conflict of Philosophy and Rhetoric," p. 403; Lisa Jardine, "Humanistic Logic," in *Cambridge History of Renaissance Philosophy*, ed. Charles Schmitt et al. (Cambridge: Cambridge University Press, 1988), pp. 173–78; Charles Lohr, "Metaphysics," ibid., pp. 591–94; Letizia Panizza, "Pico della Mirandola e il *De genere dicendi philosophorum* del 1485: L'Encomio paradossale dei *barbari* e la loro parodia," *I Tatti Studies* 8 (1999): 69–103; Grendler, *The Universities of the Italian Renaissance*, pp. 257–60.

41. *Vit.* 52–59: for the scourge in one of Savonarola's sermons, see the "Renovation Sermon" in Borelli et al., *Selected Writings of Girolamo Savonarola*, pp. 57–136; also Giovanni Di Napoli, *Giovanni Pico della Mirandola e la problematica dottrinale del suo tempo* (Rome: Desclée, 1965), pp. 486–87 on Pico's asceticism.

42. *Vit.* 55–56; Bacchelli, "Giovanni Pico," *DBI*; Bausi, "Filosofia, teologia, religione," pp. 79–81, 88.

43. *Vit.* 14–19; Bacchelli, "Giovanni Pico," *DBI*; Quaquarelli and Zanardi, *Pichiana*, no. 4, p. 413; Black, *Pico's Heptaplus*, pp. 8–9.

44. *Vit.* 21, cf. 10–11, 28–30; Black, *Pico's Heptaplus*, pp. 10–11, 131–32, 214–21, 235–39; Charles Trinkaus, "*L'Heptaplus* di Pico della Mirandola: Compendio tematico e concordanza del suo pensiero," in *Giovanni Pico della Mirandola*, ed. Garfagnini (1997), 1: 104–25; Intro., n. 41.

45. *Vit.* 18–19; Schmitt, *Gianfrancesco Pico*, pp. 16–20; Bausi, "Filosofia, teologia, religione," pp. 79–80.

46. *Vit.* 49; Schmitt, *Gianfrancesco Pico*, p. 11.

47. *Vit.* 80–93; Savonarola, *Prediche sopra Aggeo*, pp. 104, 506, which, since the friar often spoke for hours, could be a digest of a longer sermon; also Weinstein, *Savonarola and Florence*, pp. 215–16; Intro., n. 23.

48. *Vit.* 77, 85, 89–91.

49. Giannozzo Manetti, *On Human Worth and Excellence*, ed. and trans. Brian Copenhaver (Cambridge, MA: Harvard University Press, 2019), with a translation of Fazio's work in Appendix 2; Lotario dei Segni, *De miseria condicionis humanae*, ed. and trans. Robert E. Lewis (Athens: University of Georgia Press, 1978).

50. *B*, sigs. QQii^v, iv^r, iv^v, v^r, vi^r, vi^v, RR^v, ii^r, ii^v, corresponding to *Orat.* 8, 10, 27, 30, 33, 41, 46, 48, 56, and 60, but note that the last of the blank spaces (on RRrii^v) was left for a Greek quotation from the Areopagite. Chaldean language and Chaldean teachings come up in the speech at *Orat.* 10, 33, 41, 52, and 69; see also *Concl.* pp. 54–56; *App.* 1.30.

51. *Orat.* 10; *F*, fol. 147^r; also the headnote to *App.* I.

52. *Vit.* 11; *Concl.* pp. 54, 60–61; *App.* 1.30, 33.6; *W*, pp. 31, 141–42, 166–67, 197, 226; Intro., nn. 6, 7, and 44.

53. *Orat.* 5–7, 11, 27; *Bn*, pp. xi, xv–xvi, 174; Copenhaver, "Dignity," pp. 127–39.

54. *Opera Joannis Pici* (1504), sigs. i^v, v^r; Quaquarelli and Zanardi, *Pichiana*, no. 18; Schmitt, *Gianfrancesco Pico*, p. 23; James Overfield, *Humanism and Scholasticism in Late Medieval Germany* (Princeton: Princeton University Press, 1984), pp. 81–86; Erika Rummel, *The Humanist-Scholastic Debate in the Renaissance and Reformation* (Cambridge, MA: Harvard University Press, 1995), pp. 75–80; Michael Sudduth, "Pico della Mirandola's Philosophy of Religion," in Dougherty, *New Essays*, p. 63; Eric Demeuse, "Jerome Emser," in *Dictionary of Luther and the Lutheran Traditions*, ed. Timothy Wengert et al. (Grand Rapids: Baker Academic, 2017), pp. 217–18.

55. *Opera Joannis Pici* (1504), sigs. Aii^r–iv^v.

56. *Opera Joannis Pici* (1504), sigs. A^r, LXXXIV^v, LXXXX^v.

57. For the fight about Pico and Zwingli, see Copenhaver, *Magic and the Dignity of Man*, pp. 269–74, on Georg Dreydorff, Christoph Sigwart, Eduard Zeller, and Giovanni Di Napoli; Intro., n. 54.

58. *B*, fol. [1^r], sigs. QQ^v–ii; *Orat.* 4, 5, 8, 41; *Opera Joannis Pici* (1504), sigs. LXXXIV^v–VI^r; Quaquarelli and Zanardi, *Pichiana*, no. 1, p. 101; Intro., nn. 21 and 54.

59. John O'Malley, "Preaching for the Popes," in *The Pursuit of Holiness in Late Medieval and Renaissance Religion: Papers from the University of Michigan Conference*, ed. Charles Trinkaus and Heiko Obermann (Leiden: Brill, 1974), pp. 424–37; O'Malley, *Praise and Blame in Renaissance Rome: Rhetoric, Doctrine and Reform in the Sacred Orators of the Papal Court, c. 1450–1521* (Durham: Duke University Press, 1979), pp. 53–55, 111–12, 132–37; cf. Michael Dougherty, "Three Precursors to Pico della Mirandola's Roman Disputation and the Question of Human Nature in the Oratio," in Dougherty, *New Essays*, pp. 146–51.

60. Quaquarelli and Zanardi, *Pichiana*, nos. 2, 3, 19, 20, 21, 22, 23, 24, 26, 106, pp. 413–14.

61. *Orat.* 5–7; *Opera Joannis Pici* (1504), sig. LXXXVᵛ; Copenhaver, "Dignity," pp. 127–39.

62. *Orat.* 6, 9, 18, 59, 64–66; Gen. 1–2 (Vulg.); John 8:34 (Vulg.); Kristeller, "Pico and His Sources," 1.53; Di Napoli, *Giovanni Pico*, pp. 400–406.

63. *Apol.* pp. 1–10, corresponds roughly to *Orat.* 39 and 41–71. For disagreements about rhetoric, see Paul Oskar Kristeller, "Introduction," in *The Renaissance Philosophy of Man*, ed. Ernst Cassirer, Paul Oskar Kristeller, and John Herman Randall (Chicago: University of Chicago Press, 1948), p. 222; Kristeller, *Eight Philosophers*, p. 67; Kristeller, "Pico and His Sources," 1: 53; Garin, "Le Interpretazioni del pensiero di Giovanni Pico," pp. 11–12; cf. Dulles, *Princeps Concordiae*, pp. 15–16; Craven, *Giovanni Pico*, pp. 44–45, 96; and for a thorough analysis of Pico's style, Bausi, *Nec rhetor neque philosophus*; also Intro., nn. 2, 19, 20, and 25.

64. *Orat.* 8, 11, 17, 27–28, 30–31, 35–36, 39, 48, 52, 58, 60, 63–66, 68–70; Matt. 7:6, 13:44–45.

65. *Orat.* 1, 18; *Asclep.* 5–6, 11–12; also the headnote to App. II and the text at F 1; Pier Cesare Bori, "I tre giardini della scena paradisiaca del *De hominis dignitate* di Pico della Mirandola," *Annali di Storia dell'Esegesi* 13 (1996): 551–64; cf. *Bn*, p. 2; Pico, *Oration*, ed. and trans. Borghesi, Papio, and Riva, p. 109; Busi and Ebgi, *Mito, Magia, Qabbalah*, pp. xxviii–xxxi.

66. *Orat.* 10; Intro., n. 60.

67. *Orat.* 1, 8; Ter. *Haut.* 4.6.22; Ficino, *Op.* 1825; Anna de Pace, *La Scepsi, il sapere a l'anima: Dissonanze nella cerchia laurenziana* (Milan: LED, 2002), pp. 256–57; the *admiror* words are in 1–4, 7, 8, and 10; Intro., nn. 60 and 65.

68. Arist. *Eth. Nic.* 1100^{a}31–^{b}11; *Hist. an.* 503^{a}15–28; ps.-Arist., *Mir. ausc.* 832^{b}8–16; Plin. *HN* 8.120–22; 11.152, 188; 28.112–18; Plut. *Vit. Alc.* 23; *Quomodo adul.* 53D; *De soll. an.* 978E; Gell. *NA* 10.12.1; Greg. Naz. *Orat.* 4.62; *Les Emblemes de Maistre Andre Alciat, puis nagueres augmentez par ledict Alciat et mise in rime francoise avec curieuse correction* (Paris: Christien Wechel, 1542), p. 190 (88); *Desiderii Erasmi Roterodami Adagiorum chiliades quatuor et sesquicentaria* (Lyon: Gryphius, 1558), cols. 69, 817–18, 1158 (1.1.93, 3.4.1, 4.9.111).

69. *Orat.* 8, 18, 20; *Concl.* p. 55; *App.* 1.30.4; Hom. *Od.* 4.384–423, 17.485–87; Emped. fr. 108 (B117D); Pl. *Euthyd.* 288B–C; *Ion,* 541E–42A; *Phdr.* 249B; *Resp.* 381C–E, 82A–C; *Hymn. Orph.* 25 (Klutstein, *Orph.,* p. 75); Diog. Laert. 8.14, 77; Calcid. *In Tim.* 197; Greg. Naz., *Orat.* 4.62; *Koran* 2:65, 171; 7:166, 176, 179; Alciato, *Emblemes,* pp. 248–49 (115). For Ficino's efforts to mitigate Platonic errors about transmigration, see James Hankins, *Plato in the Italian Renaissance* (Leiden: Brill, 1990), 1: 358–59.

70. *Orat.* 8, 11; *F* 8; *B,* sig. QQ^v; Intro., nn. 51–53.

71. *Orat.* 15, 17.

72. *Orat.* 15, 17; Intro., n. 63.

73. *Orat.* 15–20, 26, 31, 33, and for other "Fathers," see *Orat.* 1; *Concl.* p. 68; *App.* 1.33.65; Black, *Pico's* Heptaplus, pp. 26–27; Intro., n. 32.

74. *Orat.* 7–8, 13–17, 31–32, 48, 55, 57, 65–66, 69; a recent synthesis of Moshe Idel's many writings about Abulafia, which are the best guides to this difficult material, is his *Kabbalah in Italy,* pp. 30–105, 154–63, 219–35, 419. For another approach to the structure of the speech, based on a theory about stages of its composition, see Bori and Marchignoli, *Pluralità,* pp. 35–84.

75. Iambl. *Protrep.* 8.17–21, 35.14–22; Ps.-Dion. *MT* 997A–1001A; Abulafia, *Ve-zot,* fols. 120^v, 131; *W,* pp. 109, 134–35.

76. *Orat.* 7, 14, 16–17, 19, 26–28, 30–31, 33, 56–57, 67; *Concl.* pp. 56, 61; App. 1.30.3, 33.3.

77. *Orat.* 7–8, 11, 19–20, 24, 29, 35; ps.-Dion. MT 1001A; Intro., n. 69.

78. *Orat.* 7–8, 48; *Concl.* p. 56; App. 1.30.10; ps.-Dion. EH 376A, 377B; Abulafia, *Secr.*, fols. 341^v–2^r, 377^r–8; Andrew Smith, *Porphyry's Place in the Neoplatonic Tradition: A Study in Post-Plotinian Neoplatonism* (The Hague: Nijhoff, 1974), pp. 83–99; Moshe Idel, *Messianic Mystics* (New Haven: Yale University Press, 1998), pp. 65–77; Norman Russell, *The Doctrine of Deification in the Greek Patristic Tradition* (Oxford: Oxford University Press, 2004); Stephen Finlan and Vladimir Kharmalov, *Theôsis: Deification in Christian Theology* (Eugene: Pickwick Publications, 2006); Moshe Idel, *Ben: Sonship and Jewish Mysticism* (New York: Continuum, 2007), pp. 507–14; Idel, "Kabbalistic Backgrounds," pp. 28–35; Copenhaver, *Magic in Western Culture*, pp. 76–79.

79. *Orat.* 24; *Concl.* p. 7; App. 1.7.2–4; Abulafia, *Ve-zot*, fol. 122^v; Davidson, *Alfarabi, Avicenna and Averroes*, pp. 3–126, 209–32, 258–356; Intro. at n. 27 on Elia.

80. *Orat.* 19; Ibn Tufayl, "Hayy bin Yaqzan," in *Medieval Islamic Philosophical Writings*, ed. M. Khalidi (Cambridge: Cambridge University Press, 2005), pp. 146–47; Maimonides, *Guide*, I, 93^a, 122^a; Alfred L. Ivry, *Maimonides' Guide of the Perplexed: A Philosophical Guide* (Chicago: University of Chicago Press, 2016), pp. 44, 74, 80, 255; Bacchelli, "Pico traduttore di Ibn Tufayl."

81. *Orat.* 17–18; Tg. ps.-J. Gen. 28:12 (Etheridge 252); Midr. Gen. 68:12; Bahir, pp. 169, 196; Zohar I, 19^a; Borelli et. al., *Selected Writings of Girolamo Savonarola*, pp. 3–32; David Jeffrey, *A Dictionary of Biblical Tradition in English Literature* (Grand Rapids: Eerdmans, 1992), pp. 388–90.

82. *Concl.* p. 61; App. 1.33.2; Ezek. 1:15–28: Maimonides, *Guide*, 3^a; Ivry, *Maimonides' Guide*, pp. 148–53.

83. *Orat.* 4, 8, 13–14, 16, 20, 24, 26, 28, 30–34, 42, 52, 55, 57–58, 64–66, 68–69; Raffaele Starrabba, "Guglielmo Raimondo Moncada, Ebreo convertito siciliano del secolo XV," *Archivio Storico Siciliano*, n.s. 3 (1878): 16–91; François Secret, "Qui était l'orientaliste Mithridate?" *Revue des Études Juives* 116 (1957): 96–102; Busi, "The Kabbalistic Library of

Giovanni Pico della Mirandola," pp. 167–96; Campanini, "Guglielmo Raimondo Moncada," pp. 49–88; Shlomo Simonsohn, "Guglielmo Raimondo Moncada: Un converso alla convergenza di tre culture: ebraica, Cristiana e islamica," in Perani and Pepi, *Guglielmo Raimondo Moncada*, pp. 23–31; Busi and Ebgi, *Mito, Magia, Qabbalah*, pp. lxxvi–lxxix; Wirzubski's "Introduction" in Flavius, *Sermo*, pp. 11–76.

84. *Orat.* 36–45; Intro., nn. 72 and 73.

85. *Orat.* 46–54.

86. *Orat.* 20, 24, 40, 46, 50, 53; *Concl.* p. 1; App. 1.2.

87. *Orat.* 53, 71; *Vit.* 24–25, 35, 37, 43; *Concl.* p. 28; App. 1.23.1; Charles Schmitt, "Gianfrancesco Pico's Attitude toward his Uncle," in *L'Opera e il pensiero di Giovanni Pico della Mirandola*, 2: 313, pointed out that "although the younger Pico began his career as a philosopher from roughly the same point as Giovanni ended his, he ultimately moved to a position almost exactly the opposite," especially on the issue of concord; also Intro., n. 11.

88. Brucker, *Historia critica*, 4.55–61, 353–55; Voltaire, *Essai sur les moeurs*, ed. R. Pomeau (Paris: Garnier, 1963), 2.89; Leo Catana, *The Historiographical Concept 'System of Philosophy': Its Origin, Nature, Influence and Legitimacy* (Leiden: Brill, 2008), pp. 23, 29–31.

89. *Orat.* 71; *Vit.* 41, 47; B, sig. QQ^v; App. V; Pasquale Villari, *The Life and Times of Girolamo Savonarola*, trans. L. Villari (London: Unwin, 1888), 1.74–76, 86–88, 134, 148–49, 167, 169, 244–45; 2.418; Villari, *The Life and Times of Niccolò Machiavelli*, trans. L. Villari (London: Unwin, 1892), 1.145–46; Intro., n. 18.

90. *Orat.* 36–40; *Vit.* 47; Aquinas, *Ver.* 2.3.19; Schmitt, *Gianfrancesco Pico*, pp. 86–87; Paul Cranefield, "On the Origin of the Phrase '*Nihil est in intellectu quod non prius fuerit in sensu*,'" *Journal of the History of Medicine and Allied Sciences* 25 (1970): 77–80.

91. *Orat.* 47; *Concl.* pp. 1, 28–30; App. 1.2, 23.

92. Pico, *Dell'Ente*, ed. Bacchelli and Ebgi, pp. 216–18, 226–28, 240–42, 246, 248, 254, 258, 274–80, 300, 312, 316, 342, 371; Intro., nn. 18 and 88.

93. *Orat.* 54, 56–57; Copenhaver, *Magic in Western Culture*, pp. 363–427; Intro., nn. 73 and 86.

94. *Orat.* 56–60; *Concl.* p. 48; App. 1.27.45; 31.2, 15; Pl. *Leg.* 899B; ps.-Arist. *Mund.* 397^{b}14–18; Al-Kindi, *De radiis*, ed. M.-T. d'Alverny and F. Hudry, in *Archives d'histoire doctrinale et littéraire du moyen âge* 41 (1974): 215–59; William of Auvergne, *Opera* (Paris: Deluyne, 1674), pp. 45, 69–70, 159–65; Roger Bacon, *De secretis operibus artis et naturae et de nullitate magiae*, ed. John Dee (Hamburg: Froben, 1618), pp. 21–70; Copenhaver, *Magic in Western Culture*, pp. 102–26, 245–71; Copenhaver, *The Book of Magic*, pp. 143–49, 296–97, 347–81; Intro., n. 72 on magic in the structure of the speech. For Ficino's magic, see especially James Hankins, "Ficino, Avicenna and the Occult Powers of the Soul," in *Tra antica sapienza e filosofia naturale: La magia nell'Europa moderna*, Atti del convegno (Firenze, 2–4 ottobre 2003, Istituto Nazionale di Studi sul Rinascimento), ed. Fabrizio Meroi and Elisabetta Scapparone, 2 vols. (Florence: Leo S. Olschki, 2007), 1: 35–52.

95. *Orat.* 28, 56–62; Anthony Kenny, *The Five Ways: St. Thomas Aquinas' Proofs of God's Existence* (Notre Dame: University of Notre Dame Press, 1980).

96. Copenhaver, *Magic in Western Culture*, pp. 272–427.

97. Copenhaver, *Magic in Western Culture*, pp. 367–75, 404–27.

98. *Orat.* 62–68.

99. *Orat.* 66–68.

100. *Orat.* 68; *Concl.* pp. 60–69; App. 1.33.

101. *Orat.* 64, 66–67; *Concl.* pp. 61, 63–65, 68; App. 1.32.66; August. *Trin.* 10.10–12.15; Idel, *Kabbalah in Italy*, pp. 89–138; Intro., nn. 74 and 112.

102. Abulafia, *Ve-zot*, fol. 120^v; Deut. 33:7; Ps. 45:8; Prov. 10:30; Lam. 3:49–60; *b. Ber.* 7a; Intro, n. 74.

103. Gen. 1:1–2; Deut. 4:11, 5:20; Isa. 34:11; Ezek. 1:4; Zech. 2:5; *b. Hag.* 12^a; *Zohar* I, 11^b; Intro., n. 99.

104. *Orat.* 2.

105. *Orat.* 65; Intro., n. 81.

106. *Orat.* 63–68; Intro., n. 73.

107. *Orat.* 55, 66–69, 71.

108. *Concl.* pp. 58–60, 62–63; App. 1.32; 34.17; *Apol.* pp. 52–53; Ps. 36:9 (Vulg. 35); *W*, pp. 141–43, 197; Klutstein, *Orph.*, pp. 29, 109–10; Copenhaver and Kokin, "Egidio da Viterbo's Book on Hebrew Letters."

109. *Concl.* pp. 58, 61; App. 1.32.5, 33.6; *W*, pp. 31, 141–42, 166–67, 197, 226; Pico to Benivieni, November 12, 1486, in Pico, *Lettere*, p. 155 (50); also Léon Dorez, "Lettres inédites de Jean Pic de la Mirandole (1482–1492)," *Giornale Storico della Letteratura Italiana* 25 (1895): 352–61, p. 358; Intro., n. 106. In the 1486 printing of the *Conclusions*, which does not number individual theses (see App. I), the count in the headnote of the final set of *T1* theses is seventy-one—most likely a printer's error, like two other mistakes: one in the heading of the sixth set (*Concl.* p. 50), where the number of theses, 10, was left out; and another in the ninth set, whose fourth thesis (App. 1.31.4; *Concl.* p. 56) refers mistakenly to thesis 46 of the third set as 47 (App. 1.25.46; *Concl.* p. 39). A different suggestion is that Pico himself caused this last confusion when "one thesis was dropped from that section [the third set] at a late date": see Farmer, *Syncretism in the West*, pp. 183, 412–13, 422–23, 494–46. Pico was certainly moving fast at the end of 1486: the headnote to *T2* (App. 1.22; *Concl.* p. 28) promises that ten sets of theses will follow, but eleven were printed. Nonetheless, another error in the fourth set—only twenty-nine theses under a headnote that mentions thirty-one, by transposing the last two characters of xxix to xxxi (App. 1.26; *Concl.* pp. 41–44)—can also be explained as the printer's without claiming that "two theological theses were apparently removed from Pico's text during a hasty last-minute revision." If the prince had second thoughts about these theological theses, he should have thought again, since nine of the twenty-nine printed were to be condemned.

110. *Orat.* 8; *Concl.* pp. 55, 62; App. 1.30.7, 33.11; Exod. 14:19–21; Ps. 116:15; Abulafia, *Secr.*, fols. 341ᵛ–42ʳ, 377ʳ–78; Intro, nn. 69, 77, 78, and 93; Copenhaver, "Number, Shape, and Meaning in Pico's Christian Cabala," pp. 46–60.

111. *Orat.* 68; Bacchelli, *Giovanni Pico e Pier Leone da Spoleto*, pp. 63–69; Brian Ogren, *Renaissance and Rebirth: Reincarnation in Early Modern Italian Kabbalah* (Leiden: Brill, 2009), pp. 217–20; Intro., nn. 4, 35, 44, 97–99.

112. *Orat.* 15, 28, 44, 54–55, 68–71; *Concl.* pp. 25, 27–28, 61, 63, 66, 68; Intro., n. 7.

113. App. 1.21.33; *Concl.* p. 27; Scholem, *Kabbalah*, pp. 96–116.

114. *Concl.* pp. 26–28, 61, 63–68; App. 1.21.14, 17, 29, 47; 33.4–7, 14–15, 20, 28, 32–34, 37, 47; Intro., n. 4.

115. *Orat.* 19, 63, 68–72; *Concl.* pp. 14, 18–22, 61–65, 68; App. 1.16.2; 17; 33.5, 6, 20, 33, 34, 59, 66; Proclus, *The Elements of Theology*, ed. and trans. E. R. Dodds (Oxford: Clarendon Press, 1963), pp. 220–23, 234–37, 252–54; Anagnine, *Giovanni Pico*, pp. 226–33; Intro., n. 100.

IOANNIS PICI MIRANDULAE
VIRI OMNI DISCIPLINARUM GENERE
CONSUMATISSIMI VITA
PER IOANNEM FRANCISCUM
ILLUSTRIS PRINCIPIS GALEOTTI
PICI FILIUM EDITA

A LIFE OF GIOVANNI PICO
DELLA MIRANDOLA,
A MAN SUPREMELY ACCOMPLISHED
IN LEARNING OF EVERY KIND,
TOLD BY GIANFRANCESCO,
SON OF THE ILLUSTRIOUS
PRINCE GALEOTTO PICO

Ioannes Franciscus Picus Mirandula Ludovico Mariae Sfortiae Vicecomite Anglo Mediolanensium Duci salutat.

1   Qui virorum illustrium vitas, illustrissime princeps, lectionibus posterorum exaratas tradiderunt alii id egere ut eorum nomina quibus aut sanguinis necessitudine devincti aut parta disciplina obnoxii reddebantur edaci vetustate non exolescerent sed ab oblivionis iniuria prorsus vindicarentur, quod pietatis genus Plinio avunculo Plinius et Plotino praeceptori Porphyrius exhibuerunt. Alii vero id ipsum—et quidem auspicatius—effecere ut scilicet non tam aeternae defunctorum memoriae quam superstitium comparandae vitae consulerent, ideoque Hilarionis Hieronymum, Athanasium Antonii, Martini Severum, Paulinum Ambrosii studia indefessi, mores exactissimos, opera praeclarissima chartis mandasse comperimus, unde et Dei gloria se per orbem diffudit et homines ad bene beateque vivendum et doctrina et moribus etiamnum concitantur.

2   Quorum illectus exemplis operaepretium me facturum putavi si vitam Ioannis Pici stilo prosequerer, tum ut patruo eidemque praeceptori cuius spiritalibus beneficiis auctus et cumulatus sum quasi debitum munus exolverem tum ut hominem et nostro et futuris saeculis proponerem admirandum. Eius enim exemplo mortales et ad frugalitatem institui et impendentis obitus possunt admoneri sed et doctrina abunde locupletari cum inter omnifariam litteratos (ne citem antiquitatem) extra omnem aleam principem locum obtinuerit.

3   Invidiosum fortasse verbum sed proculdubio verum, sed his compertum qui eum intus et in cute—ut dici solet—exploravere. Nec illis futurum absonum qui quinque illum novisse linguas, humanam et divinam philosophiam calluisse, cunctasque hausisse disciplinas quae in usu sunt mortalium, sed quasdam eruisse de

Gianfrancesco Pico della Mirandola salutes Ludovico Maria Sforza, Viscount of Angera, Duke of the Milanese.

Most Illustrious Prince: of those who have passed down lives of   1
illustrious men in writing for posterity to read, some have done
this so that the jaws of time would not eat up the names of those
to whom they had become bound by ties of blood or obligated for
what they learned: from then on, they were to be protected from
the threat of oblivion. This was the type of dutiful affection that
Pliny showed to Pliny, his uncle, and Porphyry to his teacher, Plotinus. Of course, others did this — and their way was better — not
so much to look after the eternal memory of the dead as to secure
the life of those left behind, as I have learned that Jerome did for
Hilarion, Athanasius for Anthony, Severus for Martin and Paulinus for Ambrose, putting their tireless efforts, shining deeds and
scrupulous conduct on paper both to spread God's glory through
the world and to excite people even now to lead good and blessed
lives by their teaching and their morals.

Attracted by their examples, I thought it worthwhile to take my   2
pen and recount Giovanni Pico's life, both to pay a debt to my
uncle, if I could, and likewise to a teacher who blessed me abun-
dantly with spiritual favors. But I also wanted to put this person
on display for our own age and future ages to admire. For by Pico's
example mortal men can be instructed in moderation, warned that
death is nigh but also enriched by copious learning since, without
question, he has taken first place among the learned everywhere —
not to speak of antiquity.

This statement may be offensive, yet it is true beyond doubt,   3
established by those who have investigated the claim *inside and
out* — as the saying goes. Nor will it ring false to those who have
ever recognized his mastery of five languages, his skill in philosophy, human and divine, his deep learning in every subject familiar

tenebris, quasdam etiam excogitasse, nec dum undena triteride perfunctum aliquando noverint.

4   Fidem amplissimam facient commentationes illae nunquam satis pro meritis celebratae quae in praesentia prodeunt in publicum *Heptaplus, Apologiaque* et tractatus *De ente et uno* aliaque compluscula. Omnia adeo illustria suapte natura totque sapientum virorum comendata iudiciis ut qui eadem vel damnet vel minus probet aut non summis efferat laudibus protinus idem contra se ferre sententiam vel ignoratae litteraturae vel malevoli animi suspitioni sit. Invidere ei tam multi possint quam vel omnes admirari vel paucissimi imitari vel nemo reprehendere.

5   Reliquae illius scriptiones sequenti ordine invulgabuntur, potissimum astrologicae pestis confutationes multis laboribus elucubratae multis suspiriis ab hominibus bene institutae mentis et expectatae et flagitatae. Multaque opera a nobis in unum ex litturato et multas in partes discerpto exemplari redactae: quae proxime foras exibunt ut quam citissime fieri possit vivifico suo splendore caligantes oculos et tabifico superstitionum vapore infectos illustrent. Hos libros si a tractandis regni negotiis feriatus interdum degustaveris.

6   Fies extra omnem controversiam certior astrologorum dogmata meracissimas esse nugas et veluti somnia delirantium eorumque praestigias his monumentis patefieri. Quibus lectis atque intellectis vanitatis istius professores—qui nostrates imitati ranas diu coaxaverunt nisi in apertam inciderint insaniam—Macedonicarum more conticescent, id quod forte inter disceptandam super hoc negotio me tibi aliqua ex parte testificatum memini.

7   Haec interim libenti suscipies animo quae nulli magis quam tibi dicanda censui ut meam in te fidem et observantiam—quam dum

to mortals, though there were some that he dug up from the shadows, also some that he invented — and before his thirty-first year was done.[1]

Plentiful proof will come from these studies — a *Heptaplus*, an   4
Apology, a treatise *On Being and the One* and several others — never given the praise that they deserve but now made public. All are so remarkable in their own right and favored by views of so many wise judges that if anyone condemns them or thinks little of them or fails to praise them straight to the skies, that person should be suspected of bringing a verdict against himself — either that he is ignorant of the material or else has evil intentions. Many may envy, very few may imitate, and no one may criticize what everyone admires in Pico.

The rest of his writings will be published in a series to follow —   5
especially proofs against the plague of astrology produced by much hard work, both awaited and demanded by right-minded people. There are also many works that I have put together from a blotted copy torn into pieces: they will come out next, as quickly as possible, so that their life-giving brilliance can light up our dim vision which has been infected by the corrosive mist of superstition. You may sample these books now and then when on holiday from the business of your realm.

They will make you more confident — indisputably so — that   6
the theories of astrologers are the purest nonsense, like dreams of crazy people, and that their juggleries are exposed by these documents. Once you have read and understood them, the professors of this rubbish, who have imitated our frogs and have kept on croaking until they have plainly gone mad, should go silent like the Macedonian kind — as I have shown you in part, if I recall, while discussing this business.[2]

Meanwhile, I hope you'll be happy to have this. I decided that I   7
ought to present it to no one but you so that you might understand that my trust and respect for you — which you have taken to

tuis mererem stipendiis perspectam et exploratam habuisti — non modo non traditam oblivioni sed et perseverare et augescere indies agnosceres. Non ingratam etiam me tibi rem facturum sum ratus quando ea librorum dignitas sit ut inscribi eos sibi maximi reges honestum semper et gloriosum sint arbitrati.

8   Reliquum est ut quo te amore prosequor ad bipartitae iustitiae obeunda munera exhorter atque adiugiter comminiscendum invitem (quod prudentissimi principis semper est officium) non tam honorem quam onus esse quod regnes ut spectatis circumquaque quae et hominem et principem hominem obsideant impedimentis eadem moderatissimis affectibus superare possis aeternamque tibi felicitatem promereri.

9   Vale, princeps clarissime. Mirandulae kalendas Marcii MCCCCLXXXXVI.

be assured and well known as long as I have deserved your support — are not just unforgotten: they endure and increase day by day. I also thought that what I have produced would not displease you since the value of books is such that the greatest rulers have always thought it honorable and glorious to accept dedications in them.

What remains, while sending you my love, is for me to urge you 8 to undertake duties that do justice twice, while continuously inviting you to bear in mind (always the obligation of the wisest prince) that it is not so much an honor as a burden for you to rule. By tempering the passions, you may overcome the obstacles besetting you on every side — as a man and as a prince — and earn for yourself eternal happiness.

Farewell, noblest prince. From Mirandola, March 1, 1496.   9

IOANNIS PICI MIRANDULAE VIRI OMNI DISCIPLINARUM GENERE CONSUMATISSIMI VITA PER IOANNEM FRANCISCUM ILLUSTRIS PRINCIPIS GALEOTTI PICI FILIUM EDITA

1 Ioannis Pici patrui mei vitam scribere orsus, praefandum lectoribus imprimis duco — ne aut quod fratris filius aut quod discipulus fuerim me aliquid in gratiam blandientium more dicturum suspicarentur — nihil familiae nihilque beneficiis, quae maxima profecto in me extiterunt, ficticia laude repensum. Tantum quippe ab adulatione seiuncta est narratio mea quantum abfuit adulandi necessitas. Tantumque cavi ne me vel mentitum vel vehementem in laudibus legentes arbitrarentur, si quicquid de ipso conceperam litteris tradidissem, ut illud fuerit fortasse periculum ne parcum potuerint vel ipsaemet virtutes excelsae vel earum assertores coarguere. Quod vel hoc argumento videre licet, cum plurimum doctorum nostrae aetatis hominum — et ex primoribus quidem — elucubratissimae scriptiones non modo his quae sumus dicturi locupletissimum reddiderint testimonium, sed dum uteretur hac luce, et postquam eam cum potiore commutavit, in eius me et morum et doctrinae praeconiis praecelluerint. Quarum nonnullas in huius libri calce post commentationes ipsius adscribi iussi ut firmior testibus non gentiliciis fides adhiberetur.

2 Paternum genus — licet ab Constantino Caesare per Picum pronepotem a quo totius familiae cognomentum memoriae proditum

A LIFE OF GIOVANNI PICO DELLA MIRANDOLA, A MAN SUPREMELY ACCOMPLISHED IN LEARNING OF EVERY KIND, TOLD BY GIANFRANCESCO, SON OF THE ILLUSTRIOUS PRINCE GALEOTTO PICO

Having set out to write a life of Giovanni Pico, my uncle, I reckon   1
I must first tell my readers that I have paid no one back with fic-
tional praise either for the sake of my family or on account of
kindnesses shown to me, as great as they have been. I hope no one
will suppose I would say anything ingratiating, like a flatterer, because I was my uncle's disciple and his brother's son. In fact, having no need to flatter him, my story is the farthest thing from
flattery. So hard have I tried to prevent readers from thinking of
my praises as lies or overdone that — had I written down whatever
I thought about him — I ran the risk that his outstanding talents
themselves, or their promoters, could blame me for being stingy.
This is especially evident from writings of great seriousness by
learned men of our day — the best of them, in fact. They have not
only supplied plentiful testimony for what I shall say but have
even outdone me in lauding his conduct and teachings, both while
he lived and after he left this life for a better one. I have had some
of their statements added at the end of this book — coming after
his own thoughts — in order to confirm my story with witnesses
who are not relatives.[3]

Setting aside his father's family — even though its origins are   2
said go back to the Emperor Constantine through a great-
grandson, Picus, from whom the whole family is said to have

sit traxisse primordia—missum facientes, ab ipso tempore nativi-
tatis sumemus initium, tum quod familiae forsan non minus honoris ille contulerit quam acceperit, tum quod proprias animi
dotes reliquaque totius vitae et obitus seriem prae se ferentia, quae
vel propriis aut auribus aut oculis hausi, vel ab gravissimis excepi
testibus, aperienda duxerim, posthabitisque et stemmate et prae-
claris avorum facinoribus recensenda.

3   Anno a partu Virginis tertio et sexagesimo supra milesimum et
quadringentesimum, Pio secundo Pontifice Maximo ecclesiae prae-
side et Federico tertio habenas imperii Romani moderante, mater
Iulia ex nobili Boiardorum familia Ioanni Francisco patri ultimo
eum partum peperit. Iam enim Galeottum maiorem natu, ex quo
sum genitus, et Antonium Mariam, sororesque duas enixa fuerat.
Quarum altera Leonello iam coniugi Albertum Pium ex Carpi
principibus unum edidit, nunc Rodulphi principis Gonzagae con-
sors. Altera Pino Ordelapho, Forolivensi Principe, cui iampridem
nupserat, vita functo, Montis Agani Comiti secundas nuptias con-
cessit.

4   Prodigium haud parvum ante ipsius ortum apparuit. Visa enim
circularis flamma est supra parientis matris astare cubiculum mox-
que evanescere, fortasse nobis insinuans orbiculari figurae intellectus perfectione simillimum eum futurum qui inter mortales eadem
hora proderetur, universoque terrae globo excellentia nominis
circumquaque celebrandum, cuius mens semper caelestia, ignis
instar, petitura esset, cuiusque ignita eloquia flammatae menti
consona Deum nostrum, qui ignis comburens est, totis viribus
quandoque celebratura, sed statim obtutibus hominum, ut illa
evanuit, occulenda.

5   Legimus quippe doctissimorum etiam sanctissimorumque hominum ortus insolita quandoque signa aut praecessisse aut sub-
sequuta fuisse, veluti eorum incunabula infantium ab aliorum
caetu divino nutu segregantia summisque rebus gerendis natos

taken its name—I shall begin from the time of his birth, both because he may have given the family no less honor than he got from it and also because I considered famous ancestral deeds and pedigree less important. I decided to open with his own gifts of mind and then review the whole course of his life and passing, as I observed it with my own eyes and ears or as I took it from the most authoritative witnesses.[4]

In the year 1463 after the Virgin Birth, when Pius II was Supreme Pontiff and chief Defender of the Church and Frederick III held the reins of the Roman Empire, Pico's mother Giulia, of the noble Boiardo family, gave birth to him, making Gianfrancesco a father for the last time. Already born were an older child, Galeotto, whose son I am, as well as Antonio Maria and two sisters besides. One of the sisters, when she married Leonello, gave birth to an only son, Alberto Pio, the Prince of Carpi, though now she is the wife of Prince Rodolfo Gonzaga. Long ago, the other sister married Pino Ordelaffi, Prince of Forlì, and when he died, she gave her hand to the Count of Montagnano in a second marriage.[5]

Quite striking was an omen that appeared before Pico was born. As his mother gave birth, a circle of flame stood over the bedroom and soon vanished, perhaps telling us that, in the perfection of his intellect, the one who joined our mortal company at that moment would closely reflect the shape of this sphere as his fame encircled the whole globe, traveling all around it with extraordinary reputation. Like fire, his thoughts would always reach for heaven, and his fiery eloquence, suited to a mind ablaze, would someday praise our God, a burning fire, with all its energy, and then, when the fire went out, the flame would suddenly be hidden from human sight.

I have read this, in fact: when very learned people were born— also the very holy—unusual signs sometimes preceded or followed, as if it were God's will to distinguish those infants in their cradles from others and indicate which were born to do great

3

4

5

indicantia. Sic, ut omittam reliquos, examen apium Ambrosii magni ora lustravit, in eaque introgressum est, dein exiens altissimumque volans seque inter nubila condens, paternos aspectusque aliorumque qui aderant visus elusit. Quod praesagium Paulinus plurifaciens scriptorum eius favos nobis indicasse disseruit, qui caelestia dona enuntiarent et mentes hominum de terris ad caelum erigerent.

6   Forma autem insigni fuit et liberali—procera et celsa statura, molli carne, venusta facie in universum, albenti colore decentique rubore interspersa, caesiis et vigilibus oculis, flavo et inaffectato capillitio, dentibus quoque candidis et aequalibus.

7   Sub matris imperio ad magistros disciplinasque delatus, ita ardenti animo studia humanitatis excoluit ut brevi inter poetas et oratores tempestatis illius praecipuos nec iniuria collocandus esset. In discendo quidem celerrimus erat, prompto adeo ingenio praeditus, ut audita semel a recitante carmina et directo et retrogrado ordine mira omnium admiratione recenseret tenacissimaque retineret memoria. Quod caeteris contra evenire solet, nam qui celeri sunt ingenio natura fieri saepe solet ut non multum memoria valeant, qui vero cum labore percipiunt tenaciores perceptorum evadant.

8   Dum vero quartum et decimum aetatis annum ageret, matris iussu—quae sacris eum initiari vehementer optabat—discendi iuris pontificii gratia Bononiam se transtulit. Quod cum biennium degustasset meris id inniti traditionibus conspicatus, alio deflexit—non tamen absque bonae frugis foetura. Quando iam puer et quidem tenellus ex epistolis summorum pontificum quas decretales vocant epitomen quandam seu breviarium compilaverit. Quo omnes concisius quam fieri potuit sanctionum illarum sententias conclusit—consummatis professoribus opus non tenue.

9   Sed secretarum naturae rerum cupidus explorator, tritas has semitas derelinquens, intellectus speculationi philosophiaeque

things. If I may skip other cases, a swarm of bees buzzed around the mouth of great Ambrose, went inside, came out and flew high enough to pass into the clouds and out of sight, thus escaping the gaze of relatives and others who were there. Paulinus, who made much of this portent, explained that it showed us how the Saint's writings were honeycombs that told about heaven's gifts, thereby lifting human thoughts from earth to heaven.[6]

My uncle's appearance was striking and aristocratic — tall and proud in stature, with smooth skin, generally good looks, complexion on the pale side with a nice mix of ruddiness, eyes blue-gray and alert, blond hair left natural, teeth white and even.

After his mother directed him to be sent off to teachers and lessons, he was so eager to acquire learning that in a short time he found a place — and rightly so — among the best poets and orators of the day. He learned so very rapidly, in fact, and was so well endowed with quick intelligence, that once he heard any verses recited, he would astonish everyone by repeating them both forward and backward, and then he would store them in his unfailingly retentive memory. Others usually have the opposite experience, since those who are naturally quick-witted, as it happens, typically lack good memories, while those who work hard to learn turn out to be better at holding on to their learning.[7]

In his fourteenth year and at his mother's direction — since her strongest desire was to have him take holy orders — he moved to Bologna to study canon law. After trying this for two years and seeing that its basis was merely traditional, he turned elsewhere — though not without producing some good results. While still a boy and quite green, he compiled a kind of epitome or abridgment from the letters by supreme pontiffs that they call decretals. He included all their decisions in statements as concise as he could make them — no light task even for experienced professors.[8]

Longing to explore nature's secrets, however, and leave well-worn paths behind, he gave himself entirely to intellectual

cum humanae tum divinae se penitus dedidit. Cuius enanciscen-
dae gratia, non tantum Italiae sed et Galliarum litteraria gymnasia
perlustrans, celebres doctores tempestatis illius — more Platonis et
Apollonii — scrupulosissime perquirebat, operam adeo indefessam
studiis illis impendens ut consumatus simul et theologus simul et
philosophus imberbis adhuc et esset et haberetur.

10   Iamque septennium apud illos versatus erat, quando humanae
laudis et gloriae cupidus — nondum enim divino amore caluerat, ut
palam fiet — Romam migravit. Inibique ostentare cupiens quanta
eum a summissoribus inposterum maneret invidia, nongentas de
dialecticis et mathematicis, de naturalibus divinisque rebus quaestiones proposuit, non modo ex Latinorum petitas archulis Grae-
corumque excerptas scriniis sed ex Hebraeorum etiam mysteriis
erutas Chaldaeorumque arcanis atque Arabum vestigatas.

11   Multa item de Pythagorae Trimegistique et Orphaei prisca et
suboscura philosophia, multa de Cabala — hoc est secreta Hebraeorum dogmatum receptione cuius et Origenes et Hilarius ex
nostris potissimum comminiscuntur — quaestionibus illis intexuit.
Multa etiam de naturali magia quam non parvo interstitio ab impia et scelesta separari edocuit, idque multorum testimonio ele-
gantissime comprobavit. Nec duo et septuaginta nova dogmata
physica et methaphysica, propria inventa et meditata ad quascunque philosophiae quaestiones elucidandas accommodata defue-
runt. His novam per numeros philosophandi institutionem ad-
nexuit. Cunctaque simul publicis locis quo facilius vulgarentur
affixit, pollicitus se soluturum eis impensas qui ex remotis oris
disceptandi gratia Romam se contulissent.

12   Verum obtrectatorum simultate, quae semper velut ignis alta
petit, nunquam efficere potuit ut dies altercationis praestitueretur.

reflections and philosophy both human and divine. To achieve this, while traveling through learned schools not only in Italy but also in France, he took great care—in the manner of Plato and Apollonius—to seek the outstanding teachers of the day. So tireless were his efforts spent on study that, while still beardless, he became expert both in theology and in philosophy, and people recognized him as such.[9]

Then, after staying with those teachers for seven years, because 10 he desired human fame and glory—and had not yet felt the heat of God's love, as we shall see—he traveled to Rome. There, wishing to make a show of how much the envious would keep grumbling about him, he proposed nine hundred questions on dialectics, mathematics, science and theology, seeking and finding them not only in collections of Latin writings and on bookshelves of the Greeks but also in Hebrew mysteries that he had dug up and even from Chaldean and Arab arcana that he had tracked down.

Into these questions he also wove many points about the an- 11 cient and rather obscure philosophy of Pythagoras, Trismegistus and Orpheus and many things also about Kabbalah—a secret tradition of Hebrew doctrines mentioned by Origen and Hilary, the best informed about it of our writers. There were many items as well about natural magic which, as he explained it, is quite unlike the irreligious and criminal kind, and he gave a very nice confirmation of this with testimony from many authorities. There were also seventy-two new statements about physics and metaphysics, discovered and developed by himself and suited to shed light on various philosophical problems. To these he added a new theory about doing philosophy with numbers. And he posted all of this at the same time in public places as a quick way to make it known, promising to pay the expenses of those who would travel to Rome from far away to join the debate.[10]

Because of hostility from his critics, which like fire always seeks 12 the heights, he could never manage to get a date scheduled for the

Ob hanc causam Romae annum mansit, quo tempore vitiligatores illi palam eum et libero examine non audebant aggredi. Sed strophis potius e cuniculis sugillare clanculariisque telis suffodere pestifera corrupti invidia—ita enim arbitrati sunt plurimi—conabantur. Livorem hunc vel hac ratione sibi maxime eum monuisse existimatum est quod multi qui, vel ambitione fortassis vel avaritia, litterario negotio diu incubuerant notam sibi fore autumarent si iuvenis ille—aggestis atavorum opibus multaque doctrina quasi fertilis ager luxurians—in prima orbis urbe de naturalibus divinisque rebus deque multis per plura saecula nostris hominibus non accessis periclitari doctrinam et ingenium non vereretur.

13   Et cum nihil adversus doctrinam veris machinis moliri posse animadverterent, attulisse in medium tormenta calumniae tredecimque ex nongentis quaestiones rectae fidei suspectas acclamavisse. Quibus forte se iunxisse nonnullos qui quaestiones illas utpote insuetas eorum auribus ut pie ita fortasse parum erudite et zelo fidei et praetextu religionis incesserent. Quas tamen quaestiones non pauci—et quidem celebrati theologiae doctors—ceu pias et mundas prius approbaverant eisdemque subscripserant. Quorum coetu Bonfranciscus Regiensis Episcopus annumeratus est, vir omnigena doctrina acerrimoque iudicio et morum gravitate praeclarus: qui Romae ad Pontificem Maximum ea tempestate pro Ferrariensium duce agebat legatus. Adversus tamen eum blaterones illi nihil attentarunt, cum forte ab eis labefactari eius famam non posse vererentur, quando quicquid tractasset correctioni matris ecclesiae et Pontificis submisisset.

14   At is famae istaec dispendia non perpessus *Apologiam* edidit— varium certe opus et elegans multaque rerum scitu dignarum

dispute. For this reason he remained in Rome for a year, but during this period the thugs never dared to attack him openly in a fair contest. Instead, they tried to taunt him with tricks and traps and undermine him with concealed aggression because, as most people reckoned, they were sick with poisonous envy. It was thought that the chief sources of these malicious threats against him were the many people long involved in learned affairs, who, perhaps out of greed or ambition, believed they would be disgraced if this young man — who had piles of ancestral wealth and was a fertile field ripe with learning — had no qualms about going to the world's leading city to test his genius and learning in science, theology and many subjects untouched by our people for many centuries.[11]

When they realized that real weapons could not damage his 13 learning, these same enemies brought the artillery of calumny into the fray and charged that thirteen of the nine hundred questions cast doubt on the true faith. Some may have joined them who had never heard of such questions, of course, since their learning was small, and perhaps they acted against them out of piety or zeal for the faith and to make a show of their scruples. Yet there were quite a few — famous teachers of theology, in fact — who had already endorsed these questions, approving them as devout and untainted. Counted in this group was Bonfrancesco, the Bishop of Reggio, a person of the most varied learning and keenest judgment, who was renowned for strict morality: he was then in Rome — sent to the Supreme Pontiff as the Duke of Ferrara's ambassador. Those fools never tried anything against the Bishop, however, probably because they feared they could do nothing to shake his reputation, since he had submitted everything he discussed to Mother Church and the Pope for correction.[12]

But Pico, who would not tolerate such losses to his reputation, 14 brought out an *Apology* — a many-sided and refined work, to be sure, loaded with information about things worth knowing and

cognitione refertum vigintique tantum noctibus elucubratum. Qua editione luce clarius conspici datum est non tam conclusiones Catholicos potuisse sensus recipere quam illos qui prius adlatraverant insolentiae et ruditatis coarguendos esse, librumque ipsum et quae scripturus erat imposterum matris ecclesiae eiusque praesidis[1] sanctissimo iudicio christianissimi hominis more committens. Id enim vel expresse vel tacite fieri oportere persuasissimum est, quasique illud[2] Augustini proferret: errare possum, haereticus esse non possum, quando alterum sit hominis proprium, alterum perversae et obstinatae voluntatis.

15   Sed ubi Innocentius octavus, Pontifex Maximus, accepit per editionem *Apologiae* interpretatas conclusiones illas quae prius calumniis infestatae fuerant in Catholicum sensum et a nota criminis relevatas, referentibusque nonnullis quibus conclusionum examen demandatum fuerat decipulas opponi posse fidelibus si nonnullae quaestionum illarum — crudae quidem et inexplicitae disceptandarum more iacebant — passim vagarentur, libelli lectione quo continebantur interdixit. Quae omnia per Alexandri sexti, Pontificis Maximi, sub quo nunc vivimus, diploma quod breve nominant liquido visuntur, quod cum *Apologia* ipsa impressoribus tradere exarandum duximus.

16   Verum in ipso *Apologiae* calce, quod postea Pontifex auctoritate praestitit quibus ille poterat rationibus antea factitaverat. Obsecraverat quippe amicos et inimicos, doctos et indoctos, ut *Apologiam* legerent, libellum vero ipsum conclusionum inexplicitarum praeterirent illectum quando in eo plurima continerentur quae non passim vulganda triviis sed secreto congressu inter doctos et paucos disputanda susceperat.

finished after only twenty nights of intense labor. This publication let people see, clearer than daylight, not just that his conclusions could have Catholic meanings but also that those who had been yipping at him were guilty of arrogance and ignorance. On his best Christian behavior, he also delivered the book itself, and what he would write later, to the most holy judgment of Mother Church and her Protector. For he was completely persuaded that this had to be done, either implicitly or explicitly, and he came close to quoting something from Augustine: *I can make a mistake, but I can't be a heretic*, because the one is human, while the other arises from a will that is evil and obstinate.[13]

However, even when Innocent VIII, the Supreme Pontiff, 15 granted that conclusions previously misrepresented and rendered unsafe were interpreted by the published *Apology* with Catholic meaning and freed of criminal stain, the Pope still forbade the reading of the book that contained the conclusions. This happened after some of those commissioned to examine the statements replied that some might set traps for the faithful if they were spread around everywhere — and indeed they had been issued as raw and undeveloped questions, in the manner of propositions for dispute. All this is evident from a document, called a *brief*, of Alexander VI, the Supreme Pontiff, under whom we now live, which I caused to be published along with the *Apology* when I brought it to the printers.[14]

But right at the end of the *Apology*, in fact, Pico had already 16 used the arguments he could muster to achieve what the Pope eventually accomplished by his ruling. The truth is that he pleaded with friends and enemies, learned and unlearned, to read the *Apology* but to leave his little book of undeveloped conclusions unread because it contained many points that he had taken up *not to spread them around everywhere on street corners but to debate them in a private meeting with a small number of experts.*

17   Scolasticamque exercitationem more academiarum meditatus, multa veterum philosophorum—Alexandri scilicet et Averrois aliorumque quam plurium—impia dogmata proposuisse, quae semper publice[3] et privatim asseverat, professus fuerat, praedicaverat non minus a verae rectaeque philosophiae quam a fidei semitis declinare. Atque in hunc modum de libello illo *Nongentarum Conclusionum* verba faciens apologeticum opus conclusit: qui ergo me oderunt, ideo illa non legant quia nostra sunt; qui me amant, ideo non legant quia ex illis quae mea sunt cogitare plurima possent quae non sunt nostra.

18   Caeterum immensa Dei bonitate, quae ex malis etiam bona elicit, effectum esse—quemadmodum mihi rettulit—iudicabat ut calumnia illa falso a malevolis irrogata veros errores corrigeret. Eique in tenebris aberranti ut quantum exorbitasset a tramite veritatis contueri posset ceu splendidissimum iubar illucesceret. Prius enim et gloriae cupidus et amore vano succensus muliebribusque illecebris commotus fuerat. Feminarum quippe plurimae ob venustatem corporis orisque gratiam—cui doctrina amplaeque divitiae et generis nobilitas accedebant—in eius amorem exarserunt, ab quarum studio non abhorrens, parumper via vitae posthabita in delicias defluxerat.

19   Verum simultate illa experrectus, diffluentem luxu animum retudit et convertit ad Christum atque feminea blandimenta in supernae patriae gaudia commutavit. Neglectaque aura gloriolae quam affectaverat, Dei gloriam et ecclesiae utilitatem tota coepit mente perquirere adeoque mores componere, ut posthac vel inimico iudice comprobari posset.

20   Cumque de ipso gloriosa statim fama et per vicinas et per remotas oras volitare occepisset, plures ex philosophis qui eruditissimi habebantur ad eum—tanquam ad mercaturam bonarum

Because he had planned a school exercise for academic pur-   17
poses, as he explained, many of his propositions were teachings by
ancient philosophers—*like Alexander, Averroes and quite a few others
besides*—which he had always, in *public and private*, declared to be
ungodly, and he had given notice that they deviated *not just from the
paths of faith but also from true and correct philosophy*. Furthermore, he
brought this work of self-defense to a conclusion by speaking
about his book of 900 *Conclusions* as follows: *those who hate me, then,
let them not read these statements because they are mine; those who love
me, let them not read them because from statements that are mine they
might think up many that are not mine.*[15]

On the other hand, since God's generosity is boundless and   18
brings good even out of evil, my uncle reckoned—as he told me—
that the spiteful people who made false charges against him set his
own errors straight: as he wandered in the dark, this dazzling illumination came to him like a radiant beam of light, letting him
see how far he had strayed from the true path. Until then, in fact,
he longed for glory while false love fueled his fires and the wiles of
women stirred them up. Because of his handsome body and good
looks—in addition to learning, abundant riches and a noble lin-
eage—many women fell passionately in love with him, and since
he was not reluctant to pursue them, he neglected to control himself and lapsed into dissipation for a time.

But when dissension woke him up, he pulled his spirit back   19
from dissolute indulgence and turned to Christ, exchanging the
charms of women for the joys of his homeland on high. Ceasing to
care for the trifling, glittering glory that he had desired, he began
seeking God's glory and the welfare of the Church with his whole
mind, tempering his behavior so much that, from then on, he
could win approval even from an unfriendly judge.[16]

As soon as Pico's fame and glory began to spread both near and   20
far, many philosophers known as experts quickly flocked to him—
as if, in Cicero's phrase, he were a *warehouse of culture*. They came

artium, ut inquit Cicero—confluebant, vel ob commovenda lit-
teralia certamina vel, quibus inerat rectior mentis sententia, ad
audienda tenendaque recte vivendi salubria dogmata—quae tanto
magis expetebantur quanto ab homine doctissimo pariter et no-
bilissimo profluebant, qui quandoque devios mollitudinis voluptariae anfractus sectatus fuerat. Videntur enim ad disciplinam
morum auditorum mentibus inserendam ea plurimum habere momenti quae et suapte natura sint bona et a praeceptore converso ad
iustitiae semitas ex distorto et obliquo libidinum calle proficiscan-
tur. Elegiaco carmine amores luserat, quos quinque exaratos libris,
religionis causa ignibus tradidit. Multa itidem rhythmis lusit He-
truscis quae pari causa par ignis absumpsit.

21   Sacras deinde litteras ardentissimo studio complexus, statim in
templo Dei ceu frugum primitias, octavum tunc et vigesimum annum agens, de operibus sex dierum Geneseos et die quietis *Hep-
taplum* obtulit—opus quippe et perfectum ingenio et elaboratum
industria, cum sublimibus philosophorum dogmatis tum profun-
dissimis nostrae Christianae theologiae misteriis refertissimum,
septemplicique varia enarratione connexum septemnario capitum
numero cuilibet septennae expositioni conserto libri nomini maxime quadrans. Quod tamen ob erutas e naturae gremio res et
difficiles divinarum quaestionum evolutiones atque ob prophetae
reconditissima sensa sermonisque elegantiam, non se passim philosophiae et eloquentiae rudibus offert, sed pretiosae illius et rarae
supellectilis usus paucis paratur. Quod et ipse animadvertens, in
eiusdem proemii calce mentionem de hac re non illepidam fecit.

22   Cum primum sacras degustavit litteras, non tantum veram
sapientiam sed et veram eloquentiam invenisse laetabundus ex-
ultabat. Multaque ut omittam ab eo Testamenti Novi allata

either to join in learned debates or, if their attitudes were more righteous, because they could learn rules of good conduct worth keeping — teachings all the more in demand because their author, an immensely learned person of great nobility, had sometimes stumbled down alleys of easy sensuality. It seems that moral precepts have more force and stick better in the minds of learners if they are both correct in their own terms and also produced by a teacher who has turned toward paths of justice and away from broken trails of desire with their twists and detours. Love poems composed in elegiac verse, which he had written out in five books, he threw in the fire for religion's sake. Likewise, for the same reason, a fire of the same kind consumed lyrics that he put into Tuscan rhythms.[17]

Then, during his twenty-eighth year, after embracing sacred letters with zeal and passion, he immediately offered up his first fruits in God's temple — a *Heptaplus* on the works of the six days of Genesis and the day of rest. The result was perfected by his genius, of course, developed diligently and methodically, filled not only with the deepest mysteries of our Christian theology but also with lofty teachings by philosophers: it tells its story in seven different ways, linked by chapters seven in number, each containing its own version of the sevenfold account framed by the book's title. However, because of material dug up from the depths of nature, because of theological problems that make hard reading, because of meanings completely concealed by the prophet and because the expression is refined, the book is not accessible at every point to people uneducated in philosophy and language, though it permits a few to use this rare and valuable resource. Because Pico was also aware of this, he mentioned it gracefully at the end of the same proem to the book.[18] 21

Once he had a taste of Sacred Scripture, he rejoiced and exulted that he had found not just real wisdom but also real eloquence. If I may leave aside much of his praise for the New Testament, he 22

praeconia, Pauli epistolas oratorum omnium scriptionibus eloquentia praestare dicebat—Tullii etiam ipsius Demosthenisque
primarii, ut inquit ille, dicendi artificis—lucubrationes nominatim
citans, non quod essent, ut illae calamistris inustae et corrasis
undique fucis et cincinnis constipatae, sed ut veram et solidam et
redolerent et saperent eloquentiam, veris sententiis vera arte suf-
fultam—essentque, ut dicam brevius, Aegyptiorum opibus non
consulto suffarcinatae.

23   Omnia porro Veteris Legis eloquia consummatissimae scientiae
et sapientiae plena praedicabat. Quod etsi cum alii tum Augustinus in libro *De doctrina christiana* luculenter ostenderit—Septimius-
que Tertulianus, Eusebius Pamphili, et Cassiodorus affirment—
grammaticos, rhetores, oratores, philosophosque omnes priscos
eloquentiae et doctrinae suae fluenta ex divinarum scripturarum
fontibus epotasse, ipse tamen aliis innumeris rationibus prosequebatur: quarum partem in *Heptapli* celebratissimae[4] exordiis inque
ipso secundae expositionis proemio videre operaeprecium est.

24   Inter tot iuges divinae legis evolutiones, secundo anno ab *Heptapli* editione opusculum etiam *De ente et uno* decem capitibus distinctum absolvit—breve quidem corpore sed amplum viribus, sed
altissimis et philosophorum dogmatis et theologicis sensibus un-
dequaque respersum. Quo superius ente non esse unum sed sibi
invicem respondere aequalique esse ambitu ostendit. Controver-
siamque super ea re a Platonis Aristotelisque sectatoribus habitam
recensuit, asseverans Academicos illos qui contrarium conten-
derunt verum Platonis dogma non assequutos sensuumque prorsus communionem inter Aristotelem et Platonem de uno et
ente—sicut et de reliquis in universum, etsi verba dissiderent—
demonstraturus erat non defuisse. Ultimo quoque operis capite
totam disputationem ad institutionem vitae et morum emendatio-
nem non minus ingeniose quam religiose convertit.

used to say that the eloquence of Paul's letters surpassed all the writings of the orators, whose works he cited by name—Cicero and even Demosthenes himself, whom he called a grand master of speaking. Paul's works, unlike theirs, were not beautified with pretty curls or smeared with fancy paints. Their scent and taste was of real, true eloquence, based on real skill and real doctrine—in a word, not deliberately stuffed with the fabled *wealth of Egypt*.[19]

Furthermore, my uncle would state that all the sayings of the 23 Old Law were full of the most perfect knowledge and wisdom. Even though Augustine in his book *On Christian Teaching*—supported by others like Tertullian, Eusebius and Cassiodorus—showed quite clearly that all the ancient grammarians, rhetoricians, orators and philosophers drank their waters of learning and eloquence from springs of Sacred Scripture, Pico still pursued this point with countless other arguments. Those that he stated in the proem to his much celebrated *Heptaplus* are worth looking at, and also the material in the proem to the second part.[20]

In the second year after publishing the *Heptaplus*, during this 24 sustained inquiry into the divine Law, he also finished a little study, *On Being and the One*, divided into ten chapters—small in bulk, to be sure, but full of energy and punctuated everywhere with teachings and insights of great depth gathered from philosophers and theologians. He showed in this book that the One is not above Being but that they correspond and have the same extension. He reviewed the controversy on this issue between followers of Plato and Aristotle, claiming that those Academics who argued the contrary point had not followed Plato's genuine teaching and that a demonstration of complete consensus between Aristotle and Plato on Being and the One had not been lacking—nor generally on other issues, even though their words might differ. In the final chapter of the book, with no less intelligence than reverence, he also turned *the whole conversation toward teaching how to live and correct one's behavior.*

25   Adversum quod opus Antonius Faventinus, egregius alioquin
philosophus, nonnulla quatuor epistolis obiectamenta protulit.
Quarum tribus ipse respondit, quartae vero—vel quia fideliter
delata non fuit vel quia ex praescriptis responderi posse putavit vel
alia quapiam de causa quae iusta tamen credenda est—mentionem
quod sciverim non habuit. Cui nos postquam decessit e vita, ne
falsa vel latrandi malevolis vel sinistri aliquid credendi rudibus
praeberetur occasio, respondendi munus obivimus, illudque potissimum curavimus ut ex praecedentibus ipsius sententiis fuisse
magna ex parte responsum monstraremus.

26   Vidimus etiam nonnulla Platonica vernaculo sermone ab eo di-
gesta: in quibus multa ad priscorum theologiam enodandam fa-
cientia, multa in aenigmatibus et scirpis abstrusa sapientum sensa
reserantia deprehenduntur. Quae forsan maius ocium nacti Latina
reddere tentabimus, ne tanti hominis supereminens doctrina hisce
de rebus, maxime pervia quibusque vulgi ante ora feratur.

27   Hactenus de perfectis lucubrationibus quas ante mortem emi-
serat veluti nuntios et anteambulones praeclarorum operum quae
conceperat et procudebat. Vetus enim Testamentum interpreta-
menti iam facibus illuminarat, id ipsum muneris ut Novo praestaret accinctus. Nec eos tantum, quos litterae series ferre poterat,
sensus protulerat, sed in his locis, quae tres alios divinorum elo-
quiorum proprios latura fuerant,[5] superaedificabat. Graecisque et
Hebraeis exemplaribus nostrorum codicum discordes sententias
conferebat. Sed hoc potissimum in eius mente consitum fuit, hoc
de universis propositis quae in commentandi genere conceperat
altius insedit: ut aliorum dogmata non adduceret, utpote quae iam
haberentur, legerentur, noscerentur. Sed sua prorsus inventa et

Antonio da Faenza, otherwise an eminent philosopher, wrote 25
four letters to bring various objections against this work. Pico
himself responded to three of the letters but, as far as I know, he
did not mention the fourth — either because it was not delivered as
promised or because he thought that an answer could be found in
what he had already written or for some other credible reason.
After he died, lest this give the malicious an opportunity to keep
snapping at him or permit the ignorant to believe something sinis-
ter, I made it my business to reply to Antonio, and my chief concern was to show that the best part of my response came from my
uncle's previous statements.[21]

I have also seen some Platonic materials condensed by Pico in 26
the *volgare*: in them many things are perceived as untangling the
theology of the ancients, many as unlocking ideas concealed by
sages in allegories and riddles. When I have more time, I may try
to put these into Latin so that the towering teaching on such matters of so great a mind will not be readily available for any ordinary
person to look at.[22]

So much for the completed efforts that he had sent out before 27
his death like heralds and ambassadors of brilliant works that he
had developed and was hammering out. In fact, the torches of his
interpretation had already illuminated the Old Testament, and his
aim was to prepare himself for the same task with the New. He
not only offered those senses that the literal order could support,
but upon the same passages he also built additional meanings
leading to the three other senses of the divine writings. From cop-
ies of the Greek and Hebrew he would also compare statements
disagreeing with our Latin texts. But this especially was planted in
his mind, deep down in all his thinking about the genre of commentary: not to introduce what others taught, since this was available, examined and already known. Instead he would discuss just

meditata dissereret ut propriis non alienis facultatibus famelicas
veritatis animas pro virile saturaret.

28   Post haec, Hebraico idiomate pollens, de veritate translationis
Hieronymi adversus Hebraeorum calumnias libellum edidit —
necnon defensionem pro LXX interpretibus quantum ad Psalmos
attinet adversus eosdem. Libellum item de vera temporum supputatione conscripsit.

29   Postremo ad debellandos septem hostes ecclesiae animum apu-
lerat. Qui enim nec Christo nec illius paret ecclesiae et, quod est
sequens, eius est hostis, aut impius existens nullum recipit credendum dogma; sive falsis inservit idolis subque hisce simulacris
demones adorat; seu Mosaicam perditissimorum Iudaeorum ritu
legem colit; nefandumve Maomethem sequitur, detestandis illius
placitis mancipatus; aut Christianam auditu tantum — non operibus et mente sincera vitam vivens — evangelica documenta perver-
tit, Catholicaeque ecclesiae non consentiens obstinato corde re-
calcitrat; vel non casta fide sed variis adulterata prophanataque
superstitionibus evangelia suscipit; aut, licet solida nitidaque ac
constanti fide receperit, operibus adversatur.

30   Hos itaque septem, quasi duces sub quibus reliqui velut gregarii
continentur, propriis eorum armis conflicturus ad congressum ci-
taverat. Adversus impios philosophos qui nullae religionis iugo
colla depressi nullique addicti numini naturales tantum rationes
adorant, eisdem rationibus dimicabat. Veteris Testamenti sententiis propriisque Iudaicae scholae auctoramentis validissime contra
Hebraeos praeliabatur. Cum Maumethanis, Alcorano nixus, pe-
dem contulerat. Idolorum cultores et multis vulneribus et vi non
multa prostraverat.

his own findings and ideas and use his own skills, not those of other people, while doing his best to satisfy souls that were starved for truth.

Next, as his skill in the Hebrew tongue grew strong, he pro-   28
duced a tract, against slanders by the Jews, on the accuracy of Jerome's translation — also, regarding the Psalms, a defense of the
Septuagint translators against the same attackers. He also wrote a
book on the correct computation of chronologies.[23]

Last of all, he directed his thoughts toward defeating seven en-   29
emies of the Church. For one who submits neither to Christ nor
his Church and thus becomes its enemy is either ungodly and ac-
cepts no doctrine or creed; or serves false idols and worships demons under their likenesses; or goes by the law of Moses like the
utterly unredeemable Jews; or follows the abominable Mohammed, captive to his hateful beliefs; or is a Christian in name
only — not by deeds and a life lived with upright intentions — who
subverts the evidence of the Gospels by disagreeing with the
Catholic Church in stiff-necked defiance; or receives the Gospels
with an impure faith, defiled and profaned by various superstitions; or else he opposes the Gospels by his deeds, even while accepting scripture with a complete, clear and steady faith.

These seven, then, who hold the rest of the herd together and   30
lead them, were challenged by him to fight a battle using their own
weapons. As for ungodly philosophers who bent their necks to the
yoke of no religion, pledging themselves to no deity and worship-
ping only natural reasons, he attacked them with the same reasons. He engaged the Jews mightily with statements from the Old
Testament and with their own stipulations from Jewish scholarship. Armed with the Koran, he warred against the Mohammed-
ans. He gave the idolaters many wounds and defeated them with
little effort.[24]

31   Superstitionibus vanis irretitos, eos praesertim qui divinatricem
colunt astrologiam, et verae philosophiae et peculiaribus rationibus astrologorum acriter taxaverat, duodecimque iam libris et quidem absolutissimis ex tredecim ad hoc destinatis eorum deliria
insectatus fuerat. Demum hydromantiam, geomantiam, pyroman-
tiam, haruspicinam et caetera id genus inania sigillatim explose-
rat.[6] Sed in prophetantes astrologos cuneum ex professo direxerat
totisque viribus arietem temperaverat, quando eorum dogmatis,
futilibus quidem et nullius momenti, superstitiones caeterae suis
erroribus fulcimenta aucupentur, vel inspectae geneseos momenta
trutinantes, vel in eligendis horis aut hexagonos aut trigonos
aspectus quos benignos vocant conciliantes—et eiusmodi reliqua
quibus nec insanus Orestes accederet.

32   Nec contentus astrologiam omnem funditus evertisse, ut
ostenderet nostri temporis astrologis—Graecae potissimum linguae ignaris—vanissimam omnium professionum astrologiam per-
versis translationibus vaniorem (si dici potest) effectam, Ptolomaei
Fructus, quos *Centiloquium* vulgo nuncupant, interscribendum adversus eosdem quasi aliud agens e Graeco in Latinum sermonem
vertit, et elegantissima expositione honestavit. Quo in libro plura,
ut ita dixerim, errata quam verba vulgata illa translatione contineri
demonstrat, quam tamen semper in archanis veluti pretiosum
thesaurum custodierunt eiusdem cultores ignavi.

33   De Christi fide perperam sentientes nec matris ecclesiae pa-
rentes imperio—quos usitatiori vocabulo nominamus haereti-
cos—et Novo Instrumento et rationibus egregia obiurgatione in-
cessiverat. Nonaginta fere haereses in propatulo habentur. Verum
ille cuncta rimatus ducentas invenit, quas sigillatim non modo

Confronting those ensnared by ridiculous superstitions, his re-   31
proaches—drawn from genuine philosophy as well as arguments
supported by astrologers—were especially fierce against devotees
of divinatory astrology. He assailed their delusions in the twelve
books that he finished in full, out of thirteen planned on this
topic. There, case by case, he proceeded to jeer at divining with
water, earth, fire, entrails and other such nonsense. But he made it
clear that he would lead his forces and aim all the power of his
weaponry against astrologers who made prophecies because, even
though their teachings were useless and ineffective, other superstitions would look to these errors for support. This would be done
by examining points on a horoscope and calculating with them or
by connecting trigon aspects or hexagons, the figures called *friendly*,
in order to choose favorable times—along with other such practices that Orestes in his madness would never go near.[25]

Not satisfied with undermining astrology at its foundations, he   32
translated Ptolemy's *Harvest*, commonly called the *Hundred Sayings*,
from Greek into Latin. He wanted to show the astrologers of our
time—especially those ignorant of the Greek language—that their
subject, the most useless of all, was made even more useless (if one
can say such a thing) by distorted translations. While attacking
them, he wrote out his Latin version of the Greek separately between the lines, embellishing it with very careful comments. He
pointed out that Ptolemy's book, in the received version, contained
more mistakes than words, as it were, and yet its ignorant advo-
cates kept this translation in their secret places to guard it like
precious treasure.[26]

Citing the New Testament and invoking reason, he moved   33
against those whose views about faith in Christ were wrong and
who disregarded the rule of Mother Church—people whom we
more commonly call heretics. His reproof was remarkable. We
generally take the number of heresies to be about ninety. But he
investigated them all and found two hundred, proposing not only

eliminare et profligare proposuerat sed et pariter docere qua ex parte philosophiae non rite percepta suos errores traxissent aut furcillassent.

34   In Christianos postremo quorum fides sine operibus visitur vehementer invectus fuerat. Necnon diligenter exploraverat qui fieri posset ut ignem in meditullio terrae constitutum homines credant, quo perpetuo datura sunt paenas damnatorum corpora ceteraque, id genus tam animae quam corporis inexcogitata supplicia, immensa quoque deitatis visae gaudia quibus animae corporibus iunctae beantur, atque dictis ecclesiae quae ad credendum compellunt obaudientes non sint. Et nihilominus passim debacchentur in vitia divitiisque incumbant cumulandis, nihilque minus formidetur ab eis quam paenae aut affectetur quam regnum Dei. Pro morborum item qualitate idoneam opem admovere tentabat: tetros scilicet morbos et suapte natura impuros acribus acerbisque medicaminibus inurere; ea vero vulnera quae minori infecta malitia depravataque forent cicatricemque obducere desiderarent lenibus placabilibusque fovere; adeptis vero valitudinem et recidiva metuentibus saluberrimas potiones celebrataque antidota praeparare.

35   Multa alia opera fuerat exorsus quibus sperari poterat futurum ut philosophiae studia in universum eliminatis erroribus explosaque barbarie reflorerent. Inter haec potissimum Platonis et Aristotelis numerabatur concordia, quam iam coeptam brevi perfecturus erat si vita comes paucis adhuc annis superfuisset.

36   Ita enim philosophiam ab incunabulis lactando nutriverat et ad usque nostra tempora perduxerat adultam ut nostrae tempestatis philosopho nil amplius aut in Graecis aut in Latinis aut in barbaris codicibus desyderandum esset. Citasset udum Thaletem, ignitum Heraclitum, circumfusumque atomis Democritum. Orpheus item

to defeat and banish them one by one but also to show where the errors came from and which part of philosophy had been misinterpreted in order to prop them up.[27]

Finally, he launched a powerful attack against Christians who plainly have *faith but no works*. He turned his attention to asking how such people could believe that a fire has been put in the center of the earth to punish the bodies of the damned forever, how they could believe that other torments of this sort have been devised for body and soul, and also believe that souls joined to bodies have the boundless joy of seeing God, and yet they would not obey statements by the Church that require these beliefs. Still, despite all this, while such people go completely mad with vice and labor at heaping up riches, punishments are the least of their worries and their concern is never the Kingdom of God. Pico also tried to apply a remedy suited to the type of each affliction: namely, for repulsive sicknesses filthy in their nature, to burn them away with harsh and corrosive drugs; for injuries less dangerous and disfiguring, to treat them gently with soothing medicines and let them scar over; but to provide the most wholesome tonics and best-known antidotes for those who gain health and fear losing it.[28]

He had begun many other works in the hope that philosophical studies might flourish again everywhere when errors were eliminated and barbarians were driven away. He counted concord between Plato and Aristotle as the most important of these projects, and, since he had already started it, he would have finished quickly had he lived a few more years.[29]

So much did he nourish philosophy by raising it from infancy and leading it toward maturity in our own time that a philosopher of our era would no longer have needed texts in Greek, Latin or barbarian languages. My uncle would have summoned up Thales with his moisture, Heraclitus ablaze and Democritus among a swarm of atoms. Orpheus also, with Pico's help and support,

34

35

36

et Pythagoras priscique alii eius ope et gratia in academiam con-
venissent. Postremo philosophiae principes — Plato scilicet, fabularum velamentis mathematicisque involucris constipatus, et Aristoteles, vallatus motibus — dextera data fidem futurae amiciciae
sanxissent.

37   Inter Averroim quoque et Avicennam, inter Thomam et Scotum, qui iam diu conflictaverant, si non pacem in universum in
multis tamen impetrasset inducias, quando in eorum pluribus
controversiis, si quispiam dissidentia verba rimetur attentius et
exactius libret, scrupulosiusque vestigans, cutem deferens, intror-
sum ad imas latebras profundaque penetralia mente pervadat,
unionem sensuum in disseparatis pugnantibusque verbis citra am-
biguitatem comperiet. Neotericorum turba partim pro meritis,
partim pro culpis et honorata fuisset et taxata. Totus igitur Deo
dicatus ecclesiam quibus poterat armis defendebat: atque lati-
tantem (ut aiunt) e Democriti puteo veritatem educebat, et ignorantiae gramen inexpugnabile quo multorum mentes praefocantur
subnascentesque pernitiosas herbas abrumpebat penitus et detrun-
cabat.

38   Sed mors adveniens tot tantarumque vigiliarum laborem et ex-
cultae lucubrationis partum inanem fere reddidit, hocque potissimum fuit in causa: ut plurimas, quamquam magna ex parte exas-
ciatas et dedolatas, imperfectas commentationes dereliquerit quod
scilicet sibi ipsi tantum, non autem nobis scribebat. Nam sicut
celeri in commentando ingenio, ita veloci in scribendo manu fuit.
Et cum antea pulcherrimos litterarum characteres deliniaret, factum erat ut ex usu nimiae in commentando velocitatis vix eorum
quae exarabat capax existeret. Huc etiam et illuc scribere solitus
erat, vetusta interdum supervenientibus novis obliterans, ea propter exoleta quaedam et dispuncta repperi, quaedam saltim et velli-
catim exarata, omnia denique adeo confusa et inordinata ut sylvae
aut farragines putarentur.

would have come together in an academy with Pythagoras and other ancients. After this, the *princes of philosophy* would have pledged *friendship* for the future — Plato, under a heavy cloak of myth and veils of mathematics, as well as Aristotle, barricaded by the senses.[30]

Pico would also have arranged a truce on many issues, if not universal peace, between Averroes and Avicenna, between Thomas and Scotus, though they had long been in conflict: if someone were to dig inside the discordant words in their various controversies and weigh them more carefully, laying back the skin to investigate with more precision and reaching within mentally to what is hidden deep inside, he would discover a sharing of meanings — beyond ambiguity — among contrary and clashing terms. Some of the modern crowd would have been honored for their services, and some would have been censured for their faults. Wholly dedicated to God, then, my uncle defended the Church with weapons available to him: at one moment he hauled *truth up from the well of Democritus* (as they say), and at another, after ripping up the ineradicable weeds of ignorance that choked so many minds, he lopped off every sickly shoot that grew beneath them.[31]   37

But efforts born of so much hard work and lost sleep were made nearly useless when death arrived, and mainly for one reason: even though he had roughed out most of his remarks and smoothed them off, he left them unfinished because he was writing only for himself, of course, not for us. In fact, as quickly as his mind produced these notes, his hand moved just as rapidly to write them down. Even though he used to shape the letters in his handwriting beautifully, the practice of taking notes so quickly left him barely in control of what he put on paper. Out of habit he had also written all over the page and blotted out old comments while adding new ones, so that I found some discarded and erased, others put down piecemeal in patches, everything mixed up, disorganized and a tangled mess to look at.[32]   38

39   Ex libro septemplici quem adversus hostes ecclesiae praetitula-
verat, pars illa quae divinaculos astrologos genethliacosque potissimum insectatur ab incude, ut dici solet, ad limam perducta fuit.
Quam non parvo tamen labore nec mediocri cura ab exemplari li-
turato et paene discerpto deprompsimus. Quo in opere summum
philosophum, summum theologum, summum oratorem, acerri-
mum Christi ecclesiae propugnatorem — incomparabili praeditum
ingenio quod in cunctis ipsius commentationibus cernitur — se
demonstrat.

40   Quaedam item minutula non tornata adhuc apud me comperi,
interpretationem dumtaxat dominicae orationis regulasque bene
vivendi circiter quinquaginta, breves profecto nimis et inexplicitas.
Quas in multa capita si vixisset deducturus omnino fuerat. Duas
quoque ad Deum deprecatorias, quarum unam rhithmis Hetrus-
cis, elegiaco metro alteram: qua gravioribus defatigatum quandoque studiis animum cantando ad lyram mulcere posset composue-
rat. Primis enim adolescentiae annis genus omne musicae artis
adeo excoluerat ut excogitata per ipsum modulamina notataeque
debitis concentibus harmoniae celebres haberentur.

41   Plurima quoque in eius scriniis quanquam inordinata pervidi-
mus, ex quibus tamen utile aliquid, praesertim Psalmorum enarrationem, compilari posse putaverim. Sed et epistolae circiter L — di-
versis editae temporibus, tum familiares, tum doctrinales, tum
adhortatoriae — emersere, una cum oratione quam Romae, si
disputare contigisset, habiturus fuerat. Quae non tam iuvenis
quartum et vigesimum annum nondum nati perspicacissimum ingenium et doctrinam uberrimam redolet, quod et cunctae ipsius
scriptiones faciunt quam fertilissimae ipsius eloquentiae locupletissimum nobis testimonium praebet.

42   Stilo quidem valde probando usus est semper, non ascito sed
ingenuo, multiformi etiam pro rerum varietate, qui etsi totum, ut

From the book in seven parts that he planned against enemies   39
of the Church, the part whose main targets are amateur prophets,
astrologers and horoscope-mongers had gone *from the anvil to the*
file, as the saying goes. With considerable effort and trouble, I took
it from a blotted copy that was almost falling apart. In this book
Pico proves himself to be a superb philosopher, a superb theologian, a superb orator and a fierce champion of Christ's Church —
armed with the unmatched genius that one sees in all his writings.[33]

In my house I have also found various small pieces that still   40
have rough edges — an exposition, but no more than that, of the
Lord's Prayer, and about fifty rules of good conduct that are quite
short and very undeveloped. Had he lived, he would have worked
all this up into many chapters. He also composed two pleas for
God's mercy, one in Tuscan rhythms, the other in elegiac meter;
when weightier pursuits wore him out, he would take up his lute
to sing these prayers and ease his mind. In his early years, as a
young man, he had pursued every kind of musical art, so much
that melodies arranged by him were considered famous, also har-
monies that he marked up especially for singing.[34]

Although many things that I searched through in his cabinets   41
were disorganized, I imagine that something useful might still be
extracted from them, in particular a commentary on the Psalms.
About fifty letters turned up as well — some written at various
times to family and friends, some to teach, others to exhort — together with a speech that he would have given in Rome if the debate had happened. Like all his writings, this product of a young
man not yet twenty-four years old not only displays penetrating
intelligence and abundant learning but also gives us plentiful evidence of his very fruitful eloquence.[35]

The style he used was always commendable, certainly, not de-   42
rivative but native to him while also conforming to a wide variety
of subjects, and even if he used up the whole *medicine chest of*

aiunt, Isocratis myrothecion consumpserit, munditiae tamen et decorae maiestatis ornamenta servavit. Nam et celebrata illa dicendi genera—quorum tria Gellius, Macrobius quattuor enarrat—ex commentationibus ipsius nec impendio colliguntur. Ibi copiosum in quo Cicero dominari fertur, breve quod Salustio ascribitur, siccum Frontoni datum, pingue et floridum in quo Plinium et Symachum lascivisse prodiderunt. At forte copiam hanc Brutus non vocasset elumbem nec Salustius immoderatam. Siccitatem quoque Frontonis humectatam, Salustii brevitatem elongatam, flores et pinguedinem Plinii latiori in campo deportatas non difficile recto iudicio orator deprehendet. Adde his Livii lacteum fontem—forte sine Patavinitate, ut ille inquit—adiectis flosculis plurimis Apulei.

43   Verum non hic in mutuata a Graecis philosophia se exercuit, non in Atticis noctibus, non in fictis saturnalibus ad laudandam prope Vergilii *Aeneidem* fabricatis, non in Romana historia, non in mera historia naturae altissimis difficilibusque speculatis[7] vacua. Sed in admiranda illa mundi fabrica in incessendis sacrosanctae Catholicae ecclesiae hostibus desudavit, in eliminandis astrologis fatigatus est. In theologicis quaestionibus excutiendis, in Aristotelis et Platonis concordia laboravit, in enarranda sacra eloquia incubuit, in commonendis et adhortandis amicis navavit operam.

44   Verum hanc de qua agimus eloquentiam tantum aberat ut affectaret ut eos potius damnaret qui pigmentata lenocinia scrupulosius exquirentes omnes ingenii vires in vestigandis vocabulorum originibus accommodabant. Quae omnia plurimos eo propensius in eius admirationem convertere quod inter eorum litteras diu et propensissime versatus esset qui Latinas litteras eloquentiae floribus refertas non sunt professi. Patiantur haec aequo animo nimii antiquitatis amatores, nam haec, etsi concisius compendiosiusque, tamen eo forte verius quo me doctiores et Hermolaus Barbarus et

Isocrates, as they say, he still kept the trappings of his grandeur neat and seemly. It takes no effort to collect well-known types of expression from his writings — the three described by Gellius, the four by Macrobius. They display *the versatile kind where Cicero is said to prevail, the concise manner ascribed to Sallust, the dry approach attributed to Fronto, also the lush and lively type that Pliny and Symmachus toyed with.* Brutus would not have called Pico's *versatility flaccid,* I imagine, nor would Sallust say it was *overdone.* Moreover, no critic with good taste has any trouble seeing Fronto's dryness irrigated, Sallust's brevity stretched out and Pliny's luxuriant vitality carried far afield. Add *pure waters* from Livy — perhaps without the Paduan idiom, as my uncle called it — and throw in many little blossoms from Apuleius.[36]

But Pico was not one to busy himself with *Attic evenings* or philosophy borrowed from Greece, with Roman history or storybook *saturnalia* closely scripted to glorify Vergil's *Aeneid,* or with simple research on nature devoid of the deepest and most difficult observations. Instead, to assail the enemies of the most holy Catholic Church, he sweated over the miracle of the world's making while wearing himself out to get rid of astrologers. To examine theological problems, he worked on a concord between Plato and Aristotle, and he pondered the Sacred Scriptures while toiling zealously to encourage and exhort his friends.[37]

But the eloquence involved was so free of affectation that he strongly condemned those who applied all their mental energy to tracking down etymologies and took pains to paint themselves up like pimps. All this made many readers more inclined to admire him because, for a long time, his own very strong inclination was to favor prose by writers who did not stuff their Latin with flowers of eloquence. Those who love antiquity to excess will suffer such eloquence in a calm spirit, even though it is rather concise and abbreviated; yet, for all that, it is perhaps more honest than the

43

44

Baptista Carmelita et Marsilius Ficinus et Matheus Bossus et ple-
rique alii doctissimi et eloquentissimi viri prodidere.

45   Bibliothecas amplas tam Latinorum quam Graecorum incredi-
bili celeritate et perlegit et excerpsit, nullasque—si modo facultas
data—commentationes illectas praeteriit. De priscis ecclesiae doctoribus tantum cognitionis adeptus fuerat quantum credere difficile est, etiam in eo qui in ipsis solum evolvendis totum vitae
tempus consumpsisset. De neotericis vero theologis—qui eo stilo
sunt usi quem Parisiensem vulgo nuncupant—tantum iudicii
apud eum residebat ut si quis ex improviso abstrusam illorum
cuiuspiam maleque explicitam quaestionem enucleandam petiisset,
tanta ingenii fertilitate adaperiebat, tanta solertia reserabat, ut di-
ceres doctoris illius universa dicta prae oculis et innumerato
habuisse.

46   Cunctasque pari modo familias agnoverat, cunctas scedas ex-
cusserat, nec uni illorum sic addictum credas—qui nostris hominibus mos est—ut caeteros aspernaretur. Ipse enim a teneris sic
institutus fuit, sic animatus, ut in illis veritatem quaereret parique
honore, quousque illa elucesceret inventam veneraretur—privata
affectione nudatus. Quid tamen de singulis sentiret qui in universum famosiores habentur, in *Apologiae* proemio, cum de barbaris,
Graecis, Latinisque philosophis proprietates peculiaresque laudes
retulerit, videre datur.

47   Thomam vero Aquinatem, quando interloquendum de his philosophis theologisve qui Gallico more disceptando scripsere mentio fieret, prae omnibus laudare consueverat, utpote solidiori prae
aliis veritatis basi nitentem. Eum quoque in *Heptaplo* nostrae
theologiae splendorem nominat. De hoc percunctatus creber-
rime—et a me ipso—idem respondit. Nec oppositum suadere

eloquence that comes from Ermolao Barbaro, Battista the Carmelite, Marsilio Ficino, Matteo Bosso and many other quite erudite and eloquent men who are more learned than I am.[38]

With unbelievable speed, he read whole libraries of Greek and Latin books from end to end, taking notes and leaving no text unread—provided he had access to it. The knowledge he gained of the Church's early teachers was so extensive that even if a person had spent a whole lifetime reading them and only them, such an achievement would have been hard to believe. So great were his resources for evaluating modern theologians—those whose style is usually called Parisian—that if someone surprised him with a puzzle poorly presented by one of them and needing to be cracked, he would lay it open with such fruitful insight and explain it so cleverly that you would say he had all the statements by that teacher listed to see in front of him.[39]   45

He knew all their schools equally well and examined every scrap of paper, but you should not think of him as so committed to any one of them—our own practice nowadays—that he would dismiss the others. From an early age, by education and disposition, he respected them all equally as he sought the truth in them, and—without cover of personal favor—he honored it wherever he found it gleaming through. However, for those generally considered the more famous thinkers, you can see how he felt about each of them in the preface to the *Apology*, where he gave descriptions of barbarian, Greek and Latin philosophers and reported their special features and merits.[40]   46

When discussing philosophers or theologians who were said to write disputatiously, in the French manner, he usually praised Thomas Aquinas more than the others because the foundation of truth that Thomas relied on was firmer than theirs. In the *Heptaplus* he also calls Thomas *the glory of our theology*. People—myself included—kept questioning him about this, and he kept giving that same answer. Furthermore, no one should be led to a contrary   47

cuiquam debent nonnulla quae in eius apologetico continentur disputanda, alioquin Thomae opinionibus ex professo adversantia. Cum iuvenis admodum esset gloriaeque tunc cupidus in urbe celebratissima, Gorgiae Leontini more, quascunque tutando partis[8] famam aucuparetur. Adde quod ex decem millibus propositionum tribus tantum aut quatuor non consentire, sed et adversari id non convincunt.

48   Disceptandi porro peritissimus fuit: frequentemque et impensissimam operam litterariis agonibus, dum ferveret animus, impendit. In obiectando facile Scoti acumen et vigilantiam, Francisci acrimoniam, copiam et multitudinem Aureoli deprehendi potuissent, nec deesse nodos illos, multiplicibus flexionibus complicitos — nec tam titillantibus argutiis quam gravitate subnixos. In respondendo Thomae fortitudinem et robur, Alberti amplitudinem cerni datur. Verum his conflictibus nuncium pridem remiserat et magis atque magis id muneris in dies perosus fuerat.

49   Adeoque detractabat ut Herculi Estensi Ferrariensium Duci et internunciis et se ipso enixissime postulanti, ut dum Generalis praedicatorum fratrum synodus Ferrariae celebraretur, disceptare non aegre ferret. Diu obsequi reluctatus fuerit, multis tamen rogatibus annuens principi illi cuius amor in ipsum non mediocris exstiterat morem gessit. Vnde datum est ambigi solercior ne an eloquentior, doctior an humanior appareret. Ex ore quidem disceptantis talis semper animi patebat alacritas ut de re comi et placida potius quam subacida et difficili altercari videretur, quapropter qui ab ore pendebant audientes in mirum eius amorem excitabantur. Sed frequens ei adagium inerat munus id esse dialectici, non philosophi.

50   Aiebat item eas disputationes prodesse quae placido animo ad vestigandam perquirendamque veritatem privatis in locis

view by debating points included in his apologetic treatise, even where they oppose the views of Thomas. For in the world's most populous city, at a moment when he was very young and lusting for glory, he chased after fame like Gorgias of Leontini by defending any and all sides. Besides, only three or four propositions out of a thousand disagree with Thomas, which does not make him an opponent.[41]

Furthermore, he was a very skilled debater: with his mind on   48
the boil, he worked constantly on academic competitions and spent heavily on them. When it was his turn to object, one could detect the ready subtlety and alertness of a Scotus, the sharpness of a Francis and the rich complexity of an Auriol all tied together, knotted up and turning every which way — though the foundation was still serious, not just witty entertainment. When he responded, one could see the strength and courage of a Thomas and the breadth of an Albert. But with every passing day he found his role in these contests more and more repugnant and had long since said farewell to them.[42]

His withdrawal went quite far. When the General of the Do-   49
minicans was about to convene a synod in Ferrara, Ercole d'Este — the Duke of Ferrara himself — as well as his representatives, begged and pleaded with him to be kind enough to debate there. For a long while he refused to give in, though he finally complied with the many entreaties from this Prince in order to humor someone who had no small regard for him. The upshot was to make it hard to say whether he seemed more expert or eloquent, more learned or stylish. Since good cheer was written on his face, the content of the debate appeared to be friendly and polite, not harsh or nasty, and those who listened closely to his words were moved to become surprisingly fond of him. But he often cited a maxim that described this as a debater's duty, not a philosopher's.

He also used to say that helpful disputations are those con-   50
ducted quietly to seek the truth and find it, apart from spectators

semotisque arbitris exercebantur, at illas obesse plurimum quae in propatulo fiebant, ad ostentandam doctrinam vel ad captandam vulgi auram atque imperitorum applausum. Vixque posse fieri omnino censebat ut honoris cupidini, qua frontivagi illi disputatores exagitantur, inseparabili vinculo annexum[9] non sit illius cum quo disputatur desyderium infamiae confusionisque—letale vulnus animae venenumque charitatis mortiferum.

51   Latuit eum nihil omnino quod pertineret ad captiunculas cavillasque sophistarum et Suiseticas quisquilias quae calculationes vocantur; hae mathematicae commentationes sunt subtilioribus— ne dixerim an morosioribus—excogitationibus naturalibus applicatae. Verum etsi in eis esset eruditus ac eiusmodi scriptiones legisset quas forte ad plenum non novit Italia—nulla enim tam invia et inaccessa litterarum reperiri poterant quae illius vestigio lustrata abunde explorata non essent—odisse tamen et detestari videbatur, valere meo iudicio earum communem usum animadvertens ad sociorum parandam infamiam labefactandamque in replicando memoriam, veritati vero inveniendae—cui indefessam operam navandam arbitrabatur—aut nihil aut parum conducere.

52   Sed ne plura consecter lectoremque detineam, comprehendam brevi. Enituit aliquis eloquentia, sed inscitia rerum naturae secretarum dehonestatus est. Alius peregrinas linguas sed universa philosophorum decreta non calluit. Priscorum alius inventa perlegit, non nova dogmata concinnavit. Scientiae ab altero hominum tantum et humanae gloriae causa, non Christianae rei publicae emolumento et divinae et humanae, quaesitae sunt. Ille vero cuncta haec pari studio ita complexus fuerat ut turmatim et coacervatim in eum confluxisse viderentur—nec ut multi qui non aliquo uno excellentes omnium participes sunt, sed in omnibus usque adeo profecerat scientiis, ut quamlibet ex his in ipso considerasses, eam

and in private settings, but that debates are mostly harmful when held in public to make a show of learning, capture popular attention or get applause from the ignorant. He reckoned it could almost never happen that the lust for reputation that drives these debaters to ramble so boldly would not be linked unbreakably with a desire to confuse and disgrace an opponent — a deadly poison to kill love and injure the soul fatally.[43]

He was all too aware of what comes with sophistical fallacies 51 and dodges, also the swill for the Pigheaded called 'calculations': these are mathematical experiments applied to physical constructions with exquisite — not to say peevish — precision. Even though he was well-informed in these matters and had read writings about them that may not have been widely known in Italy — for there was no literature so impenetrable or out of reach that he had not tracked it down and explored it fully — he still seemed to despise and abominate the Calculators. In my opinion, he recognized that the effect of their widespread use is to equip one's allies for disgrace and destroy their memory as respondents. But for finding the truth — a task to be worked on tirelessly, in his view — they do little good or none.[44]

Not to follow more leads and hold the reader back, I shall give 52 a brief summary. One person's eloquence has been brilliant, but ignorance of nature's secrets has shamed him. One has mastered foreign languages but not every finding of the philosophers. One has examined discoveries by the ancients yet has produced no new teachings. Another has sought knowledge only for the sake of mankind and human glory, not to benefit the Christian commonwealth which is divine as well as human. But so much did my uncle embrace with equal zeal all such accomplishments that they seemed to converge on him in floods and heaps — not like the many people who participate in everything but excel at nothing, but as one who made progress in every branch of knowledge — so that no matter which subject you were to examine in him, you

sibi propriam et peculiarem elegisse iudicavisses. Haec quoque eo admirabiliora erant cum a se ipso vi ingenii et veritatis amore quasi absque praeceptore assequutus esset, ut quasi de ipso illud quod de se dicebat Epicurus possimus proferre—se sibi ipsum scilicet fuisse magistrum.

53 Ad quos mirabiles effectus tam parvo temporis spatio producendos quinque ego causas convenisse repperi: incredibile ingenium; tenacissimam memoriam; facultates amplas quibus ad coemendos tum nostrae tum Graecae tum barbarae linguae libros adiutus est (septem quippe aureorum nummum milia rettulisse mihi memoria repeto in asciscendis sibi usque ad diem illam omnifariae litteraturae voluminibus erogasse); iuge et infatigabile studium; contemptionem postremo terrenarum rerum. Hunc igitur si prisca illa aetas Laconum tempore protulisset, si Aristoteli credimus, divinum illum virum appellauisset.

54 Sed virtutes intellectus iam ut arbitror relinquendae videntur et nunc praeclarae eius animae partes quae actiones spectant prosequendae. Exactissimique mores in publicum educendi sunt ut flammatus ipsius in Deum animus innotescat, ut erogatae in egenos divitiae collaudentur, ut his qui tandem divinae legi sunt addicti referendi gratias in bonorum omnium auctorem quam cumulatissime paretur occasio.

55 Triennio igitur priusquam diem obiret, ut posthabitis dominandi curis in alta pace degere posset, securus quo sceptra caderent, cuncta patrimonia quae Mirandulae Concordiaeque possidebat—hoc est tertiam partem earum—mihi nescio an dono an venditione tradidit. Quod factum postea Maximilianus Augustus—qui nobis est Rex et dominus (ut ita dixerim) immediatus neque enim alium tot saeculis quot est exaedificata Mirandula atque Concordia nisi qui successive in regali imperialive Romanorum throno consideret recognovimus—Caesarea liberalitate firmavit.

would conclude that he had chosen it as his own specialty. Even more astonishing was that he achieved this on his own, by force of intellect and love of truth, and essentially without an instructor, so that we might say of him what Epicurus stated about himself — that he was *his own teacher*.[45]

My own conclusion is that five causes came together to produce these amazing results in so short a space of time: unbelievable intelligence; an exceedingly tenacious memory; great wealth to help him buy books in our own Latin and in Greek and barbarian languages (I remember his telling me one day that he had spent seven thousand gold coins up to that point to acquire books on all kinds of topics); constant, tireless study; and finally, contempt for worldly things. Had Sparta produced such a person in ancient times, that age would have called him a *divine man* — if we believe Aristotle.[46]

But now I suppose the time has come to leave Pico's mental powers behind and attend to the splendid faculties of soul that bear on his actions. His very stringent requirements for conduct must also be brought out in public so that we can see how his mind was on fire for God, so that the money he spent on the needy will earn praise, and finally so that those pledged to God's law may have every opportunity to give thanks to the Maker of everything good.

Three years before he died, then, because he wanted to find deep peace and leave the cares of ruling behind him without worrying where scepters might fall, he passed on to me all his inherited property in Mirandola and Concordia — a third of those territories — though whether this was a sale or a gift is unclear. After this was done, the Emperor Maximilian showed a Caesar's generosity by confirming the transaction: he is our King and liege lord (so to speak) because, for the many centuries since Mirandola and Concordia were built up, we have recognized no one but a royal and imperial heir to the throne of the Romans.[47]

53

54

55

56   Quicquid autem ex hoc negotio pecuniarum acceperat partim
pauperibus elargitus est, partim in emendis agris unde et ipse et
eius familiares alerentur exposuit, nominatimque Corbulas in agro
Ferrariensi multis aureorum milibus nummum sibi comparaverat.
Multa itidem vasa argentea preciosasque supellectilis partes in
pauperum usus distribuit. Mensa mediocri contentus fuit, reti-
nente tamen nonnihil lautitiae prioris quantum ad fercula et ad
vasa argentea pertineret. Diebus singulis preces ad Deum suis horis effundebat. Pauperibus semper, si qui occurrerant, pecunias
tribuebat. Nec eo contentus, Hieronymo Benivenio—civi Floren-
tino litterato homini, quem pro magna in ipsum charitate proque
morum integritate dilexit plurimum—demandaverat ut propriis
pecuniis semper subveniret egenis, nuptum quoque virgines trad-
deret, eique statim, ut erogatos nummos quam primum restituere
posset, renuntiaret. Id enim muneris ei delegaverat quo facilius
veluti fido internuntio pauperum civium calamitates et miserias
quae ipsum latuissent relevare quiret.

57   Dedit et saepius quod silentio praetereundum non puto de corpore proprio elemosinas. Scimus plerosque, ut verbis utar Hieronymi, porrexisse egentibus manum, sed carnis voluptate et illecebris superatos. At ipse propriam carnem, diebus illis potissimum
qui Christi cruciatus et mortem nostrae salutis gratia repraesen-
tant, in summi illius beneficii memoriam delictorumque expiationem caedebat: meisque oculis saepius, cuncta in Dei gloriam redeant, flagellum vidi.

58   Vultu hilari semper erat et placido, adeoque miti natura ut nunquam se fuisse turbatum multis etiam audientibus testatus sit.
Recolo mihi interloquendum dixisse, in nullum eventum, ut res
pessime cederent, ira commoveri posse credere—nisi scrinia

Part of any money that my uncle got from this arrangement, 56
however, he distributed to the needy, spending the rest to improve
lands that would support him and his household. He expressly
mentioned buying property in Corbola in the region of Ferrara for
several thousand gold coins. For the same purpose, he handed out
silver plate and valuable items of furniture to be used for the poor.
He was happy to eat little, though he maintained some of his former luxury in silver plate and the dishes served. Every day at regular hours he poured out prayers to God. If any poor people turned
up, he always had money to give them. Feeling that this was not
enough, he asked Girolamo Benivieni—a citizen of Florence and
man of letters of whom he was very fond because of his blameless
conduct and great affection for my uncle—to keep using his own
funds to help the needy. He also wanted Girolamo to see that
young women got married and then inform him immediately so
that he could cover the expenses right away. He gave Girolamo
this task because it would be easier for him, as a reliable go-
between, to provide relief for poor townspeople whose sufferings
and misfortunes were unknown to him.[48]

Quite often he also gave alms from his own body, and I think I 57
should not remain silent about them. We know that many people
have held out a hand to the needy—to repeat Jerome's words—
but have also been defeated by pleasure and lures of the flesh. But
my uncle beat his own flesh, especially on those days that mark
Christ's suffering and death for the sake of our salvation, to com-
memorate that best of all good deeds and atone for his sins: I have
often seen the lash with my own eyes, and may it all be for the
glory of God.[49]

He always looked cheerful and calm, and he was naturally so 58
serene that he claimed never to have been bothered even when
many people came to hear him. We were talking once, and I remember him telling me that he believed nothing could make him
angry, no matter how badly things might turn out—unless he

quaedam deperirent quibus elucubrationes eius et vigiliae reconditae stipabantur. Sed cum animadverteret pro Deo optimo maximo eiusque ecclesia laborare, eisdemque omnia opera, studia, actionesque dedicavisse, et id fieri minime posse nisi aut eo iubente aut permittente, confidebat se non contristatum iri.

59   O felicem mentem! Quae iam nullis posset adversis deprimi, nullis quoque commodis (ut palam fiet) extolli. Non illum certe universae philosophiae peritia, non Hebraeae non Chaldaeae Arabicaeque linguae, ultra Latinam et Graecam, cognitio tumidum reddiderant. Non amplae divitiae, non generis nobilitas inflaverant. Non corporis pulchritudo et elegantia, non magna peccandi licentia in mollem illam et spatiosam multorum viam revocare poterant. Quid igitur poterat esse tam admirabile quod illius quiret mentem pervertere? Quid inquam supra illum esse poterat qui, ut verbis Senecae utar, supra Fortunam erat, cum illam — sive secundis flatibus tumidam sive adversis reflatibus humilem, aliquando contempserit — ut eius mens Christo et supernae patriae civibus spiritali glutino copuleretur?

60   Quod vel hoc argumento liquido percipitur. Quod dum ecclesiae officia et dignitates, a plerisque nostri temporis — proh dolor! — licitatas auctionatasque, non paucos videret expetere, flagitare, suspirare, enixissime mercari, ipse a duobus regibus per internuntios oblatas — testes adsunt gravissimi, testis ego — se sacris initiari nolle respondens repudiavit. Alter vero quidam cum saeculi dignitates et amplos reditus se daturum spopondisset[10] si regem eius adiret, conspicatus angulum non relinqui in quem se conderet ademptaque esse cuncta suffugia, tale illi dedit responsum: ut intelligeret se non dignitates aut divitias expetere sed potius, ut Deo et studiis vacare posset, illas neglegisse.

were to lose the writing cases packed with hard work that cost him so much sleep. But when he considered that he was laboring for almighty God and his Church, that he had dedicated to them all his efforts, inquiries and actions, and that none of this was possible without God's direction or permission, he was confident that it would not make him unhappy.

What a fortunate attitude! Adversity could not weigh him 59 down nor (as we shall see) would he exult in success. Skill in every part of philosophy, in knowledge of the Hebrew, Chaldean and Arabic languages, not to speak of Latin and Greek — none of this puffed him up, you may be sure. Neither great riches nor a noble pedigree swelled his head. His body was handsome and graceful, yet not even great sin and dissolution could call him back to the broad, easy path that many follow. What, then, could be so astonishing that it could corrupt his mind? Tell me: *what could be beyond reach of this person who*, in Seneca's phrase, *stood beyond Fortune's reach* — she whom he always scorned, whether fair breezes blew her along or contrary winds brought her low — and, by a spiritual bond, kept his mind linked with Christ and with the citizens of his heavenly home?[50]

The evidence for this observation is clear. Although he saw 60 people doing their best to traffic in Church offices, many of them begging and pleading for titles that have been bought and sold in our day — what a scandal! — he himself refused offers sent to him through intermediaries by two kings, replying that he did not want to take holy orders; two very serious people, as I also can testify, were present to witness this. When another person promised to give him temporal titles and a full income if he would approach his king for them, my uncle saw that he had no corner left to hide in and that all his cover was gone, so this is the answer he gave: please to understand that he had was not seeking titles and riches but rather shunning them so that he could free himself for God and his studies.

61   Ferrariae quoque cum ex amicis quidam Pandulpho Collenutio
Pisaurensi — iurisconsulto, perspicacis ingenii viro et multifariae
lectionis quo amico familiarissime utebatur — suassissent ut eum
adduceret quibuscunque rationibus posset ad cardinalatus dignitatem petendam vel certe si eam Pontifex offerret, quod multis
futurum videbatur, amplectendam. Idque Pandulphus subhaesi-
tans pertentasset, quippe qui non ignarus esset omnia illum malle
quam huiusmodi honoribus commisceri. Ipse, qua erat animi mag-
nitudine, responderi protinus propheticum illud per epistolam ius-
sit, non sunt cogitationes meae cogitationes vestrae, contemplans
forte de bonis ecclesiae, quorum pars maxima pauperibus hereditario iure debetur, magnificos ducere apparatus non oportere.

62   Sanctissimorum item hominum exempla ante oculos posita —
Ambrosii scilicet, Augustini, Martini caeterorumque — qui episco-
patus dignitatem oblatam effugerunt diuque id muneris antequam
obirent detractaverunt. Quid quod et non modo ab cardinalatu
ipso, sed et ab suprema Summi Pontificii potestate sanctissimum
Celestinum se abdicasse legerat, ipsumque totius Christianae rei
publicae humeris onus excussisse — onus vere, cum subeuntibus
maximum paretur praemium invitis scilicet et parendi tantum iu-
vandique gratia illud amplectentibus?

63   Persuassimum erat viro philosopho non esse laudis cumulasse
divitias, non quaesisse honores, sed renuisse, et umbratilem re-
nuendo gloriam, veram adipisci, quae semper virtutes ceu comes
individua et assecla comitatur. Humanam gloriam vel pro nihilo
habebat, aiebatque saepius famam vivis non nihil, mortuis minime
profuturam.

64   Tantumque propriam aestimasse doctrinam agnovimus quantum utilitati ecclesiae et eliminandis explodendisque adversis erroribus conduceret. Quinetiam ad eam perfectionis metam

Some of his friends from Ferrara also persuaded Pandolfo Col- 61
lenucio of Pesaro — a jurist, an avid reader and a man of acute intelligence to whom Pico was very close — to use whatever reasons
he could to convince him to seek a Cardinal's office or certainly to
accept it if the Pope should offer it to him, which many thought
would happen. Since Pandolfo was aware of all the things my uncle would prefer to getting mixed up in such honors, he was less
than convinced, but he gave it a try. Pico, drawing on his greatness
of spirit, immediately saw to it that Pandolfo should get his answer by letter with that saying of the prophet — *my thoughts are not
your thoughts*. Perhaps his idea was that resources owned by the
Church, which by right of inheritance should be mainly for the
poor, ought not to yield pomp and splendor.

Also before his eyes were exemplary deeds of the greatest 62
saints — namely Ambrose, Augustine, Martin and others — who
fled the rank of bishop when it was offered and refused such employment for a long time before accepting it. Had he also read
about the most blessed Celestine? He renounced not only a Cardinal's office but also the absolute power of a Supreme Pontiff, thus
removing the burden of the whole Christian commonwealth from
his shoulders. This office truly is a burden, even though it brings
an enormous reward to those who submit unwillingly and accept it
only to be helpful and obedient.[51]

The greatest attraction to someone who was a philosopher was 63
not to pile up riches while seeking honors but to refuse them and,
by refusing a mere shadow of glory, to attain the real thing, which
always accompanies virtues as their inseparable attendant and aco-
lyte. Pico had really no regard at all for human glory, and he often
used to say that fame amounts to something for the living, but for
the dead it will be nothing.[52]

As for his own learning, I realized that he valued it only to 64
promote the Church's welfare, expel her enemies and eliminate
their errors. I saw that he had reached even this goal of perfection:

pervenisse percepimus — ut scilicet parum curaret si eius commentationes non sub proprio nomine publicitus ederentur, dum tamen id ipsum quod sub Pici nomine facturae fuerant afferrent hominibus emolumenti; minimumque aliis amplius affici libris praeterquam Veteri Novoque Testamento, aetatisque residuum in eis semper volvendis consumere statuisse — nisi publica eum stimularet utilitas cum videret tot et tanta quae conceperat et parturierat passim ab omnibus non efflagitari modo sed et immatura exigi.

65   Minutulumque quantulumcunque devoti vel seniculi vel aniculae affectum in Deum pluris quam omnem eius humanarum divinarumque rerum noticiam faciebat. Admonebatque saepissime familiares interloquendum ut animadverterent quantum laborant nutantque[11] mortalia, quamque caducum et fluxum quod vivimus, quam firmum et stabile quod sumus futuri — sive scilicet detrudamur ad inferos sive sublevamur[12] ad caelos — hortabaturque ut ad Deum amandum converterent et incitarent mentes, quod opus praeponderaret cuicunque quam in hac vita habere possemus cognitioni.

66   Hoc etiam in libello ipso *De ente et uno* luculentissime est exsecutus, quando ad Angelum Politianum, cui librum nuncupavit, in ipsa disputatione conversus haec verba effatus fuerit:

> Sed vide, mi Angele, quae nos insania teneat. Amare Deum dum sumus in corpore plus possumus quam vel eloqui vel cognoscere. Amando plus nobis proficimus, minus laboramus, illi magis obsequimur. Malumus tamen semper per cognitionem nunquam invenire quod querimus quam amando possidere id quod non amando frustra etiam inveniretur.

Illud quoque divi Francisci: tantum scit homo quantum operatur, illius in ore frequens fuerat.

to worry little about publishing his ideas under his own name—
provided that their being published under the Pico name would be
of some profit to people. At this point he cared hardly at all for
books other than the Old Testament and the New, and he had
resolved to spend the rest of his life studying them always—were
it not that the public good spurred him on when he noticed that
much of his output and many of his thoughts were not only
widely in demand everywhere but were being requested even before they were ready.[53]

Feeling for God, no matter how slight, in some devout old man   65
or grandmother moved him more than all his knowledge of theology and the arts and sciences. And when he talked with friends,
he would very often warn them to notice how much we mortals
toil and stagger, how frail and fleeting our present lives are, but
how firm and enduring things will be for us in the future—
whether we are shoved down into hell, in other words, or raised
up to heaven—and he would urge them to turn their minds
around and awaken them to love God, a task that outweighs any
knowledge that we can get in this life.

He also followed this up splendidly in his little book *On Being*   66
and the One, dedicated to Angelo Poliziano, whom he addressed in
these words while debating him:

> See the madness that grips us, Angelo. While we are in the
> body, we can love God better than we can describe or know
> him. By loving, we help ourselves more, struggle less and
> please him better. Yet instead of loving we always prefer to
> get knowledge and never find what we seek, in order to have
> what would be useless without love even if we found it.

He also used to repeat a remark by Saint Francis: *a person knows
only as much as he labors for.*[54]

67 Caeterum liberalitas sola in eo modum excessit, tantumque
aberat ut aliquid curae terrenis rebus apponeret ut etiam incuriosi-
tatis naevo macularetur. Ab amicis quoque saepius admonitum
comperimus ut in totum divitias non contemneret, asseverantibus
id sibi probro dari cum vulgatum foret, sive id verum sive falsum,
furti dispensatoribus praebuisse occasionem. Nihilominus mens
illa, quae semper contemplandis perscrutandisque totius naturae
consiliis inhaerebat, demittere se facile non poterat ad haec infima
abiectaque pensiculanda.

68 Memini, dum Ferrariae cum eo obversarer, obsonatorem pagella
quadam oblata expensarum approbationem expetere. Quo viso
mirabundus exstiti, percunctatusque illum mentemne ad id quod
retroactis temporibus neglexerat apposuisset. Respondit fami-
liaris[13] non modo ab eo efflagitasse sed exegisse ut id subiret officii,
quibus ut morem gereret factitaverat, tantum vero curae quantum
prius habuisse. Quinetiam dum eius dispensator primarius eum
interpellasset ut eius pecuniarum quas per multos annos con-
tractaverat dispunctionem fieri iuberet, quo securius menti suae
consuleret, atque eiusmodi libros coram attulisset, talia eidem
verba respondisse percepimus: Scio me quam saepissime abs te et
potuisse et posse fraudari. Quapropter libratione expensarum harum opus non est. Si tibi debeo, quamprimum nummos exsolvam.
Si mihi debes, vel in presentia si potes, vel in posterum si non
adest facultas, debita relue.

69 Amicos vero semper multa indulgentia tractavit, quibuscum
hortatoriis ad benevivendum locutionibus uti solebat. Hominem
novi qui, dum eius doctrina fretus et fama secum loqueretur, et
haberetur sermo de moribus, duobus tantum ipsius verbis commo-
tum ut via vitiorum deserta mores reformaverit. Verba fuerunt
eiusmodi: si Christi mortem nostri amore perpessam prae oculis
haberemus, propriam quoque identidem cogitando caveremus a

Otherwise, only his generosity went beyond bounds, and he 67
put so little store in the here and now that heedlessness was another blemish in him. I find that friends also often warned him
not to be completely contemptuous of wealth, insisting that people
would think him guilty — rightly or wrongly — of giving his agents
an opportunity to steal. Yet that mind of his, always fixed on
grand purposes of nature that had to be investigated and understood, could not easily stoop to fuss over these utterly petty trivi-
alities.

I remember, when I was with him in Ferrara, that a grocer of- 68
fered him a receipt for expenses and asked him to approve it.
Stunned to see this, I questioned him and asked whether he was
bothering with something he had neglected in times past. He answered that when people close to him not only requested but demanded that he do his duty, he did so to keep them happy, though
he worried no more about it than he ever had. I actually witnessed
the following scene. To put his own mind at ease, my uncle's head
steward nagged him to order an accounting of funds that he had
handled for many years. When he brought the appropriate books
to put in front of his master, I heard my uncle reply with words
like these: I realize that I may have been cheated by you quite
frequently — and that this still might happen. This is why there is
no need to balance these books: if I owe you, I'll pay you back the
money directly; if you owe me, either settle the debt now, if you
can, or else pay later, if you lack the means at present.

He always treated his friends very kindly, in fact, and he used to 69
have conversations with them to urge them to live righteously. I
know a man who spoke with him because he had confidence in his
celebrated learning. When my uncle gave him a talk about morality, just a single pair of statements moved him to abandon the path
of vice and reform his conduct. The statements were like these:
keep the death that Christ endured out of love for us constantly
before our eyes; then we would avoid vice if we also meditated on

vitiis. Modestiam et comitatem in eos admirabilem exhibuit quos non a viribus aut fortuna probatos sibi devinciendos duxerat sed et a moribus[14] et doctrina. Eos tamen qui quantulumcunque pollerent litteris vel saltem bonarum artium studiis navos aptosque inspiceret diligere consueverat. Similitudo namque amoris est causa, et erga sapientem virum — ut teste Philostrato, Apollonius inquit — affinitas quaedam est. Scientiam quoque perficere hominem qua homo est, perfectum vero bonitatem consequi, super alios vero probos[15] esse diligendos non ambigitur.

70   Caeterum nihil ei intolerabilius quam, ut verbis Horatii utar, superba civium potentiorum limina. Militiam quoque saeculi et coniugale vinculum perosus fuerat. Interrogatusque inter iocandum quid ei ad alterum subeundum onus ferendumque et necessitate cogente et optione data levius videretur, haesitabundus aliquantulum nutabundusque necnon pauxillum subridens coniugium respondit, cui non tantum esset et servitutis annexum et periculi quantum militiae.

71   Libertatem enim supra modum dilexerat quam et natura sic affecta et philosophiae studia suggesserant. Vagumque ob id plurimum extitisse illum autumo nec propriam sibi unquam sedem delegisse, licet Florentiae saepius et Ferrariae quandoque commoraretur. Quarum alteram civitatem sibi quasi domicilium praestituisse putaverim quod scilicet in ea, post Bononiam, primum litterarum studia coluerat, illiusque princeps eum mirifice diligeret quadamque veluti affinitate coniunctus — utpote ex cuius ego sorore, scilicet Blancha Maria Estensi, natus sim. Nec etiam longe nimis esset a patria quando triginta tantum passuum milibus ab Mirandula orientem solem versus Ferraria distet.

72   Alteram sive aeris amaenitate sive plurium amicorum suavitate sive ingeniorum subtilitate dilexit plurimum et incoluit. Quos inter litterario amore duos sibi potissimum devinxit: Angelum scilicet Politianum, virum Graece Latineque doctissimum necnon

our own deaths in the same way. He showed remarkable modesty and courtesy to those he thought he should keep close to him, not because he liked their power or good fortune, but for their conduct and learning. Yet usually he chose friends with a bit of literary talent or those whom he considered at least fit and eager for higher learning. For *likeness is a cause of love*, and in the case of a wise man, it is a kind of *affinity* — as Apollonius said, according to Philostratus. There is also no doubt that knowledge perfects a human *as* human, who then, thus perfected, achieves goodness, but the righteous are surely to be loved above others.[55]

Besides, he had no patience at all for Horace's *proud portals of the mighty*. He also despised civic employment and the bond of marriage. Asked in a joking way which of these burdens would be the lighter to bear if he had a choice and were forced to pick, he wavered, hesitated a bit and then replied with a slight smile that it was marriage, where the slavery involved was not so great as in public service and the danger was less.[56]

His love of freedom was boundless because by nature he was so inclined and because his studies of philosophy told him so. This was why he kept wandering, I believe, and never chose a place of his own, though he stayed in Florence rather often and sometimes in Ferrara. I suppose the latter city offered him a home of sorts, especially because, after Bologna, it was where he first began serious studies and because its prince was remarkably fond of him and connected by a special family alliance — since I was born to that prince's sister, of course, Bianca Maria d'Este. Nor was Ferrara too far from his native place, only thirty miles away from Mirandola to the east.

It was the other city that he liked best — Florence — and he lived there because of the pleasant climate or else for his many agreeable friends with their refined intellects. Love of learning brought him especially close to two of them: one was Angelo Poliziano, a man of enormous erudition in Latin and Greek, well

70 .

71

72

variarum litterarum florum[16] refertum ac prope vindicem Romanae linguae; alterum Marsilium Ficinum Florentinum, hominem omnifaria litteratura redolentem sed maximum ex his qui nunc vivunt Platonicum, cuius opera in Academicis sibi vendicandis usus fuerat.

73   Exterioris latriae cultus non multum diligens fuerat. Non de eo loquimur quem observandum praecipit ecclesia — gestasse quippe[17] prae oculis eum vidimus — sed de his caerimoniis mentionem facimus quas nonnulli, posthabito vero cultu Dei, qui in spiritu et veritate colendus est, prosequuntur et provehunt. At internis affectibus ferventissimo Deum amore prosequebatur. Interdum etiam alacritas illa animi propemodum elanguescebat et decidebat, maiori quandoque nixu vires assumens. Adeoque in Deum exarsisse illum memini, ut cum Ferrariae in pomario quodam de Christi amore colloquentes longis spatiaremur ambulacris, in eiusmodi verba proruperit: Tibi haec dixerim in arcanis recondito. Opes quae mihi reliquae sunt, absolutis consummatisque elucubrationibus quibusdam, egenis elargiar, et crucifixo munitus, exertis nudatisque pedibus, orbem peragrans per castella, per urbes, Christum predicabo. Accepi postea illum mutavisse propositum, nam[18] praedicatorum ordini se addicere statuisse.

74   Interim eorum quae conceperat operum quaeque inchoaverat maturabat editionem. Sed millesimo quadringentesimo nonagesimo quarto anno redemptionis nostrae, dum ipse secundum et trigesimum aetatis annum impleret Florentiaeque moraretur, insidiosissima correptus est febre. Quae adeo in humores et viscera grassata est ut nullum non medicamentorum genus adhibitum contempserit, eumque omnino naturae satisfacere intra tertium decimum diem coegerit. Sed quemadmodum in infirmitate se gesserit, licet eo tempore ab eo procul essem, narrare tamen non desinam quae ab gravissimis testibus qui aderant acceperim.

75   Quale illud. Cum post sumptum eucharistiae sacramentum sigillum ei crucifixi Christi offeretur ut inde plenos amoris haustus

supplied with fruits of various literatures and, for all practical purposes, the champion of Rome's language; the other was Marsilio Ficino, a Florentine noted for learning of every kind, but the greatest living expert on Plato, whose work my uncle called upon to claim Plato's followers in the Academy as his own colleagues.[57]

He did not much care for external devotions in worship. I am   73
not talking about services that the Church has commanded us to attend—he certainly did so, as I saw—but ceremonies that some pursue and promote while neglecting real worship of God, who must be revered in the spirit and the truth. In his feelings, however, my uncle approached God with love that burned hot inside him. Yet now and then, even his eager mind faded and almost failed, though sometimes the struggle made him stronger. Once in Ferrara, as we walked in an orchard along rows of trees and talked together about Christ's love, I remember him blazing with such passion for God that words like these burst out of him: Let me tell you this, and keep it secret. After I have finally finished a few big projects, I shall give the rest of my wealth to the needy and I shall preach Christ—armed with the crucifix, barefoot and shoeless, roaming the world's cities and high places. Later I heard that he changed his plan, for he decided to join the Order of Preachers.[58]

Meanwhile he was finishing an edition of projects that he had   74
been thinking about and some that he had started. But in the year 1494 of our salvation, as he was completing his thirty-second year while staying in Florence, a very nasty fever took hold of him. It attacked his humors and bowels with a force that defied any medicine used against it, and within thirteen days the fever forced him to pay his debt to nature. I was far away at the time, but I shall not fail to tell how he conducted himself as he declined, using what I have heard from reliable witnesses who were present.

This, for example. After he took the sacrament of the eucharist,   75
they held an image of Christ crucified in front of him so that,

ob ineffabilis illius passionis nostrae salutis gratia memoriam, priusquam exhalaret animam, sumere posset—fortissimum dumtaxat adversus quaecunque adversa munimen validissimumque contra iniquos daemones propugnaculum. Interrogantique mox seniori an firmiter crederet veram esse illam Dei veri verique hominis imaginem, qui qua Deus est ante tempus et aevum ab ipso Patre Deo cui aequalis in omnibus genitus esset, deque Spiritu Sancto qui et Deus est, ab ipsoque et Patre (quae tria unum sunt) coeterne manante, in utero Mariae semper virginis conceptus esset in tempore, qui famem, qui sitim, qui labores, aestus, vigilias perpessus esset, qui demum—pro contractis ab Adae semine sordibus nostris abluendis proque reseranda ianua coeli—maxima qua genus humanum charitate complectabatur, preciosissimum sanguinem et sponte et libentissime in ara crucis effudisset, caeteraque id genus recenseri quandoque solita, non modo se credere sed et certum esse responderit.

76   Et item illud. Cum Alberto Pio, sororis filio quem nominavimus inter huius *Vitae* initia, iuveni et ingenio et bonarum artium studiis et moribus conspicuo, eadem ratione qua Alexander ex Aphrodisiade et Themistius in *Auscultatoriorum* librorum proemio fortitudinem e physicis contemplationibus sumi contra mortis metum declaravit—quam mox sententiam usurpavit Averrois— conanti (inquam) Alberto mortis confinia reddere placabiliora, in hunc modum verba reddiderit: non illa dumtaxat ratione pacari animum, non finem mortis cruciatibus poni sed hac potissimum— quod Dei sui offensis terminus iam poneretur quando breviusculum vitae eius tempus crebriores in Deum offensas non contenturum arbitraretur.

77   Et illud praeterea. Quando pluribus ex praedicatorum collegia probatissimis testibus—et Alberto ipso paulo ante citato—

before he breathed out his soul, he could remember and drink deep from the love that brought Christ such unspeakable suffering for the sake of our salvation—this was his strongest defense against any hostile power and the mightiest bulwark against wicked demons. Then a Church elder asked him if he firmly believed the crucifix to be a true image of the true God who is truly human, who before endless time, as God, comes from the same God, the Father, by whom he was begotten equal to the Father in all respects. Then he was asked about the Holy Spirit who is also God, flowing coeternally (since the three are one) from the Father and Christ, who in time was conceived in Mary's womb—the Ever Virgin—and who endured hunger, thirst, toil, heat and sleeplessness until at last, to wash away the filth of Adam's seed that has infected us and to unlock heaven's gates, he shed his most precious blood on the altar of the cross, willingly and most joyfully, embracing humankind with the greatest love of all. Other such customary points were reviewed, and he answered not only that he believed them but that he was sure of them.[59]

This also. Alberto Pio, the son of a sister whom I mentioned at the beginning of this *Life*, was a well-behaved young man with obvious talent for the life of the mind. He declared that one should not fear death but take courage from thinking about nature for the same reasons given by Alexander of Aphrodisias and by Themistius in the preface to his books on the *Physics*—a view then taken over by Averroes. When Alberto (and this is my point) tried to make death's approach more bearable, my uncle replied with words like these: what mainly set his mind at ease was not so much being done with the agonies of dying as this: realizing that a limit would now be set on his offenses against God, since he thought that the small bit of time remaining to him in this life left little room for more frequent trespasses.[60]

And this besides. After he revealed to several upstanding witnesses from a Dominican convent—as well as the Alberto just 76

77

revelaverit caeli reginam ad se nocte adventasse miro fragrantem
odore, membraque omnia febre illa contusa confractaque refovisse,
seque morti omnino non concessurum promisisse, hilari placi-
doque ore in strato dum aegrotaret iacuisse compertum est. Atque
inter mortis aculeos quos sustinebat, quasi coelos sibi patefactos
cerneret loqui solitum salutantesque omnes et operam suam, ut
moris est, pollicentes, blandissimo ab eo sermone et receptos et
exosculatos.

78   Ab servis item omnibus, si cui molestus forte fuisset, ignosci
sibi postulasse certiores facti sumus. Quibus ante acto anno testamento caverat victum aliis et tegumentum dum viverent, aliis
pecunias pro meritis erogari. Haeredes Florentini xenodochei
pauperes instituit—eorum dumtaxat quae moveri non poterant,
mobilium vero, Antonium Mariam fratrem.

79   Quanta vero molestia eius obitus infimos et summos omnium
gradus affecerit, testes sunt Italiae principes, urbes et populi, testes
hi reges quos supra citavimus, testis iterum Caroli Galliarum regis
benignitas et gratia, silentio non praetereunda. Cui cum Florentiam adventanti ut inde Romam peteret Neapolitanum regnum
expugnaturus, gravi eum laborare aegretudine nuntiatum fuisset,
duos statim medicos ad eum, legatorum etiamnum fungentes offi-
cio, visitatum et opitulatum ipse transmiserit. Litterasque quas et
vidimus et legimus propria subscriptas manu dedit, plenas et humanitatis et earum pollicitationum quas et magnanimi regis beni-
volentissimus animus et praeclarae virtutes aegrotantis exigebant.
Ei quippe tum fama notissimus erat, tum quadam familiaritate
coniunctus. Nam ab eo in Galliis, dum Parisios inviseret, honori-
fice exceptus fuerat. Enimvero qui eum dum vixit toti orbi et
multis saeculis admirandum praestitit, ita eius obitum non minus
celebrem et inauditum celebrari decrevit.

222

mentioned—that the Queen of Heaven had come to him at night with a marvelously sweet smell, that she restored every part of his body, wracked and worn out by fever, and promised that he would never yield to death, they found him lying on his sickbed with a calm and happy expression. And while suffering the stings of death, he kept talking as if he saw the heavens open up for him to kiss, greet and speak sweetly to everyone who hailed him there and, in the customary way, promised to help him.[61]

All his servants also assured me that he begged their forgiveness 78 in case he had offended any of them. A year before, he had provided by will for some to be fed and clothed for as long as they lived, for others to be paid money as they deserved. He also gave an inheritance to poor people in a hospice for strangers in Florence—just the real property, while the furnishings went to his brother, Antonio Maria.[62]

His death brought great distress to one and all, of low degree 79 and high. Witnesses are Italy's princes, cities and peoples, kings whom I named before are witnesses, nor can we fail to mention another witness—King Charles of France, in his courtesy and generosity. When he was advancing on Florence to go from there to Rome and conquer the Kingdom of Naples, and he was informed that my uncle was suffering a grave illness, he promptly sent two physicians to visit him and bring help, though they were still serving on his diplomatic staff. He also sent a letter and signed it himself. I read it and saw that it was full of the sympathy and assurances that one would expect, given the extraordinary goodwill of this magnanimous monarch and the celebrated gifts of the one lying ill. My uncle was very well known by reputation, of course, but there was also a personal connection. For the King had received and honored him when he visited Paris. During his life, Charles endorsed him as a marvel for the whole world and for the ages, and since his exceptional death was no less praiseworthy, he decided that praise was due again.[63]

80   Quocirca ea in praesentiarum referenda puto quae meis auribus
hausi dum Florentiae quo illius infirmitate percepta, licet non tem-
pestive, me contuleram, in aede sacra quae Sanctae Reparatae dicitur, Hieronymum Savonarolam Ferrariensem, ex praedicatorum
ordine virum et theologiae consultissimum et praeclarissimum fa-
matissimumque sanctimonia, sacras habentem ad Florentinum
populum conciones audirem. Sed prius sacrarum litterarum igna-
ros Apulei verbis admonere consilium est: ne crassis auribus et
obstinato corde ea putent mendacia quae auditu nova vel visu ru-
dia vel certe supra captum cogitationis ardua videantur. Quae si
paulo altius exploraverint, non modo compertu evidentia verum
etiam factu facillima sentient. Is igitur e pulpito declamitans, quae
sum dicturus cunctis qui aderant insinvauit.

81   Arcanum tibi, O Florentia, pandendum est, quod equidem
ita verum est quam proverbium illud apud te frequens Ioannis evangelii.[19] Subticuissem profecto, sed ad dicendum com-
pellor, et qui mihi praecipere potest ut haec palam facerem
imperavit. Neminem porro vestrum puto fuisse qui Ioannem
Picum Mirandulam non noverit. Magnis ille a Deo beneficiis
magnisque gratiis cumulatus, multifariaque praeditus disciplina fuerat. Nulli forte mortalium tam celebre obtigit ingenium. Magnam in eo iacturam fecit ecclesia. Arbitrarer, si
diutius ei vitae spatium prorogatum fuisset, cunctos qui oc-
tingentis ab hinc annis decessere, ob scriptionum monumenta quae reliquisset, excelluisse.

82   Hic mecum obversari solitus erat secreta palam facere, ex
quibus noveram internis eum locutionibus a Deo ad religionem citari, unde afflatibus hisce obsequi cupiens non semel
obtemperare proposuerat. Verum divinis beneficiis male gra-
tus vel ab sensibus evocatus, detractabat labores (delicatae

For this reason and in the circumstances, I think I should add   80
my report of what I heard with my own ears in Florence, having
hurried there after learning of Pico's illness, though I did not ar-
rive in time. In the holy church called Santa Reparata, I listened to
devotional addresses given to the Florentine people by Girolamo
Savonarola of the Order of Preachers, an expert theologian from
Ferrara also renowned for outstanding sanctity. But first I mean to
use words from Apuleius to warn those ignorant of Sacred Scripture: since *their hearing is dull and their hearts stubborn, not to treat as
false what seems strange to hear or hard to see or plainly difficult to grasp
by thinking.* If people only looked a little deeper, they would find
such things not only evident from their own experience but also
quite easily done. Orating from the pulpit, then, Savonarola made
known to everyone present what I am about to say.[64]

A mystery is to be laid out before you, Florence, truly as real   81
as that maxim from John's Gospel that you often repeat. I
might have stayed silent, in fact, but I am forced to speak
because He who has the power to rule me has commanded
me to make this public. Now I think that not one of you did
not know Giovanni Pico della Mirandola. God's abundant
kindnesses and many favors equipped him with learning of
various kinds. Perhaps no mortal possessed such abounding
talent. For the Church his loss was great. Had his life been
preserved for a longer time, I believe he would have outdone
everyone who died during the last eight hundred years, as
shown by the written records that he left.[65]

He used to come to me and reveal his secrets, from which   82
I knew that God had called him to religion by speaking inside him, and, wishing to comply with these inspirations, he
proposed more than once to obey. Since he was ungrateful
for God's generosity, however, or else because he was en-
chanted by the senses, he shirked his task (his character was

quippe temperaturae fuerat) vel arbitratus eius opera religionem indigere differebat ad tempus: hoc tamen non ut verum sed ut a me coniectatum et praesumptum dixerim.

83   Ob id duobus ei annis flagellum interminatus sum si opus quod ei Deus patrandum proposuerat negligenter exsequeretur. Rogabam—fateor—Deum identidem ut caesus aliquantulum viam quae ex alto eidem ostensa fuerat tandem capesseret. Non hoc quaesivi quo perculsus est. Non hoc putaveram at id Deo decretum fuit—ut vitam hanc relinqueret, praeclaraeque coronae in caelis preparatae partem amitteret, famamque et nominis celebritatem quae ad summum cumulum si vixisset fuerat habiturus ad plenum non assequeretur.

84   Verum benignissimus iudex clementissime erga ipsum se habuit. Atque ob elemosinas larga et effusissima manu pauperibus elargitas et orationes quae ad Deum instantissime effusae sunt, effectum est ut nec eius anima in sinu Patris adhuc super caelos exultet nec ad inferos deputata perpetuis tormentis crucietur, sed purgatorio igni ad tempus mancipata temporarias paenas luat. Quod in hac parte libentissime dixerim ut qui eum noverunt, et hi potissimum qui eius beneficiis cumulati fuere, suffragiis adiuvent.

85   Haec et plura alia vir Dei clara voce asseveravit, se addens non latuisse ob mendatia eiusmodi, si qua miscerentur, verbi Dei praecones dignos effici de quibus aeternum summeretur supplicium, nec non adiciens diebus aliquot haec sibi in universum fuisse comperta. Sed—propter verba quae Virginem dixisse sibi aegrotus affirmaverat—nutabundum[20] stetisse formidasseque diu, ne ille demonum opera fuisset illusus, quando ob eius mortem Virginis pollicitatio frustraretur. Verum tamen innotuisse sibi defunctum

soft, to be sure), or he thought he should put it off for a while because his work was needed by the faith: I state this not as a fact but as my guess and assumption.[66]

For two years, then, I threatened him with the lash if he neglected to follow through on the task that God had set out and assigned to him. Again and again I asked God to cut him down a bit—I admit it—so that he would take the road that had been shown to him from on high. But I did not seek what killed him. This was not my idea but God's decision—that he leave this life, lose part of the shining crown waiting for him in heaven and not attain the reputation and celebrity that would have come to him in full had he lived.

But this most kindly Judge showed him extraordinary mercy. Because of the abundant charity that flowed from his hand to the poor and the prayers that he poured out to God so earnestly, the result was that his soul does not yet exult in the Father's embrace beyond the skies, nor has he been sent to Hell to suffer perpetual torment, but for a time he has been assigned to Purgatory to pay temporal penalties. Accordingly, I was quite ready to say this to those who knew him, especially those who gained so much from his kindnesses, so that they might help him with their support.[67]

The man of God declared this and much else in his clear voice, adding that he was not unaware that messengers of God's word would deserve eternal punishment if they mixed statements about such a matter with lies. He also noted that the whole business had been known to him for some days. But—because of words that the Virgin spoke, as the dying man confirmed—he remained hesitant for a while, fearing that demonic activity might have deceived my uncle, since the Virgin's promise about his death was empty. Then he realized that an equivocal use of 'death' had misled the

83

84

85

69

aequivocatione mortis deceptum cum illa de secunda et aeterna locuta fuisset, hic de prima et temporaria credidisset.

86   Quod si quis dixerit hominem hunc vel hypocrisi fuisse mentitum vel fantasmatis ludificatum vel daemonum praestigiis circumventum, is — nisi aut male de fide sentiens aut mentis emotae sit — fateatur necesse est, Deum multifarie foelicitatem eorum miseriamque qui animam effudissent viventibus et revelasse iam et revelare posse. Eodemque temporis spacio eos quibus haec palam fiunt certiores reddere se non a visis aut spectris illudi sed vera esse quae aut mente aut oculis cernant et videant.

87   Tantae vero et doctrinae et auctoritatis virum, tantae probitatis et prudentiae, quorum in Aristotelis philosophiam compendiaria theoremata, monitiones publicae, praeclarissima interpretamenta in sacra eloquia, futurorum contingentium praedictiones quae evenisse ad lineam omnis fere novit Italia, sanctissimaque vitae conversatio testatissimam pridem fecere fidem, in principe templo tam celebratae urbis, haec ut vera, ut inconcussa tenenda, tot milibus hominum veritate non comperta pronuntiasse, nemo nisi malevolus inficiabitur. Adde quod dum non nihil super id negocii sciscitarer, virum qui sermoni interfuerat adiisse concionatorem audivi ac eidem — ut ea plus haberent roboris quae vulgaverat — rettulisse defunctum vallatum igne sibi apparuisse et professum ingratitudinis adhuc paenas dare.

88   Quinetiam monacha quaedam multis praeclara vaticiniis quaeque ipsi dum viveret multa futura praedixit quae adamusim evenere. Inter reliqua hoc unum protulit biennio antequam e vita migrasset: eum liliorum tempore — opera et hortatu fratris Hieronymi, de quo mentionem fecimus — praedicatorum fratrum

deceased, since Mary had been talking about the second death that lasts forever, though my uncle believed it was the first and temporary death.

But if anyone should claim that this Girolamo was a lying 86 hypocrite duped by phantoms or deceived by demonic illusions, such a person—unless he has lost his mind or has not kept the faith—must acknowledge that God has had and still has many ways of revealing to the living whether those who have breathed their last are happy or suffering. And in the same moment God can assure those to whom such things are revealed that they are not deluded by visions or ghosts but that what they see with their eyes and perceive with their minds is real.[68]

This Girolamo is a man of enormous learning and authority, of 87 immense wisdom and righteousness. Think of his comprehensive propositions on Aristotle's philosophy, his warnings to the public, his absolutely dazzling interpretations of Sacred Scripture, his predictions of future events found to be exact almost everywhere in Italy and also his most holy way of life. All this has long since given him such indisputable credence that no one, except out of spite, would deny that he checked his facts before telling thousands of people, in the main church of a famous city, that such things were true and unshakably solid. Add this too: while I was still making inquiries into this affair, I heard that a man who was present for the sermon came up to the speaker and—to give more weight to what had been divulged—told him that the dead man had appeared to him walled in by fire and confessing that he was still paying the price of his ingratitude.[69]

There was also a nun, renowned for many prophecies, who had 88 given my uncle accurate predictions of many things while he was alive. Among other announcements, she made this one two years before he left this life: that in the time of lilies—with support from Brother Girolamo, whom I have mentioned, and at his urging—he would pledge himself to the convent of the Preaching

collegio se dicaturum, eodemque tempore Florentinam quandam familiam quam Pactiam nuncupant tunc exulantem ad patriam redituram. Complures ad quos haec fama pervenerat super hac liliorum nomenclatura demirabantur, loqui eam arbitrantes de verno tempore quo lilia florescunt. Sed lilium hoc Galliarum regem exstitisse compertum est talibus utentem insignibus. Qui pridie quam ille religionem profiteretur[21] — ita enim voverat antequam moreretur — et quatriduo postquam extorris illa familia se contulit in urbem patriam, magno comitatu Florentiam ingressus est, iter per Hetruriam faciens, Neapolitanum regnum vi et armis in ditionem vindicaturus.

89   Verum antequam finem faciam, praefari iterum paucula in calce operis non inutile puto. Videor enim mihi videre ad revelationes has veluti ad lunae umbram baubantes molossos, quibus adhuc offula, prioribus fortasse non contentis, obicienda est, ne frustra latratibus aera verberent. Video item dementibus excuti risum. Video his qui sciolos se arbitrentur summoveri ludum.

90   Qui forte ob non persolutum religionis votum igne[22] torqueri animas non debere contendent — nec divino afflatos spiritu tempestate nostra reperiri homines qui Christi colloquiis perfruantur. At si peccata non morte sed venia digna purgatorio igni esse plectenda arbitrarentur, iustos et[23] paenas dare non mirarentur. Item si servum qui voluntatem Domini sciens non adimplevit — teste Veritate — multis vapulaturum non ignoraverint, hunc qui Dei voluntatem noverat et implere distulit, etsi a noxis quibusque aliis fuisset immunis, supplicia luere non extasim paterentur.

91   Alia ex parte rudem et insulsam eorum astutiam mirari satis non possum, qui cum Christum pro hominibus mortuum credant,

Friars, at the same moment when a certain Florentine family named Pazzi, then in exile, would return to their native land. Many who heard this story were puzzled by the word 'lilies,' supposing that she meant the time when lilies bloom—in Spring. But they learned that this lily was the King of France, who used the lily as his device. On the day before my uncle made his commitment to religion—as he vowed before he died—and four days after that banished family moved back to their native city, the King entered Florence with a large escort and journeyed through Tuscany, meaning to claim authority over the Kingdom of Naples by force of arms.[70]

Before I finish, however, I think it worthwhile to restate a few things as I end this work. For it appears to me that some people look at these revelations like hounds baying at shadows cast by the moon. So that they will not keep whipping the air with their ridiculous barking, I must throw out more scraps in case what they already have has not satisfied them. I also see these lunatics shaking with laughter. I see them straining to hold back their jokes because they think they know something. 89

Maybe they would claim that souls should not be tortured with fire for failing to keep a vow to enter the religious life—also that in our time no one is inspired by the spirit of God to have conversations with Christ. Yet if they think that sins not mortal but venial ought to be punished with the fire of Purgatory, it should not surprise them that the just too are penalized. Likewise, assuming it has not escaped them that a servant would receive many lashes if he knew his master's will but did not fulfill it—and the Truth is our witness here—then it should come as no surprise that this person, who knew God's will and yet postponed carrying it out, would suffer torments even though he was discharged of any other crimes.[71] 90

As for the other issue, I cannot wonder enough at the crude, clumsy cunning of those who believe that Christ died for mankind 91

73

eosdem homines alloqui eundem facile posse non credant — vehe-
mentiorique argumento — virginis matris angelorumque beato-
rumve hominum spirituum affatibus participes eosdem mortales
homines non posse fieri. Animadvertendum eis profecto foret inferiora omnia per superiora gubernari, Dionysio etiam Areopagita
teste in libro *De hierarchia caelesti*; separatisque mentibus inferioris
gradus et naturae, quibus hominum cura demandata est, per su-
periores mentes quae iterum vel a supremis vel ab ipso Deo divina
mysteria hauriunt illuminari; hominesque divino afflatos spiritu
easdem revelationes accipere, hominum multitudini cum expedit
patefaciendas. Sacrosancta haec divinitatis lex quod ab eodem
Dionysio libro *Caelestis hierarchiae* edocemur: ut per prima sequen-
tia ad augustissimam lucem subvehantur.

92   Ignari proculdubio sunt divinarum litterarum, insolentis quoque et pervicacis ingenii, nam in illis conspici datur divina futura
mysteria non tantum per bonos sed per scelestos homines et
pseudoprophetas quandoque patefacta. Quid prohibet huic fidem
non habere[24] qui et doctrina et tot virtutibus pollet multaque iam
futura quae nunc evenere praedixit, et hoc non somniculose testatus sed asseveranter affirmans. Adde quod Aristotelis philosophia
his non reclamet et Platonica suffragentur, licet pro gravi testimonio nisi scripturae divinae auctoritatem non acceperim. Sed
extraria haec quandoque citare non absurdum est ut malevolorum
tela in auctores maiore vi quam venerint revertantur.

93   Verum ad nosmet ipsos iam redeundum est, quibus non tam
maerendum est quod talem amisimus quam quod habuimus et
habemus gratias agendum regi cui vivunt omnia. Quippe[25] morta-
lis vitae munere perfunctus — diuque cum habitantibus Cedar

yet cannot bring themselves to believe that he speaks quite readily to these same people, and — on stronger evidence — that the same mortal men can share in conversation with the Virgin Mother, angels and spirits of sainted humans. Surely they must realize that everything lower is ruled by something higher, even as Dionysius the Areopagite testifies in his book *On the Celestial Hierarchy*; that separated minds of a lower grade and nature, entrusted with the care of humans, are illuminated by higher minds who in turn drink in divine mysteries from the highest minds or from God himself; and that humans inspired by the divine spirit receive these same revelations when it is best to disclose them to many people. This is the most sacred law of theology that Dionysius teaches us in the same book *On the Celestial Hierarchy*: that those who follow the first beings are raised up by them to the most sacred Light.[72]

With their haughty and headstrong attitude, these people are   92
ignorant of theology, no doubt, since a theological principle is that we see divine mysteries revealed for the future not only through good people but also through the wicked and sometimes through *false prophets*. What prevents them from trusting this Girolamo, so strong in learning and virtue, who has predicted many future events that have already happened by now? And he has testified not with dreams but in demonstrative declarations. Note also that Aristotle's philosophy does not contradict these claims, while Platonists support them, though I would not accept this evidence as serious apart from the authority of Sacred Scripture. Yet sometimes it is not foolish to cite this outside evidence so that weapons hurled at authorities by the malevolent might fly back at them with greater force.[73]

But now I must return to my own task, which is not so much   93
to mourn losing such a person as to give thanks to the King, in whom all things live, for what we have had and still have. After my uncle put down the burden of mortal life — having long kept

quos luce non pauca perfuderat conversatus — inaccessibile et infinitum supernae patriae lumen iamiam ingrediens, ineffabili divinitate, nobis etiam in dies laturus opem, sine fine fruetur.

FINIS

company with those who *dwell in Kedar*, and having brought them no little illumination — he now advances toward the unapproachable and endless light of our homeland on high, and he will enjoy without end the divinity that is beyond telling and also, day by day, bring help to us.[74]

THE END

ORATIO IOANNIS PICI MIRANDULANI CONCORDIAE COMITIS

AN ORATION BY GIOVANNI PICO, COUNT OF MIRANDOLA AND CONCORDIA

ORATIO IOANNIS PICI
MIRANDULANI CONCORDIAE
COMITIS[1]

1   Legi, patres colendissimi, in Arabum monumentis, interrogatum Abdalam Sarracenum quid in hac quasi mundana scena admirandum maxime spectaretur, nihil spectari homine admirabilius respondisse. Cui sententiae illud Mercurii adstipulatur: Magnum, o Asclepi, miraculum est homo.

2   Horum dictorum rationem cogitanti mihi non satis illa faciebant, quae multa de humanae naturae praestantia afferuntur a multis: esse hominem creaturarum internuntium, superis familiarem, regem inferiorum; sensuum perspicacia, rationis indagine, intelligentiae lumine naturae interpretem; stabilis aevi et fluxi temporis interstitium, et (quod Persae dicunt) mundi copulam, immo hymeneum—ab angelis, teste Davide, paulo deminutum. Magna haec quidem, sed non principalia, idest quae summae admirationis privilegium sibi iure vendicent. Cur enim non ipsos angelos et beatissimos caeli choros magis admiremur?

3   Tandem intellexisse mihi sum visus cur felicissimum proindeque dignum omni admiratione animal sit homo, et quae sit demum illa conditio quam in universi serie sortitus sit, non brutis modo, sed astris, sed ultramundanis mentibus invidiosam—res supra fidem et mira! Quidni? Nam et propterea magnum miraculum et admirandum profecto animal iure homo et dicitur et existimatur. Sed quae nam ea sit audite, patres, et benignis auribus pro vestra humanitate hanc mihi operam condonate.

AN ORATION BY GIOVANNI PICO, COUNT OF MIRANDOLA AND CONCORDIA

In Arab memorials, Most Reverend Fathers, I have read about 1
Abdala, a Saracen: when asked what was the most astonishing
sight to be seen on this *stage* of the world—so to speak—he answered that there was nothing to see more astonishing than man.
Supporting his opinion is that saying of Mercury: *man is a great
miracle, Asclepius*.[1]

I was not satisfied—*thinking over* the basis for these state- 2
ments—with claims often made for mankind's outstanding nature: that among creatures man is a go-between, the intimate of
higher beings and ruler of those below; that he is an interpreter of
Nature, having keen senses, a searching reason and shining intelligence; that he is an *interval* between fixed eternity and flowing
time and (as the Persians say) the *bond*—no, the *wedding knot*—of
the world, *a little lower than the angels*, according to David. These
reasons are great, to be sure, but they are not the chief reasons,
those that would truly establish the height of astonishment as
man's due. Why should those angels and heaven's blessed choirs
not astonish us more?[2]

At last I seem to have understood why man is the most fortu- 3
nate of animals, why he deserves all the astonishment, and just
what standing he has been given in the universal order to make
him the envy not only of beasts but also of stars and hypercosmic
minds—a wonderful and unbelievable fact! And why not? For
with good reason man is judged a great miracle and called a truly
astonishing animal. Hear what this means, Fathers: in a spirit
of generosity turn a kindly ear to this work of mine, and bear
with me.[3]

4   Iam summus Pater architectus Deus hanc quam videmus mun-
danam domum, divinitatis templum augustissimum, archanae legibus Sapientiae fabrefecerat. Supercaelestem regionem mentibus
decorarat; aethereos globos aeternis animis vegetarat; excrementa-
rias ac feculentas has[2] inferioris mundi partes omnigena anima-
lium turba complerat. Sed, opere consumato, desiderabat Artifex
esse aliquem qui tanti operis rationem perpenderet, pulchritudinem amaret, magnitudinem admiraretur. Idcirco iam rebus omnibus (ut Moses Timaeusque testantur) absolutis, de producendo
homine postremo cogitavit.

5   Verum nec erat in archetipis unde novam sobolem effingeret,
nec in thesauris quod novo filio hereditarium largiretur, nec in
subselliis totius orbis ubi universi contemplator iste sederet. Iam
plena omnia; omnia summis, mediis infimisque ordinibus fuerant
distributa. Sed non erat paternae Potestatis in extrema faetura
quasi effetam defecisse; non erat Sapientiae consilii inopia in re
necessaria fluctuasse; non erat benefici Amoris ut qui in aliis esset
divinam liberalitatem laudaturus, in se illam damnare cogeretur.
Statuit tandem optimus Opifex ut cui dari nihil proprium poterat,
ei[3] commune esset quicquid privatum singulis fuerat. Igitur hominem accepit, indiscretae opus imaginis, atque in mundi positum
meditullio sic est alloquutus.

6   Nec certam sedem, nec propriam faciem, nec munus ullum
peculiare tibi dedimus, o Adam, ut quam sedem, quam faciem, quae munera tute optaveris, ea pro voto, pro tua sententia habeas et possideas. Definita caeteris natura intra
praescriptas a nobis leges cohercetur. Tu, nullis angustiis
cohercitus, pro tuo arbitrio, in cuius manu te posui, tibi

Our Father on high, God the *Master Builder*, had already ap-   4
plied laws of arcane Wisdom to construct this cosmic house that
we see, this most majestic temple of divinity. The region above the
heavens he had adorned with minds; he had enlivened the ethereal
spheres with eternal souls; and with a motley multitude of animals
he had filled up these *waste and feculent parts of the world below*. But
when his work was done, the *Artificer* wanted someone to assess
the reason for so great an undertaking, to love its beauty, to be
astonished by its immensity. Therefore, after everything was finished (as Moses and Timaeus testify), he gave thought at last to
making man.[4]

But in the archetypes there was nothing from which he could   5
fashion a new child, no riches in the treasury for a new son to in-
herit, no place anywhere on the benches of the All where this
contemplator of a universe might sit. For all the places were full,
every one allotted to its order — high, middle and low. And yet it
was no part of a fatherly *Power* to fail exhausted in the last stage of
breeding, no part of *Wisdom* to waver for want of counsel in a moment of need, no part of bountiful *Love* to force someone to condemn divine liberality in his own case and then praise it when
others were helped. So in the end the best *Workman* decided that
he to whom nothing of his own could be given should share whatever was reserved for every other being. Therefore, he took man as
a work with *no distinct image*, stationed him in the *midregion* of the
world and spoke these words to him.[5]

No fixed seat, no special look, nor any particular gift of your   6
own have we given you, Adam, so that what seat, what look,
what gifts you choose for yourself, those you may have and
hold as you wish, according to your purpose. For others, a
definite nature is confined within laws that we have pre-
scribed. With no strictures confining you, you will deter-
mine that nature by your own choice, which is the authority

illam praefinies. Medium te mundi posui, ut circumspiceres inde comodius quicquid est in mundo. Nec te caelestem neque terrenum, neque mortalem neque immortalem fecimus, ut tui ipsius quasi arbitrarius honorariusque plastes et fictor, in quam malueris tute formam effingas. Poteris in inferiora, quae sunt bruta, degenerare; poteris in superiora, quae sunt divina, ex tui animi sententia regenerari.

7   O summam Dei Patris liberalitatem, summam et admirandam hominis foelicitatem, cui datum id habere quod optat, id esse quod velit! Bruta, simul atque nascuntur, id secum afferunt — ut ait Lucilius, e bulga matris — quod possessura sunt. Supremi spiritus aut ab initio aut paulo mox id fuerunt, quod sunt futuri in perpetuas aeternitates. Nascenti homini omnifaria semina et omnigenae vitae germina indidit Pater, quae quisque excoluerit, illa adolescent, et fructus suos ferent in illo. Si vegetalia, planta fiet; si sensualia, obrutescet; si rationalia, caeleste evadet animal; si intellectualia, angelus erit et Dei filius. Et si, nulla creaturarum sorte contentus, in unitatis centrum suae se receperit, unus cum Deo spiritus factus, in solitaria Patris caligine, qui est super omnia constitutus omnibus antestabit.

8   Quis hunc nostrum chamaeleonta non admiretur? Aut omnino quis aliud quicquam admiretur magis? Quem non immerito Asclepius Atheniensis, versipellis huius et se ipsam transformantis naturae argumento, per Protheum in mysteriis significari dixit — hinc illae apud Hebreos et Pythagoricos methamorphoses celebratae. Nam et Hebreorum theologia secretior nunc Enoch sanctum

under which I have put you. I have set you up as the center of the world so that you will be better placed to survey what the world contains. And we have made you neither heavenly nor earthly, neither mortal nor immortal, so that on your own, as molder and maker, specially appointed to decide, you may shape yourself in the form that you prefer. You can sink back into lower forms that are beasts; from your own resolute spirit, you can be born again to higher forms that are divine.[6]

O the supreme generosity of God the Father! This is man's supreme and astonishing good fortune, to whom it is given to have what he chooses, to be what he wants. From the moment of birth—*from the mother's belly*, as Lucilius says—beasts bring with them what they will have. Either from the beginning or a little later, spirits above have been what they will be for all the eternities. In man at birth the Father has planted seeds of every kind and sprouts of every type of life, and if anyone cultivates them, they will grow and bear their fruit in him. If the seeds he tends are vegetal, the man will be a plant. If they are sensual, he will grow into a beast. If they are rational, he will turn into a heavenly animal. If they are intellectual, he will be an angel and a son of God. And if he is not *contented* with the lot of creatures and draws himself into the center of his own unity, becoming a spirit and one with God, this one who has been set above everything will stand ahead of them all and absolutely apart in the Father's *darkness*.[7] 7

Who would not be astonished at this *chameleon* of ours? Or who would be any more astonished at anything else? It was not wrong of the Athenian Asclepius to say that he is signified by Proteus in the mysteries, by reason of his shapeshifting and self-changing nature—hence those metamorphoses solemnized by Hebrews and Pythagoreans. For with their more secret theology, Hebrews too sometimes transform the blessed Enoch into an 8

in angelum divinitatis, quem vocant מטטרון,[4] nunc in alia alios numina reformant; et Pythagorici scelestos homines et[5] in bruta deformant et, si Empedocli creditur, etiam in plantas. Quos imitatus
Maumeth illud frequens habebat in ore, qui a divina lege recesserit
brutum evadere. Et merito quidem: neque enim plantam cortex,
sed stupida et nihil sentiens natura; neque iumenta corium, sed
bruta anima et sensualis; nec caelum orbiculatum corpus, sed recta
ratio; nec sequestratio corporis, sed spiritalis intelligentia angelum
facit.

9   Si quem enim videris deditum ventri, humi serpentem hominem, frutex est, non homo, quem vides. Si quem in fantasiae quasi
Calipsus vanis praestigiis caecutientem et, subscalpenti delinitum
illecebra, sensibus mancipatum, brutum est, non homo, quem
vides. Si recta philosophum ratione omnia discernentem, hunc
venereris: caeleste est animal, non terrenum. Si purum contempla-
torem, corporis nescium, in penetralia mentis relegatum, hic non
terrenum, non caeleste animal: hic augustius est numen humana
carne circumvestitum.

10   Ecquis hominem non admiretur, qui non immerito in sacris
litteris Mosaicis et Christianis nunc omnis carnis, nunc omnis
creaturae appellatione designatur, quando se ipsum ipse in omnis
carnis faciem, in omnis creaturae ingenium effingit, fabricat et
transformat? Idcirco scribit Euantes Persa, ubi Chaldaicam theologiam enarrat, non esse homini suam ullam et nativam imaginem,
extrarias multas et adventitias. Hinc illud Chaldeorum: ቡልናው ሀ
ሐያ ማጠበበ ማሥታኄ ዊናዳ. ማመሐለጸተ ጋረማህ ከ መከ,[6] idest
homo variae ac multiformis et desultoriae naturae animal.

angel of divinity, whom they call מטטרון, and sometimes they change others into other divine powers. Pythagoreans also transmute wicked people into beasts and, if Empedocles is to be believed, even into plants. Imitating them, Maumeth often used to say that whoever strays from divine law turns into a beast. And this is surely right: for it is not bark that makes a plant but a dull and unfeeling nature; not hide that makes a beast of burden but a brutish and sensual soul; not a spherical body but *right reason* that makes a heavenly orb; not removing the body but spiritual intelligence that makes an angel.[8]

If you see a person who has surrendered to the belly, for example, snaking along the ground, what you see is a vegetable, not a human. If you see someone blinded by false enchantments of fantasy, like a victim of Calypso, charmed into scratching where it itches and enslaved by the senses, what you see is no human but a beast. But if you find a philosopher distinguishing everything by *right reason*, this is a person you should honor: this is a heavenly animal, not of the earth. And if you see a pure contemplator, unaware of the body, withdrawn to the mind's sanctuary, this is an animal neither earthly nor heavenly — a more majestic divinity cloaked in human flesh.[9]

Is there anyone who would not find man astonishing, then, the one that Sacred Scripture, Mosaic and Christian, rightly calls *all flesh* or sometimes *every creature*, seeing that he is the one who transforms, forges and fashions himself with the look of all flesh, with every creature's abilities? For this reason, when he explains the Chaldean theology, Euanthes the Persian writes that man is born with no image of his own, that his images are many, alien and accidental. Hence that saying of the Chaldeans: በረፐ ሀ ሐይ ሚጠበ ሚሥተነ ፚናጿ ሚሞሐለጿተ ጋረማሀ ከ ውከ, which means that *a man is a living thing whose nature is variable, manifold and inconstant*.[10]

87

11   Sed quorsum haec? Ut intelligamus (postquam hac nati sumus conditione, ut id simus quod esse volumus) curare hoc potissimum debere nos, ut illud quidem in nos non dicatur: cum in honore essemus, non cognovisse similes factos brutis et iumentis insipientibus. Sed illud potius Asaph prophetae: dii estis et filii Excelsi omnes, ne, abutentes indulgentissima Patris liberalitate, quam dedit ille liberam optionem e salutari noxiam faciamus nobis. Invadat animum sacra quaedam et Iunonia⁷ ambitio, ut mediocribus non contenti anhelemus ad summa, adque illa — quando possumus, si volumus — consequenda totis viribus enitamur. Dedignemur terrestria, caelestia contemnamus, et, quicquid mundi est denique posthabentes, ultramundanam curiam eminentissimae divinitati proximam advolemus. Ibi, ut sacra tradunt mysteria, Seraphin, Cherubin et Throni primas possident; horum nos, iam cedere nescii et secundarum impatientes, et dignitatem et gloriam emulemur. Erimus illis, cum voluerimus, nihilo inferiores.

12   Sed qua ratione aut quid tandem agentes? Videamus quid illi agant, quam vivant vitam. Eam si et nos vixerimus — possumus enim — illorum sortem iam equaverimus.

13   Ardet Saraph charitatis igne; fulget Cherub intelligentiae splendore; stat Thronus iudicii firmitate. Igitur si actuosae addicti vitae inferiorum curam recto examine susceperimus, Thronorum stata soliditate firmabimur. Si ab actionibus feriati in opificio Opificem, in Opifice opificium meditantes, in contemplandi ocio negociabimur, luce cherubica undique corruscabimus. Si charitate ipsum Opificem solum ardebimus, illius igne, qui edax est, in saraphicam effigiem repente flammabimur. Super Throno — idest iusto

88

But what is my purpose in all this? To help us understand this   11
point: once born into this condition of being what we want to be,
we ought to take utmost care that this not be said against us, that
while we were held in honor, we did not recognize that we became like
stupid and unthinking beasts of burden. Better that other line from the
prophet Asaph: *you are gods and all sons of the Most High,* telling us
not to abuse the Father's generosity at its most indulgent and turn
the free choice that he granted us from a help into a harm. Because we are not *content* with middling things, let a holy *ambition*
like Juno's possess our spirit; let us climb for the heights, panting;
and let us strive with all our might to reach them — since we can
do it if we will it. Let us scorn things of earth, let us despise those
of heaven, and then, leaving behind whatever belongs to the world,
let us fly up to the hypercosmic court nearest the most exalted divinity. There, as the sacred mysteries say, Seraphim, Cherubim
and Thrones hold the first places; since we cannot abide second
place and cannot yield, let us be their rivals for rank and glory.
Once we will it, in nothing shall we be their inferiors.[11]

But what method shall we use, and how in the end shall we do   12
it? Let us see what they do and what life they live. And if we live
that life — as we can, in fact — we shall have made our destiny
equal to theirs.

A Seraph burns with the fire of love; a Cherub flashes with the   13
brilliance of intelligence; a Throne stands steadfast in judgment.
Thus, if after due deliberation we are bent on a *life full of action* and
accept concern for lower things, we shall stand firm with the solidity of Thrones. If we have detached from active matters, we shall
be engaged in the disengagement of contemplation as we reflect
upon the *Workman* in the work and the work in the *Workman,* and
we shall gleam with Cherubic light all about us. If in love we burn
only for that *Workman,* in likeness to the Seraph we shall suddenly
blaze with his devouring fire. Above the Throne — a just judge, in

iudice—sedet Deus iudex saeculorum. Super Cherub—idest contemplatore—volat atque eum quasi incubando fovet. Spiritus enim
Domini fertur super aquas—has inquam quae super caelos sunt,
quae apud Iob Dominum laudant antelucanis hymnis. Qui Saraph—idest amator—est in Deo; est et Deus in eo: immo et Deus
et ipse unum sunt.

14   Magna Thronorum potestas, quam iudicando, summa Sara-
phinorum sublimitas, quam amando assequimur. Sed quo nam
pacto vel iudicare quisquam vel amare potest incognita? Amavit
Moses Deum quem vidit, et administravit iudex in populo quae
vidit prius contemplator in monte. Ergo medius Cherub sua luce
et saraphico igni nos praeparat et ad Thronorum iudicium pariter
illuminat.

15   Hic est nodus primarum mentium, ordo Palladicus, philosophiae contemplativae praeses. Hic nobis et aemulandus primo et
ambiendus atque adeo comprehendendus est unde et ad amoris
rapiamur fastigia et ad munera actionum bene instructi paratique
descendamus. At vero operae precium, si ad exemplar vitae cherubicae vita nostra formanda est, quae illa et qualis sit, quae actiones,
quae illorum opera, prae oculis et in numerato habere. Quod cum
nobis per nos, qui caro sumus et quae humi sunt sapimus, consequi non liceat, adeamus antiquos patres qui de his rebus utpote
sibi domesticis et cognatis locupletissimam nobis et certam fidem
facere possunt.

16   Consulamus Paulum apostolum, vas electionis, quid ipse, cum
ad tertium sublimatus est caelum, agentes Cherubinorum exercitus
viderit. Respondebit utique, Dyonisio interprete, purgari illos,
tum illuminari, postremo perfici. Ergo et nos, cherubicam in terris
vitam emulantes, per moralem scientiam affectuum impetus cohercentes, per dialecticam rationis caliginem discutientes, quasi

other words—God sits to judge the ages. Above the Cherub—the contemplator—he hovers and keeps him warm as if brooding over him. For *the Spirit of the Lord is borne upon the waters*—those waters, I say, that are *above the heavens*, and they, according to Job, *praise* the Lord in *daybreak* hymns. One who is a Seraph—a lover—is *in God*; also, God is *in him*: or rather, he and God *are one*.[12]

Great is the power of Thrones, and we attain it by judging, but the greatest exaltation, attained when we love, belongs to Seraphim. Yet how can anyone judge or love what is unknown? Moses loved the God whom he saw, and as *judge over the people* he administered the law which, as contemplator, he had already seen on the mountain. In between, then, the Cherub both prepares us with its light for Seraphic fire and in the same manner lights our way toward the judgment of Thrones.[13]   14

This is the knot of primary minds, the order of Pallas, protector of contemplative philosophy. This we must first emulate and also seek and indeed embrace in order to be carried off from there to the heights of love and then descend, well instructed and prepared for duties of action. But truly, if we are to form our lives on the model of the Cherubic life, it is worthwhile to keep before our eyes what that life is and what it is like—to have in readiness what those angels do and what their activities are. Because we *mind the flesh* and *smell like dirt*, however, we may not attain this on our own, so let us go to the ancient Fathers who can give us a sure and completely reliable account of matters that they are at ease with and are familiar to them.[14]   15

Let us consult the apostle Paul, the *chosen vessel*, and ask what he saw the armies of Cherubim doing when he was raised *to the third heaven*. He will answer without fail, while Dionysius interprets, that they are *cleansed, then enlightened and finally completed*. We too, then, emulating the Cherubic life on earth, checking emotional impulses with moral knowledge, dispelling the darkness of reason through dialectic, let us cleanse the soul by washing away   16

ignorantiae et vitiorum eluentes sordes animam purgemus, ne aut
affectus temere debacchentur aut ratio imprudens quandoque deliret. Tum bene compositam ac expiatam animam naturalis philosophiae lumine perfundamus, ut postremo divinarum rerum eam
cognitione perficiamus.

17   Et ne nobis nostri sufficiant, consulamus Iacob patriarcham,
cuius imago in sede gloriae sculpta corruscat. Admonebit nos pater sapientissimus in inferno dormiens, mundo in superno vigilans.
Sed admonebit per figuram (ita eis omnia contingebant): esse scalas ab imo solo ad caeli summa protensas, multorum graduum serie distinctas, fastigio Dominum insidere, contemplatores angelos
per eas vicibus alternantes ascendere et descendere. Quod si hoc
idem nobis angelicam affectantibus vitam factitandum est, quaeso
quis Domini scalas vel sordidato pede vel male mundis manibus
attinget? Impuro, ut habent mysteria, purum attingere nephas.

18   Sed qui hi pedes? Quae manus? Profecto pes animae illa est
portio despicatissima, qua ipsa materiae tanquam terrae solo innititur, altrix inquam potestas et cibaria, fomes libidinis et voluptariae mollitudinis magistra. Manus animae cur irascentiam non
dixerimus, quae appetentiae propugnatrix pro ea decertat, et sub
pulvere ac sole praedatrix[8] rapit quae illa sub umbra dormitans
helluetur? Has manus, hos pedes — idest totam sensualem partem
in qua sedet corporis illecebra quae animam obtorto, ut aiunt,
detinet collo — ne a scalis tanquam prophani pollutique reiciamur,
morali philosophia quasi vivo flumine abluamus.

19   At nec satis hoc erit, si per Iacob scalam discursantibus angelis
comites esse volumus, nisi et a gradu in gradum rite promoveri, et
a scalarum tramite deorbitare nusquam, et reciprocos obire excursus bene apti prius instructique fuerimus. Quod cum per artem

the filth of ignorance and vice so that our emotions will not rage in fury nor reason ever go mad and foolish. Then let us bathe the soul, purified and well settled, with the light of natural philosophy so that finally we may complete it with knowledge of divinity.[15]

Not to limit ourselves to our own people, let us consult the patriarch Jacob, whose gleaming *image is carved in the Glory Seat.* As he sleeps in the lower world and watches in the world above, this wisest of Fathers will warn us. But he will use a figure (those sages used to do everything this way) to give us his warning: that a ladder reaches from the ground below to the summit of heaven, marked off in a series of many steps, with the Lord seated at the top, while up and down the ladder angels of contemplation take turns moving back and forth. Yet if we are to aspire to the angelic life and must keep doing the same, who (I ask) will be wicked enough to touch the Lord's ladder with dirty feet or hands unclean? *For the impure to touch the pure is sacrilege,* as the mysteries teach.[16] 17

What are these feet, then, and these hands? The foot of the soul, surely, is that utterly worthless part that leans on matter as on the dirt of the ground, a nutritive and feeding power, I mean— tinder for lust and mistress of voluptuary softness. As for the soul's hands, why not call them its raging part that rushes into battle to defend the appetites, plundering in *daylight and dust* to snatch something and gorge on it while *snoozing in the shade?* These hands, these feet—the whole sensual part where, so they say, *the lure of the body hangs like a noose round the soul's neck*—let us wash them in moral philosophy's living waters lest we be turned away from the ladder, desecrated and defiled.[17] 18

But if we want to join angels speeding up and down Jacob's ladder, this washing will not be enough unless we have first been instructed and well prepared to advance *from rung to rung* as the rites require, never leaving the way of the ladder to *charge off* on some alternate path. After we have completed this preparation through 19

sermocinalem sive rationariam erimus consequuti, iam cherubico spiritu animati, per scalarum idest naturae gradus philosophantes, a centro ad centrum omnia pervadentes, nunc unum—quasi Osyrim—in multitudinem vi titanica discerpentes descendemus, nunc multitudinem—quasi Osyridis membra—in unum vi phebea colligentes ascendemus, donec, in sinu Patris, qui super scalas est, tandem quiescentes, theologica felicitate consumabimur.

20   Percontemur et iustum Iob, qui fedus iniit cum Deo vitae prius quam ipse ederetur in vitam, quid summus Deus in decem illis centenis millibus qui assistunt ei potissimum desideret. Pacem utique respondebit—iuxta id quod apud eum legitur, qui facit pacem in excelsis. Et quoniam supremi ordinis monita medius ordo inferioribus interpretatur, interpretetur nobis Iob theologi verba Empedocles philosophus. Hic duplicem naturam in nostris animis sitam, quarum altera sursum tollimur ad caelestia, altera deorsum trudimur ad inferna, per litem et amicitiam, sive bellum et pacem, ut sua testantur carmina, nobis significat. In quibus se lite et discordia actum, furenti similem, profugum a diis in altum iactari conqueritur.

21   Multiplex profecto, patres, in nobis discordia: gravia et intestina domi habemus et plus quam civilia bella. Quae si noluerimus, si illam affectaverimus pacem quae in sublime ita nos tollat ut inter excelsos Domini statuamur, sola in nobis compescet prorsus et sedabit philosophia.

22   Moralis primum: si noster homo ab hostibus indutias tantum quaesierit, multiplicis bruti effrenes excursiones et leonis iurgia, iras animosque contundet. Tum si rectius consulentes nobis perpetuae pacis securitatem desideraverimus, aderit illa et vota nostra liberaliter implebit—quippe quae caesa utraque bestia, quasi icta porca—inviolabile inter carnem et spiritum foedus sanctissimae

the art of speaking or reasoning, and now animated by a Cherubic
spirit, philosophizing along the rungs of the ladder (or Nature),
passing through all things from center to center, at one moment
we will *descend*, using the power of Titans to tear the One, like
Osiris, into many, while at another moment we will *ascend*, using
the power of Phoebus to gather the manifold, like limbs of Osiris,
into the One, until at last, *resting* in the bosom of the Father, who
is above the ladder, we shall be consumed in theological bliss.[18]

Let us also question Job the *just*—who made a *covenant* with the
God of life before he began his own life—about what God Almighty desired most of all in those *hundreds of thousands* who stand
near him. His answer will surely be *peace*—in keeping with what
one reads in his book, *who makes peace on high*. And since the
middle order interprets the warnings of the highest order for those
below, it is the philosopher Empedocles who should interpret for
us the words of Job the theologian. As his poems show, the philosopher uses *strife* and *friendship*—*war* and *peace*—to symbolize
for us the twofold nature sited in our souls, the one lifting us to
the heavens above, the other plunging us down to hell. He laments
in these poems about being driven like a madman by strife and
discord, cast into the depths and exiled from the gods.[19]

Discord certainly takes many forms in us, Fathers: at home our
fights are violent and inside us—*wars worse than civil*. If we reject
them, if we are to strive for a *peace* that lifts us so high that we will
be set among the Lord's exalted, only philosophy can calm us
within and put a complete stop to these struggles.[20]

At first this will be moral philosophy: she will check the *wild
excesses* of the many-formed beast, as well as the lion's brawling,
raging and pride, if *our man* seeks only a truce from the enemy.
Then, if we think better of it and want the security of perpetual
peace for ourselves, morality will come with generous answers to
our prayers, and—once both beasts have been killed like pigs at a
sacrifice—this philosophy will ratify an inviolable covenant of the

20

21

22

pacis sanciet. Sedabit dyalectica rationis turbas, inter orationum pugnantias et sillogismorum[9] captiones anxie tumultuantis. Sedabit naturalis philosophia opinionis lites et dissidia, quae inquietam hinc inde animam vexant, distrahunt et lacerant. Sed ita sedabit ut meminisse nos iubeat esse naturam, iuxta Heraclytum, ex bello genitam, ob id ab Homero contentionem vocitatam.

23   Idcirco in ea veram quietem et solidam pacem se nobis praestare non posse, esse hoc dominae suae, idest sanctissimae theologiae, munus et privilegium. Ad illam ipsa et viam monstrabit et comes ducet. Quae procul nos videns properantes, Venite — inclamabit — ad me qui laboratis[10] venite et ego reficiam vos; venite ad me et dabo vobis pacem quam mundus et natura vobis dare non possunt.

24   Tam blande vocati, tam benigniter invitati, alatis pedibus quasi terrestres Mercurii in beatissimae amplexus matris evolantes, optata pace perfruemur — pace sanctissima, individua copula, unianimi amicitia qua omnes animi in una mente, quae est super omnem mentem, non concordent adeo sed ineffabili quodammodo unum penitus evadant. Haec est illa amicitia quam totius philosophiae finem esse Pythagorici dicunt. Haec illa pax quam facit Deus in excelsis suis, quam angeli in terram descendentes annuntiarunt hominibus bonae voluntatis, ut per eam ipsi homines, ascendentes in caelum, angeli fierent.

25   Hanc pacem amicis, hanc nostro optemus saeculo, optemus unicuique domui quam ingredimur, optemus animae nostrae, ut per eam ipsa Dei domus fiat, ut — postquam per moralem et dyalecticam suas sordes excusserit, multiplici philosophia quasi aulico apparatu se exornarit, portarum fastigia theologicis sertis coronarit — descendat Rex gloriae et cum Patre veniens mansionem faciat apud eam. Quo tanto hospite si se dignam praestiterit — quae est

holiest *peace* between flesh and spirit. Dialectic will calm the turmoils of reason as it swings agitated between quarrels of oratory
and quibbles of syllogistic. Natural philosophy will settle disputes
and disagreements of opinion that come from all sides to worry,
distract and torment the restless soul. But it will calm us by also
compelling us to remember that Nature was born of war, according to Heraclitus, which is why Homer called it *contention*.[21]

From philosophy, therefore, we cannot get true rest and lasting   23
peace; this is a gift from philosophy's mistress — from most holy
theology — and only hers to give. Philosophy will show us the way,
keep us company and lead us to her. When theology sees us far
off, hastening toward her, *come to me* — she will shout — *you who are
weary with toil, and I will restore your strength. Come to me*, and I will
give you the *peace* that the *world* and Nature cannot supply.[22]

Called so sweetly, invited so kindly, flying on *winged feet* like   24
earthly Mercuries to the embrace of our most blessed mother, we
will take delight from the *peace* that we have longed for — the holiest *peace*, the unbroken bond, the friendship of the *single-souled*
wherein all our spirits do not so much converge in the one Mind
above every mind as, in some unsayable way, emerge as absolutely
one. This is the friendship that Pythagoreans say is the end of all
philosophy. This is the *peace* that God *makes on high*, which angels
descending to earth have announced *to men of goodwill* so that
through this *peace* these same men, ascending to heaven, might be
made into angels.[23]

Let us wish this *peace* for our friends, for our time, for every   25
house we enter; let us wish it for our soul, so that through it she
might be made a *house of God*; and then — after she has shaken off
her filth through morals and dialectic, after she has fitted herself
out in *courtly splendor*, or manifold philosophy, after she has decked
the tops of her *gates with garlands* of theology — the *King of Glory*
may descend and, coming with the Father, make his *dwelling* with
our soul. If she proves herself worthy of so great a guest — so vast

illius immensa clementia—deaurato vestitu quasi toga nuptiali,
multiplici scientiarum circumdata varietate, speciosum hospitem,
non ut hospitem iam sed ut sponsum excipiet, a quo ne unquam
dissolvatur dissolvi cupiet a populo suo, et domum patris sui,
immo se ipsam oblita, in se ipsa cupiet mori ut vivat in sponso, in
cuius conspectu preciosa profecto mors sanctorum eius—mors,
inquam, illa (si dici mors debet plenitudo vitae), cuius meditatio-
nem esse studium philosophiae dixerunt sapientes.

26   Citemus et Mosen ipsum, a sacrosanctae et ineffabilis intelligentiae fontana plenitudine, unde angeli suo nectare inebriantur,
paulo deminutum. Audiemus venerandum iudicem nobis in deserta huius corporis solitudine habitantibus leges sic edicentem:

> Qui polluti adhuc morali indigent, cum plebe habitent extra
> tabernaculum sub divo, quasi Thessali sacerdotes interim se
> expiantes. Qui mores iam composuerunt, in sanctuarium re-
> cepti, nondum quidem sacra actractent, sed prius dyalectico
> famulatu, seduli Levitae philosophiae sacris ministrent. Tum
> ad ea et ipsi admissi, nunc superioris Dei regiae multi-
> colorem, idest sydereum aulicum ornatum, nunc caeleste
> candelabrum septem luminibus distinctum, nunc pellicea ve-
> lamenta[11] in philosophiae sacerdotio contemplentur; ut post-
> remo, per theologicae sublimitatis merita in templi adita re-
> cepti, nullo imaginis intercedente velo divinitatis gloria
> perfruantur.

Haec nobis profecto Moses et imperat et imperando admonet, excitat, inhortatur, ut per philosophiam ad futuram caelestem gloriam, dum possumus, iter paremus nobis.

is his mercy—wearing a golden garment like a wedding gown, clothed in the manifold variety of knowledge, she will now welcome the fair guest no longer as a guest but as a spouse. Wishing never to part from him, she will want to be parted from her people and from her own father's house. Yes, and ever forgetful of herself, she will wish to die in herself that she might live in her spouse, *in whose sight the death of his saints is truly precious*—that *death*, I mean (if one should use *death* for life in its fullness) that sages have said one *practices* when doing philosophy.[24]

Let us call on Moses himself, only a little lower than the flowing plenty of sacrosanct and ineffable intelligence from which angels get drunk on their nectar. We who dwell in the body's lonely wilderness, we shall attend to this honored judge as he declares the laws to us: 26

> Those who are unclean and still need moral teaching, let them dwell with the people outside the *Tabernacle* while they purify themselves in the open air like *priests from Thessaly*. Those who have put their conduct in order and are allowed in the *sanctuary* may still not touch the sacred articles but must first have done service in dialectic and assist with the rites as philosophy's diligent *Levites*. Once accepted in those ceremonies, in the philosophical *priesthood* they may first contemplate the many-colored curtain, hung with stars, in God's palace on high; next the heavenly *candelabra* ornamented with *seven lights*; and finally the *coverings of skin*; until at last, having been received into the temple's inner sanctum through the merits of an exalted theology, and with no *image* in between to veil the *glory* of the Godhead, they may enjoy it to the full.

This surely is what Moses commands and, in commanding, warns, rouses and exhorts us, while we can, to plan our journey through philosophy to the heavenly glory that will come.[25]

27   Verum enimvero, nec Mosayca tantum aut Christiana mysteria sed priscorum quoque theologia harum, de quibus disputaturus accessi, liberalium artium et emolumenta nobis et dignitatem ostendit. Quid enim aliud sibi volunt in Graecorum archanis observati initiatorum gradus, quibus primo, hercle,[12] per illas quas diximus quasi februales artes, moralem et dialecticam, purificatis, contingebat mysteriorum susceptio? Quae quid aliud esse potest quam secretioris per philosophiam naturae interpretatio? Tum demum ita dispositis illa adveniebat ἐποπτεία, idest rerum divinarum per theologiae lumen inspectio. Quis talibus sacris initiari non appetat? Quis, humana omnia posthabens, fortunae contemnens bona, corporis negligens, deorum conviva adhuc degens in terris fieri non cupiat, et aeternitatis nectare madidus mortale animal immortalitatis munere donari? Quis non Socraticis illis furoribus a Platone in *Fedro* decantatis, sic afflari non velit ut alarum pedumque remigio hinc—idest ex mundo qui est positus in maligno—propere aufugiens, ad caelestem Hierusalem concitatissimo cursu feratur?

28   Agamur, patres, agamur Socraticis furoribus, qui extra mentem ita nos ponant ut mentem nostram et nos ponant in Deo! Agemur[13] ab illis utique, si quid est in nobis ipsi prius egerimus. Nam si et per moralem affectuum vires ita per debitas competentias ad modulos fuerint intentae ut immota invicem consonent concinentia, et per dyalecticam ratio ad numerum se progrediendo moverit, Musarum perciti furore caelestem armoniam intimis auribus combibemus. Tum Musarum dux Bacchus, in suis mysteriis—idest visibilibus naturae signis—invisibilia Dei philosophantibus nobis ostendens, inebriabit nos ab ubertate domus Dei, in qua tota si, uti Moses, erimus fideles, accedens sacratissima theologia duplici furore nos animabit.

29   Nam in illius eminentissimam sublimati speculam, inde et quae sunt, quae erunt quaeque fuerint insectili metientes aevo, et

Yet in truth not only Mosaic and Christian mysteries but also 27
the *theology of the ancients* shows us the value as well as the benefits
of those liberal arts that we have come to debate. What else might
they mean, those stages observed in the secret rites of the Greeks
by initiates who gained admittance to mysteries after first, to be
sure, being purified by arts that we have called *cleansing,* so to
speak: the moral and dialectical? What else can this be but interpreting Nature's hidden part with philosophy? Then at last came
that ἐποπτεία, that gazing upon divinity by the light of theology,
to those thus prepared. Who would not want to be initiated in
such rites? Putting all human things behind, scorning fortune's
goods, careless of the body's welfare, who would not wish to dine
with gods while still dwelling on earth and get the gift of immortality while still mortal, drunk on the *nectar* of eternity? Who
would not wish to be so inspired by those Socratic frenzies sung
by Plato in the *Phaedrus* that he would be carried off, rushing away
from here—from a *world that lies in wickedness,* that is—to take a
quick trip with *wings and feet stroking* to the *heavenly Jerusalem?*[26]

Let us be swept up, Fathers, swept up by Socratic frenzies that 28
take us *outside the mind,* putting us and our minds in God! They
will certainly sweep us up if we have first swept up what is in us.
For if moral philosophy has tuned the forces of emotion and set
them to harmonize with one another in due measure and tranquil
concord, and if reason has moved in cadence with dialectic, then,
stirred by the frenzy of the Muses, our inward ears will drink deep
of the heavenly symphony. Next, as Bacchus *leads the Muses* while
we philosophize and he shows us *God's* invisible *things* in his mysteries—Nature's visible signs—he will *make us drunk on the flowing
bounty of God's house,* where holiest theology will come to ensoul us
with a double frenzy if, like Moses, we are *faithful in all of this.*[27]

Lifted now to the topmost height of theology's *watchtower,* and 29
from there taking the measure—by a time beyond division—of
what is, what will be, and what might be, then gazing up at prime-

primaevam pulchritudinem suspicientes, illorum Phebei vates, huius alati erimus amatores, et ineffabili demum charitate quasi aestro perciti, quasi Saraphini ardentes extra nos positi, numine pleni, iam non ipsi nos, sed ille erimus, ipse qui fecit nos.

30 Sacra Apollinis nomina, si quis eorum significantias et latitantia perscrutetur misteria, satis ostendent[14] esse deum illum non minus philosophum quam vatem. Quod cum Ammonius satis sit exequutus, non est cur ego nunc aliter pertractem. Sed subeant animum, patres, tria delphica praecepta oppido his necessaria qui non ficti sed veri Apollinis, qui illuminat omnem animam venientem in hunc mundum, sacrosanctum et augustissimum templum introgressuri[15] sunt. Videbitis nihil aliud illa nos admonere quam ut tripartitam hanc, de qua est praesens disputatio, philosophiam totis viribus amplectamur. Illud enim μηδὲν ἄγαν—idest nequid nimis—virtutum omnium normam et regulam per mediocritatis rationem, de qua moralis agit, recte praescribit. Tum illud γνῶθι σεαυτόν—idest cognosce te ipsum—ad totius naturae nos cognitionem, cuius et interstitium et quasi cynnus natura est hominis, excitat et inhortatur. Qui enim se cognoscit, in se omnia cognoscit, ut Zoroaster prius, deinde Plato in *Alcibiade* scripserunt. Postremo, hac cognitione per naturalem philosophiam illuminati, iam Deo proximi εἶ—idest es—dicentes, theologica salutatione verum Apollinem familiariter proindeque foeliciter appellabimus.

31 Consulamus et Pythagoram sapientissimum, ob id praecipue sapientem, quod sapientis se dignum nomine nunquam existimavit. Praecipiet primo ne super modium sedeamus—idest rationalem partem qua anima omnia metitur, iudicat et examinat—ociosa desidia ne remittentes amittamus, sed dyalectica exercitatione ac regula et dirigamus assidue et excitemus. Tum cavenda in primis duo nobis significabit, ne aut adversus solem emingamus,

val beauty, we shall sing prophecies about those times like Phoebus, and we shall be winged lovers of that beauty until at last,
driven wild by desire with a love beyond telling and transported
beyond ourselves like burning Seraphs, full of divine power, we
shall be ourselves no longer, but shall be Him, the very One who
made us.[28]

Apollo's sacred names — if anyone searches out their meanings   30
and hidden mysteries — will show quite plainly that this god is no
less a philosopher than a prophet. Since Ammonius has tracked
this down, there is no need now for me to investigate farther. But
consider three Delphic maxims, Fathers, as just what they need
who are about to move within the holiest and most majestic temple of the true Apollo — not the pretended one — the one who
lights every soul that comes into this world. You will see that they warn
us just to embrace with all our might the three-part philosophy
that we are now debating. In fact, the saying μηδὲν ἄγαν — *nothing in excess* — rightly prescribes a norm and a rule for all virtues
through the method of the mean presented by morality. Another
saying, γνῶθι σεαυτόν — *know yourself* — rouses and exhorts us to
know the whole of Nature, in which man's nature is an *interval*
and, as it were, a *coupling.* One who actually knows himself also
knows all things in himself, as Zoroaster first and then Plato in
the *Alcibiades* have written. Finally, enlightened by this knowledge
through natural philosophy, now close to God and saying to him
εἶ — *you are* — with this theological greeting we address the true
Apollo as a friend and hence happily.[29]

Let us also consult the very wise Pythagoras, wise most of all   31
because he never thought himself worthy to be called a *wise man.*
His first rule is *not to sit on the bushel* — on the rational part, that is,
by which the soul measures, judges and weighs everything — lest
we lose it by giving way to sluggish idleness and not taking care to
stimulate and regulate it by the rule and practice of dialectic. Then
he will show us by signs that two things especially are to be

aut inter sacrificandum ungues resecemus. Sed postquam per moralem et superfluentium voluptatum fluxas eminxerimus appetentias, et unguium praesegmina quasi acutas irae prominentias et animorum aculeos resecuerimus, tum demum sacris—idest de quibus mentionem fecimus Bacchi mysteriis—interesse, et cuius pater ac dux merito Sol dicitur, nostrae contemplationi vacare incipiamus.

32   Postremo ut gallum nutriamus nos admonebit—idest ut divinam animae nostrae partem divinarum rerum cognitione quasi solido cibo et caelesti ambrosia pascamus. Hic est gallus cuius aspectum leo—idest omnis terrena potestas—formidat et reveretur. Hic ille gallus cui datam esse intelligentiam apud Iob legimus. Hoc gallo canente, aberrans homo resipiscit. Hic gallus in matutino crepusculo, matutinis astris Deum laudantibus, quotidie commodulatur. Hunc gallum moriens Socrates, cum divinitatem animi sui divinitati maioris mundi copulaturum se speraret, Esculapio—idest animarum medico—iam extra omne morbi discrimen positus, debere se dixit.

33   Recenseamus et Chaldeorum monumenta: videbimus (si illis creditur) per easdem artes patere viam mortalibus ad felicitatem. Scribunt interpretes Chaldei verbum fuisse Zoroastris alatam esse animam, cumque alae exciderent, ferri illam praeceps in corpus, tum illis subcrescentibus ad superos revolare. Percunctantibus eum discipulis quo pacto alis bene plumantibus volucres animos sortirentur: Irrigetis, dixit, alas aquis vitae. Iterum sciscitantibus unde has aquas peterent, sic per parabolam (qui erat hominis mos) illis respondit:

Quatuor amnibus paradisus Dei abluitur et irrigatur; indidem vobis salutares aquas hauriatis. Nomen ei qui ab aquilone ቅሥ⳩ት,[16] quod rectum denotat; ei qui ab occasu ከ⳿ጸር⳿ነ,[17]

avoided, *making water while facing the sun* and *cutting our nails during a sacrifice*. But after we have voided our eager floods of overflowing pleasure with morality, and after we have cut back the sharp edges of wrath and spines of animosity as if clipping our nails, then at last we may begin to join the rites—those mysteries of Bacchus that I have mentioned—and free ourselves for contemplation where the Sun is rightly called *Father* and *Guide*.[30]

Lastly he will warn us to *feed the cock*—to nourish *our soul's divine part*, in other words, with knowledge of divinity as if with *solid food* and heavenly *ambrosia*. This is the cock whose sight the lion— every earthly power, in other words—*fears* and respects. This is the cock to which *understanding* was given, as we read in Job. When this *cock crows*, the human who strays returns to his senses. This is the cock that times its daily round by the dim light of early dawn, when the *morning stars* give praise to God. This is the cock that the dying Socrates—who hoped *to join his spirit's divinity to the divinity of a greater world*—said that he owed to Aesculapius, physician of souls, once he was past all threat of illness.[31]

Let us also review the memorials of the Chaldeans: we shall see (if one believes them) that a path to happiness lies open to mortals through the same arts. Chaldean translators write that one of Zoroaster's sayings was that the *soul has wings*, and when her wings drop off, the soul falls headlong into the body, but she flies back to the gods when they grow again. His disciples asked him how to get souls that fly with well-feathered wings: *Drench your wings*, he said, *in the waters of life*. Then they wanted to know where to look for the source of these waters, and he answered them with a parable (which was this person's custom):

> God's paradise is washed and watered by four rivers: drink waters from them that will save you. The name of the one that comes from the north is ቀሡት, which means *righteous*; the one that comes from the west is ኩጽርጎ, which signifies

32

33

quod expiationem significat; ei qui ab ortu ⵏⵓⵐⵍⵔ,[18] quod lumen sonat; ei qui a meridie ⵍⵔⵁⵀⵊⵝⵔⵜ,[19] quod nos pietatem interpretari possumus.

34   Advertite animum et diligenter considerate, patres, quid haec sibi velint Zoroastris dogmata: profecto nihil aliud nisi ut morali scientia, quasi undis hibericis, oculorum sordes expiemus; dialectica, quasi boreali amussi,[20] illorum aciem lineemus ad rectum; tum in naturali contemplatione debile adhuc veritatis lumen, quasi nascentis solis incunabula, pati assuescamus, ut tandem per theologicam pietatem et sacratissimum deorum[21] cultum, quasi caelestes aquilae, meridiantis solis fulgidissimum iubar fortiter perferamus. Hae illae forsan et a Davide decantatae primum, et ab Augustino explicatae latius, matutinae, meridianae et vespertinae cognitiones. Haec est illa lux meridialis quae Saraphinos ad lineam inflammat et Cherubinos pariter illuminat. Haec illa regio quam versus semper antiquus pater Abraam proficiscebatur. Hic ille locus ubi immundis spiritibus locum non esse et Cabalistarum et Maurorum dogmata tradiderunt.[22]

35   Et si secretiorum aliquid mysteriorum fas est vel sub aenigmate in publicum proferre, postquam et repens e caelo casus nostri hominis caput vertigine damnavit et (iuxta Hieremiam) ingressa per fenestras mors iecur pectusque male affecit, Raphaelem caelestem medicum advocemus, qui nos morali et dialectica uti pharmacis salutaribus liberet. Tum ad valitudinem bonam restitutos iam — Dei robur — Gabriel inhabitabit, qui nos per naturae ducens miracula, ubique Dei virtutem potestatemque indicans, tandem sacerdoti summo Michaeli nos tradet, qui sub stipendiis philosophiae emeritos theologiae sacerdotio quasi corona preciosi lapidis insignet.

atonement; from the east comes ⲓⳑⲋⳑ, indicating *light*; and
from the south comes ⳑ-ⳍⲟⳅⳜ⳿⳿, which we can translate as
piety.[32]

Attend to this, Fathers, and consider carefully what these doc-   34
trines of Zoroaster might mean. Surely they mean nothing else
but to wash filth from our eyes with moral knowledge, as if with
waters from the far west, and to align their vision and correct it
with dialectic, as if with a straight edge from the north. Then, by
contemplating Nature, we may get our eyes used to bearing the
light of truth while it is still faint, like the new Sun as it rises, so
that later, through theological piety and the most sacred worship
of God, we may, like eagles in the sky, bravely endure the Sun's full
brightness, blazing at noon. These, perhaps, are *morning, noon and
evening perceptions* that David first sang about and Augustine explained more fully. This is the midday light that shines directly on
the Seraphim to set them on fire and, with equal effect, light up
the Cherubim. This is the country that old Father Abraham was
always heading for, the place where unclean spirits have no place,
as doctrines of Moors and Kabbalists teach.[33]

And if it is lawful to disclose any part of the more secret mys-   35
teries, even *darkly*, consider this: after a swift fall from heaven has
injured *our man's head* with dizziness, and (according to Jeremiah)
after *death has entered through the windows* to afflict our *heart* and
liver, we should call on Raphael, a heavenly physician, to use morals and dialectic like *healing* drugs in order to free us. Once we
have been restored to good health, Gabriel — God's strength — will
dwell within us, to lead us through Nature's wonders, pointing out
God's might and power all around us and finally handing us over
to the high priest Michael, who will bestow on us, after we have
served our time in philosophy, the priesthood of theology, like a
crown of precious gems.[34]

36   Haec sunt, patres colendissimi, quae me ad philosophiae studium non animarunt modo sed compulerunt. Quae dicturus certe
non eram, nisi his responderem qui philosophiae studium in principibus praesertim viris, aut his omnino qui mediocri fortuna vivunt, damnare solent. Est enim iam hoc totum philosophari—
quae est nostrae aetatis infoelicitas—in contemptum potius et
contumeliam quam in honorem et gloriam. Ita invasit fere omnium mentes exitialis haec et monstrosa persuasio, aut nihil aut
paucis philosophandum, quasi rerum causas, naturae vias, universi
rationem, Dei consilia, caelorum terraeque mysteria prae oculis,
prae manibus exploratissima habere nihil sit prorsus—nisi vel gratiam inde aucupari aliquam vel lucrum sibi quis comparare possit.
Quin eo deventum est ut iam—proh dolor!—non existimentur
sapientes nisi qui mercennarium faciunt studium sapientiae, ut sit
videre pudicam Palladem—deorum munere inter homines diver-
santem—eiici, explodi, exsibilari, non habere qui amet, qui faveat,
nisi ipsa, quasi prostans et praefloratae virginitatis accepta merce-
dula, male paratum aes in amatoris arculam referat.

37   Quae omnia ego—non sine summo dolore et indignatione—in
huius temporis non principes sed philosophos dico, qui ideo non
esse philosophandum et credunt et praedicant quod philosophis
nulla merces, nulla sint praemia constituta, quasi non ostendant
ipsi, hoc uno nomine, se non esse philosophos quod cum tota
eorum vita sit vel in quaestu vel in ambitione posita, ipsam per se
veritatis cognitionem non amplectuntur. Dabo hoc mihi, et me
ipsum hac ex parte laudare nihil erubescam, me nunquam alia de
causa philosophatum nisi ut philospharer, nec ex studiis meis, ex
meis lucubrationibus mercedem ullam aut fructum vel sperasse
alium vel quaesiisse quam animi cultum et a me semper plurimum
desideratae veritatis cognitionem. Cuius ita cupidus semper et
amantissimus fui ut, relicta omni privatarum et publicarum rerum
cura, contemplandi ocio totum me tradiderim, a quo nullae

These are reasons, Reverend Fathers, that have not just excited   36
me to study philosophy but have forced me to it. To be sure, I
would not need to make this point except to reply to those who
make a habit of condemning the study of philosophy, especially in
people of rank — or generally in those of some means. Today, in
fact — so unlucky is our age — *any philosophizing at all* brings contempt and abuse rather than honor and glory. This monstrous and
deadly conviction, that *no one or only a few should do philosophy*, has
possessed almost every mind, as if it were worth nothing for a
careful hand and eye to examine the *causes of things, Nature's ways,*
the *world's structure, God's purposes* and *mysteries of heaven and earth* —
except to gain goodwill or turn a profit. This is how things are:
what a pity! None are thought wise unless they trade on the *pursuit of wisdom:* we see the *chaste Pallas* — who dwells among humans
as a gift from the gods — driven away with hoots and hisses, un-
loved and friendless unless she sells herself and then returns to her
lover's money box the ill-gotten coin taken in cheap trade for her
deflowered virginity.[35]

I make all these charges — in great distress and with provoca-   37
tion — not against princes of this age but against philosophers,
since it is they who believe and proclaim that one should not philosophize because there is no *pay* for philosophers, no *profit*. Apparently they do not realize that such talk by itself shows them
not to be philosophers and not to love knowledge of truth for its
own sake, while they go on planning their whole lives for advan-
tage and ambition. As for me, I shall go so far as to praise myself
and not blush, on this account: that I have never philosophized for
any other reason but to do philosophy, nor have I sought or hoped
for any other *profit* or product from my studies and my long hours
except to develop my mind and know the truth that I have always
chiefly desired. Of this I have always been so fond and so enam-
ored that I have put aside all concern for private or public affairs
to give myself wholly to contemplative quiet, and thus far no

invidorum obtrectationes, nulla hostium sapientiae maledicta vel potuerunt ante hac vel in posterum me deterrere poterunt. Docuit me ipsa philosophia a propria potius conscientia quam ab externis pendere iudiciis, cogitareque semper non tam ne male audiam, quam ne quid male vel dicam ipse vel agam.

38   Equidem non eram nescius, patres colendissimi, futuram hanc ipsam meam disputationem quam vobis omnibus, qui bonis artibus favetis et augustissima vestra praesentia illam honestare voluistis, gratam atque iocundam, tam multis aliis gravem atque molestam; et scio non deesse qui inceptum meum et damnarint ante hac et in praesentia multis nominibus damnent. Ita consueverunt non pauciores—ne dicam plures—habere oblatratores quae bene sancteque aguntur ad virtutem quam quae inique et perperam ad vitium.

39   Sunt autem qui totum hoc disputandi genus et hanc de litteris publice disceptandi institutionem non approbent, ad pompam potius ingenii et doctrinae ostentationem quam ad comparandam eruditionem esse illam asseverantes. Sunt qui hoc quidem exercitationis genus non improbent, sed in me nullo modo probent, quod ego hac aetate, quartum scilicet et vigesimum modo natus annum, de sublimibus Christianae theologiae mysteriis, de altissimis philosophiae locis, de incognitis disciplinis, in celebratissima Urbe, in amplissimo doctissimorum hominum consessu, in Apostolico Senatu disputationem proponere sim ausus. Alii, hoc mihi dantes quod disputem, id dare nolunt quod de nongentis disputem quaestionibus, tam superfluo et ambitiose quam supra vires id factum calumniantes.

40   Horum ego obiectamentis et manus illico dedissem si ita quam profiteor philosophia me edocuisset, et nunc, illa ita me docente, non responderem si rixandi iurgandique proposito constitutam hanc inter nos disceptationem crederem. Quare obtrectandi omne

complaints from the envious, no curses from enemies of wisdom have been able to deter me, nor shall they in the future. Philosophy herself has taught me to trust my own conscience, not what others think, and always to concern myself to avoid the evil that I might say or do, not the evil opinion of others.[36]

I have been far from unaware, Most Reverend Fathers — you supporters of the liberal arts who with your august presence have chosen to honor this disputation of mine which will follow — that as welcome and pleasing as this is to all of you, it is just as irksome and offensive to many others. And there are those, I realize, who have already damned my project and keep damning it under many headings. So it is that good and holy actions leading to virtue have usually had as many critics sniping at them — or more, dare I say? — as there are false and wicked acts that lead to vice.[37]   38

There are some besides who do not accept *this type* of disputation at all, this practice of debating ideas in public: they insist that its point is to put learning on parade and make a display of cleverness, not to promote knowledge. Others do not really reject the sort of thing I am doing. It is just *my* doing it that they do not accept at all because, being barely twenty-four years of age, I have dared to propose a disputation on sublime mysteries of Christian theology, on philosophy's deepest problems and on teachings not yet recognized, and because I have dared offer to debate in the most populous of all cities, before the grandest gathering of the most learned people, in the Apostolic Senate. Still others, allowing me to dispute, wish not to allow me to dispute 900 questions, misrepresenting what I have done as excessive, ambitious and beyond my ability.[38]   39

I would have yielded to these objections instantly had I been so instructed by the philosophy that I profess, and now, even as I am instructed by it, I would not respond if I thought that the debate arranged for us were a pretext for squabbles and scraps. So in our   40

lacessendique propositum, et quem[23] scribit Plato a divino semper
abesse choro, a nostris quoque mentibus facessat livor, et an dispu-
tandum a me, an de tot etiam quaestionibus, amice incognoscamus.

41   Primum quidem ad eos qui hunc publice disputandi morem
calumniantur, multa non sum dicturus, quando haec culpa — si
culpa censetur — non solum vobis omnibus, doctores excellentissimi, qui saepius hoc munere non sine summa et laude et gloria
functi estis, sed Platoni, sed Aristoteli, sed probatissimis omnium
aetatum philosophis mecum est communis. Quibus erat certissi-
mum nihil ad consequendam quam quaerebant veritatis cognitionem sibi esse potius quam ut essent in disputandi exercitatione
frequentissimi. Sicut enim per gymnasticam corporis vires firmiores fiunt, ita dubio procul in hac quasi litteraria palaestra
animi vires et fortiores longe et vegetiores evadunt. Nec crediderim
ego aut poetas aliud per decantata Palladis arma, aut Hebreos cum
ברזל שלחכמים, ferrum sapientum,[24] symbolum esse dicunt, significasse nobis quam honestissima hoc genus certamina adipiscendae
sapientiae oppido quam necessaria. Quo forte fit ut et Caldei in
eius genesi qui philosophus sit futurus illud desiderent, ut Mars
et[25] Mercurium triquetro aspectu conspiciat, quasi si hos congres-
sus, haec bella substuleris, somniculosa et dormitans futura sit
omnis philosophia.

42   At vero cum his qui me huic provinciae imparem dicunt, diffici-
lior est mihi ratio defensionis. Nam si parem me dixero, forsitan
immodesti et de se nimia sentientis; si imparem fatebor, temerarii
et inconsulti notam videor subiturus. Videte quas incidi angustias,
quo loco sim constitutus! Dum non possum sine culpa de me pro-
mittere quod non possum mox sine culpa non praestare. Forte
et illud Iob afferre possem, spiritum esse in hominibus,[26] et cum
Timotheo audire: nemo contemnat adolescentiam tuam.

thoughts let there be no occasion for goading and vilifying, nor for the envy that is *always absent from the divine choirs* (as Plato writes), and let us inquire like friends about whether I should dispute and whether about so many questions.[39]

First, to those who misrepresent this custom of disputing in 41 public, I shall have little to say, since this fault — if it is deemed a fault — is not only all of yours to share with me, most eminent doctors, who have often done this duty with great honor and praise, but also Plato's and Aristotle's, along with all the most acclaimed philosophers of every age. To them it was absolutely certain that nothing made them more fit to gain the knowledge of truth that they sought than constant practice at disputation. Just as the body's strength becomes more vigorous through physical exercise, the strength of the mind undoubtedly grows livelier and hardier in this *gymnasium* of ideas. When poets keep singing about the *arms of Pallas* or when Hebrews say that the *iron of sages*, ברזל שלחכמים, is their symbol, I would have thought they were giving us a sign for contests just like this most honorable kind, which is absolutely necessary for acquiring wisdom. This may be why Chaldeans also find it desirable, in the geniture of one who is to be a philosopher, that Mars should also look on Mercury in trine aspect, as if all philosophy would grow tired and drowsy if one were to do away with these contests and clashes.[40]

Against those who say I am unfit for this duty, my plan of de- 42 fense is truly more difficult. For if I say that I am fit for it, I may seem given to immodesty and self-regard, but if I concede that I am not fit, I will appear thoughtless and reckless. See what a bind I find myself in, what a situation! Without being blamed, I cannot promise from my own resources the very thing that I cannot withhold, without being blamed. Perhaps I should also mention that saying of Job, *this is the Spirit in men*, and listen with Timothy: *let no one despise your youth*.[41]

43   Sed ex mea verius hoc conscientia dixero: nihil esse in nobis
magnum vel singulare. Studiosum me forte et cupidum bonarum
artium non inficiatus, docti tamen nomen mihi nec sumo nec ar-
rogo. Quare et quod tam grande humeris onus imposuerim, non
fuit propterea quod mihi conscius nostrae infirmitatis non essem,
sed quod sciebam hoc genus pugnis — idest litterariis — esse peculiare: quod in eis lucrum est vinci. Quo fit ut imbecillissimus quisque non detrectare modo sed appetere ultro eas iure possit et debeat, quandoquidem qui succumbit beneficium a victore accipit,
non iniuriam, quippe qui per eum et locupletior domum — idest
doctior — et ad futuras pugnas redit instructior. Hac spe animatus,
ego infirmus miles cum fortissimis omnium strenuissimisque tam
gravem pugnam decernere nihil sum veritus. Quod tamen temere
sit factum nec ne, rectius utique de eventu pugnae quam de nostra
aetate potest quis iudicare.

44   Restat ut tertio loco his respondeam qui numerosa proposita-
rum rerum multitudine offenduntur, quasi hoc eorum humeris
sederet onus et non potius hic mihi soli quantuscumque est labor
esset exanclandus. Indecens profecto hoc et morosum nimis, velle
alienae industriae modum ponere, et — ut inquit Cicero — in ea re
quae eo melior quo maior, mediocritatem desiderare. Omnino tam
grandibus ausis erat necesse me vel succumbere vel satisfacere. Si
satisfacerem, non video cur quod in decem praestare quaestionibus
est laudabile in nongentis etiam praestitisse culpabile existimetur.
Si succumberem, habebunt ipsi, si me oderunt, unde accusarent; si
amant, unde excusent. Quoniam in re tam gravi, tam magna, tenui
ingenio exiguaque doctrina adolescentem hominem defecisse venia
potius dignum erit quam accusatione. Quin et iuxta poetam:

. . . si deficiant[27] vires, audacia certe
laus erit: in magnis et voluisse sat est.

But from my own conscience I will say this, and it is quite true: 43
there is nothing grand or special about me. I have not denied being studious and fond of the liberal arts, perhaps, yet I do not call
myself learned or pretend to be. So when *I shouldered so great a
burden,* this was not because I was unaware of my weakness, but
because I knew the peculiar nature of this kind of combat — the
learned kind: I knew that *one wins by being beaten.* Accordingly,
even the most helpless person should not shirk such a fight; on the
contrary, he should deliberately seek it, since what the loser gets
from the winner is help, not harm, and after his loss he goes home
the richer — knowing more — and is better equipped to fight in the
future. Encouraged by this hope, I have no fear of fighting so hard
a battle against the strongest and swiftest — *weak soldier* that I am.
If anyone is to judge whether it was rash of me to do so, would
not the outcome of the battle be better proof than my age?[42]

In the third place, it remains for me to reply to those who are   44
offended by the vast number of my propositions, as if *this burden
rested on their shoulders,* as if it were not I who will carry it —
alone — to the end, however heavy the labor. This is unseemly and
overbearing, is it not, *to set a limit to another's enterprise* and — as
Cicero says — *to look for a half-measure in something that gets better by
getting bigger?* Having ventured so much, obviously I must fail or
succeed. If I succeed, I don't see why what earns praise in ten
questions should deserve blame even in 900. If I fail, those who
hate me will have grounds to accuse me, those who love me to
forgive. For a young man of slight talent and small learning to have
lost in an effort so great and so grave will warrant pardon more
than accusation. According to the poet,

> where strength is wanting, surely daring wins praise;
> for great deeds, just to have willed is enough.[43]

45   Quod si nostra aetate multi, Gorgiam Leontinum imitati, non modo de nongentis sed de omnibus etiam omnium artium quaestionibus soliti sunt, non sine laude, proponere disputationem, cur mihi non liceat, vel sine culpa, de multis quidem, sed tamen certis et determinatis disputare? At superfluum — inquiunt — hoc, et ambitiosum. Ego vero non superfluo modo, sed necessario factum hoc a me contendo. Quod et si ipsi mecum[28] philosophandi rationem considerarent, inviti etiam fateantur plane necesse est.

46   Qui enim se cuipiam ex philosophorum familiis addixerunt — Thomae videlicet aut Scoto, qui nunc plurimum in manibus, faventes — possunt illi quidem vel in paucarum quaestionum discussione suae doctrinae periculum facere. At ego ita me institui ut in nullius verba iuratus me, per omnes philosophiae magistros funderem, omnes scedas excuterem, omnes familias agnoscerem. Quare, cum mihi de illis omnibus esset dicendum, ne si privati dogmatis defensor reliqua posthabuissem, illi viderer obstrictus, non potuerunt, etiam si pauca de singulis proponerentur, non esse plurima quae simul de omnibus afferebantur. Nec id in me quisquam damnet quod me, quocumque ferat tempestas, deferar hospes. Fuit enim cum ab antiquis omnibus hoc observatum, ut omne scriptorum genus evolventes nullas quas possent commentationes illectas praeterirent, tum maxime ab Aristotele, qui eam ob causam ἀναγνώστης — idest lector — a Platone nuncupabatur. Et profecto angustae est mentis intra unam se Porticum aut Achademiam continuisse. Nec potest ex omnibus sibi recte propriam selegisse qui omnes prius familiaritates[29] non agnoverit. Adde quod in unaquaque familia est aliquid insigne, quod non sit ei commune cum caeteris.

47   Atque ut a nostris, ad quos postremo philosophia pervenit, nunc exordiar. Est in Ioanne Scoto vegetum quiddam atque discussum, in Thoma solidum et aequabile, in Egidio tersum et

But if many in our day have imitated Gorgias of Leontini and   45
have been praised for it, making it a practice to arrange disputations not just on 900 questions but *on all questions in all the arts,*
why may I not dispute about topics that are many, yes, but a limited number on specific points, and do so without blame? This is
excessive and ambitious, they say. But my contention is not just
that it is not excessive. What I have done is necessary besides. The
fact is that if they too would join me in thinking about how philosophy works, they would admit—though not happily—that the
necessity is plain enough.[44]

Those who are committed to any of the schools of philoso-   46
phy—favoring Thomas or Scotus, for example, who are now so
widely read—they indeed can test their learning by discussing just
a few questions. But I have resolved to *swear by no one's teaching* and
extend my inquiry to all masters of philosophy, *to examine every
scrap of paper* and get to know all the schools. Therefore, since I
must speak about all these philosophers, defending no one's dogma
lest I seem bound to it while neglecting the rest, I have no
choice—even in making a few points about each philosopher—
but to raise many questions about all of them together. Let no one
condemn me if I go as a guest *where a tempest takes me.* In fact, all
the ancients followed this rule: to skip no books without reading
them as they examined writers of every kind. This was especially
true of Aristotle, whom Plato therefore called ἀναγνώστης or
reader. To have confined oneself within a single Porch or Academy
is surely the mark of a narrow mind. Only one who has already
made friends with all philosophers can have *picked out* what truly
suits him from all of them. Add the fact that there is something
distinctive about each and every group, something not shared with
others.[45]

Let me start here with our own people, at the point where phi-   47
losophy has finally arrived. In John Scotus there is something
lively and discerning, in Thomas something solid and balanced,

exactum, in Francisco acre et acutum, in Alberto priscum, amplum et grande, in Henrico — ut mihi visum est — semper sublime et venerandum. Est apud Arabes in Averroe firmum et inconcusum, in Avempace, in Alpharabio grave et meditatum, in Avicenna divinum atque Platonicum. Est apud Graecos in universum quidem nitida, in primis et casta philosophia; apud Simplicium locuplex et copiosa, apud Themistium elegans et compendiaria, apud Alexandrum constans et docta, apud Theophrastum graviter elaborata, apud Ammonium enodis et gratiosa.

48   Et si ad Platonicos te converteris — ut paucos percenseam — in Porphirio rerum copia et multiiuga religione delectaberis; in Iamblico secretiorem philosophiam et barbarorum mysteria veneraberis; in Plotino privum quicquam non est quod admireris, qui se undique praebet admirandum, quem de divinis divine, de humanis longe supra hominem docta sermonis obliquitate loquentem sudantes Platonici vix intelligunt. Praetereo magis novitios: Proculum asiatica fertilitate luxuriantem, et qui ab eo fluxerunt, Hermiam, Damascium,[30] Olympiodorum et complures alios, in quibus omnibus illud τὸ θεῖον — idest divinum — peculiare Platonicorum simbolum, elucet semper.

49   Accedit quod, si qua est secta[31] quae veriora incessat dogmata et bonas causas ingenii calumnia ludificetur, ea veritatem firmat, non infirmat, et velut motu quassatam flammam excitat, non extinguit.

50   Hac ego ratione motus, non unius modo — ut quibusdam placebat — sed omnigenae doctrinae placita in medium afferre volui, ut hac complurium sectarum collatione ac multifariae discussione[32] philosophiae ille[33] veritatis fulgor, cuius Plato meminit in *Epistolis*, animis nostris quasi sol oriens ex alto clarius illucesceret. Quid erat si Latinorum tantum — Alberti scilicet, Thomae, Scoti, Egidii,

something clean and precise in Giles, shrewd and sharp in Francis, august, capacious and grand in Albert, in Henry something always sublime and revered — so it seems to me. Among the Arabs, Averroes is steady and unshaken, Avempace and Alfarabi serious and thoughtful, Avicenna godlike and Platonic. Among the Greeks philosophy is clear, on the whole, and in the first thinkers also pure. In Simplicius it is opulent and abundant, in Themistius elegant and parsimonious, in Alexander consistent and learned. Theophrastus works things out painstakingly, while Ammonius is uncomplicated and accessible.[46]

And if you turn to Platonists — to list only a few — in Porphyry   48
you will enjoy rich content and a complex piety; in Iamblichus you will pay respects to a more secret philosophy and *mysteries* of barbarians; and in Plotinus you will find nothing particular to amaze you because everything he offers is altogether amazing, making the Platonists *sweat to barely understand him* because his indirect and learned language speaks divinely about the divine and about the human in terms far beyond human. The more recent Platonists I omit: Proclus, abounding in Asiatic fecundity, and those who followed him, Hermias, Damascius, Olympiodorus and several others, in all of whom that special *symbol* of the Platonists — τὸ θεῖον, the divine — always gleams forth.[47]

Beyond this, if there is any *sect* that attacks truer doctrines and   49
mocks well-meant thoughts with slander, this makes truth stronger, not weaker, like a flame that flares when fanned, stirred up and not snuffed out.[48]

Moved by this reasoning, I have decided to put ideas of all sorts   50
into play, not just those of one doctrine (as some would prefer), so that — after many sects have been compared and philosophies of many kinds discussed — the *flash* of truth that Plato mentions in the *Letters* will light up our minds and clarify them, like the Sun rising from the deep. If we dealt only with philosophy by Latins — Albert, Thomas, Scotus, Giles, Francis, and Henry — and left out

Francisci, Henricique — philosophia, obmissis Graecorum Arabumque philosophis, tractabatur, quando omnis sapientia a barbaris ad Graecos, a Graecis ad nos manavit? Ita nostrates semper in philosophandi ratione peregrinis inventis stare et aliena excoluisse sibi duxerunt satis. Quid erat cum Peripateticis egisse de naturalibus, nisi et Platonicorum accersebatur Achademia? Quorum doctrina et de divinis semper inter omnes philosophias, teste Augustino, habita est sanctissima, et a me nunc primum — quod sciam, verbo absit invidia — post multa saecula sub disputandi examen est in publicum allata.

51   Quid erat et aliorum quot quot erant tractasse opiniones si, quasi ad sapientum symposium asymboli accedentes, nihil nos quod esset nostrum, nostro partum et elaboratum ingenio, afferebamus? Profecto ingenerosum est, ut ait Seneca, sapere solum ex commentario et, quasi maiorum inventa nostrae industriae viam praecluserint, quasi in nobis effaeta sit vis naturae, nihil ex se parere quod veritatem, si non demonstret, saltem innuat vel de longinquo. Quod si in agro colonus, in uxore maritus odit sterilitatem, certe tanto magis infecundam animam oderit illi complicita et associata divina mens, quanto inde nobilior longe proles desideratur.

52   Propterea non contentus ego, praeter communes doctrinas, multa de Mercurii Trismegisti prisca theologia, multa de Caldeorum, de Pythagorae disciplinis, multa de secretioribus Hebreorum addidisse mysteriis. Plurima quoque per nos inventa et meditata de naturalibus et divinis rebus disputanda proposuimus.

53   Proposuimus primo Platonis Aristotelisque concordiam a multis ante hac creditam, a nemine satis probatam. Boetius apud Latinos id se facturum pollicitus, non invenitur fecisse unquam quod semper facere voluit. Simplicius apud Graecos idem professus,

philosophies by Greeks and Arabs, what good would it do, seeing that all wisdom came from barbarians to Greeks and from Greeks to us? For this reason, our own people have always thought it enough in their method of philosophizing to stand on what *strangers have found* and to improve what came from elsewhere. Why study Nature with Peripatetics without also summoning Platonists from the Academy? Their theological doctrine, according to Augustine, was always considered the holiest of all philosophies, and now for the first time, after many centuries—as far as I know, begrudging no one—I have brought it forward for public scrutiny through disputation.[49]

But why discuss the views of so many others and—like coming 51 *empty-handed to a banquet* of sages—contribute nothing of one's own, nothing born of one's own talent and nurtured by it? Surely it is beneath us, as Seneca says, to *take wisdom only from textbooks* and bring forth nothing of our own that suggests the truth at least remotely, even while giving no proof, as if *ancestral discoveries* blocked the way to our own enterprise and Nature's force were *spent* in us. If a farmer hates *sterility* in his field and a husband in his wife, surely all the greater will be the hatred of a *divine Mind* when joined and commingled with an *infertile soul*, since the desired child is nobler by far.[50]

For this reason I am not content to have added, beyond the 52 usual doctrines, much about the *ancient theology* of Mercurius Trismegistus, much from teachings of Chaldeans and Pythagoras, much from more secret mysteries of Hebrews. I have also proposed for disputation many things that I have discovered and devised on topics natural and divine.[51]

To begin, I have proposed the concord between Plato and Aris- 53 totle that many have accepted before now but no one has managed to prove. Among the Latins, Boethius promised to do it, but no one has found that he ever did what he always wanted. Among the Greeks, Simplicius announced the same plan, and would that he

utinam id tam praestaret quam pollicetur! Scribit et Augustinus in *Achademicis* non defuisse plures qui subtilissimis suis disputationibus idem probare conati sint—Platonis scilicet et Aristotelis eandem esse philosophiam. Ioannes item Grammaticus, cum dicat apud eos tantum dissidere Platonem ab Aristotele qui Platonis dicta non intelligunt, probandum tamen posteris hoc reliquit. Addidimus autem et plures locos in quibus Scoti et Thomae, plures in quibus Averrois et Avicennae sententias quae discordes existimantur concordes esse nos asseveramus.

54   Secundo loco quae in philosophia cum Aristotelica tum Platonica excogitavimus nos, tum duo et septuaginta nova dogmata physica et methaphysica collocavimus, quae si quis teneat poterit—nisi fallor, quod mihi erit mox manifestum—quamcumque de rebus naturalibus divinisque propositam questionem longe alia dissolvere ratione quam per eam edoceamur quae et legitur in scolis et ab huius aevi doctoribus colitur philosophiam. Nec tam admirari quis debet, patres, me in primis annis, in tenera aetate, per quam vix licuit—ut iactant quidam—aliorum legere commentationes, novam afferre velle philosophiam, quam vel laudare illam si defenditur, vel damnare si reprobatur. Et denique, cum nostra inventa haec nostrasque sint litteras iudicaturi, non auctoris annos, sed illorum merita potius vel demerita numerare.

55   Est autem et praeter illam alia quam nos attulimus nova per numeros philosophandi institutio, antiqua illa quidem et a priscis theologis—a Pythagora praesertim, ab Aglaophemo, a Philolao, a Platone prioribusque Platonicis observata—sed quae hac tempestate, ut praeclara alia, posteriorum incuria sic exolevit, ut vix vestigia ipsius ulla reperiantur. Scribit Plato in *Epinomide* inter omnes liberales artes et scientias contemplatrices praecipuam maximeque divinam esse scientiam numerandi. Quaerens item cur homo animal sapientissimum, respondet quia numerare novit, cuius sen-

had produced as much as he pledged. In his *Academics*, Augustine also writes that many, using the most sophisticated arguments, tried to show the same thing—namely, that Plato's philosophy and Aristotle's are the same. Likewise John the Grammarian: he says that Plato disagrees with Aristotle only for those who fail to understand what Plato said—though John left the proof for posterity to supply. I have also added several passages in which I assert that statements by Scotus and Thomas, by Averroes and Avicenna, agree in several places where they are thought to disagree.[52]

Next, having thought deeply about Aristotle's philosophy as well as Plato's, I then put together seventy-two novel teachings in physics and metaphysics, and—unless I have made a mistake that will soon be obvious to me—anyone who masters them will be able to solve any problem posed about nature or divinity by using a method far different from the philosophy taught to us, the one read in schools and respected by teachers in our time. In my early years, Fathers—at a tender age when, as some would have it, one can barely read works by others—I have chosen to put forward a new philosophy, which should give rise not so much to amazement as to praise, if I can defend it, or to condemnation, if it is rejected. In the end, when people judge my discoveries and these writings of mine, what should count is their merits or defects—not the author's age.[53]

Beyond what I have mentioned so far, there is another novel method that philosophizes with numbers; in fact, the *ancient theologians* used it in antiquity—Pythagoras especially, as well as Aglaophemus, Philalaos, Plato and the earlier Platonists. But it withered away when our later age neglected it, along with many other brilliant achievements, and in our time one finds hardly a trace of it. Plato writes in the *Epinomis* that among all the liberal arts and the sciences of contemplation, the supreme and preeminently *divine science* is that of numbering. When he asks why man is the wisest animal, his answer is that he *knows how to count*, a

54

55

tentiae et Aristoteles meminit in *Problematis*. Scribit Abumasar
verbum fuisse Avenzoar Babilonii eum omnia nosse qui noverat
numerare. Quae vera esse nullo modo possunt, si per numerandi
artem eam artem intellexerunt cuius nunc mercatores imprimis
sunt peritissimi; quod et Plato testatur, exerta nos admonens voce
ne divinam hanc arithmeticam mercatoriam esse arithmeticam intelligamus. Illam ergo arithmeticam quae ita extollitur, cum mihi
videar post multas lucubrationes exploratam habere, huiusce rei
periculum facturus, ad quatuor et septuaginta quaestiones quae
inter physicas et divinas principales existimantur responsurum per
numeros publice me sum pollicitus.

56   Proposuimus et magica theoremata, in quibus duplicem esse
magiam significavimus. Quarum altera daemonum tota opere et
auctoritate constat, res medius fidius execranda et portentosa. Altera nihil est aliud, cum bene exploratur, quam naturalis philosophiae absoluta consumatio. Utriusque cum meminerint Graeci, illam, magiae nullo modo nomine dignantes, γοητείαν nuncupant,
hanc propria peculiarique appellatione μαγείαν, quasi perfectam
summamque sapientiam, vocant. Idem enim, ut ait Porphyrius,
Persarum lingua magus sonat quod apud nos divinorum interpres
et cultor.

57   Magna autem—immo maxima, patres—inter has artes disparilitas et dissimilitudo. Illam non modo Christiana religio sed omnes leges, omnis bene instituta respublica damnat et execratur.
Hanc omnes sapientes, omnes caelestium et divinarum rerum stu-
diosae nationes approbant et amplectuntur. Illa artium fraudulen-
tissima, haec altior sanctiorque philosophia; illa irrita et vana, haec
firma, fidelis et solida. Illam quisquis coluit semper dissimulavit,
quod in auctoris esset ignominiam et contumeliam; ex hac summa
litterarum claritas gloriaque antiquitus et pene semper petita. Illius nemo unquam studiosus fuit vir philosophus et cupidus discendi bonas artes; ad hanc Pythagoras, Empedocles, Democritus,

remark that Aristotle also recalls in the *Problems*. Abumasar writes that Avenzoar of Babylon used to say that *a person who knows numbers knows everything*. There could be no truth at all in this if by the art of numbering they meant the technique in which *merchants* are now the great experts, for Plato also testifies and loudly warns us not to understand this *divine arithmetic* as the arithmetic of *commerce*. Of this much esteemed arithmetic, then, I am ready to make a trial, having spent long hours exploring it to my own satisfaction. And I have promised to use numbers in replying publicly to seventy-four questions considered fundamental for divine and natural knowledge.[54]

I have also proposed theorems about magic, taking the word   56 *magic* in two senses. One, which relies entirely on the activity and authority of demons, is a monstrous and accursed thing — as God is my witness. The other, when well investigated, is nothing more than the final realization of natural philosophy. Although the Greeks mention both, they call the former γοητεία, never dignifying it with the word *magic*, while for the latter they use μαγεία, the special name suited to it as the highest and perfect wisdom. In the Persian tongue, as Porphyry says, the word *magus* means the same thing as our *interpreter* or *worshipper of the divine*.[55]

But between these arts is a great — no, Fathers, the very great-   57 est — *difference and disparity*. Not only the Christian religion but all laws and every well-ordered state condemn and curse the former. All sages, all nations that study the heavenly and divine, approve and embrace the latter. One is *the most dishonest of arts*, the other a higher and holier philosophy; one is hollow and useless, the other solid, strong and reliable. Whoever practiced the one has always concealed it because it would bring disgrace and abuse on the person who tried it; from the other, ever since antiquity, people have almost always sought great fame and cultural distinction. No philosopher wishing to learn the liberal arts was ever a student of the former; *for the latter, Pythagoras, Empedocles, Democritus and Plato*

Plato discendam navigavere, hanc praedicarunt reversi et in archanis praecipuam habuerunt. Illa ut nullis rationibus, ita nec certis
probatur auctoribus. Haec, clarissimis quasi parentibus honestata,
duos precipue habet auctores: Xamolsidem, quem imitatus est
Abbaris Hyperboreus, et Zoroastrem—non quem forte creditis,
sed illum Oromasi filium.

58   Utriusque magia quid sit Platonem si percontemur, respondebit
in *Alcibiade* Zoroastris magiam non esse aliud quam divinorum
scientiam qua filios Persarum reges erudiebant, ut ad exemplar
mundanae reipublicae suam ipsi regere rempublicam edocerentur.
Respondebit in *Charmide* magiam Xamolsidis esse animi medici-
nam, per quam scilicet animo temperantia, ut per illam corpori
sanitas comparatur. Horum vestigiis postea perstiterunt Carondas,
Damigeron, Apollonius, Hostanes et Dardanus. Perstitit Home-
rus, quem, ut omnes alias sapientias, ita hanc quoque sub sui
Ulixis erroribus dissimulasse in poetica nostra theologia aliquando
probabimus. Perstiterunt Eudoxus et Hermippus, perstiterunt fere
omnes qui Pythagorica Platonicaque mysteria sunt perscrutati. Ex
iunioribus autem qui eam olfecerint tres reperio, Alchindum Ara-
bem, Rogerium Baconem et Guilielmum Parisiensem.

59   Meminit et Plotinus, ubi naturae ministrum esse et non Artifi-
cem magum demonstrat. Hanc magiam probat asseveratque vir
sapientissimus, alteram ita abhorrens ut, cum ad malorum daemonum sacra vocaretur, rectius esse dixerit ad se illos quam se ad illos
accedere. Et merito quidem: ut enim illa obnoxium mancipa-
tumque improbis potestatibus hominem reddit, ita haec illarum
principem et dominum.

60   Illa denique nec artis nec scientiae sibi potest nomen vendicare;
haec altissimis plena misteriis profundissimam rerum secretissima-
rum contemplationem et demum totius naturae cognitionem com-
plectitur. Haec, intersparsas Dei beneficio et interseminatas[34]

traveled abroad, preached it when they returned and gave it a high place in their secrets. No arguments support the former, and no competent authorities approve it. The latter, ennobled somehow by eminent parents, has two authors especially: Zalmoxis, whom Abaris from the Far North imitated, and Zoroaster—not perhaps the one you think, but the famous *son of Oromasus.*[56]

If we question Plato about the magic of these two sages, he will 58 answer in the *Alcibiades* that *Zoroaster's magic* is nothing but the *knowledge of divinity* that Persian kings taught their sons so that they might learn to rule their commonwealth on the model of the cosmic commonwealth. He will answer in the *Charmides* that the magic of Zalmoxis is medicine *for the mind* and that it makes the mind *temperate* just as medicine makes the body *healthy.* Charondas, Damigeron, Apollonius, Ostanes and Dardanus later stayed on their trail. Homer too kept up with this, concealing magic—along with all other kinds of wisdom—under the wanderings of his Ulysses, as I shall prove someday in my *poetic theology.* Eudoxus and Hermippus also kept it going, like almost all who have made a thorough study of Pythagorean and Platonic mysteries. Among more recent authorities, I also find three who had picked up the scent of magic: Alkindi the Arab, Roger Bacon and William of Paris.[57]

Plotinus also mentions it where he shows that the *magus is Na-* 59 *ture's minister,* not her Artificer. This man of the loftiest wisdom approves and confirms the one magic and abhors the other so that, when he was summoned to rites of evil demons, he said it was *better that they should come to him than he to them.* And rightly so: for as the one magic exposes and enslaves man to unclean powers, the other makes him their lord and prince.[58]

In the end, one magic cannot claim the name of art or science, 60 while the other is full of the deepest mysteries, including the most profound contemplation of the most abstruse secrets and leading at last to knowledge of Nature as a whole. Not so much by work-

mundo virtutes quasi de latebris evocans in lucem, non tam facit
miranda quam facienti naturae sedula famulatur. Haec universi
consensum, quem significantius Graeci συμπάθειαν dicunt, in-
trorsum perscrutatius rimata, et mutuam naturarum cognationem
habens perspectatam, nativas adhibens unicuique rei et suas illece-
bras — quae magorum ἴυγγες nominantur — in mundi recessibus,
in naturae gremio, in promptuariis arcanisque Dei latitantia miracula, quasi ipsa sit Artifex, promit in publicum; et sicut agricola
ulmos vitibus, ita magus terram caelo, idest inferiora superiorum
dotibus virtutibusque maritat.[35]

61   Quo fit ut quam illa prodigiosa et noxia, tam haec divina et
salutaris appareat, ob hoc praecipue: quod illa hominem, Dei
hostibus mancipans, avocat a Deo; haec in eam operum Dei admirationem excitat, quam propensa charitas, fides ac spes certissime
consequuntur. Neque enim ad religionem, ad Dei cultum quicquam promovet magis quam assidua contemplatio mirabilium
Dei. Quae ut per hanc de qua agimus naturalem magiam bene
exploraverimus, in Opificis cultum amoremque ardentius animati,
illud canere compellemur: pleni sunt caeli, plena est omnis terra
maiestate gloriae tuae.

62   Et haec satis de magia, de qua haec diximus quod scio esse
plures qui, sicut canes ignotos semper adlatrant, ita et ipsi saepe
damnant oderuntque quae non intelligunt.

63   Venio nunc ad ea quae ex antiquis Hebraeorum mysteriis eruta
ad sacrosanctam et catholicam fidem confirmandam attuli. Quae
ne forte ab his quibus sunt ignota commentitiae nugae aut fabulae
circumlatorum existimentur, volo intelligant omnes quae et qualia
sint, unde petita, quibus et quam claris auctoribus confirmata, et

ing wonders as by diligently serving Nature as she works them, this other magic calls out of hiding into the light powers *sown* by a gracious God and *scattered* over the world. After probing deep into that universal accord that the Greeks more tellingly call συμπάθεια, after examining how natures are kin to one another, and applying to each and every thing its inborn charms — named ἴυγγες by the Magi — this magic makes public, as if it were the Artificer, wonders concealed in the world's secret parts, in Nature's heart, in God's hideaways and storerooms, and, as a farmer *marries elm to vine*, so a magus joins earth to heaven, linking things below to properties and powers of those above.[59]

So it is that this magic is as divine and helpful as the other is 61 dreadful and harmful, for this reason especially: that the other leads man away from God by enslaving him to God's enemies, while this one excites man to that astonishment at God's works whose absolutely certain effects are *hope, faith and a love* that is always willing. For there is no greater stimulus to religion or to any worship of God than constantly contemplating God's marvels. After exploring them carefully through this natural magic of which I speak, we shall be stirred to love and worship their Creator with a hotter passion, and then we shall be forced to sing that famous song: *full are the heavens, full is the whole earth with your glory's greatness.*[60]

And this is enough about magic: I have made these statements 62 about it because I know there are many who — as *dogs always bark* at those unknown to them — also often denounce and detest what they do not understand.[61]

I come now to what I have unearthed from ancient mysteries of 63 the Jews and have brought forward to confirm the most holy and Catholic faith. So that people who know nothing about these mysteries might not mistakenly regard them as fallacious nonsense or fabulous *conjurations*, I want everyone to understand what they are, what their features are, where they come from, who has confirmed

quam reposita, quam divina, quam nostris hominibus ad propugnandam religionem contra Hebreorum importunas calumnias sint necessaria.

64   Scribunt non modo celebres Hebreorum doctores, sed ex nostris quoque Hesdras, Hilarius et Origenes, Mosen non Legem modo quam quinque exaratam libris posteris reliquit sed secretiorem quoque et veram Legis enarrationem in monte divinitus accepisse. Praeceptum autem ei a Deo ut Legem quidem populo publicaret, Legis interpretationem nec traderet litteris, nec invulgaret. Sed ipse Iesu Nave tantum, tum ille aliis deinceps succedentibus sacerdotum primoribus, magna silentii religione revelaret. Satis erat per simplicem historiam nunc Dei potentiam, nunc in improbos iram, in bonos clementiam, in omnes iustitiam agnoscere, et per divina salutariaque praecepta ad bene beateque vivendum et cultum verae religionis institui. At mysteria secretiora et sub cortice Legis rudique verborum praetextu latitantia, altissimae divinitatis archana, plebi palam facere, quid erat aliud quam dare sanctum canibus et inter porcos spargere margaritas? Ergo haec clam vulgo habere, perfectis communicanda — inter quos tantum sapientiam loqui se ait Paulus — non humani consilii, sed divini praecepti fuit.

65   Quem morem antiqui philosophi sanctissime observarunt. Pythagoras nihil scripsit nisi paucula quaedam, quae Damae filiae moriens commendavit. Egyptiorum templis insculptae Sphinges hoc admonebant, ut mistica dogmata per enigmatum nodos a prophana multitudine inviolata custodirentur. Plato, Dionisio[36] quaedam de supremis scribens substantiis, per enigmata — inquit — dicendum est ne, si epistola forte ad aliorum pervenerit manus, quae tibi scribimus ab aliis intelligantur. Aristoteles libros *Methaphysice*, in quibus agit de divinis, editos esse et non editos dicebat. Quid plura? Iesum Christum, vitae magistrum, asserit Origenes multa revelasse discipulis, quae illi, ne vulgo fierent comunia, scribere

them and on what eminent authority, how remote they are, how divine, and how much our people need them to do battle for religion against savage slanders by Jews.[62]

Not only famous teachers of the Jews but also our Esdras, Hilary and Origen write that what God gave Moses on the mountain was not just the Law that he recorded for posterity in five books but also a true and more secret reading of the Law. God's command to Moses was indeed to make the Law public to the people but not to divulge the interpretation of the Law or write it down. Moses was to reveal it only to Jesus Nave, and he in turn to the high priests who succeeded him, under a strict rule of silence. From the simple story there was enough to recognize God's power here, there his wrath at the wicked, his mercy to the good, his justice to all, and from the divine and saving commandments there was enough to learn how to live a good and holy life and to worship in a true religion. But to disclose more secret mysteries to people — arcana of supreme divinity concealed beneath the *bark of the Law* and rough surface of its words — what would that be but to *give something holy to dogs and cast pearls before swine?* Hence it was a matter of divine command, not human judgment, to keep secret from the populace what should be told to the perfect — the only ones with whom Paul says that he *speaks about Wisdom.*[63]

Ancient philosophers observed this custom scrupulously. Pythagoras wrote only a few little phrases that he trusted to his daughter Dama as he died. Sphinxes carved on temples in Egypt used to give this warning — that intricate riddles were to keep mystic dogmas safe from the common crowd. Plato, writing to Dionysius about the highest beings, says *I must speak in riddles so that no one else may understand what I write you, in case my letter falls into another's hands.* Aristotle used to say that the books of the *Metaphysics* that deal with theology were *published and not published.* What more to add? Origen claims that the master of life, Jesus Christ, revealed much to his disciples that they decided not to write down

64

65

noluerunt. Quod maxime confirmat Dyonisius Areopagita, qui
secretiora mysteria a nostrae religionis auctoribus ἐκ νοὸς εἰς
νοῦν διὰ μέσου λόγου, σωματικοῦ μὲν, ἀυλοτέρου δὲ ὅμως,
γραφῆς ἐκτός[37] — idest ex animo in animum, sine litteris, medio
intercedente verbo ait fuisse transfusa.

66   Hoc eodem penitus modo cum ex Dei praecepto vera illa Legis
interpretatio Moisi deitus tradita revelaretur, dicta est Cabala,
quod idem est apud Hebreos quod apud nos receptio: ob id scilicet quod illam doctrinam non per litterarum monumenta sed ordi-
nariis revelationum successionibus alter ab altero quasi hereditario
iure reciperet. Verum postquam Hebrei, a Babilonica captivitate
restituti per Cyrum et sub Zorobabel instaurato templo, ad repa-
randam Legem animum appulerunt. Esdras, tunc ecclesiae prae-
fectus, post emendatum Moseos librum, cum plane cognosceret
per exilia, caedes, fugas, captivitatem gentis Israeliticae institutum
a maioribus morem tradendae per manus doctrinae servari non
posse, futurumque ut sibi divinitus indulta caelestis doctrinae arcana perirent, quorum commentariis non intercedentibus durare
diu memoria non poterat, constituit ut, convocatis qui tunc super-
erant sapientibus, afferret unusquisque in medium quae de mysteriis Legis memoriter tenebat, adhibitisque notariis in LXX volu-
mina (tot enim fere in sinedrio sapientes) redigerentur.

67   Qua de re ne mihi soli credatis, patres, audite Esdram ipsum sic
loquentem:

      Exactis XL diebus, loquutus est Altissimus dicens: Priora
      quae scripsisti in palam pone, legant digni et indigni, novis-
      simos autem LXX libros conservabis ut tradas eos sapientibus

in order to keep it from becoming common knowledge. Dionysius the Areopagite confirms this better than anyone: he says that the founders of our religion transmitted the more secret mysteries ἐκ νοὸς εἰς νοῦν διὰ μέσου λόγου, σωματικοῦ μὲν, αὐλοτέρου δὲ ὅμως, γραφῆς ἐκτὸς—*from mind to mind, without writing, and only speech mediating between them.*[64]

Since that true interpretation of the Law divinely bestowed on 66
Moses was revealed by God's command in just the same way, it was called *Kabbalah*, which is the Hebrew word for our *reception*; this is because one person would *receive* that teaching from another, not through written records but from a regular succession of revelations, as if by a law of inheritance. But after Cyrus brought the Jews back from captivity in Babylon and the Temple was restored under Zorobabel, they turned their attention to recovering the Law. Once Esdras, then the leader of the Assembly, had corrected the book of Moses, he saw clearly that after exiles, massacres, escapes and the captivity of the people of Israel, the custom of passing the Law from person to person could not be kept as the elders had established it. He also realized that secrets of heavenly doctrine divinely granted to them would perish since the memory of them could last no longer without the support of written texts. So Esdras arranged for sages who then survived to be called together and for each to contribute what he remembered of the mysteries of the Law, and scribes were brought in to compile these contributions in 70 volumes (for that was roughly the number of sages in the Sanhedrin).[65]

In this matter, Fathers, no need to trust my word alone. Hear 67
what Esdras himself has to say:

> After 40 days had passed, the Most High spoke, saying, *make public what you have written first, let the righteous and unrighteous read, but the 70 most recent books you shall hold back to*

de populo tuo; in his enim est vena intellectus et sapientiae fons et scientiae flumen. Atque ita feci.

Haec Esdras ad verbum. Hi sunt libri scientiae Cabalae. In his libris merito Esdras venam intellectus, idest ineffabilem de supersubstantiali deitate theologiam, sapientiae fontem, idest de intelligibilibus angelicisque formis exactam methaphisicam, et scientiae flumen, idest de rebus naturalibus firmissimam philosophiam esse clara imprimis voce pronuntiavit. Hi libri Sixtus Quartus Pontifex Maximus, qui hunc sub quo vivimus feliciter Innocentium VIII proxime antecessit, maxima cura studioque curavit ut in publicam fidei nostrae utilitatem Latinis litteris mandarentur. Iamque cum ille decessit, tres ex illis pervenerant ad Latinos.

68   Hi libri apud Hebreos hac tempestate tanta religione coluntur ut neminem liceat nisi annos XL natum illos attingere. Hos ego libros non mediocri impensa mihi cum comparassem, summa diligentia indefessis laboribus cum perlegissem, vidi in illis — testis est Deus — religionem non tam Mosaicam quam Christianam. Ibi Trinitatis mysterium, ibi Verbi incarnatio, ibi Messiae divinitas, ibi de peccato originali, de illius per Christum expiatione, de caelesti Hyerusalem, de casu daemonum, de ordinibus angelorum, de purgatoriis, de inferorum paenis, eadem legi quae apud Paulum et Dyonisium, apud Hieronymum et Augustinum quotidie legimus. In his vero quae spectant ad philosophiam, Pythagoram prorsus audias et Platonem, quorum decreta ita sunt fidei Christianae affinia ut Augustinus noster immensas Deo gratias agat quod ad eius manus pervenerint libri Platonicorum. In plenum nulla est ferme de re nobis cum Hebreis controversia de qua ex libris Cabalistarum ita redargui convincique non possint, ut ne angulus quidem reliquus sit in quem se condant. Cuius rei testem gravissimum

*pass them on to sages of your people. For in them is a vein of intellect
and a spring of wisdom and a river of knowledge.* And so have I
done it.

These are the exact words of Esdras. These are books on the
knowledge of Kabbalah. Esdras was right to declare, before anyone
and in a voice of singular clarity, that in these books there is a *vein
of intellect,* or an ineffable theology of supersubstantial divinity; a
spring of wisdom, or a finished metaphysics of intelligible and angelic forms; and a *river of knowledge,* or a most certain philosophy
of Nature. The Supreme Pontiff, Sixtus IV, who ruled just before
Pope Innocent VIII, under whom we are fortunate to live, saw to
it with great care and diligence that these books were put into
Latin for the general good of our faith. And now that he has
passed away, three of them have come down to readers of Latin.[66]

So scrupulously are these books revered by Jews of our time 68
that they permit no one under the age of forty to touch them.
After I had bought them for myself at no small cost and had read
through them with the greatest attention and unremitting labor, I
saw in them — so help me God — a religion not so much Mosaic as
Christian. There I read about the mystery of the Trinity, about the
Incarnation of the Word, about the divinity of the Messiah, about
original sin, its atonement through Christ, the heavenly Jerusalem,
the fall of demons, the orders of angels, about purgatory and pains
of hell, reading the same things we read every day in Paul and
Dionysius, in Jerome and Augustine. But where these books bear
on philosophy, you might actually be hearing Pythagoras and
Plato, whose teachings are so closely related to the Christian faith
that our Augustine gives great thanks to God because books by
Platonists came into his hands. All in all, there is hardly any point
of contention between us and the Jews on which these books by
Kabbalists cannot defeat and rebut them, leaving them no corner
to hide in. I have a most impressive witness to this fact in Antonio

habeo Antonium Cronicum, virum eruditissimum, qui suis au-
ribus, cum apud eum essem in convivio, audivit Dactylum,
Hebreum peritum huius scientiae, in Christianorum prorsus de
Trinitate sententiam pedibus manibusque descendere.

69   Sed ut ad meae redeam disputationis capita percensenda, attulimus et nostram de interpretandis Orphei Zoroastrisque carmini-
bus sententiam. Orpheus apud Graecos ferme integer, Zoroaster
apud eos mancus, apud Caldeos absolutior legitur. Ambo priscae
sapientiae crediti patres et auctores. Nam, ut taceam de Zoroastre,
cuius frequens apud Platonicos non sine summa semper venerati-
one est mentio, scribit Iamblicus Calcideus habuisse Pythagoram
Orphycam theologiam tanquam exemplar ad quam ipse suam fin-
geret formaretque philosophiam. Quin idcirco tantum dicta Pythagorae sacra nuncupari dicunt, quod ab Orphei fluxerint insti-
tutis; inde secreta de numeris doctrina et quicquid magnum
sublimeque habuit Graeca philosophia ut a primo fonte manavit.
Sed — qui erat veterum mos theologorum — ita Orpheus suorum
dogmatum mysteria fabularum intexit involucris et poetico velamento dissimulavit, ut si quis legat illius *Hymnos*, nihil subesse
credat praeter fabellas nugasque meracissimas.

70   Quod volui dixisse ut cognoscatur quis mihi labor, quae fuerit
difficultas ex affectatis enigmatum syrpis, ex fabularum latebris
latitantes eruere secretae philosophiae sensus, nulla praesertim in
re tam gravi, tam abscondita inexplorataque adiuto aliorum inter-
pretum opera et diligentia. Et tamen oblatrarunt canes mei minutula quaedam et levia ad numeri ostentationem me accumulasse,
quasi non omnes quae ambiguae maxime controversaeque sunt
quaestiones, in quibus principales digladiantur achademiae, quasi

Cronico, a man of immense learning. When I was dining at his house, with his own ears he heard Dattilo, a Jew skilled in this science, accept a thoroughly Christian position on the Trinity *from top to toe.*[67]

But to get back to listing topics of my disputation, I have also 69 added my views on interpreting poems by Orpheus and Zoro-aster. In Greek one reads Orpheus almost intact, but Zoroaster is mutilated in that language, more complete in Chaldean. Both are thought to be Fathers and founders of ancient wisdom. Now to leave Zoroaster aside — since Platonists speak of him frequently and always with the greatest reverence — Iamblichus of Chalcis writes that Pythagoras treated Orphic theology as a model for forming and fashioning his own philosophy. Indeed, they claim that sayings of Pythagoras were called sacred only for this rea-son — because they came from the teachings of Orpheus whence, as from a primal spring, flowed a secret doctrine of numbers and anything of the great and sublime that Greek philosophy pos-sessed. Orpheus, however, wrapped his mysterious doctrines in folds of myth — in the way of ancient theologians — concealing them so well under a veil of poetry that anyone who reads his *Hymns* would think there was nothing beneath them but fables and the purest nonsense.[68]

I have decided to mention this so that people would recognize 70 the work I have done, the trouble I have faced in digging out meanings from a secret philosophy hidden in *weeds* of farfetched riddles and obscurities of myth, especially since, in a matter so serious, so recondite and so unexplored, I have done this without aid or attention from other interpreters. And still *those dogs of mine have been barking* and complaining that I have piled up petty trivi-alities to make a show of quantity, as if all my questions were not those most doubted and debated, those that have great academies crossing swords, as if I had not brought them — those who pick at

non multa attulerim his ipsis—qui et mea carpunt et se credunt philosophorum principes—et incognita prorsus et intentata.

71   Quin ego tantum absum ab ea culpa ut curaverim in quam paucissima potui capita cogere disputationem, quam si, ut consueverunt alii, partiri ipse in sua membra et lancinare voluissem, in innumerum profecto numerum excrevisset. Et, ut taceam de ceteris, quis est qui nesciat unum dogma ex nongentis, quod scilicet de concilianda est Platonis Aristotelisque philosophia, potuisse me—citra omnem affectatae numerositatis suspitionem—in sexcenta, ne dicam plura, capita deduxisse, locos scilicet omnes in quibus dissidere alii, convenire ego illos existimo, particulatim enumerantem? Sed certe—dicam enim, quamquam neque modeste neque ex ingenio meo—dicam tamen quia dicere me invidi cogunt, cogunt obtrectatores: volui hoc meo congressu fidem facere, non tam quod multa scirem quam quod scirem quae multi nesciunt.

72   Quod ut vobis re ipsa, patres colendissimi, iam palam fiat, ut desiderium vestrum, doctores excellentissimi, quos paratos accinctosque expectare pugnam non sine magna voluptate conspicio, mea longius oratio non remoretur, quod foelix faustumque sit, quasi citante classico iam conseramus manus.

FINIS

me and think themselves princes among philosophers — problems
entirely unknown and untried.[69]

So far am I from being guilty as charged, in fact, I have taken   71
care to confine my disputation to as few topics as I could. Had I
wanted to do as others do, had I divided my disputation and torn
it into pieces, their number would quickly have become number-
less. Also, letting other things pass, does not everyone know that
just one proposition of the 900, the one about reconciling the
philosophies of Plato and Aristotle, could have led me — beyond
any suspicion of deliberately piling the numbers up — to propose
hundreds of theses, not to say more, if I had worked point by
point through those issues where others find discord but I find
harmony? But certainly — even though it is immodest and not my
manner, I shall say it — I shall say it because the envious force me,
the malicious force me to say it: yes, by arranging this gathering of
mine I have wished to convince people not so much that I know
many things as that *I know what many do not know.*[70]

And now, Most Reverend Fathers, to put the facts before you,   72
to let my oratory no longer delay what you want, most excellent
doctors, as I watch you — and greatly enjoy the moment — while
you await the fight, *prepared and girded* for it, now let us give battle,
for this is the hour of our great good fortune, and the trumpet
calls.[71]

THE END

APPENDIX I

Selections from Pico's 900 Conclusions

Persons, topics, or texts named in the headnote of each set of theses, thirty-nine in all, are in the second column below. Pico planned two groups of theses, 400 (*T1*) and 500 (*T2*), for a total of 900. Since the theses were not numbered in the 1486 edition, keeping track of them while producing the book will have been hard: the third column gives the number of theses *stated* in the heading of each set of theses in 1486. The 1532 edition numbered every thesis, without counting the eleven corollaries: the fourth column counts the theses *numbered* in 1532, but not the eleven corollaries. Although 901 is the total count (ignoring the omission in *T2* 34) of what was *stated* in 1486, 900 theses were *numbered* in the 1532 edition — despite an error of LXXI for LXXII in the heading of the last set.

	Name	Theses Stated 1486	Theses Numbered 1532
T1			
1	Albert the Great	16	16
2	Thomas Aquinas	45	45
3	Francis of Meyronnes	8	8
4	John Duns Scotus	22	22
5	Henry of Ghent	13	13
6	Giles of Rome	11	11
7	Averroes	41	41
8	Avicenna	12	12
9	Alfarabi	11	11
10	Isaac of Narbonne	4	4

	Name	Theses Stated 1486	Theses Numbered 1532
11	Abumaron	4	4
12	Maimonides	3	3
13	Mohammed of Toledo	5	5
14	Avempace	2	2
15	Theophrastus	4	4
16	Ammonius	3	3
17	Simplicius	9	9
18	Alexander	8	8
19	Themistius	5	5
20	Plotinus	15	15
21	Adelandus	8	8
22	Porphyry	12	12
23	Iamblichus	9	9
24	Proclus	55	55
25	Pythagoras	14	14
26	Chaldeans	6	6
27	Mercurius Trismegistus	10	10
28	Kabbalists	47	47
T2			
29	Unusual Reconciling	17	17
30	Dissenting	80	80
31	Unusual New	71	71
32	Theological	31	29
33	Plato	62	62
34	*Book of Causes*	0	10
35	Mathematics	85	85
36	Zoroaster	15	15
37	Magic	26	26
38	*Orphic Hymns*	31	31
39	Kabbalah	71	72

Selections

Headnotes in roman font are from the 1486 edition, with numbers of theses as stated and uncorrected.

I

*The thirteen theses condemned initially by Innocent VIII
in the order of Pico's defense in the* Apology

1 Christ did not truly, and as far as real presence is concerned, descend to Hell, as proposed by Thomas and on the shared approach, but only in regard to the effect. (*Concl.* p. 42; *Apol.* p. 11)

2 The second is that for a mortal sin in limited time the penalty due is not unlimited in time but only limited. (*Concl.* p. 43; *Apol.* p. 33)

3 Neither the cross of Christ nor any image should be adored with the adoration of worship, even in the way that Thomas proposes. (*Concl.* p. 42; *Apol.* p. 37)

4 I do not assent to the usual statement by theologians who say that God can supposit any nature whatever, but I grant this only for a nature able to reason. (*Concl.* p. 42; *Apol.* p. 41)

5 There is no knowledge that gives us more certainty of Christ's divinity than magic and Kabbalah. (*Concl.* p. 57; *Apol.* p. 47)

6 If one takes the usual approach to the possibility of suppositing with regard to any creature whatever, I say that, without the substance of bread changing into Christ's body or without eliminating the breadness, it can happen that Christ's body is on the altar in keeping with the reality of the sacrament because the statement would occur in speaking about a possibility, not about being so. (*Concl.* p. 41; *Apol.* p. 60)

7 It is more reasonable to believe that Origen is saved than to believe him damned. (*Concl.* p. 44; *Apol.* pp. 75–76)

8 I state this as acceptable, and I would assert it firmly except that what theologians usually say is the opposite, and yet I maintain that this statement is acceptable in itself, as follows: that just as no one's opinion is exactly thus and so because he wants to have this opinion, no one believes it to be true in this way exactly because he wants to believe it so.

Corollary: It is not in a person's free power to believe an article of faith to be true when he pleases and to believe it not to be true when he pleases. (*Concl.* p. 43; *Apol.* p. 99)

9 Anyone who says that an accident cannot exist unless it exists *in* will be able to hold to the sacrament of the Eucharist even while holding that the substance of bread does not remain. (*Concl.* p. 42; *Apol.* p. 103)

10 The words *this is my body* that are said in the consecration are taken materially, not as signifying. (*Concl.* p. 42; *Apol.* 105)

11 Christ's miracles are the most certain evidence of his divinity not because of what was done but because of how it was done. (*Concl.* p. 57; *Apol.* 106)

12 Saying of God that he is an intellect or that he understands is less appropriate than saying of an angel that it is a rational soul. (*Concl.* p. 39; *Apol.* p. 108)

13 The soul understands nothing actually and distinctly except itself. (*Concl.* p. 40; *Apol.* p. 109)

2

Headnote on page 1 of the 1486 edition.

Giovanni Pico della Mirandola will dispute his own views in public — as well as those of Chaldeans, Arabs, Hebrews, Greeks, Egyptians and Latins — about the statements listed, numbering nine hundred, about dialectical, moral, natural, mathematical, metaphysical, theological, magical and Kabbalist topics. In stating them, he has imitated not the splendid Roman tongue but the way the most famous disputants talk in Paris, since this is the custom of almost all philosophers in our day. Propositions to be disputed are stated separately for nations and heads of sects, though without distinction for parts of philosophy — all mixed together in an assortment.

Conclusions following the teaching of Latin philosophers and theologians: Albertus Magnus, Thomas Aquinas, Henry of Ghent, John Scotus, Giles of Rome and François de Meyronnes.

3

Conclusions 16 in Number Regarding Albert

1 Intelligible species are not needed, and positing them is not appropriate for good Peripatetics.

5 In intension and remission, form varies not as to essence but as to existence.

4

Conclusions 22 in Number Regarding John Scotus

6 Any undivided is an undivided through an individuating difference of its own, called a *just-this-ness*.

5

Conclusions 11 in Number Regarding Giles Of Rome

7 A higher angel illuminates a lower one not by showing it a luminous object or by dividing what is united in itself and making it particular but because it gives comfort to the intellect of the lower one and makes it strong.

6

Headnote on page 7 of the 1486 edition.

Conclusions Regarding the Teaching of Arabs Who Generally Declare Themselves To Be Peripatetics: Averroes, Avicenna, Alfarabi, Avempace, Isaac, Abumaron, Moses and Mohammed.

7

Conclusions 41 in Number Regarding Averroes

2 In all humans there is a single intellective soul.

3 Supreme human happiness comes when the Agent Intellect connects with a potential intellect as its form; other Latin writers that I have read have interpreted that continuation wrongly and perversely, and especially John of Jandun, who on nearly all points of philosophy has completely corrupted and distorted the teaching of Averroes.

4 While holding the unity of the Intellect, it is possible that after death my soul remains so particularly mine that I do not share it with everyone.

35 The essence of anything and its existing are the same in reality.

8

Conclusions 12 in Number Regarding Avicenna

9 Odor is multiplied up to the sense according to real — not intensional — existence.

9

Conclusions 11 in Number Regarding Alfarabi

9 Species exist in a middle state — a mode between spiritual and material existence.

10 In regard to spiritual existence, any species is formally a cognition.

10

Headnote from page 12 of the 1486 edition.

Conclusions Regarding Greeks Who Declare the Peripatetic View: Theophrastus, Ammonius, Simplicius, Alexander and Themistius.

11

Conclusions 3 in Number Regarding Ammonius.

2 A rational soul does not join directly with a body as its instrument.

12

Conclusions 8 in Number Regarding Alexander of Aphrodisias

1 The rational soul is immortal.

13

Conclusions 5 in Number Regarding Themistius

2 I believe the Agent Intellect that only illuminates to be in Themistius what Metatron is in Kabbalah.

14

Headnote on page 14 of the 1486 edition.

Conclusions Regarding the Teaching of Philosophers called Platonists: Plotinus of Egypt, Porphyry of Tyre, Iamblichus of Chalcis, Proclus of Lydus and the Arab Adelandus

15

Conclusions 15 in Number Regarding Plotinus

2 Not all the soul descends when it descends.

4 After death a soul that has sinned either in an earthly or in an airy body lives the life of a beast.

7 Human happiness is supreme when our particular intellect is fully and wholly conjoined with the First Intellect.

16

Conclusions 8 in Number Regarding the Arab Adelandus

1 The Agent Intellect is nothing other than the part of the soul that stays above and does not fall.

6 Since, as Abdala said, seeing dreams shows strength of imagination and understanding them shows strength of intellect, then whoever sees them in the usual way does not understand them.

8 All the sages of India, Persia, Egypt and Chaldea believe in the movement of souls between bodies.

17

Conclusions 55 in Number Regarding Proclus

7 By the one and many, whole and parts, bounded and unbounded that we have from the *Parmenides,* understand a second group of the trinity as intelligibles intellected by dividing that group into three.

9 Plato represents a third group of the second trinity with three boundaries — extremes, completed and by figure.

13 The second trinity of the intellected hebdomad is the trinity of Curetes called undefiled by the *Theology.*

21 It befits hypercosmic gods to resemble what exists and to pass on that mutual sympathy and sharing that they get from resembling one another.

22 Although this resembling befits the guiding gods described in the previous conclusion, it still comes to befit the middle group of their trinity because the first group has conjoined directly and by substance with intellected gods and a third blends in with the next kinds.

24 The Jupiter in the guiding trinity is substantivated, the Neptune is vivified and the Pluto reverts.

30 Even though the whole trinity of hypercosmic gods may be called Persephone, in Greek its first unity is still called Diana, the second Persephone and the third Minerva, while the barbarians say that Hecate comes first, Soul second and Power third.

31 According to the preceding conclusion, what Proclus thought can explain one of the sayings of Zoroaster in the Greek version, although the reading and explanation are different in Chaldean.

32 The third trinity of hypercosmic gods is called Apollo, and reversion befits it.

33 A trinity that watches and preserves accompanies Persephone's trinity at her side.

47 Every middle order abides, stable in the one before, and in itself supports the one that follows.

48 Just as the first Trinity after Unity is everything as intelligible, commensurate and bounded in form, so the second Trinity is everything as living, true and unbounded in form, and the third is all of this as belonging properly to the mixture and beautiful in form.

49 The first Trinity only abides, the second abides and processes, the third turns back after processing.

52 By the place beyond the heavens, we should understand that for the second trinity this is more intelligible than intellected,

more intellected than intelligible for the hollow below the heavens, and for the heavens sharing equally in both.

18

Conclusions 14 in Number Regarding the Mathematics of Pythagoras

5 Through One, the Three and Seven we know that in Pallas what unifies the discrete is a causal power of Intellect that also blesses.

19

Conclusions 6 in Number Regarding a Belief of Chaldean Theologians

5 The intelligible ordering is not within an intellectual ordering, as Amosis the Egyptian said: it is above the whole intellectual hierarchy, unparticipated in the depths of primal Unity and hidden in the gloomy primal darkness.

20

Conclusions 10 in Number Regarding the Ancient Teaching of Mercurius Trismegistus the Egyptian

7 God warns man about things to come in six ways: through dreams, omens, birds, entrails, inspiration and the Sibyl.

10 Within everyone are ten tormentors: ignorance, grief, inconsistency, lust, injustice, extravagance, deceit, envy, fraud, anger, recklessness, malice.

Corollary: The ten tormentors described in the previous conclusion according to Mercury, as one who thinks deeply about it will see, correspond in Kabbalah to the evil grouping of ten with its governors, of whom I have had nothing to say in the Kabbalist conclusions because this is a secret.

21

Kabbalist Conclusions 47 in Number Regarding the
Secret Teaching of Hebrew Kabbalist Sages,
May We Always Remember Them Well

1 Just as a human being and lower priest sacrifices souls of nonreasoning animals to God, so Michael, a higher priest, sacrifices souls of animals that reason.

2 There are nine hierarchies of angels, whose names are Cherubim, Seraphim, Hasmalim, Haiot, Aralim, Tarsisim, Ophanim, Thephsarim and Isim.

4 Adam's sin was to cut the Kingdom off from other Plants.

6 The great North Wind is the source of all souls in general, just as other Days are sources of some souls but not of all.

11 They say that out of Eden comes a river that divides into four headwaters, meaning that out of the second Numeration comes the third that divides into the fourth, fifth, sixth and tenth.

14 One who knows the southern Attribute in the group on the right will know why every journey of Abraham always goes to the South.

17 Wherever Scripture mentions love between male and female, we are given a mystical representation of *Tiferet*'s conjunction with the Congregation of Israel or of *bet*'s with *Tiferet*.

19 The letters of a name of the evil demon who is the Prince of This World and of a Name of God, the Triagrammaton, are the same, and one who knows how to arrange their transposition will derive the one from the other.

22 Although there are many ways to group the chariots, yet, insofar as this applies to the mystery of phylacteries, two chariots

are to be grouped so that one chariot is made from the second, third, fourth and fifth, and they are the four phylacteries that *vav* puts on, and the sixth, seventh, eighth and ninth make the second chariot, and they are the phylacteries that the final *he* puts on.

24 When Job said, "who makes peace on high," he understood the Southern Water, the Northern Fire and their Commanders, of whom nothing more should be said.

29 The four-letter name of God composed of *mem, sade, pe* and *sade* should be attributed to the Kingdom of David.

33 In the whole Law there are no letters whose forms, ligatures, separations, twisting, direction, defect, excess, smallness, greatness, crowning, closing, opening and order do not reveal secrets of the ten Numerations.

36 Sodom sinned by severing the Last Plant.

37 By the secret of the prayer before dawn we should understand nothing other than the Attribute of Piety.

38 Just as outward Fear is lower than Love, so is the inward higher than Love.

39 From the preceding conclusion one understands why Abraham is praised in Genesis because of Fear even though we know that he did everything out of Love through the Attribute of Piety.

41 Every good soul is a new soul coming from the East.

44 When the soul grasps whatever it can grasp and is joined to a higher soul, it will rub off its earthly covering and will be rooted up from its place and joined with divinity.

47 They hold that the order in which the influences of the Numerations come forth is expressed by saying *amen*.

22

Headnote on page 28 of the 1486 edition.

Conclusions numbering 500 that follow my own opinion, divided ten ways into physical, theological, Platonic and mathematical theses, unusual theses that state or reconcile opinions, Chaldean, Orphic, magical and Kabbalist theses. In all of them I propose nothing as asserted or acceptable except insofar as the Most Holy Roman Church judges it either true or acceptable — also its most worthy head, the Supreme Pontiff, Innocent VIII — and anyone is thoughtless who does not submit the judgment of his own thinking to the Pope's judgment.

23

Unusual Conclusions Numbering 17 and
Following My Own Opinion to Reconcile Statements
That Seem Absolutely Incompatible
First by Aristotle and Plato, Then by Other Teachers

1 There is no problem, natural or theological, about which Aristotle and Plato do not agree in meaning and substance, though they may seem to differ in words.

4 On the subject of theology, Thomas, Scotus and Giles are in harmony on basics and at the root, although in branches and at the surface of words one of them may seem quite out of tune with another.

24

Philosophical Conclusions Numbering 80 and Following My
Own Opinion Which, While Disagreeing with the Usual
Philosophy, Still Do Not Differ Much from the
Usual Way of Doing Philosophy

1 A universal species can be drawn directly from a species existing in an external sense.

2 A second intention is a being of reason disposed through the mode of qualitative form to arise from a mental act as a consequence but not an effect.

3 No first intention nor second intention is anywhere a subject.

6 A singular is not understood by the intellect — neither in fact nor even in the view of Aristotle, the Commentator and Thomas.

16 A tractate on suppositions does not belong to a logic.

44 If Thomas says that, according to Aristotle, the Intelligences are in a genus, he will oppose himself no less than Aristotle.

53 If Thomas says that, according to Aristotle, there are accidents in the Intelligences, he will contradict not only Aristotle but himself.

25

Unusual Conclusions Numbering 71 and
Following My Own Opinion That Bring
New Teachings into Philosophy

1 Just as the existence of properties is preceded by quidditive existence, so is quidditive existence preceded by unitary existence.

46 Given any object that can be practiced, an act that practices it is nobler than an act that theorizes about it — other things being equal.

49 Saying of God that he is an intellect or intelligent is less appropriate than saying of a rational soul that it is an angel. (twelfth thesis defended in *Apol.* p. 108)

60 The soul understands nothing except itself actually and distinctly. (thirteenth thesis defended in *Apol.* p. 109)

71 Empedocles, by strife and friendship in the soul, means nothing but the power in it that leads up and the power that leads down, which I believe to be analogous to Eternity and Beauty in knowledge of the *Sefirot*.

26

Conclusions in Theology Numbering 31
Following My Own Opinion and
Quite Different from the Usual Way of
Talking about Theology

1 Anyone who says that an accident cannot exist unless it exists *in* will be able to hold to the sacrament of the Eucharist even while holding that the substance of bread does not remain. (ninth thesis defended in *Apol.* p. 103)

2 If one takes the usual approach to the possibility of suppositing with regard to any creature whatever, I say that, without the substance of bread changing into Christ's body or without eliminating the breadness, it can happen that Christ's body is on the altar in keeping with the reality of the sacrament because the statement would occur in speaking about a possibility, not about being so. (sixth thesis defended in *Apol.* p. 60)

8 Christ did not truly, and as far as real presence is concerned, descend to Hell, as proposed by Thomas and on the shared approach, but only in regard to the effect. (first thesis defended in *Apol.* p. 11)

10 The words *this is my body* that are said in the consecration are taken materially, not as signifying. (tenth thesis defended in *Apol.* p. 105)

13 I do not assent to the usual statement by theologians who say that God can supposit any nature whatever, but I grant this only for a nature able to reason. (fourth thesis defended in *Apol.* p. 41)

14 Neither the cross of Christ nor any image should be adored with the adoration of worship, even in the way that Thomas proposes. (third thesis defended in *Apol.* p. 37)

18 I state this as acceptable, and I would assert it firmly except that what theologians usually say is the opposite, and yet I maintain that this statement is acceptable in itself, as follows: that just as no one's opinion is exactly thus and so because he wants to have this opinion, no one believes it to be true in this way exactly because he wants to believe it so.

Corollary: It is not in a person's free power to believe an article of faith to be true when he pleases and to believe it not to be true when he pleases. (eighth thesis defended in *Apol.* p. 99)

19 Were it not for sayings by saints who in their statements seem plainly to say the opposite, I would assert this firmly with the conclusion following it, yet I assert them as acceptable and as capable of being defended by reasoning, and the first is that mortal sin in itself is a limited evil.

20 The second is that for a mortal sin in limited time the penalty due is not unlimited in time but only limited. (first thesis defended in *Apol.* p. 33)

29 It is more reasonable to believe that Origen is saved than to believe him damned. (seventh thesis defended in *Apol.* pp. 75–76)

27

Conclusions Following My Own Opinion and
Numbering 62 on Plato's Teaching
on Which Few Statements Are Made Here
Because the First Unusual Conclusion Undertakes
to Examine the Whole of Plato's Teaching

1 By triadic numbers that Plato, in the *Timaeus*, puts in a triangle signifying the soul, we are advised how far to go, in numbering forms, by the nature of what the first forming form is. But by dyadic numbers posited in the same place, we are advised, by the

nature of what a middle term is in general, about how far to coordinate middle terms with the two posited extremes.

36 From Plato's demonstration in the *Phaedrus* of the soul's immortality there is proof not only for our souls, as Proclus, Hermias and Syrianus believe, nor for every soul, according to Plotinus and Numenius, nor only for the world-soul, as Posidonius thinks, but the proof applies for any heavenly soul and immortality is the conclusion.

45 The sentience in nature posited by Alkindi, Bacon, William of Paris and some others — but especially all the Magi — is nothing other than the sentience in the vehicle posited by Platonists.

51 If Plato's statement in the *Phaedrus* is correctly understood — that unless a person's soul gazed on the realities it would not have come into this ensouled being — one will understand that the view of Plotinus asserting the transmigration of souls into beasts is not Plato's teaching.

28

Conclusions about Mathematics
Following My Own Opinion and Numbering 85

1 Mathematical sciences are not real.

5 Just as Aristotle would be correct to say that the ancients — had they taken 'mathematicals' not in a formal sense but materially — went wrong in thinking about nature because they treated physical things as mathematicals, so it is absolutely correct that moderns who use mathematics to discuss natural problems have destroyed the foundations of natural philosophy.

11 There is a way through numbers to investigate and understand everything knowable. To verify this conclusion I promise that I will use a method of numbers to answer the 74 questions that follow.

29

Headnote on page 52 of the 1486 edition.

Questions That He Promises To Answer With Numbers.

12 Whether there is A God.
13 Whether he is infinite.
14 Whether he is the cause of all things.

30

Conclusions Numbering 15 Following My Own Opinion
on Understanding Sayings of Zoroaster
and His Chaldean Expositors

1 What Chaldean translators say about Zoroaster's first saying, on a ladder from Hell to the First Fire, signifies nothing other than a series of natures extending through the cosmos from matter, without a rung, to the One who is above every rung.

2 I say that by mysterial powers in the same place the translators understand nothing other than natural magic.

3 What the translators say about Zoroaster's second saying, on a double air, water and earth, means just that any element that can be divided into pure and impure has reasoning and unreasoning tenants, while an element that is only pure has reasoning tenants only.

4 In the same place, roots of the earth can mean nothing but a vegetating life, which matches statements by Empedocles who even posits a metempsychosis into plants.

6 Statements by Chaldean translators about aphorism 11 on the double drunkenness of Bacchus and Silenus are completely

intelligible through statements by Kabbalists about the double wine.

7 What the translators say about aphorism 14 is completely intelligible through what Kabbalists say about the death of the kiss.

8 By the three-layered wrapping in aphorism 17, the Magi understand nothing but the soul's threefold dwelling—heavenly, spiritual and earthly.

9 From the preceding conclusion you can understand something about the garments of skin that Adam made for himself— also about the skins that were in the Tabernacle.

10 In the translators understand nothing other than the Intellect by *Boy*.

31

Conclusions about Magic Numbering 26
Following My Own Opinion

1 All magic used by people today and which the Church rightly bans, has no solidity, no foundation and no truth because it depends on the power of enemies of primal truth, these dark powers that pour the darkness of deceit into minds disposed to evil.

2 Natural magic is licit and not forbidden, and I propose the following theses according to my own opinion about general principles of a theory for this science.

3 Magic is the practical part of natural knowledge.

4 From this conclusion and number 47 of the unusual theses on new teaching, it follows that magic is the noblest part of natural knowledge.

5 In heaven or on earth there is no power, separated seedwise, that a magus cannot unify and activate.

6 Any astonishing effect that occurs, whether it is magic or Kabbalah or some other kind, must be referred chiefly and mainly to the glorious and blessed God, whose grace rains down supercelestial waters of wondrous power every day on contemplative people of good will.

7 Christ's deeds cannot have been done either by a method of Kabbalah or by a method of magic.

8 Christ's miracles are the most certain evidence of his divinity not because of what was done but because of how it was done. (eleventh thesis defended in *Apol.* 106)

9 There is no knowledge that gives us more certainty of Christ's divinity than magic and Kabbalah. (fifth thesis defended in *Apol.* p. 47)

10 What the magus who is human does artificially, nature has done naturally by making the human.

13 Doing magic is nothing but marrying the world.

15 No magical action can have any effect unless it has an act of Kabbalah, explicit or implicit, linked with it.

23 Except the threefold and tenfold, any number is material in magic, but those are formal, and in magical arithmetic they are numbers of numbers.

25 Just as characters belong to an act of magic, so numbers belong to an act of Kabbalah, and lying between the two is a use of letters that avoids either extreme.

26 Just as something untouched by mediating causes happens by the influence of the First Agent when this is specific and unmediated, so by an act of Kabbalah, if the Kabbalah is pure and unmediated, something happens that no magic touches.

32

Conclusions Numbering 31 Following My Own Opinion
on a Way to Understand the Hymns of Orpheus as about
Magic, Namely, a Secret Wisdom of Divine and Natural
Things That I Was the First to Discover in Them

4 Just as David's hymns are wonderfully useful for an act of
Kabbalah, so are the hymns of Orpheus useful for an act of true,
licit and natural magic.

5 Numbered under the figure of the Pythagorean tetractys,
the number of the *Orphic Hymns* is the same as the number by
which the threefold God created the world.

12 By the eightfold number of maritime hymns a property of
bodily nature is pointed out to us.

20 From the septet of hymns attributed to the Father's Mind —
hymns of Protogonus, Pallas, Saturn, Venus, Rhea, Law and Bacchus — one who understands and thinks deeply can conclude
something about the end of time.

21 The effect of the preceding hymns is nothing without an act
of Kabbalah, whose special result is to put every figural, continuous and discrete quantity into practice.

24 He will not get drunk on any Bacchus who has not first
been joined to his own Muse.

33

Kabbalist Conclusions Numbering 71
Following My Own Opinion and Providing
Powerful Confirmation of the Christian Religion
from the Very Principles of Hebrew Sages

1 Whatever the rest of the Kabbalists may say, the first distinction that I would make divides knowledge of Kabbalah into

knowledge of *Sefirot* and *Shemot*, similar to theoretical and practical knowledge.

2 Whatever other Kabbalists may say, I would divide the visionary part of Kabbalah into four, corresponding to the fourfold division of philosophy that I have usually proposed. First is what I call knowing how to revolve the alphabet, corresponding to the part of philosophy that I call comprehensive philosophy. The second, third and fourth part is the threefold *Merkabah*, corresponding to a threefold particularizing philosophy about divine, middle and sensible natures.

3 Knowledge that is the practical part of Kabbalah puts into practice all formal metaphysics and lower theology.

4 *Ensoph* is not to be numbered along with other Numerations because it is the unity of those Numerations, removed and uncommunicated, not the unity of any grouping.

5 Any Hebrew Kabbalist, following principles and statements of the knowledge of Kabbalah, is forced inevitably to grant precisely — without addition, subtraction or variation — what the Catholic faith of Christians declares about the Trinity and each divine person, Father, Son and Holy Spirit.
Corollary: Not only those who deny the Trinity but those who treat it in any way differently than the Catholic Church treats it — as do Arians, Sabellians and the like — can plainly be refuted if principles of Kabbalah are accepted.

6 Someone with a deep knowledge of Kabbalah can understand that the three great fourfold names of God contained in the secrets of Kabbalists ought to be assigned to the three persons of the Trinity through a wondrous allocation so that the name אהיה belongs to the Father, the name יהוה to the Son, the name אדני to the Holy Spirit.

7 No Hebrew Kabbalist can deny that the name Jesus, if we interpret it according to the method and principles of Kabbalah, signifies precisely all of this and nothing else, as follows: God, the

Son of God and the Wisdom of the Father united through the third person of the Deity (who is the hottest fire of Love) to human nature in the unity of the supposit.

8 From the preceding conclusion one can understand why Paul said that Jesus was given the name that is above every name and why it is said that every being in heaven, on earth and in the infernal regions bends the knee at the name of Jesus; this also has great Kabbalist meaning, as anyone who knows Kabbalah deeply can understand on his own.

10 What Kabbalists call מטטרון is beyond doubt what Orpheus names Pallas, Zoroaster the Mind of the Father, Mercury the Son of God, Pythagoras Wisdom, Parmenides the Intelligible Sphere.

11 The way (though Kabbalists leave it unspoken) in which rational souls are sacrificed to God by an archangel happens only by the soul's parting from the body, not the body's parting from the soul—except secondarily, as it happens in the death of the kiss, of which it is written: the death of his saints is precious in the sight of the Lord.

13 One who works at Kabbalah and mixes in nothing extraneous, if he stays long at the work, will die from *binsica*, and if he makes a mistake in the work or comes to it unpurified, he will be devoured by Azazel through the Attribute of Judgment.

14 Through the letter ש or *shin* that stands in the middle of the name Jesus we get meaning from Kabbalah—that the world was completely at rest, as if at its completion, when *iod* was joined with *vav* as it was done in Christ, who was really God's Son and a human being.

15 Through the name *iod he vav he*, the ineffable name that Kabbalists say will be the Messiah's name, we plainly recognize that he will be God, Son of God made man through the Holy Spirit, and that after him a Paraclete will descend upon mankind in order to perfect the human race.

16 From the mystery of the three letters that are in the term

shabbat or שבת, we can use Kabbalah to explain that the world keeps its Sabbath when the Son of God becomes human, and that the Sabbath will come for the last time when humans are reborn in the Son of God.

17 One who knows what the Purest Wine is for Kabbalists will know why David said *I will be made drunk on the bounty of your house*, and what the drunkenness was that the ancient prophet Musaeus called happiness, and what each of these Bacchi signifies according to Orpheus.

20 If Kabbalists attend to their interpretation of this term אז, which means *then*, they will be greatly enlightened about the mystery of the Trinity.

21 One who has joined a statement of the Kabbalists, saying that the Numeration called Just and the Redeemer is also called *zeh*, with a statement by Talmudists, saying that Isaac went like *zeh* carrying his cross, will see that what was prefigured in Isaac was fulfilled in Christ.

28 Through the term *et* that appears twice in the text, *in the beginning God created heaven and earth*, I believe that Moses means the creation of an intellectual nature and an animate nature which in the natural order came before the creation of heaven and earth.

30 Following their own principles, Kabbalists must necessarily grant that the true Messiah will have been such that we may truly say of him that he is God and God's Son.

32 If we connect the double *alef* in the text, *the scepter will not be taken away* and so on, to the double *alef* in the text, *God had me from the beginning*, and to the double *alef* in the text, *but the earth was empty*, we will understand by a method of Kabbalah that Jacob spoke there of the true Messiah who was Jesus of Nazareth.

33 Through this term איש, written with *alef*, *iod* and *scin* and meaning *man*, which is applied to God in the phrase *Man of War*, we are given an absolutely complete reminder of the mystery of the Trinity through a method of Kabbalah.

34 By the name הוא, the mystery of the Trinity along with the possibility of the Incarnation is revealed to us through a method of Kabbalah; this name, because it is written with the three letters *he, vav* and *alef*, is a name most properly applied to God, and this is most consistent not only with the Kabbalists, who often say it explicitly, but also with the theology of Dionysius the Areopagite.

36 From the preceding conclusion one can understand why Kabbalists say that God clothed himself in ten garments when he created the world.

37 One who understands the subordination of Piety to Wisdom in the grouping on the right will understand perfectly through a method of Kabbalah how Abraham in his Day saw the Day of Christ through a straight line and rejoiced.

38 The effects that followed the death of Christ should convince any Kabbalist that Jesus of Nazareth was the true Messiah.

39 From this conclusion and from the thirtieth above, it follows that any Kabbalist must grant that Jesus, when asked who he was, gave exactly the right answer, saying, I who speak to you am the Beginning.

41 In Kabbalah one can know through the mystery of the closed *mem* why Christ sent a Paraclete after him.

42 From principles of Kabbalah one knows how right Jesus was to say *before Abraham was born I am.*

47 Whoever knows the Attribute of the North Wind in Kabbalah will know why Satan promised Christ the kingdoms of the world if he would fall down and adore him.

56 If he is expert in Kabbalah, one who knows how to extend the quaternary into the denary will have a method for deriving the Name of 72 letters from the ineffable Name.

57 From the preceding conclusion one who understands formal arithmetic can understand that working through the *Shemhamforash* is proper to a rational nature.

59 Anyone who thinks deeply about the fourfold arrangement

of things—first, the unity and stability of remaining, second procession, third reversion, fourth blissful reunion—will see that the letter *bet* works first with the first letter, medially with a middle letter and last with the last letters.

60 From the preceding conclusion a thoughtful person can understand why the Law of God—of which it is written that it is spotless, that it was with God to put everything together, that it transforms souls, that it acts to bear fruit in its time—begins with the letter *bet*.

61 From the same conclusion one can know that the same Son who is the Father's Wisdom is the one who unites all things in the Father, through whom all were made, by whom all are returned and in whom at last all keep the Sabbath.

62 One who has thought deeply about the novenary number of beatitudes that Matthew writes about in the Gospel will see that they fit wonderfully with the novenary of nine Numerations that come beneath the first, which is the unapproachable abyss of the Deity.

63 Just as Aristotle himself concealed under the guise of philosophical speculation and obscured by terse expression the more divine philosophy that the ancient philosophers veiled under fables and stories, so Rabbi Moses of Egypt in the book that Latins call the *Guide for the Perplexed* embraces mysteries of Kabbalah through hidden interpretations of deep meaning while seeming through the outer bark of words to proceed philosophically.

65 It is more correct that *amen* should say *Tiferet* and Kingdom, as the method of number shows, than that it should say Kingdom only, as some suppose.

66 I relate our soul to the ten *Sefirot* in this way: through her unity she goes with the first, through intellect with the second, with the third through reason, the fourth through higher desire, the fifth through higher wrath, the sixth through free will, as she turns back through all of this to those above with the seventh and

with the eighth toward those below, then with the ninth mixing both, through indifference or cleaving to each in turn rather than holding back from both, and she goes with the tenth by her power to dwell in the first Dwelling.

67 Through a saying of Kabbalists that the heavens are made of fire and water, in one stroke we are shown both a theological truth about the *Sefirot* themselves and the philosophical truth that the elements are in the heavens only with regard to active power.

68 One who knows what the denary is in formal arithmetic and recognizes the nature of the first spherical number will know what I still have not read in any Kabbalist, which is that in Kabbalah this is the foundation of the secret of the Great Jubilee.

72 Just as a true astrology teaches us to read in the book of God, so Kabbalah teaches us to read in the book of the Law.

34

Colophon and Final Notice on pages 69 and 70 of the 1486 edition.

Printed at Rome by the work of the Honorable Eucharius Silber, alias Franck, on the seventh day of December in the year 1486 since the Lord's incarnation during the reign of the Supreme Pontiff, Innocent VIII, in the third year of his papacy.

These conclusions will be disputed only after Epiphany. Meanwhile they will be published in all the universities of Italy. And if any philosopher or theologian, even from distant parts of Italy, wishes to come to Rome and debate, the same Lord who intends to dispute also promises to cover the costs of travel from his own resources.

APPENDIX II

An Incomplete Early Draft of the Oration

Source: Florence, Biblioteca Nazionale Centrale, MS Palatino 885, fols.
143–53

This part of MS Palatino 885, first published by Eugenio Garin,
was copied from a draft of the *Oration* earlier than the final version, which was probably finished by December 1486, when Pico
published the *Conclusions*, but was not printed in full until 1496 in
Gianfrancesco Pico's collection of his uncle's works. In 1487 Pico
had only the latter part of the speech printed in his *Apology*, and
the Palatino is more complete for the previous part. In the manuscript's current state, one of its eleven leaves (fol. 146) is out of
order. At about 3,100 words, the draft is less than half the length
of the version published in 1496. At three points, sections of the
text had already fallen out of the copy from which the Palatino
was made, but the Palatino gives no indication of the gaps. Did
the copyist not notice them? Or did he see them but wanted a
close replica — including obvious mistakes — of the copy available
to him?[1]

The first piece missing from the Palatino corresponds to most
of paragraphs 20 through 25 of the 1496 version, where Job and
supernal peace are the subjects. On fol. 149[r], the manuscript has
percontemur et iustum Iob, qui foedus citemus et Mosem ipsum. . . ,
showing no break between *foedus,* where the gap starts, and *citemus,*
the first word of paragraph 26. Two other gaps correspond to paragraphs 27–29, on Bacchus and the Socratic frenzies, and 31–32, on
Pythagorean maxims — although the last rupture is not as sharp.

Otherwise, the manuscript transmits a state of the speech written before most of the final version was ready. This considerably

shorter draft also shows a few differences in order of exposition and contains a few passages not used in the final version. Paragraph 46 of the draft names Flavius Mithridates as Pico's language teacher, for example, but the 1496 version never mentions him. Large parts of that version missing from the draft — and perhaps not yet written — present most of Pico's self-defense as a disputant (paragraphs 36–46), his overview of the *Conclusions* (51–55), and the accounts of magic and Kabbalah (56–72) at the end of the speech.[2]

Before the draft was revised and Flavius was eliminated, Pico's relations with his translator and teacher of Kabbalah may not yet have hit bottom. The draft does not include the part of the 1496 version (paragraphs 63–68) devoted to Kabbalah, which the draft mentions only once (34). The last propositions printed in the *Conclusions*, toward the end of 1486, were seventy-two theses on Kabbalah: the absence of a full treatment of this topic from the draft suggests a date earlier rather than later in 1486, if not in the previous year, and the same goes for Pico's praise of Flavius.

The manuscript is untitled and names no author, but the copyist has been identified as Giovanni Nesi, who dedicated his *Oracle of a New Age* to Gianfrancesco Pico. He finished this book in September 1496, five months after Gianfrancesco published the final version of the *Oration*. Nesi's *Oracle* was *piagnone* propaganda, showing his sympathies for other friends of Savonarola, like the two Picos: this project could have motivated him to copy a manuscript of the *Oration*. Perhaps he reproduced the defects of what he copied because he wanted to work fast. But once Gianfrancesco put his much fuller version in print, Nesi had no reason to rely on the draft. Moreover, since he was close to Gianfrancesco, he may have seen the final version before it was published, once the nephew found a fuller text of Pico's speech after his uncle died on November 17, 1494. Circumstances suggest that Nesi copied the draft between that date and March 20, 1496, when Gianfrancesco released his collection of Pico's writings.[3]

Greek words (paragraphs 27, 28, 46) in a Latin text of this period are no surprise, but not so for Arabic letters (1), words in Hebrew (8, 41), and even more words in Ethiopic script (10, 33). Since Flavius knew these languages and advertised his skill in Ethiopic — utterly exotic in his day — he was almost certainly the source of Pico's belief that 'Chaldean' was a language like Hebrew, Aramaic, or Syriac though written in Ethiopic characters. But if Flavius was no longer in touch with Pico's friends in Florence after 1489 — according to the current consensus — who wrote the exotic characters in Nesi's manuscript? And why would Pico have wanted to put them there?[4]

An answer to the second question comes easier: *pour épater les bourgeois*. The good burghers were Pico's learned friends — shown by arcane erudition that the prince's learning, compared to theirs, was as Hyperion to a satyr. Even Poliziano would have been dazzled. For Pico to have meant such a manuscript to impress other intellectuals is more than plausible. That he would have relied on it in Rome to read his speech aloud is less likely — because of the exotic passages.

Had he opened the speech by pronouncing the Arabic in the first paragraph as *al-rajul* and then explaining it with *idest hominem*, an audience could have followed him. Likewise for paragraph 8 and 'Metatron' in Hebrew. In both cases, if the orator had Arabic or Hebrew on the page in front of him, he could easily have remembered a single word or name even without a prompt in Latin. As he read paragraph 10, however, and saw ten words in Ethiopic script, what would he have said? The script encodes a mixture of Hebrew and Aramaic — unintelligible to his listeners without the Latin that follows. The same problem, Hebrew and Aramaic words written in Ethiopic script, comes up in paragraph 33.

Our reading of *al-rajul* follows Bausi's text. But Angelo Piemontese, an expert on Persian and Arabic paleography, calls *al-rajul* a bad (*impertinente*) choice. Accepting Nesi as the scribe, he says that the Arabic is a "tracing" which is "crude" and hard to make out. He concludes that the signs on this page are not letters of a word but elements of a cryptogram. Perhaps so: Pico loved a good puzzle. Piemontese's solution amalgamates several Hebrew names of God in a few signs: this too would have pleased the prince. But if the orator planned to read his *Oration* aloud from an ancestor of the Palatino, how could he utter a cryptogram? Maybe someone in a crowd of learned prelates (or their staff) might recognize a little spoken Arabic — but not a piece of code.[5]

The draft (not Nesi's copy of the draft, the Palatino) was written some months, at least, before Pico could have needed a version to read in Rome. Such a reading text might have replaced Ethiopic characters with Roman letters to write Hebrew and Aramaic words. But this hypothetical text does not correspond to the text in Gianfrancesco's 1496 collection, where blank spaces were left in paragraphs 10 and 33 — though not in paragraph 1, where the Arabic occurs. Gianfrancesco's printer had type for Greek but not for Arabic, nor for Hebrew, Aramaic, or Ethiopic — the likeliest contents for blanks in the 1496 edition where the draft has Ethiopic script. Bausi's superb edition uses the draft to correct Gianfrancesco's text for Latin and Hebrew, and we have adopted most of these readings. The evidence of the draft is just as good, we believe, for the Ethiopic characters not shown in Bausi's text but thoroughly discussed in his notes.

Bausi based his decision on the "obscurity and uncertainty" of the Ethiopic passages first interpreted by Wirszubski. Aggravating the difficulty are (1) Nesi's role as the copyist of the draft, (2) the orthography and evolution of Ethiopic characters, and (3) the anomalous use of the script by Flavius and Pico to write non-

Ethiopian languages. This last complication means that the script—Ge'ez, a syllabary for several languages spoken in Ethiopia and elsewhere in northeast Africa—cannot be checked against any language normally encoded by it. Moreover, differences between signs in the syllabary—about two dozen alphabetic letters vocalized by scores of variations, larger and smaller, on the same signs—may be meaningful but hard to see in the Palatino, which was written during just one phase of the syllabary's evolution, after more than a millennium of development and probably not by a native or expert user of Ge'ez.[6]

There is no reason to think that Nesi was experienced with Ethiopic script. It is not impossible, however, that he simply reproduced Ethiopic characters mechanically, by drawing each letter like a picture without having any sense of its phonetic value or relation to other letters. If he did not write the Ethiopian passages, a different scribe could have been competent, more or less, in writing them but still lack the skill of a native or experienced user. Furthermore, we cannot know exactly what forms of Hebrew or Aramaic words were intended by Flavius or Pico. Hence, Bausi's judgment of obscurity is correct. Nonetheless, to the inexpert eyes (our own) of yet more readers who read no Ethiopian language, the script in the Florence manuscript seems to map well, more or less, on to the consonantal and vocalic sounds of the corresponding words in Hebrew and Aramaic. *Caldaeum est, non legitur*: as a guide to the evidence of the Palatino, this response may be more prudent than ours, though perhaps not as helpful to readers.

Otherwise, the text that follows is our transcription of *F*, checked against the edition in Bausi's *Appendice*. Unlike Bausi we have noted cancellations and preserved errors because of the importance of this unique document. Paragraph numbers correspond to those in *Orat*. The order of the paragraphs is somewhat different, however: we have followed the paragraph order of the manuscript, apart from the text on the misplaced leaf, which we have restored to its proper place. The redaction was preserved without a title.

NOTES

1. Eugenio Garin, "La Prima redazione dell' *Oratio de hominis dignitate*," in *La Cultura filosofica del rinascimento italiano* (Milan: Bompiani, 1994); *Bn*, pp. 141–92; Intro. at nn. 5–6, 32, 71, 105.

2. Intro. at n. 82. Bausi, who also edits the Palatino redaction in his *Appendice*, prints in italics the places where F differs from Ba.

3. *Bn*, pp. x, 159–60; Weinstein, *Savonarola and Florence*, pp. 192–205; Christopher Celenza, *Piety and Pythagoras in Renaissance Florence: The Symbolum Nesianum* (Leiden: Brill, 2001), pp. 34–52.

4. Intro. at nn. 50–52.

5. Angelo Michele Piemontese, "Pico, Moncada e Abdala Sarracenus nella *Oratio de hominis dignitate*," in *Flavio Mitridate mediatore fra culture nel contesto dell'ebraismo siciliano del xv secolo*, ed. Mauro Perani and Giacomo Corazzol (Palermo: Officina di Studi Medievali, 2012), pp. 105–36.

6. Getatchew Haile, "Ethiopic Writing," in *The World's Writing Systems*, ed. Peter Daniels and William Bright (Oxford: Oxford University Press, 1996), pp. 569–76.

The Palatino Redaction of the Oratio

Legi, patres colendissimi, in Arabum monumentis Abdalam pro-   1
phetam Sarracenum, cum eum rogarent eius discipuli quid in hac
quasi mundana[1] scena admirandum maxime spectaretur, الرجل,[2]
idest hominem, respondisse. Cui sententiae illud Mercurii astipu-
latur: Magnum, O Asclepi, miraculum est homo.

Horum dictorum rationem cogitanti mihi non satis illa facie-   2
bant, quae multa de humanae naturae praestantia afferuntur a
multis: esse hominem creaturarum internuntium, superis familiarem, regem inferiorum; sensuum perspicacia, rationis indagine,
intelligentiae lumine naturae interpretem; stabilis aevi et fluxi[3]
temporis interstitium, et (quod Magi dicunt) mundi copulam,[4]
immo hymeneum—ab angelis, teste Davide, paulo deminutum.
Magna haec quidem, sed non principalia, idest quae summe admirationis privilegium iure sibi vendicent. Cur enim non ipsos angelos et beatissimos caeli choros magis admiremur?

Tandem intellexisse mihi sum visus cur felicissimum proinde-   3
que dignum omni admiratione animal sit homo, et quae sit demum[5] illa conditio quam in universi serie sortitus sit, non brutis
modo, sed astris, sed ultramundanis mentibus invidiosam—res
supra fidem et mira! Quidni? Nam et propterea magnum miraculum et admirandum profecto animal iure homo et dicitur et existimatur. Sed quaenam ea sit audite, patres, pro vestra humanitate
hanc mihi operam condonate.

Iam summus Pater architectus Deus hanc quam videmus mun-   4
danam domum, divinitatis templum augustissimum, archanae legibus Sapientiae fabrefecerat. Supercaelestem regionem mentibus
decorarat; aethereos globos aethernis animis vegetarat; excremen-
tarias ac feculentas has mundi inferiores partes omnigena anima-
lium turba complerat. Sed opere consumato, desiderabat artifex
esse aliquem qui tanti operis rationem perpenderet, pulchritudi-

nem amaret, magnitudinem admiraretur. Iccirco iam rebus omnibus (ut Moses Thimaeusque testantur) absolutis, de producendo homine postremo cogitavit.

5   Verum nec erat in archetypis unde novam sobolem effigiet, nec in thesauris quod novo filio hereditarium largiatur, nec in subselliis totius orbis ubi universi contemplator iste sederet. Iam plena omnia; omnia summis, mediis infimisque ordinibus fuerant distributa. Sed non erat paternae Potestatis in extrema faetura quasi effaetam defecisse; non erat Sapientiae consilii inopia in re necessaria[6] fluctuasse; non erat benefici Amoris ut qui in aliis divinam esset liberalitatem laudaturus in se illam damnare cogeretur. Statuit tandem optimus Opifex ut cui dari nihil proprium poterat, ei commune esset quicquid privatum singulis fuerat. Igitur hominem accepit, indiscretae opus imaginis, atque in mundi positum meditullio sic est allocuutus.

6   Nec certam sedem, nec propriam faciem nec munus ullum peculiare tibi dedimus, o Adam, ut quam sedem, quam faciem, quae munera tute optaveris, ea pro voto, pro tua sententia habeas et possideas. Definita ceteris natura intra praescriptis a nobis leges coercetur. Tu, nullis angustiis coercitus, pro tuo arbitrio, in cuius manu te posui, tibi illam praefinies. Medium tete mundi posui, ut circumspiceres inde commodius quicquid est in mundo. Nec te caelestem neque terrenum, neque mortalem neque immortalem fecimus, ut, tui ipsius quasi arbitrarius plastes et fictor, in quam malueris tute notam effingas. Poteris in inferiora, quae bruta sunt, degenerare; poteris in superiora, quae sunt divina, ex tui animi sententia regenerari.

7   O summam Dei patris liberalitatem, summam hominis foelicitatem, cui datum id habere quod optat, id esse quod velit! Bruta, protinus[7] quam nascuntur, id secum afferunt — ut ait Lucilius, e vulva matris — quod possessura sunt. Supremi spiritus aut ab

initio aut paulo mox id fuerunt, quod sunt futuri in perpetuas
ethernitates. Nascenti homini omnifaria semina et omnigenae vitae germina indidit Pater, quae quisque excoluerit, illa[8] adolescent,
et fructus suos ferent in illo. Si vegetalia, planta fiet; si sensualia,
obrutescet; si rationalia, daemon evadet et caeleste animal; si intellectualia, angelus erit et Dei filius. Et si, nulla creaturarum sorte
contentus, in unitatis centrum suae se receperit, unus cum Deo
spiritus factus, in solitaria Patris caligine, quae est super omnia,
constitutus omnibus antestabit.

Quis hunc nostrum chameleonta non admiretur? Aut omnino   8
quis quicquam aliud admiretur magis?. Quem non immerito Asclepius Atheniensis, versipellis huius et se ipsam transformantis
naturae argumento, per Protheum in mysteriis significari dixit—
hinc illae apud Hebreos et Pythagoricos methamorphoses celebratae. Nam et Hebreorum theologia secretior nunc Enoch sanctum me[9] angelum divinitatis, quem vocant מטטרן,[10] nunc in alia
alios numina reformant; et Pythagorici scelestos homines et in
bruta deformant et, si Empedocli creditur, etiam in plantas. Quos
imitatus Maumeth illud frequens habet in ore, qui a divina lege
recesserit brutum evadere. Neque enim plantam cortex, sed stupida et nihil sentiens natura; nec iumenta corium, sed bruta anima
et sensualis; nec daemonem orbiculatum corpus, sed recta ratio;
nec sequestratio corporis, sed spiritualis intelligentia angelum facit.

Si quem enim videris deditum ventri, humi serpentem homi-   9
nem, frutex est, non homo, quem vides. Si quem in phantasie
quasi Calipsus vanis praestigiis caecutientem et subscalpenti delinitum illecebra, sensibus mancipatum, brutum est, non homo,
quem vides. Si recta philosophum ratione omnia discernentem,
hunc venereris: caeleste est animal, non terrenum. Si purum con-
templatorem corporis nescium, in penetralia mentis relegatum, hic
augustius est numen, humana carne circumvestitum.

Et quis hominem non admiretur? qui non immerito in sacris   10
litteris Mosaycis et Christianis nunc omnis carnis, nunc omnis

creaturae appellatione designatur, quando se ipsum ipse in omnis carnis faciem et in omnis creaturae ingenium effingit, fabricat
et transformat. Iccirco scribit Euantes Persa, ubi Chaldaicam theologiam enarrat, non esse homini suam ullam et nativam imaginem, extrarias multas et adventitias. Hinc illud Chaldeorum:
ብረሳው ሀ ሐይ ሚጠበ0 ሚሥታኔ ፱ናጷጷ ሚሞሐለጸተ ጋረሟሀ ከ
ወከ, idest homo variae ac multiformis et desultoriae naturae animal.[11]

11   Hac igitur conditione nati, hac praediti natura, ut id simus
quod esse volumus, quid curare potissimum debemus? Certe ut
non illud quidem in nos dicatur: cum in honore essemus, non cognovisse[12] similes factos brutis et iumentis insipientibus. Sed illud
potius Asaph prophaete: dii estis et filii Excelsi omnes, ne
abutentes indulgentissima Patris liberalitate, quam dedit ille liberam optionem e salutari noxiam faciamus nobis. Invadat animum
sacra quaedam et Iunonia ambitio, ut mediocribus non contenti
anhelemus ad summa, atque[13] illa — quando possumus, si volumus — consequenda enitamur. Dedignemur terrestria, caelestia
contemnamus, et, quicquid mundi est denique posthabentes,
ultramundanam curiam eminentissimae divinitati proximam advolemus. Ibi, ut sacra tradunt mysteria, Seraphin,[14] Cherubin et
Throni primas possident; horum iam nos, cedere nescii et secundarum impatientes, et dignitatem et gloriam emulemur. Erimus
illis, cum voluerimus, nihilo inferiores.

12   Sed qua ratione, aut quid tandem agentes? Videamus quid illi
agant, quam vivant vitam. Eam si et nos vixerimus — possumus
enim — illorum sortem iam aequaverimus.

13   Ardet Seraph charitatis igne; fulget Cherub intelligentiae splendore; stat Thronus iudicii firmitate. Igitur si actuosae addicti vitae
inferiorem curam recto examine susceperimus, Thronorum stata
soliditate firmabimur. Si ab actionibus feriati in opificio Opificem,
in Opifice opificium meditantes, in contemplandi otio negotiabi-
mur, luce Cherubica undique coruscabimus. Si charitate ipsum

Opificem solum ardebimus, illius igne, qui edax est, in Seraphicam effigiem repente flammabimur. Super Throno — idest iusto iudice — sedet Deus iudex saeculorum. Super Cherub — idest contemplatore — volat atque eum quasi incubando fovet. Spiritus enim Domini fertur super aquas — has inquam quae super caelos sunt, quae apud Iob Dominum laudant antelucanis hymnis. Qui Seraph — idest amator — est in Deo, est et Deus in eo, immo et Deus et ipse unum sunt.

Sed quonam pacto aut iudicare quisquam aut amare potest in- 14 cognita? Amavit Moses Deum quem vidit, et administravit iudex in populo quae vidit prius contemplator in monte. Ergo medius Cherub sua luce et Seraphico igni nos praeparat, et ad Thronorum iudicium pariter illuminat.

Hic est nodus primarum mentium, ordo Palladicus contempla- 15 tivae philosophiae praeses. Hic nobis emulandus primo et ambiendus atque adeo comprehendendus est ut se[15] ad amoris rapiamur fastigia, et ad munera actionum bene instructi paratique descendamus. At vero operae pretium, si ad exemplar vitae Cherubicae vita nostra formanda est,[16] quae illa et qualis sit, quae actiones, quae illorum opera, prae oculis et in numerato habere. Quod cum per nos, qui caro sumus et quae humi sunt sapimus, nobis consequi non liceat, adeamus antiquos patres, qui de his rebus utpote sibi domesticis et cognatis locupletissimam nobis et certam fidem facere possunt.

Consulamus Paulum apostolum, vas electionis, quid ipse, cum 16 ad tertium sublimatus est caelum, agentes Cherubinorum exercitus viderit. Respondebit utique, Dionysio interprete, purgari illos, tum illuminari, postremo perfici. Ergo et nos, Cherubicam in terris vitam emulantes, per moralem scientiam affectuum impetus cohercentes, per dialecticam rationis caliginem discutientes, quasi ignorantiae et vitiorum eluentes sordes animam purgemus, ne aut affectus temere debacchentur aut ratio imprudens quandoque deliret. Tum bene compositam ac[17] expiatam animam naturalis philosophiae lumine perfundamus, ut postremo divinarum rerum eam cognitione perficiamus.

17 Et ne nobis nostra sufficiant, veteris legis mysteria perscrutemur. Consulamus Iacob patriarcham, cuius imago in sede gloriae sculpta coruscat. Admonebit nos pater sapientissimus in inferno dormiens, mundo in superno vigilans. Sed admonebit per figuram (ita eis omnia contingebant): esse schalas ab imo solo ad caeli summa protensas, multorum graduum serie distinctas, fastigio Dominum insidere, contemplatores angelos per eas vicibus alternantes ascendere et descendere. Quod si hoc idem nobis angelicam affectantibus vitam factitandum est,[18] quaeso quis Domini schalas vel sordidato pede vel male mundis manibus attinget? Impuro purum attingere nephas.

18 Sed qui hi pedes? Quae manus? Profecto pes animae illa est portio despicatissima, qua ipsa materiae tanquam terrae solo innititur—altrix inquam potestas et cibaria—fomes libidinis et voluptariae mollitudinis magistra. Manus animae cur irascentiam non dixerimus, quae appetentiae propugnatrix pro ea decertat, et sub pulvere ac sole praedatrix rapit quae illa sub umbra dormitans helluetur? Has manus, hos pedes, ne a schalis tanquam prophani pollutique reiciamur, idest totam sensualem partem in qua sedet corporis illecebra quae animam obtorto,[19] ut aiunt, detinet collo, morali philosophia quasi vivo flumine abluamus.

19 At nec satis hoc erit, si per Iacob schalas discursantibus angelis comites esse volumus, nisi et a gradu in gradum rite promoveri, et a schalarum tramite deorbitare nusquam, et reciprocos obire excursus bene apti prius instructique fuerimus. Quod cum per artem sermocinalem sive rationariam erimus consecuti, iam Cherubico spiritu animati, per schalarum idest naturae gradus philosophantes, a centro ad centrum omnia pervadentes, nunc unum—quasi Osyrim—in multitudinem vi Titanica discerpentes descendemus, nunc multitudinem—quasi Osyridis membra—in unum vi Phebea colligentes ascendemus, donec, in sinu Patris—qui

super schalas est — tandem quiescentes, theologica foelicitate consumabimur.

    Percontemur et iustum Iob, qui foedus. . . . [20]   20

    Citemus et Mosem ipsum, a sacrosancte et ineffabilis intelligen-   26
tiae fontana plenitudine unde angeli suo nectare inebriantur, paulo
deminutum. Audiemus venerandum iudicem sic nobis in deserta
huius corporis solitudine habitantibus leges edicentem:

> Qui mores iam composuerunt, in sanctuarium recepti, non-
> dum quidem sacra attractent sed prius dialectico famulatu
> seduli Levitae philosophiae sacris ministrent. Tum ad ea ipsi
> admissi, nunc superioris Dei regiae multicolorem, idest side-
> reum aulicum ornatum; nunc caeleste candelabrum septem
> luminibus distinctum; nunc pellicea elementa in philoso-
> phiae sacerdotio contemplentur, ut postremo, per theologicae
> sublimitatis merita in templi adyta recepti, nullo imaginis
> intercedente velo divinitatis gloria perfruantur.

Hec nobis profecto Moses et imperat et imperando admonet,
excitat, inhortatur, ut per philosophiam ad futuram caelestem gloriam, dum possumus, iter paremus nobis.

    Verum enimvero nec Mosaica tantum aut Christiana mysteria   27
sed priscorum quoque theologia harum, de quibus disputaturus
accessi, liberalium artium et emolumenta nobis et dignitatem
ostendit. Quid enim aliud sibi volunt in Graecorum arcanis observati initiatorum gradus, quibus primo — hercle — per illas quas
diximus quasi februales artes, moralem et dialecticam, purificatis,
contingebat mysteriorum susceptio? Quae quid aliud esse potest
quam secretioris per philosophiam naturae interpretatio?[21] Tum
demum ita dispositis illa adveniebat ἐποπτεία, idest rerum divinarum per theologiae lumen inspectio. Quis talibus. . . .[22]

    . . . ipsa Apollinis nomina, si quis eorum significantias perscru-   30
tetur et latitantia mysteria, satis ostendent esse deum illum non
minus philosophum quam vatem. Quod cum Ammonius satis[23] sit

exequutus, non est cur ego aliter pertractem; sed subeant animum, patres, tria Delphica praecepta oppido his necessaria, qui non ficti, sed veri Apollinis, qui illuminat omnem animam venientem in hunc mundum, sacrosanctum et augustissimum templum introgressuri sunt: videbitis nil aliud illa nos admonere, quam ut tripartitam hanc, de qua est praesens disputatio, philosophiam totis viribus amplectamur. Illud enim $\mu\eta\delta\grave{\epsilon}\nu$ $\check{\alpha}\gamma\alpha\nu$ — idest ne quid nimis — virtutem[24] omnium normam et regulam per mediocritatis rationem, de qua moralis agit, recte praescribit. Tum illud $\gamma\nu\hat{\omega}\theta\iota$ $\sigma\epsilon\alpha\upsilon\tau\acute{o}\nu$ — idest cognosce te ipsum — ad totius naturae nos cognitionem, cuius et interstitium et quasi cinnus natura est hominis, excitat et inhortatur. Qui enim se cognoscit, in se omnia cognoscit, ut Zoroaster prius; deinde Plato in Alcibiade scripserunt. Postremo, hac cognitione per naturalem philosophiam illuminati, iam Deo proximi $\epsilon\hat{\imath}$ — idest es — dicentes, theologica salutatione verum Apollinem familiariter proindeque foeliciter apellabimus.

31   Consulamus et Pythagoram. . . . [25]

33   Recenseamus et Chaldeorum monumenta: videbimus (si illis creditur) per easdem artes patere viam mortalibus ad foelicitatem. Scribunt interpretes Chaldei verbum fuisse Zoroastris alatam esse animam, cumque alae exciderent, ferri illam praeceps in corpus, tum illis subcrescentibus ad superos revolare. Percunctantibus eum discipulis quo pacto alis bene plumantibus volucres animas sortirentur: Irrigetis — dixit — alas aquis vitae. Iterum sciscitantibus unde has aquas peterent, sic per parabolam (qui erat hominis mos) illis respondit:

Quatuor amnibus paradisus Dei abluitur et irrigatur; indidem salutaris nobis aquas hauriatis. Nomen ei qui ab aquilone ቀ𝒷ᴟ†, quod rectum denotat; ei qui ab occasu ኩጿርꞌነ, quod expiationem significat; ei qui ab ortu ነሀ𝒷ር, quod lumen sonat; ei qui a meridie ር⋅ሕᴼᎵᎢ†, quod nos pietatem interpretari possumus.[26]

Advertite animum et diligenter considerate, patres, quid haec   34
sibi velint Zoroastris oracula: profecto nihil aliud nisi ut morali
scientia, quasi undis Hibericis, oculorum sordes expiemus; dialectica, quasi boreali amussi, illorum aciem lineemus ad rectum; tum
in naturali contemplatione debile adhuc veritatis lumen, quasi
nascentis solis incunabula, pati assuescamus, ut tandem per theologicam pietatem et sacratissimum deorum cultum, quasi caelestes
aquilae, meridionalis solis fulgidissimum iubar fortiter perferamus.
Hae illae et a Davide decantatae primum, ab Augustino explicatae
latius, matutinae, meridianae[27] et vespertinae cognitiones. Haec
est·illa lux meridialis quae Seraphinos cremat, inflammat ad lineam et Cherubinos illuminat. Haec illa regio quam versus semper
antiquus pater Abraam proficiscebatur. Hic ille locus ubi immundis spiritualibus[28] locum non esse et Cabalistarum et Maurorum
dogmata tradiderunt.

Et si secretiorum aliquid mysteriorum fas est in publicum pro-   35
ferre, postquam et repens e[29] caelo casus nostri hominis caput
vertigine damnavit, et — iuxta Hieremiam — ingressa per fenestras
mors iecur pectusque male affecit, Raphaelem caelestem medicum
advocemus, qui nos morali et dialectica uti pharmacis salutaribus
liberet. Tum ad valitudinem bonam restitutos iam Dei robur
Gabriel inhabitabit, qui nos per naturae ducens miracula, ubique
Dei potestatem virtutemque indicans, tandem sacerdoti summo
Michaeli nos tradet, qui sub stipendiis philosophiae emeritos
theologiae sacerdotio quasi corona pretiosi lapidis insignet.

Haec sunt, patres colendissimi, quae me ad philosophiae stu-   36
dium non animarunt adeo sed compulerunt.[30]

Quam quidem ut tam plene consequerer quam sequebar arden-   46
ter, duo in primis conducere semper existimavi. Primum id fuit, in
nullius verba iurare,[31] sed se[32] per omnes philosophiae magistros
fundere, omnes scedas excutere, omnes familias agnoscere. Vidi
ad hoc munus necessariam esse non Grecae modo et Latinae sed

Hebraicae quoque atque Chaldaicae et, cui nunc primum sub Mithridate Gulielmo harum linguarum interprete peritissimo insudare coepi, Arabicae linguae cognitionem.

50   Ferme enim omnis sapientia a barbaris ad Graecos, a Graecis ad nos[33] manavit. Ita nostrates semper in philosophandi ratione peregrinis inventis stare et aliena excoluisse sibi duxerunt satis. Sacras omnino litteras et mysteria secretiora ab Hebreis primum atque Chaldeis, tum a Graecis petere necessarium. Reliquas artes et omnifariam philosophiam cum Graecis Arabes partiuntur. Quos qui non adit, qui in illis progredietur, quando permulti hique pretiosiores eorum libri ad nostros nullo interprete pervenerunt, et horum qui pervenerunt tum plures inverterunt potius quam converterunt illi interpretes, tum certe omnibus eam caliginem obscuritatis offuderunt; ut quae apud suos facilia, nitida et expedita sunt, apud nostros scrupea facta, fusca et laciniosa studiosorum conatum eludant plurimum atque frustrentur?

46   Fuit autem cum ab antiquis omnibus observatum hoc, ut omne scriptorum genus evolventes nullas prorsus quas possent commentationes illectas praeterirent, tum maxime ab Aristotele, qui eam ob causam ἀναγνώστης — idest lector — a Platone nuncupabatur. Et profecto angustae est mentis intra unam se Porticum aut Achademiam continuisse. Nec ‹potest› ex omnibus sibi propriam recte selegisse, qui prius omnes familiaritates non agnoverit. Nemo aut fuit olim aut post nos erit cui se totam dederit veritas comprehendendam: maior illius immensitas quam ut par sit ei humana capacitas. Videas in unaquaque familia aliquid insigne quod non sit ei commune cum ceteris.

47   Atque ut a nostris, ad quos postremo philosophia pervenit, nunc exordiar. Est in Ioanne Scoto vegetum quoddam atque discussum, in Thoma solidum et aequabile, in Aegidio tersum et examinatum, in Francisco acre et acutum, in Alberto priscum, amplum et magnum, in Henrico — ut mihi visum est — semper sublime et venerandum. Est apud Arabes in Averoe firmum et in-

concussum, in Avempace, in Alpharabio grave et meditatum, in Avicenna divinum et Platonicum. Est apud Grecos in universum quidem nitida, in primis et casta philosophia. Apud Simplicium locuples et copiosa, apud Themistium elegans et compendiaria, apud Alexandrum constans et docta, apud Theophrastum graviter elaborata, apud Ammonium enodis et gratiosa.

Et si ad Platonicos te converteris — ut paucos percenseam — in Porphyrio rerum copia et multiiuga religione delectaberis; in Iamblico secretiorem philosophiam et barbarorum mysteria veneraberis; in Plotino privum quicquam non est quod admireris, qui se undique praebet admirandum, quem de divinis divine, de humanis longe supra hominem docta sermonis obliquitate loquentem sudantes Platonici vix intelligunt. Praetereo magis novicios, Proclum Asiatica fertilitate luxuriantem, et qui ab eo fluxerunt, Hermiam, Damascium, Olympiodorum et complures alios, in quibus omnibus illud τὸ θεῖον — idest divinum — peculiare Platonicorum symbolum, elucet semper.[34]   48

Acceditque,[35] si qua est haeresis quae veriora incessat dogmata et bonas causas ingenii calumnia ludificetur, veritatem[36] firmat, non infirmat, et velut motu· quassatam flammam excitat, non extinguit, sane hoc veritatis privilegio, ut vinci nesciat, et contorta in eam spicula in auctores redeant.   49

Alterum quod mihi ego ad philosophiae consecutionem utilissimum iudicavi hoc fuit, ut in disputandi exercitatione essem frequentissimus. Sicut enim per gymnasticam corporis vires firmiores fiunt, ita dubio procul in hac quasi litteraria palestra animi vires et fortiores longe et vegetiores evadunt. Nec crediderim ego aut poetas aliud per decantata Palladis arma, aut Hebreos cum ברזל, idest ferrum, שלחכמים, idest sapientum symbolum dicunt, significasse nobis quam honestissima hoc genus certamina adipiscendae sapientiae oppido quam necessaria. Quo forte fit ut et Chaldei, in eius genesi qui philosophus sit futurus, illud desiderent ut Mars Mercurium aspectu triquetro conspiciat.   41

Est autem pugnis Palladis hoc peculiare, quod in eis lucrum est 43
vinci. Quo fit ut imbecillimus quisque non detrectare modo, sed
appetere ultro illas et iure possit et debeat, quandoquidem qui
succumbit beneficium a victore accepit,[37] non iniuriam, quippe qui
per eum et locupletior domum, id est doctior, et ad futuras pugnas
redit instructior. Hac ego spe infirmus miles, et qui e tyronatus
modo rudimentis excessi, cum fortissimis omnium strenuissimisque non decertaturus, sed vincendus descendi, nil veritus (quae
est vestra excellens in omni scientiarum genere doctrina) futurum
hunc mihi congressum ad usum maximum proindeque voluptatem
non mediocrem; quam ne mihi ipse egomet morer,

72   quasi citante classico iam conseramus manus.

APPENDIX III

Abraham's Journey through the Sefirot

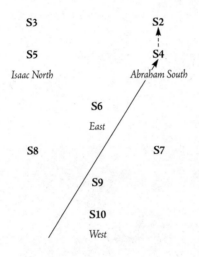

APPENDIX IV

Notabilia *to the* Life *and* Oration
in the Bologna Edition (1496)

The *notabilia* or "things worth noting" printed in the margin of the
1496 Bologna edition (B) have never to our knowledge been included in modern editions of either text before. But they were an
integral part of the way the texts were presented to contemporary
readers, and might conceivably be the work of Gianfrancesco Pico,
who edited the volume for publication. Given the interest of book
historians today in paratexts, it seemed worthwhile to include
them. The *notabilia* are keyed to the paragraph numbers.

IOANNIS PICI MIRANDULAE VITA

2   Paternum genus.
3   Mater Iulia. Ioannes Franciscus pater. Galeottus Antonius
      Maria fratres. Sorores. Albertus Pius.
4   Prodigium.
5   Ambrosius. Paulinus.
6   Forma et corporis habitudo.
7   Profectus in studiis humanitatis aetate tenella. Ingenium
      velox.
8   Ius pontificium puer caluit.
10 Nongentas disputande conclusiones Romae proposite.
11 Origines. Hilarius.
13 Bonfranciscus Regiensis episcopus.
14 Apologia.
15 Innocentius octavus pontifex. Alexander sextus.
16 Nota.
17 Alexander. Auerrois.

18 Dei bonitas.

19 Conversio ad deum.

20 Cicero. Exusta amatoria carmina.

21 Studium litterarum sacrarum.

22 Quid de sacris litteris pronuntiant Pauli epistolae.

23 Eloquia legis ueteris. Augustinus. Septimius. Eusebius.
Cassiodorus.

24 Libellus de ente et uno. Nota.

25 Antonius Faventinus.

26 Nonnulla platonica.

27 Vetus testamentum interpretatum.

28 Libellus de ueritate translationis Hieronymi. Libellus de
uera temporum supputatione.

32 Ptolomaei centiloquium e graeco in latinum uersum.

34 Nota.

35 Concordia Platonis ac Aristotelis.

40 Musica exculta

41 Epistole multiformes

42 Probatus dicendi character. Dicendi genera: copiosum,
breue, siccum, floridum et pingue.

45 Velocitas legendi.

47 Thomas Aquinas. Gorgias Leontinus.

48 Scoti acumen. Aureolus.

49 Hercules Estensis. Adagium.

51 Captiunculae sophistarum. Suiseticae quisquiliae.

53 Quinque causae mirabilium effectuum. Septem aureorum
nummum milia in comparandis
libris erogata.

56 Erogatio in pauperes. Mediocris mensa.

57 Hieronimus. Proprium corpus caesum flagris.

58 Vultus hilaris. Mitis natura. Constantia animi.

59 Quinque linguarum notitia. Seneca.

60 A duobus regibus oblatae dignitates & reiecte. Diuitiae
    propter Deum & propter studia
    neglectae.
61 Pandulphus Collenucius.
62 Ambrosius. Augustinus. Martinus. Celestinus.
63 Contemptor humanae gloriae.
64 Nota.
65 Vera Christianae mentis institutio. Quid de amando &
    cognoscendo deo in hac uita
    iudicarit.
66 Eullogium quod in ore habebat frequens.
67 Liberalitas nimia.
69 In amicos beneuolentia. Duo saluberrima remedia aduersus
    vitia. Similitudo amoris causa.
70 Horatius.
71 Libertas animi. Blancha Maria Estensis.
72 Angelus Politianus. Marsilius Ficinus.
73 Exterioris latriae cultus. Verus Dei cultus interioris latriae
    cultus. Feruor amoris in Deum.
74 Quo anno uitae sit mortuus. Qualiter in infirmitate se
    gesserit.
75 Christiani hominis finis laudandus narratur. Dei imago.
76 Albertus Pius. Alexander ex Aphrodisiade. Themistius.
    Auerrois.
77 Caeli reginam ad egrotantem nocte accessisse.
79 Obitum eius omnes gradus hominum molestia affecisse.
80 Laus fratris Hieronymi Sauonarolae. Apuleius.
81 Verba fratris Hieronymi.
84 Elemosinae. Status animae.
85 Duplex mors.
87 Laus doctrinae et probitatis fratris Hieronymi.

ORATIO IOANNIS PICI MIRANDULAE
CONCORDIAE COMITIS

1	Abdala sarracenus.
1	Mercurius.
2	Hominis dignitatis. Perse. Dauid.
4	Moses. Timaeus.
6	Voluntas libera in homine.
7	Lucilius. Nota.
8	Asclepius Atheniensis. Hebrei. Pythagorici. Empedocles. Maumeth.
9	Nota.
10	Mosaice & Christianae littere. Euantes Persa. Chaldei. Nota.
11	Asaph propheta. Seraphin. Cherubin. Throni.
13	Seraph. Cherub. Thronus. Iob.
14	Moses.
16	Paulus apostolus. Dyonisius.
17	Iacob.
18	Pes animae. Manus animae.
20	Iob. Empedocles.
21	Multiplex in nobis discordia.
22	Philosophia moralis. Dyalectica. Philosophia naturalis. Heraclitus. Homerus.
23	Sanctissima theologia.
24	Amicitia. Pythagorici. Pax optanda.
25	Preciosa in conspectu Dei mors sanctorum.
26	Moses. Sacerdotes Thessali.
27	Grecorum archana.
28	Socratici furores. Bacchus. Moses.
29	Phoebei uates.
30	Ammonius. Tria Delphica precepta. Zoroaster. Plato.

31 Pythagoras sapiens. Declaratio preceptorum Pythagorae.

32 Gallus. Iob. Socrates.

33 Chaldei. Interpretes Chaldei. Zoroaster.

34 Dauid. Augustinus. Antiquus pater Abraam. Cabaliste.
      Mauri.

35 Hieremias. Raphael. Gabriel. Michael.

37 Nota. Nota. Quid ipsum docuerit philosophia.

38 Nota.

39 Aetas auctoris.

40 Plato.

41 Poete. Hebrei. Chaldei.

42 Iob. Timotheus.

44 Cicero.

45 Gorgias Leontinus.

46 Antiquorum obseruatio. Aristoteles. Plato.

47 Ioannes Scotus. Thomas. Egidius. Franciscus. Albertus.
      Henricus. Auerrois. Auempace.
      Alpharabius. Auicenna. Simplicius. Themistius. Alexander.
      Theophrastus. Ammonius.

48 Porphirius. Iamblicus. Plotinus. Proculus. Hermias.
      Damasc‹i›us. Olimpiodorus. Plato.

50 Peripatetici. Platonici. Augustinus.

51 Seneca.

52 Mercurius Trismegistus.

53 Aristotelis Platonisque concordia. Boetius. Simplicius.
      Augustinus. Ioannes Grammaticus.

54 Duo & septuaginta dogmata physica & methaphisica.

55 Noua per numeros philosophandi institutio. Plato.
      Aristoteles. Abumasar. Auenzoar.

56 Magica theoremata. Duplex magia. Porphirius. Magus quid
      significet lingua Persarum.

57 Xamolsides. Abbaris Hiperboreus. Zoroaster.

APPENDIX V

Gianfrancesco Pico's Argumentum
to his Edition of Pico's Oration and Letters

Source: B, sign. QQ1v.

Argumentum Ioannis Francisci Pici Mirandulae etc. in *Orationem* et *Epistolas* Ioannis Pici patrui etc.

Accipe, lector, et has Ioannis Pici Mirandulae lucubrationes, leuioris curae opera, quas forte nec ipse uiuens inuulgasset nec nos, nisi celebratorum hominum crebris adhortamentis excitati.

Leges primum *Orationem* elegantissimam iuuenili quidem alacritate dictatam, sed a doctioribus prae doctrine et eloquentie fastigio sepius admiratam. Nec te moueat si plurima in eius calce conuisuntur quae et in *Apologie* sunt inserta prohemio, quando illud foras publicauerit, hanc domi semper tenuerit, nec nisi amicis comunem fecerit. Videbis pleraque antiquorum dogmata, abstrusa prius in aenigmatis et fabularum inuolucris, ingeniosissime reserata conatumque illum et robore et delinimentis oratoriis ostendere — quam priscorum sapientum poetica theologia nostre theologie mysteriis ancillaretur — atque utriusque nodis quibusdam enodatis ad litterarias palestras homines inuitare. In his enim per id tempus frequentissimus fuit quas postea, quasi grauiorum studiorum preludia ludicrasque pugnas derelinquens, ad ea, quae iam emissimus queque sumus in posterum emissuri, emolienda conuertit animum.

Leges et nonnullas epistolas (omnes enim collegisse laboriosissimum): alias familiares tum per etatem teneram tum prouectiorem scriptitatas, alias postquam totum pectus deo dicauit, sanctissimis refertas monitis exaratas. Illas et doctrinam et eloquentiam olere

copiosissime deprehendes; has et utrumque affatim sapere et Christi amorem preter hec uberrime spirare percipies.

[*English translation*]

Headnote by Gianfrancesco Pico della Mirandola to the *Oration* and *Letters* by Giovanni Pico, his uncle.

Dear reader: please also accept these less weighty efforts by Giovanni Pico della Mirandola: were he alive, he might not have made them public, nor would I have been enthusiastic had distinguished people not insisted.

First, please read an oration of the utmost elegance which, though written in the eagerness of youth, has often been admired by the learned as the pinnacle of learning and eloquence. Don't be disturbed if you notice that much of the material at the end contains passages inserted into the *Apology* as an introduction. Although he made the latter work public, he always kept the former private and shared it with no one but his friends. You'll see that he has very cleverly unlocked many recondite teachings of the ancients previously shrouded in fables and riddles. He strove mightily and with charms of oratory to show how the poetic theology of ancient sages was handmaid to the mysteries of our theology, and he tried to attract people to intellectual combat by unraveling various tangles of both. At that time he was an avid student of such matters, later abandoning them as trivial squabbles and preliminaries to serious study, as he moved on to what I have already published, then turned his attention to the work that I shall publish.[1]

You'll also read a selection of letters (since it would have been too difficult to collect them all): some are personal, written both when he was young and when he was older, while others, composed after he had given his whole heart to God, are filled with admonishments of great holiness. You'll discover that the former

196

are richly redolent of learning and eloquence, but from the latter, above and beyond their strong flavor of both those qualities, you'll also perceive that they breathe out the love of Christ in great abundance.[2]

NOTES

1. That is, the *Disputationes adversus astrologium divinatricem*, the second half of Gianfrancesco's 1496 edition of Giovanni Pico's works.

2. For Gianfrancesco's selection from Pico's letters, see the introduction to Francesco Borghesi's edition of the *Lettere*, pp. 21–32. The 1496 edition contained forty-seven of the seventy-four letters known today.

Note on the Texts and on Sources

࿐࿐࿐

EDITORIAL PRINCIPLES

The basis of both works edited here is *B*, which is the *editio princeps* (1496) of the *Life* of Pico by his nephew and also of the *Oration*; this edition was overseen by Gianfrancesco Pico.[1] The spelling in our edition follows that of *B* for both works, except that we have printed semivowel *u* as *v*. Punctuation and capitalization have been modernized. We have added paragraph numbers in accordance with the rubrics of this I Tatti series.

For the *Life*, we have checked our readings against *Y*, the Latin text prepared for the Yale Edition of the Complete Works of St. Thomas More, which records the variants of the five early editions printed before More prepared his English version (about 1510). These later editions sometimes correct obvious printing errors in *B*, and in these cases we have silently preferred the later readings. More substantive corrections taken from the later editions, as noted by *Y*, have been recorded.

For the text of *Oration* we have consulted Bausi's edition (*Ba*) with its textual notes (*Bn*). Bausi's superb critical edition of the speech has been indispensable, both for textual issues and for other information. For editorial purposes, we have not used other translations and editions of the *Oration*, many of which are considered in *Bn*.

Appendix I contains a selection, in English translation only, of those *Conclusiones* most relevant to understanding the *Oration*, especially those referred to in our commentary. A full edition and translation of the *Conclusiones* will be presented in a future volume of this I Tatti series. A partial manuscript of the speech, *F*, is described and transcribed in Appendix II. *F* corresponds mainly to the first half of the *Oration* and antedates the text in *B*.[2] Appendix III provides for the reader's convenience a diagram of Abraham's journey through the Sephirot. The *notabilia* printed with both texts are edited in Appendix IV. Appendix V provides a text and translation of Gianfrancesco Pico's *argumentum*, or headnote, to his edition of the *Oration* and a selection of his uncle's letters.

For other works by Pico published in his lifetime or shortly after, we have used the earliest Latin versions (*Apol.*, *Concl.*, *Hept.*, and *B*) rather than later editions. When Pico used the second half of the *Oration* in his *Apology*, his aim was not to introduce the *900 Conclusions*, which is a primary purpose of the speech, but to defend propositions condemned by Pope Innocent VIII. This motive makes the *Apology* a problematic witness for the speech. Its first edition fills 115 closely printed pages, which Pico claimed to have produced in less than three weeks. Working so fast, as Bausi points out, the prince had little time to make changes in the part of the *Oration* that he used—only three substantive additions, for example. By the same token, there was also little time to check the text of what he copied. In any case, *Ba* includes Bausi's collation of the *Apology* (with the text of the three additions), for which we have relied on his judgment.[3]

SOURCES

Gianfrancesco Pico's evidence for his *Life* of his uncle came mainly from his own experience, from his acquaintance with family and friends, and from Giovanni's writings, which he edited in order to produce *B*. Christian hagiography—in particular, the *Life* of Ambrose by Paulinus of Milan—gave him a narrative model. Savonarola's prophecies and preaching provided inspiration and a point of view. Although most of the authorities he mentioned and the texts he cited came from the prince's writings, Gianfrancesco was a learned person in his own right by the time he wrote this biography—at the age of twenty-six.

The biblical, classical, patristic, and medieval works that interested Gianfrancesco personally are those one might expect, though some are just decorative—works by Apuleius, Cicero, Gellius, Horace, Macrobius, Ovid, both Plinys, Quintilian, pseudo-Sallust, Seneca, Tacitus, and possibly Vitruvius among Latin authors; by Aristotle, Diogenes Laertius, and Philostratus among the pagan Greeks; and by the Areopagite, Augustine, and Lactantius among the Fathers. But when Gianfrancesco mentioned Averroes and two commentators on Aristotle—Alexander of

Aphrodisias and Themistius—some of his own views on the contentious issue of naturalism may have been taking shape.[4]

For the most part, Gianfrancesco declared his sources openly or left them in plain view. But explicit citations and obvious allusions are insufficient clues to his uncle's sources in the *Oration*—an aggressively esoteric project. For example, the speech names Proclus only once, in passing, to make a minor point about style, even though fifty-five of the nine hundred theses introduced by the speech are listed under his name. Read in light of all the theses "regarding Proclus" and in conjunction with those on Kabbalah, the most explosive theological innovation in the speech is a triad of Trinities derived from Kabbalah with help from Proclus. As for Kabbalah itself, the *Oration* names none of the authors or titles of books on that topic that the orator bragged about buying "at no small cost."[5]

The trail of influence left concealed by the speech leads far beyond authors named, titles mentioned, and transparent allusions. Some evidence has been masked so well, no doubt, that it will stay that way, and some of our identifications may be wrong. Taking that risk, we have cited sources of two kinds in the notes to our English translation of the *Oration*: *textual* sources, to identify authorities used, though often not named, by Pico to support his arguments and assertions, along with *intertextual and contextual* sources, to identify other relevant information known to Pico or available to him and also informative, we hope, to readers.

Tracking the speech's sources has required dense citation. For that reason, our notes to the *Oration* (unlike our notes to the *Life*) refer only to primary sources, although in a few exceptional cases we have cited secondary sources needed to identify primary sources. Scholars have been writing about Pico for more than five centuries. Cassirer, Garin, Gentile, and Kristeller analyzed his work from one point of view; from another perspective, Idel and Wirszubski—following in Scholem's footsteps—showed how his project was grounded in Kabbalah. Perched on the shoulders of giants while feeding on their labors, we can only wish it were possible to record their achievements in detail.[6]

Since space and time prevent paying these debts in full, suffice it to divide the *Oration*'s primary authorities and sources, textual and contextual, into four groups: first, canonical biblical texts, both Hebrew and Greek, as well as apocrypha and pseudepigrapha; next, ancient Greek and Latin writers; also patristic, medieval, and later authors; and finally, books of Kabbalah and related Hebraica.

Pico thought that Kabbalah was a lost key to the Hebrew scriptures, which fill his speech from beginning to end — from Adam's creation, Eden's rivers, and Jacob's ladder in Genesis through the wilderness journeys of the Pentateuch to visions of Ezekiel and a noncanonical Ezra. Prophets interested him more than chroniclers, but his favorites were sacred poets — especially the Psalmists. Job and the Song of Songs were valuable because of their roles in Kabbalah. But Paul was the first of the "ancient Fathers" whom he consulted — the "chosen vessel" who was born a Jew. Pico named him three times in the speech, where his Epistles and letters by other early Christians are as visible as the Gospels.

About a hundred and twenty classical texts by about fifty pagan authors are textual, intertextual, or contextual sources for the *Oration*. Most are in Latin, but a single Greek writer — Plato — produced nineteen works that informed the speech, though fewer of them (*Alcibiades, Charmides, Epinomis, Letters, Phaedrus*) are actually mentioned. Plato is the author named most often — eighteen times, ten more than Aristotle — not counting ten additional mentions of later Platonic thinkers and ideas. Besides twenty-three works by Damascius, Iamblichus, Julian, Plotinus, Porphyry, Proclus, Psellus, Simplicius, Synesius, and Timaeus of Locri, nine titles credited to Plutarch — an eclectic with Platonic instincts — were also important to Pico or may be informative to his readers. Absolutely crucial for his "poetic theology" were the fragmentary *Chaldean Oracles* and inscrutable *Orphic Hymns*. Pico's ladder with seven steps was like the route to salvation explored by the Chaldeans, whose verses Proclus read along with the *Hymns* as expressions of Platonic piety.

After tallying these texts and listing their authors, one might conclude that Pico was a Platonist — like his friend Ficino — and that his speech was a manifesto for Platonism. But the *Oration* was written to introduce the *Conclusions*, where the prince was enthusiastic about Plato, to be sure, but also fascinated by the technical side of medieval Aristotelianism. In the second group (T2) of theses that Pico claimed as his own, he dedicated a large block of sixty-one propositions to Plato, but he gave two hundred theses of the first group (T1) to Muslim and Christian scholastics, and many T2 theses are of the same type. His principle of concord started with Plato and Aristotle but also covered not only Scotus and Thomas but Averroes and Avicenna as well. Despite the prince's admiration for Plato, Ficino himself noticed—more than once—that his project and Pico's were different.[7]

Pico and his friend, who disagreed as philosophers on matters of substance, also expressed their philosophies in different ways. Pico's exchange with Barbaro, before he wrote the *Oration*, shows that he was careful and self-conscious about style. Some of the Latin classics that he used in the speech—Apuleius especially—helped him shape its exquisite language, whose elegance is sometimes labored and obscure. Like everyone else in his day who wrote Latin, the prince imitated Cicero—while dropping his name only once. Catullus, Horace, Lucan, Lucilius, Lucretius, Ovid, Plautus, Propertius, Statius, Terence, and Vergil all show up in various ways, in the text or behind it. To make the *Oration* eloquent, these Latin poets interested the orator as much as prose writers: both Plinys, Quintilian, both Senecas, Suetonius, and Valerius Maximus supplied words to live by, rules for writing, and other assorted information.[8]

Augustine, Jerome, and Origen are Church Fathers who stand out in the speech—especially Augustine. But the Platonist Areopagite is the Christian who dominates the *Oration*. Pico named him three times to interpret Paul's epistles, to authenticate an esoteric approach to Christian doctrine, and to legitimate a poetic spirituality derived from ancient Platonism. Toward the end of the speech, the Areopagite enters for the last time in a group of eminent authorities who certify "things we read every day in Paul and Dionysius, in Jerome and Augustine"—the point being that these doctrines were also teachings of Kabbalah. All the Areopagite's works—including the *Letters*—were in play, but it was the *Celestial Hierarchy* that gave Pico an angelology to reinforce the angel magic of Kabbalah.

The prince read dozens of books of Kabbalah and related Hebraica but named none of their authors or titles, although in many cases he knew both—as inventories of his library show. The two most important for his speech and for the *Conclusions* were Abraham Abulafia, whose ecstatic mysticism he found compatible with the spirituality of the Areopagite, and Menahem Recanati, who summarized the sefirotic theosophy of the *Zohar* — a basic text of Kabbalah that Pico himself may never have seen. What he did see — and often annotated — are manuscripts of Kabbalah, now in the Vatican, translated mainly by his tutor and employee, Flavius Mithridates, a whole library now being published by Giulio Busi and associates. But in his quest for secrets of Jewish sages, Pico did not distinguish systematically between Kabbalah, in the strict sense, and other texts in Hebrew and Aramaic, including Targums, Talmud, Midrash, and other rabbinic writings.[9]

Items in the following lists are cited in our notes to the English translations of the *Oration* and the *Life*. The numbers in these lists correspond *to the notes*, not to paragraph numbers.

A. Bible and Koran

Genesis	*Orat.* 4, 6, 8, 10, 12, 16, 19, 25, 32, 33
	Vit. 73
Exodus	*Orat.* 7, 13, 25, 67
Leviticus	*Orat.* 8
Numbers	*Orat.* 25, 27, 65
	Vit. 72
Deuteronomy	*Orat.* 33, 67
Ruth	*Orat.* 17
2 Samuel	*Orat.* 17
1 Chronicles	*Orat.* 25
Ezra (1 Esdras Vulgate)	*Orat.* 65
Ezra (4 Esdras Vulgate)	*Orat.* 63, 65, 66
Job	*Orat.* 12, 17, 19, 23, 31, 41
Psalms	*Orat.* 2, 4, 7, 11, 12, 17, 23, 24, 27, 30, 33, 34
Proverbs	*Orat.* 31, 40
Ecclesiastes	*Orat.* 40, 42
Song of Songs	*Orat.* 24

Isaiah	*Orat.* 4, 15, 19, 27, 28, 48, 60
	Vit. 73
Jeremiah	*Orat.* 27, 28, 30, 34
Ezekiel	*Orat.* 12, 16, 18, 25, 32
Daniel	*Orat.* 19, 35
Habakkuk	*Orat.* 60
	Vit. 72
Tobit	*Orat.* 34
Wisdom	*Orat.* 4
Ecclesiasticus	*Orat.* 8, 63
	Vit. 54
3 Enoch	*Orat.* 8
Matthew	*Orat.* 17, 22, 24, 31, 35, 42, 63
	Vit. 70, 72
Luke	*Orat.* 23, 42
John	*Orat.* 12, 22, 24, 29, 33
	Vit. 64
Acts	*Orat.* 10, 15, 24, 35, 39, 48
	Vit. 19
Romans	*Orat.* 10, 14, 27, 60, 63
1 Corinthians	*Orat.* 4, 5, 12, 34, 36, 60, 63
2 Corinthians	*Orat.* 15, 21, 63
Galatians	*Orat.* 28
Philippians	*Orat.* 14, 42
1 Thessalonians	*Vit.* 72
1 Timothy	*Orat.* 41
Hebrews	*Orat.* 25, 27, 31
James	*Vit.* 27
1 Peter	*Orat.* 10
2 Peter	*Vit.* 72
1 John	*Orat.* 26
	Vit. 72
Revelation	*Orat.* 25, 26, 27, 36, 60
Koran	*Orat.* 8, 33

B. Greek and Latin Classics

Apuleius
    Apologia   *Orat.* 7, 54, 55, 56, 57, 59
                               Vit. 29
    De dogmate Platonis   *Orat.* 4, 5
    Metamorphoses   *Orat.* 5, 10
                               Vit. 35, 43, 63
Aristotle
    De caelo   *Orat.* 54
    De divinatione per somnia   *Vit.* 71
    Ethica Eudemia   *Vit.* 44
    Ethica Nicomachea   *Orat.* 8, 9
    Historia animalium   *Orat.* 8, 59
    Meteorologica   *Orat.* 54
    [De Mirabilibus auscultationibus]   *Orat.* 8
    [*Problemata*]   *Orat.* 40, 54
    Fragments   *Orat.* 26
Caesar
    Bellum civile   *Orat.* 42
Catullus   *Orat.* 29
Calcidius
    In Platonis Timaeum   *Orat.* 5, 8
Cicero
    Academica   *Orat.* 54
    De divinatione   *Orat.* 26, 42, 57
    De finibus   *Orat.* 35, 37, 38, 43, 54, 56
                               Vit. 29
    De legibus   *Orat.* 9, 17, 57
    De natura deorum   *Orat.* 54
                               Vit. 44
    De officiis   *Orat.* 7, 54
                               Vit. 16, 29
    De oratore   *Orat.* 1, 2, 44, 46
    De senectute   *Orat.* 69

Epistulae ad Atticum	*Vit.* 35
Epistulae ad familiares	*Orat.* 45
In Verrem	*Orat.* 70
Orator ad Marcum Brutum	*Orat.* 45
Paradoxa Stoicorum	*Orat.* 48
Pro Cluentio	*Orat.* 17
Tusculanae disputationes	*Orat.* 17, 24, 30, 35, 54, 56, 69

Columella
De re rustica	*Orat.* 59

Damascius
In Phaedonem	*Orat.* 26

Digesta (Corpus iuris civilis)	*Orat.* 36, 50
Diogenes Laertius	*Orat.* 8, 9, 30, 48, 49, 55, 56, 64
	Vit. 9, 44

Empedocles
fr. 8 (from Plut. *Adv. Colt.* 1111F)	*Orat.* 19
fr. 17 (from Theophr. *De sensu* 9 = DK 31, A86)	*Orat.* 19

Firmicus Maternus	*Orat.* 40

Aulus Gellius
Noctes Atticae	*Orat.* 35, 50, 64, 69
	Vit. 35, 42

Gorgias
Helen	*Orat.* 55

Hermes Trismegistus
Asclepius	*Orat.* 1, 4, 7, 17
Corpus Hermeticum	*Orat.* 4, 50, 51
Pimander	*Orat.* 5, 51

Heraclitus
fr. 53 (from Hippolytus, *Heresies* 9.9.4)	*Orat.* 21

Homer
Iliad	*Orat.* 9, 21, 28
Odyssey	*Orat.* 9, 31, 57

Horace
    Ars Poetica   *Orat.* 42
    Carmina   *Orat.* 35
    Epistulae   *Orat.* 45
    Epodes   *Orat.* 59
    Satires   *Orat.* 29
                                 Vit. 24
Hymni Orphici   *Orat.* 14, 55, 68, 69
Iamblichus
    De mysteriis   *Orat.* 47, 56
    Protrepticus   *Orat.* 7, 30, 31
    Vita pythagorae   *Orat.* 23, 30, 47, 48, 54, 56, 64,
                                 68

Julian the Apostate
    Orations   *Orat.* 4
Lucan   *Orat.* 9, 20
Lucilius   *Orat.* 7, 31
Lucretius   *Orat.* 5, 35, 50
Macrobius
    In somnium Scipionis   *Orat.* 4, 18, 24
    Saturnalia   *Vit.* 35
Martianus Capella   *Orat.* 6, 9
Oracula chaldaica   *Orat.* 2, 4, 10, 14, 15, 18, 27, 29,
                                 32, 50, 57, 59

Ovid
    Epistulae ex Ponto   *Orat.* 61
    Fasti   *Orat.* 23
    Metamorphoses   *Orat.* 21
                                 Vit. 4
    Tristia   *Vit.* 32
Persius   *Vit.* 1
Philo
    De opificio mundi   *Vit.* 19
    De vita Mosis   *Vit.* 19

Philostratus
   Vita Apollonii   *Vit.* 9, 54
Plato
   Alcibiades   *Orat.* 29, 31, 55, 56, 57
   Apologia   *Orat.* 36
   Charmides   *Orat.* 8, 29, 40, 56, 57
   Epistulae   *Orat.* 26, 29, 45, 49, 64
   Epinomis   *Orat.* 54
   Euthydemus   *Orat.* 8
   Gorgias   *Orat.* 55
   Ion   *Orat.* 8
   Leges   *Orat.* 27, 55, 57
   Lysis   *Orat.* 40
   Meno   *Orat.* 55
   Phaedo   *Orat.* 8, 16, 23, 24, 26, 31, 57
   Phaedrus   *Orat.* 11, 26, 31, 32, 39, 57
   Philebus   *Orat.* 5
   Protagoras   *Orat.* 5, 29
   Respublica   *Orat.* 17, 27, 54, 55
   Sophista   *Orat.* 15, 26, 55
   Symposium   *Orat.* 6, 18, 26, 50, 55, 59
   Timaeus   *Orat.* 2, 4, 14, 17, 34, 57
Plautus
   Miles gloriosus   *Orat.* 37
   Poenulus   *Orat.* 61, 69
Pliny the Elder
   Historia naturalis   *Orat.* 5, 8, 14, 30, 31, 56, 57, 59
                        Vit. 2, 24
Pliny the Younger
   Epistulae   *Orat.* 42
   Panegyricus   *Vit.* 18
Plotinus   *Orat.* 6, 9, 24, 26, 55, 58, 59
Plutarch
   [*De Cons. ad Apoll.*]   *Orat.* 54

De E apud Delphos	*Orat.* 18, 25, 27, 28, 29
De Iside et Osiride	*Orat.* 16, 18, 19, 21, 26, 64
[*De liberis educandis*]	*Orat.* 30
De Pythiae oraculis	*Orat.* 27, 29, 31
Quomodo adulescens poetas audire debeat	*Orat.* 8
[*Placita philosophorum*]	*Orat.* 15
De sollertia animalium	*Orat.* 8
Vita Alcibiadis	*Orat.* 8
Porphyry	
De abstinentia	*Orat.* 55
De antro nympharum	*Orat.* 57
Vita Plotini	*Orat.* 58
Vita Pythagorae	*Orat.* 30, 31
Proclus	
Institutio theologica	*Orat.* 57
In Parmenidem	*Orat.* 2, 14
De sacrificio	*Orat.* 31, 59
In Timaeum	*Orat.* 2, 14, 54
Theologia Platonica	*Orat.* 15, 16, 26, 31, 47, 54, 57
Propertius	*Orat.* 35, 43
Psellus	
In Oracula chaldaica	*Orat.* 59
Expositio brevis	*Orat.* 4
Quintilian	
Institutio oratoria	*Orat.* 42, 45
	Vit. 29, 35, 42
[*Declamationes*]	*Orat.* 67
Sallust,	
[*Invectiva in Ciceronem*]	*Vit.* 35
Scholia in prolegomena Hermogenis	*Orat.* 55
Seneca	
Dialogi	*Orat.* 12
	Vit. 49
Epistulae	*Orat.* 9, 11, 49, 50, 57, 70
Servius	*Orat.* 50

Simplicius
  In Categorias   *Orat.* 52
Statius,
  Thebais   *Orat.* 63, 71
Suda   *Orat.* 55
Suetonius
  Domitianus   *Orat.* 24
  [Prata]   *Orat.* 70
Synesius
  Calvitii encomium   *Orat.* 59
  Dion   *Orat.* 26
  De insomniis   *Orat.* 59, 64
  Hymni   *Orat.* 4
Tacitus
  Dialogus de oratoribus *Vit.* 35
Terence
  Andria   *Orat.* 67
Timaeus of Locri   *Orat.* 2, 4
Valerius Maximus   *Orat.* 30, 50
Varro
  De lingua latina   *Orat.* 59
Vergil
  Aeneid   *Orat.* 17, 21, 23, 26, 40
                 Vit. 4
  Georgics   *Orat.* 35, 50, 59
Vita Aristotelis (anon.) *Orat.* 45, 52
Vitruvius
  De architectura   *Vit.* 29

C. PATRISTIC, MEDIEVAL, AND LATER CHRISTIAN LITERATURE

Anon.
  Ars moriendi   *Vit.* 67
  Chronicle   *Orat.* 1
  Compilatio assisiensis *Vit.* 53

Aquinas
    Scriptum super sententias   *Vit.* 40
    Sententia libri metaphysicae   *Vit.* 44
    Summa theologiae   *Vit.* 54, 70
Augustine
    De civitate Dei   *Orat.* 5, 49, 55, 67
    Contra Academicos   *Orat.* 52
    Confessiones   *Orat.* 49, 67
    De doctrina christiana   *Vit.* 19
    Enarrationes in Psalmos   *Orat.* 17, 33
    Epistolae   *Orat.* 56
    De Genesi ad litteram   *Orat.* 5, 33
    De gratia Christi   *Vit.* 13
    De haeresibus   *Vit.* 26
    Sermones   *Orat.* 34
    Soliloquia   *Orat.* 70
    De Trinitate   *Orat.* 5, 13
    De vera religione   *Orat.* 49, 67
Boethius
    Consolatio philosophiae   *Orat.* 26, 28
    In Aristotelis de interpretatione 2   *Orat.* 52
Cassiodorus
    Institutiones   *Vit.* 19
Dante
    Inferno   *Vit.* 50
    Purgatorio   *Vit.* 66
Dionysius the Areopagite (pseudo-)
    Celestial Hierarchy   *Orat.* 11, 12, 15, 19, 26, 57, 60
                                  Vit. 40, 71
    Ecclesiastical Hierarchy   *Orat.* 64
    Letters   *Orat.* 7
    Mystical Theology   *Orat.* 7, 12, 13
    On the Names of God   *Orat.* 12, 15, 27, 39
Eusebius
    Praeparatio evangelica   *Orat.* 27, 49
                                  Vit. 19

Ficino
    Opera   Orat. 8, 27, 54
    Platonica theologia   Orat. 26
Gregory the Great
    Homiliae in evangelia   Orat. 12
Gregory of Nazianzus
    Orationes   Orat. 8
Hilary of Poitiers
    Tractatus super Psalmos   Orat. 63, 65
Isidore
    Etymologiae   Orat. 9
Jerome (Hier.)
    Adversus Jovinianum   Orat. 47
    Adversus Pelagianos   Orat. 5
    Epistolae   Orat. 34
                                        Vit. 44
    In Ezechielem prophetam   Orat. 61
Lactantius
    Institutiones divinae   Orat. 48
                                        Vit. 30
    De ira Dei   Orat. 4
Origen
    Commentary on the Gospel of John   Orat. 63
    Commentary on the Gospel of   Orat. 63, 64
    Matthew
    Commentary on the Epistle to the   Orat. 63
    Romans
    Contra Celsum   Orat. 18, 54, 64
                                        Vit. 19
Paulinus of Milan
    Vita Ambrosii   Vit. 6, 50
Peter Lombard
    Sententiae in IV libris distinctae   Orat. 27, 60
Petrarch
    De vita solitaria   Vit. 50

Posidonius
  Vita Augustini   *Vit.* 50
Smaragdus of Saint-Mihiel
  In regulam sancti Benedicti   *Orat.* 42
Sulpicius Severus
  Vita Martini   *Vit.* 50
Tertullian
  Adversus Marcionem   *Orat.* 62
  Apologeticum   *Vit.* 19

D. KABBALAH AND HEBRAICA

Abraham Abulafia
  De secretis legis (Sitre tora)   *Orat.* 7, 8, 63
  Ve-zot li-Yehuda   *Orat.* 16, 18, 65
Abraham Axelrad,
  Corona nominis boni   *Orat.* 12
Bahir   *Orat.* 16, 17, 19
Expositio decem numerationum   *Orat.* 34
Expositio secretorum punctuationis   *Orat.* 11
Flavius Mithridates
  Sermo   *Orat.* 32, 67
Gersonides
  Commentary on the Song of Songs   *Orat.* 24
  Commentary on Job   *Orat.* 19
Joseph Gikatilla
  Portae iustitiae   *Orat.* 33
Liber de radicibus   *Orat.* 27
Maimonides,
  Guide of the Perplexed   *Orat.* 16, 24
Menahem Recanati,
  Commentary on the Torah   *Orat.* 24, 32, 33, 34
Midrash   *Orat.* 6, 16, 26, 27, 31, 32, 34, 40,
                                          42, 65
Pirkei avot   *Orat.* 67

Rashi	Orat. 33
Sefer yetzirah	Orat. 17
Targums	Orat. 8, 16, 26
Talmud	Orat. 8, 26, 32, 40, 65, 67
Zohar	Orat. 6, 7, 8, 10, 16, 17, 18, 19, 24,
	25, 26, 27, 31, 32, 33, 34, 41,
	65, 67

NOTES

1. For a complete listing of all editions of Giovanni Pico's works through the twentieth century, see Quaquarelli and Zanardi, *Pichiana;* the 1496 *princeps* is accessible online via the digital collections of the Munich Staatsbibliothek at https://daten.digitale-sammlungen.de/~db/0006/bs b00068573/images/

2. Luc Deitz "*De omni re scibili — et de quibusdam aliis:* A New Attempt at Understanding Pico's 900 Theses," *Neulateinisches Jahrbuch: Journal of Neo-Latin Language and Literature* 7 (2005): 295–301: this review of Farmer's edition of the *Conclusions* (see Intro., n. 108) concludes that its translation of the theses "is of limited usefulness" because it "raises a number of serious interpretative and conceptual problems." The "Palatine redaction" is also edited in Bausi's edition (*Appendice*): see App. II.

3. *Bn*, pp. 155–56, 162–66; *Apol.* pp. 3, 7.

4. *Vit.* 76 for Averroes and the commentators.

5. *Orat.* 68; Intro. at n. 114.

6. The many editions and translations of the *Oration* after Thomas More's, besides Eugenio Garin's 1942 version and before those by Bausi and by Borghesi, Papio, and Riva, constitute an archive of information and insight. See Arthur Liebert, *Ausgewählte Schriften* (Jena: Diederichs, 1905); Giovanni Semprini, "Della dignità dell'uomo," in *La Filosofia di Pico della Mirandola* (Milan: Libreria Lombardia, 1936), pp. 221–57; Herbet Rüssel, *Die Würde des Menschen nebst einigen Briefen und der Lebensbeschreibung Pico della Mirandolas* (Amsterdam: Pantheon, 1940); Bruno Cico-

gnani, *Dignità dell'uomo* (Florence: Lemonnier, 1941); Elizabeth Forbes and Paul Oskar Kristeller, "Oration on the Dignity of Man," in *The Renaissance Philosophy of Man*, ed. Ernst Cassirer, Paul Oskar Kristeller, and John Herman Randall (Chicago: University of Chicago Press, 1948), pp. 223–54; A. Robert Caponigri, trans., *Oration on the Dignity of Man*, introduction by Russell Kirk (Chicago: Regnery Gateway, 1956); Charles Wallis and Paul Miller, *On the Dignity of Man* (Indianapolis: Bobbs-Merrill, 1965); Arturo Fallico and Herman Shapiro, "Oration on the Dignity of Man," in *Renaissance Philosophy*, I: *The Italian Philosophers; Selected Readings from Petrarch to Bruno* (New York: Modern Library, 1967), pp. 141–71; Hans Reich and Frank-Rutger Hausman, *De dignitate hominis Lateinisch und Deutsch* (Bad Homburg: Gehlen, 1968); Fabio Sante Pignagnoli, *La Dignità dell'uomo* (Bologna: Edizioni Scolastiche Pàtron, 1969); Giuseppe Tognon, *Discorso sulla dignità dell'uomo* (Brescia: La Scuola, 1987); August Buck, *De hominis dignitate: Über die Würde des Menschen* (Hamburg: Meiner, 1990); Olivier Boulnois and Giuseppe Tognon, "Sur la dignité de l'homme," in Pico, *Oeuvres philosophiques* (Paris: Presses Universitaires de France, 1993); Yves Hersant, *De la dignité de l'homme* (Paris: Éclat, 1993); Vittorio Branca and Carlo Carena, *De hominis dignitate: La Dignità dell'uomo* (Milan: Silvio Berlusconi, 1994): published over Berlusconi's imprint, a misnamed speech about dignity is astonishing—but not in the way that the prince intended. In the same year his words circled back to normal scholarship in Garin, *Oratio de hominis dignitate* (Pordenone: Edizioni Studio Tesi, 1994).

7. See Intro., at nn. 12 and 84.

8. Intro., at n. 40.

9. Intro., at nn. 100–102. In addition to anonymous texts in Hebrew and Aramaic, Kibre, *The Library of Pico*, lists Abigdor ben Nathan (886); Abraham Abulafia (532, 599); Abraham bar Hiyya (526, 1037); Elia del Medigo (437); Gersonides (276); Abraham Ibn Ezra (273, 864, 879, 1016, 1055); Isaac Israeli (893); Isaiah ben Elijah di Trani (904); Jacob ibn Tibbon (895); Samuel ibn Tibbon (905); Maimonides (235, 448, 694, 894); Moses Kimhi (534); Nachmanides (300, 306, 881); Pablo de Heredia (784); Rashi (868); Menahem Recanati (993, p. 46); Saadia Gaon (754); Samuel ibn Seneh Zarza (210); and Solomon ibn Gabirol (647). The

first volume of Giulio Busi's "Kabbalistic Library of Pico della Miran-dola," *The Great Parchment: Flavius Mithridates' Latin Translation, the Hebrew Text and an English Translation*, ed. G. Busi with S. Bondoni and S. Cam-panini (Torino: Aragno, 2004), has been followed by several others. Some of the manuscripts in the Vatican collections studied by Busi and his colleagues name the authors of their texts and give titles for them.

Notes to the Texts

❧❧❧

1. praesidis *Y*] praesidi *B*
2. quasi illud *Y*
3. publice *Y*] publicae *B*
4. *corrected*: celebratissima *B*] celebratissimis *Y*
5. fuerant *Y*] fuerat *B*
6. explodere destinarat *Y*
7. speculatis, *sc.* speculationibus *B*] speculatibus *Y*
8. partis *B*] partes *Y*
9. annexum *Y*] annexus *B*
10. spondisset *Y*
11. labant nutentque *Y*
12. sublevemur *Y*
13. familiares *Y*
14. duxerat sed et a moribus *Y*] duxerat etiam et amoribus *B*
15. super aliosque probos *Y*
16. floribus *Y*
17. gestasse hunc quippe *Y*
18. et *Y*
19. *corrected*: evangelium *B, Y*
20. nutabundum *Y*] nutabundus *B*
21. voveret *Y*
22. ob posthabitum religionis ingrediendae salubrum afflatum igne *Y*
23. etiam *Y*

24. fidem habere *Y*

25. quippe qui *Y*

ORATION

1. *Tit. sic B (text proper, sign. QQ2r):* Oratio quedam elegantissima *B (contents page, a1r)*

2. has *om. B*

3. *om.* ei *B*

4. מטטרון *Ba:* מטטרן *F: blank space in B*

5. et *om. B*

6. חלקש . . . מה *F: blank space in B, ellipsis in Ba*

7. et Iunonia *om. B*

8. pedatrix *B*

9. sillogismo *B*

10. laboratis *Ba, who corrects from Matt. 11:28:* laborastis *B*

11. elementa *BBaF: corrected from Exod. 36:19:* velamentum de pellibus; *Num. 4:8:* velamento ianthinarum pellium; *and* velo divinitatis *in this sentence*

12. hercle *om. B*

13. Agamur *B*

14. ostendunt *B*

15. ingressuri *B*

16. *so F: blank spaces in B, ellipsis in Ba*

17. *so F: blank spaces in B, ellipsis in Ba*

18. *so F: blank spaces in B, ellipsis in Ba*

19. *so F: blank spaces in B, ellipsis in Ba*

20. quasi undis . . . quasi boreali amussi *Ba]* quasi boreali undis . . . quasi amussi *BF*

21. deorum *BaF:* dei *B: cf. paragraph 33*

22. illae *B*

23. quam *B*

24. cum ברזל idest ferrum שלחחכמים idest sapientum *BaF: 14 blank spaces, then* ferrum sapientum *B*

25. et *om. BaF*

26. omnibus *BBa: corrected from Job 32:8:* spiritus est in hominibus

27. deficiunt *B*

28. meam *Ba*

29. familiaritates *BaF:* familiariter *B*

30. Damascum *B*

31. secta B] haeresis *BaF*

32. discussionae *B*

33. illae *B*

34. inter sparsas . . . inter seminatas *B*

35. cognationem *Ba, with Bn p. 192:* cognitionem *B*

36. Dioni *B*

37. ἐκ νοὸς . . . εκτὸς *Ba: blank space in B*

APPENDIX II

1. ~~machina~~ *cancelled after* mundana

2. الرجل *read by Bausi*

3. et fluxi *illeg. because of water damage; restored by Bausi*

4. -upalam *illeg. because of water damage; restored by Bausi*

5. ~~ip~~ *between* demum *and* illa

6. nostra *inserted above* necessaria

7. ~~po~~ *before* protinus

8. ~~ado~~ *before* illa

9. *So F: Bausi reads* in: in *BBa*

10. מטטרון *Bausi*

11. ብረፃሠ . . . ወከ *not printed by Bausi, who refers in a note to Wirszubski's analysis and notes that F "introduces here an obscure citation in Ethiopic characters"*

12. g *before* cognivisse

13. *Bausi reads* adque *in F:* adque *BBa*

14. ~~se~~ *before* Seraphin

15. ut se (ut *superscript:* un- *before correction*): *Bausi reads* ut et *in F:* unde et *BBa*

16. forma~~ta est~~ *before correction*

17. ~~atque~~ *before* ac

18. ~~faciendum est~~ *before* factitandum est

19. *Bausi reads* abtorto *in F*

20. ~~e~~ *after* foedus; *the following passage,* iniit cum Deo . . . dixerunt sapientes, *has fallen out "for mechanical reasons," according to Bn, who explains that the break makes F—which is earlier than Pico's definitive but lost version from the end of 1486 or early in 1487—incoherent at this point; see Bn, pp. 176-81, and notes 26 and 31 below*

21. ~~interprete~~ *before* interpretatio

22. *a passage,* sacris initiari ... fecit nos, *has fallen out, as in note 26 below*

23. ~~fat=~~ *after* satis

24. *So F: Bausi reads* virtutum

25. *a passage,* sapientissimum ob id ... debere se dixit, *has fallen out, as in the following note*

26. ቄሠት, ኩጽርን, ነሀሪ *and* ራሕማፃት *not printed by Bausi; see note 17 of this Appendix*

27. ~~et~~ *before* meridianae

28. *Bausi reads* spiritibus

29. e *superscript, corrected from* est

30. *The next three paragraphs differ substantially in content and order from the corresponding material in Ba.*

31. iurare *above* iuratu *(neither cancelled)*

32. ~~se sed~~ *corrected superscript to* sed se

33. ad ~~Latinos~~ nos

34. *The next three paragraphs differ in content and order from the corresponding material in Ba.*

35. *Thus F: Bausi reads* Accedit quod, *as in Ba*

36. *Bausi silently inserts* ea *before* veritatem, *as in Ba*

37. *Bausi reads* accipit

Notes to the Translations

※※※

ABBREVIATIONS AND SIGLA

Abbreviations for biblical, classical, patristic, rabbinic, medieval, and some other sources follow examples in

The Oxford Classical Dictionary, ed. S. Hornblower and A. Spawforth (Oxford: Oxford University Press, 1996).
The SBL Handbook of Style for Biblical Studies and Related Disciplines, ed. P. Alexander et al. 2nd ed. (Atlanta: SBL Press, 2014).

ABBREVIATIONS FOR KABBALAH, HEBRAICA, AND MUSLIM TEXTS

Abbreviations for books of Kabbalah and related works in BAV, MS Vat. Ebr. 190 and 191 (= CVE) and BAV, MS Chigi A.VI.190 are based on *W*, pp. 286–92. After checking the Vatican manuscripts, we have relied on *W*'s transcriptions and on communications from Saverio Campanini for Abulafia, *Ve-zot*. Since the Latin version of Recanati, *Comm.*, is lost, we have followed *W*'s English versions from the Hebrew edition printed in Venice in 1545.

Abulafia, *Secr.*	*De secretis legis* (CVE 190)
Abulafia, *Sitre*	the Hebrew original of *De secretis legis Tora*
Abulafia, *Ve-zot*	Abraham Abulafia, *Incipit summa brevis Cabalae quae intitulatur Rabi Ieudae contenta in his propositionibus primis* (CVE 190)
Axelrad, *Cor.*	Abraham Axelrad, *Corona nominis boni* (CVE 190)
Averroes, *Beat.*	Averroes, *Tractatus de animae beatitudine*, in *Opera*, vol. 9 (Venice: Giunta, 1550), fols. 64–66
Bahir	*The Book of Bahir: Flavius Mithridates' Latin Translation, the Hebrew Text and an English Version*, ed. and trans. S. Campanini (Torino: Nino Aragno, 2005)

b. Ber., Hag., Sanh., etc.	standard form for citations of Talmud: the letter *b.* followed by the abbreviated title of the tractate: see the *SBL Handbook* above
CVE	Codici Vaticani Ebraici
Expos. decem num.	*Expositio decem numerationum* (CVE 191)
Expos. secr. punct.	*Expositio secretorum punctuationis* (CVE 190)
Flavius and Pico, *Job*	translation by Pico and Flavius, with comments by Pico, of the Book of Job, in BAV, MS Ottob. Lat. 607, ff. 3–62, partly transcribed in C. Wirszubski, "Giovanni Pico's Book of Job," *Journal of the Warbug and Courtauld Institutes* 32 (1969): 171–99
Flavius, *Sermo*	Flavius Mithridates, *Sermo de passione Domini*, ed. C. Wirszubski (Jerusalem: Israel Academy of Sciences and Humanities, 1963)
Gersonides, *SS*	*Commento al Cantico dei Cantici nella traduzione ebraico-latina di Flavio Mitridate: edizione e commento del ms. Vat. Lat. 4273 (cc. 5r–54r)*, ed. M. Andreatta (Florence: Olschki, 1999)
Gikatilla, *Port.*	Joseph Gikatilla, *Portae iustitiae* (in BAV, MS Chigi A.VI.190)
Lib. rad.	*Liber de radicibus* (CVE 190)
Midr. Gen.	standard form for citations of Midrash: see *SBLH*
Recanati, *Comm.*	Menahem Recanati, ביאור על התורה (Venice, 1545)
S1, S2, S3 . . . S10	the ten *Sefirot* in the standard array; see Intro. at note 113
Scholem (1991)	Gershom Scholem, *On the Mystical Shape of the Godhead*, trans. J. Neugroschel, ed. J. Chipman (New York: Schocken, 1991)
SY	*Sefer Yetzirah*
Tg. ps.-J.	standard form for citations of Targums: see the *SBL Handbook*, above
Zohar	*Zohar: Pritzker Edition*, ed. and trans. D. Matt et al., 12 vols. (Stanford: Stanford University Press, 2004–17)

OTHER ABBREVIATIONS

Apol.	*Apologia Joannis Pici Mirandulani Concordiae comitis* (Naples: Francesco del Tuppo, 1487). Copy used: British Library: IB.29535
App.	appendices in this book
BAV	Vatican City, Biblioteca Apostolica Vaticana
Concl.	Giovanni Pico, *[D]e adscriptis numero noningentis.* . . . (Rome: Eucharius Silber, 1486). Copy used: British Library: IB.18857
DBI	*Dizionario Biografico degli Italiani* (Rome: Treccani, 1960–). Cited from the online version at http://www.treccani.it/
Disp.	*Disputationes adversus astrologiam divinatricem,* ed. Eugenio Garin, 2 vols. (Florence: Vallechi, 1946–52)
Ficino, Op.	Marsilio Ficino, *Opera omnia,* ed. M. Sancipriano (Torino: Bottega d'Erasmo, 1959). Reprint of edition of Basel, 1576
Ficino, Pim.	Marsilio Ficino, *Mercurii Trismegisti liber de potestate et sapientia Dei,* trans. Marsilio Ficino, ed. S. Gentile (Florence: Studio per Edizioni Scelte, 1989)
Hept.	*Heptaplus Iohannis Pici Mirandulae de septiformi sex dierum Geneseos enarratione ad Laurentium Medicem* (Florence: Bartolomeo de' Libri, ca. 1489). Copy used: British Library: IB.27535
Idel (2014)	"The Kabbalistic Backgrounds of the 'Son of God' in Giovanni Pico della Mirandola's Thought," in *Giovanni Pico e la cabbalà,* ed. Fabrizio Lelli (Florence: Olschki, 2014), pp. 19–45
Intro.	the Introduction to this book
ISTC	British Library, *Incunabula Short-title Catalogue,* online at http://www.bl.uk/catalogues/istc/
KJV	King James Version of the Bible (1611)

Klutstein, *Orph.*	*Orphei carmina* and *Magica dicta magorum ex Zoroastre*, in *Marsilio Ficino et la théologie ancienne: Oracles chaldaïques, Hymnes orphiques, Hymnes de Proclus*, ed. Ilana Klutstein (Florence: Olschki, 1987)
Lewy	Hans Lewy, *Chaldean Oracles and Theurgy: Mysticism, Magic and Platonism in the Later Roman Empire*, ed. M. Tardieu, 3rd ed. (Paris: Institut des Études Augustiniennes, 2011)
MPL	J.-P. Migne, *Patrologiae cursus completus, . . . series latina* (Paris: Migne, 1841–55)
Orat.	Pico's *Oration* as edited and annotated in this book
SEP	*Stanford Encyclopedia of Philosophy,* https://plato.stanford.edu/
T1	the first four hundred theses in *Concl.*
T2	the next five hundred theses in *Concl.*
Vit.	Gianfrancesco Pico's *Life* of Pico as edited and annotated in this book
Vit. ep.	Gianfrancesco's letter of dedication to Ludovico il Moro in *Vit.*
W	Wirszubski, *Pico's Encounter*

Sigla

B	*Commentationes Ioannis Pici Mirandulae in hoc volumine contenta, quibus anteponitur vita per Iohannem Franciscum illustris principis Galeotti Pici filium conscripta . . .* (Bologna: Benedictus Hectoris, 1496). (Copy used: British Library: IB.29063–64)
Ba	the Latin text of the *Oration*, in Pico, *Discorso*, ed. Bausi
Bn	Bausi's notes and appendices in *Ba*
F	Florence, Biblioteca Nazionale Centrale, MS Palatino 885, fols. 143–53, containing a fragment of Pico's *Oration*. See App. II.

Y   the Latin text of Gianfrancesco Pico's *Life* of Pico, in *The Yale Edition of the Complete Works of St. Thomas More*, vol. I, *English Poems, Life of Pico, The Last Things*, ed. A. S. G. Edwards, K. G. Rogers, and C. H. Miller (New Haven: Yale University Press), 295–341

LIFE

1. Since Pico's thirty-first year began on February 23, 1494, it was not finished when he died in the following November. For "inside and out," see *in cute*, Pers. 3.30.

2. Plin. *NH* 11.268 describes mute frogs in Macedonia; on astrology at the Sforza court in the time of Il Moro, see Azzolini, *The Duke and the Stars*.

3. *Vit.* 69; *B*, sigs. XX^r–YYiv^v: Gianfrancesco collected two dozen "testimonies to the life, teaching and writings of Giovanni Pico della Mirandola"; for the question of inheritance, see Intro. at n. 41.

4. Verg. *Aen.* 7.48–49, 170–93; Ov. *Met.* 14.320–96; Felice Ceretti, ed., *Cronaca della Mirandola dei figli di Manfredo e della Corte di Quarantola scritta da Ingrano Bratti, continuata da Battista Papazzoni, illustrata con note e documenti*, published in *Memorie storiche della città e dell'antico ducato della Mirandola pubblicate per cura della commissione municipale di storia patria e di arti belle della Mirandola*, vol. 1 (Mirandola: Gaetano Cagarelli, 1872), pp. 13–15; Bruno Andreolli, "Pico [famiglia]," *DBI* (2015): According to Vergil and Ovid, Picus was a son of Saturn and king of Latium, turned into a woodpecker (*Picus* in Latin) by Circe. A chronicle compiled in Carpi in the fourteenth century tells the story of Euride, a daughter of Constantine's son, who married Manfred, a noble Saxon, and "gave birth to three male infants at the same time . . . whose names were Pico, Pio, and Papazano."

5. *Concl.* p. 1; *App.* 1.2; *Apol.* p. 1; *B*, sig. QQii^r; Ceretti, *I Signori che hanno dominato sulla corte di Quarantola e sulla Mirandola dal 1115 al 1707* (Mirandola: Gaetano Cagarelli, 1879); Schmitt, *Gianfrancesco Pico*, pp. 11–12; Odoardo Rombaldi, "Mirandola dai Pico agli Estensi: Problemi," in *Mi-*

randola e le terre del basso corso del Secchia dal medioevo al'età contemporanea, 1: *Territorio e società* (Modena: Aedes Muratoriana, 1984), pp. 35–43; Alma Poloni, "Pino Ordelaffi," *DBI* (2013); Andreolli, "Pico [famiglia]," *DBI* (2015); "Galeotto I Pico," *DBI* (2015); Fabio Forner, "Alberto Pio," *DBI* (2015); Elisabetta Scapparone, "Giovan Francesco Pico," *DBI* (2015); also Biondo Flavio, *Italy Illuminated*, ed. Jeffrey A. White (Cambridge, MA: Harvard University Press, 2005–16), 2: 355; *Pii Secundi Pontificis Maximi commentarii rerum memorabilium* (Frankfurt: Aubrianus, 1614), p. 174: Powerful people named Pico were active in the area between Modena and Reggio by the middle of the twelfth century. The first Giovanni Pico to be called Lord of Mirandola and Count of Concordia was given those titles by Emperor Sigismund of Luxembourg in 1432, before the family switched its primary allegiance from the Visconti to the Este. A later Giovanni, the famous philosopher, was the youngest of five children of this earlier Giovanni's son, Gianfrancesco I, who married Giulia Boiardo: Matteo Boiardo was her nephew. After Gianfrancesco I died in 1467, his two older sons, Galeotto I and Antonmaria, fought incessantly over their inheritance, while their younger brother, perhaps sheltered by his mother, stuck to his books. Efforts at sharing territory, backed by Emperor Maximilian, assigned Mirandola to Galeotto and Concordia to Antonmaria. According to Gianfrancesco's *Life* (*Vit.* 55), their brother held "a third of these territories": hence the philosopher's title, Count of Mirandola and Concordia, used by him or of him in works published in his lifetime or shortly after. After the imperial intervention failed, Galeotto I won a round in the struggle, dying in 1499. He had married Bianca Maria d'Este in 1468, a year after his father died, thus securing powerful allies at the Este court in nearby Ferrara. Gianfrancesco II, the author of this *Life*, was born to Bianca Maria and Galeotto I in 1469; he was only six years older than the subject of his biography, who was born on February 23, 1463. One of Pico's sisters, Caterina, married Leonello Pio, who died in 1477, two years after Alberto III Pio was born: his family had ruled Carpi since the early fourteenth century. Caterina's second husband, Roberto Gonzaga, was the Marquis of Mantua, where his family was as old as the Pico clan in the Modenese. Lucrezia, Pico's other sister, married Pino Ordelaffi of Forlì in 1475, five years before he died. Her second marriage may have taken her far from home, to Puglia, if the "Count of Montagnano" (*Mons Agani* or *Sagani*) was an heir of the "famous captain Giacomo da Montagano" mentioned by Biondo Flavio and Pius II. The Pope (Enea Silvio Piccolomini) reigned from 1458 to 1464, Frederick III from 1452 to 1493.

6. Paulinus, *Vit. Ambros.* 2.3; also Intro., at n. 22, for the omen and the hagiography.

7. Intro., at nn. 25–26, for Pico's good lucks and marvelous memory.

8. Ceretti, *Cronaca*, p. 155; Felix Gilbert, "Cesare Borgia," *DBI* (1971); Bacchelli, "Pico," *DBI* (2015); Grendler, *Universities*, pp. 4–5, 434–36, 443–48, 453; James A. Brundage, *The Medieval Origins of the Legal Profession: Canonists, Civilians and Courts* (Chicago: University of Chicago Press, 2008), pp. 114–18, 257–65; *Medieval Canon Law* (London: Routledge, 2013), pp. 159–60: Bologna began to award law degrees in 1217, and civil law still thrived there in Pico's time. A degree took six years to finish. Since most students were about eighteen when they began, Pico was exceptionally young. Moreover, he had been made a protonotary apostolic at the age of ten: the honor implied that his family wanted an ecclesiastical career for him; Cesare Borgia was a protonotary when he was seven. Decretals or rescripts, legally binding decisions formally recorded by a pope, began to be collected in the twelfth century, and they were still the most productive source of new church law in the fifteenth century, though their importance—like the study of canon law in general—had declined. Epitomes of decretals were common.

9. Diog. Laert. 3.6–7; Philostr. *VA* 1.18–20; Grendler, *Universities*, pp. 267–69, 285–87; Bacchelli, "Pico," *DBI* (2015): Italian universities, especially Bologna, were good places to "explore nature's secrets." Leading professors of natural philosophy also taught at the other Italian universities where Pico studied: Ferrara, Padua, and Pavia. At Padua he met Nicoletta Vernia, an eminent Aristotelian naturalist attacked for Averroism in 1489. See Intro., at nn. 27 and 78, for Elia del Medigo, an Averroist of a different kind whom Pico also knew at Padua. Apollonius is

Apollonius of Tyana, whose life, comparing him to Jesus, was written by Philostratus. The work was translated into Latin by Alamanno Rinuccini in 1472.

10. *Orat.* 64–65; *Concl.* p. 44; App. 1.7, 26.29; *Apol.* pp. 52–58, 75–76; Ceretti, *Cronaca*, pp. 149–50; Bacchelli, "Pico," *DBI* (2015): Since Pico went to Rome in 1486, his seven years of study would have started in 1479, when he studied at the University of Ferrara after leaving Bologna and the law, as in *Vit.* 8; his mother had died in the summer of 1478. The *Conclusions* were published in Rome on December 7, 1486. For the "posting" of the theses, see Intro., at n. 30. Gianfrancesco's description of their content is broadly correct. Pico refers to Origen—while making a single mention of Hilary—only twice, in one passage of the *Oration*, where the subject is Kabbalah. But one of the condemned theses deals with the problem of Origen's salvation, and Pico defended it at length in the *Apology*, where he also cited Hilary.

11. *Orat.* 36–45, 62, 70–71: Exactly when (or how often) Pico went to Rome and how long he stayed is unclear, but his "great distress" about attacks on his Roman project is very plain in the *Oration*.

12. *Concl.* p. 28; App. 1.22; Bacchelli, "Pico," *DBI* (2015): Pope Innocent made his first official move against Pico on February 20, 1487, by forbidding discussion of the theses; on March 2 he condemned seven as heretical and six others as suspect of heresy. In a headnote to the last five hundred of the nine hundred theses, Pico declared his intention to "propose nothing as asserted or acceptable except insofar as the Most Holy Roman Church judges it either true or acceptable—also its most worthy head, the Supreme Pontiff, Innocent VIII—and anyone is thoughtless who does not submit the judgment of his own thinking to the Pope's judgment." No such disclaimer precedes all the theses or the first four hundred. Since only the last five hundred are labeled *secundum propriam opinionem*, Pico probably considered such a declaration inappropriate or at least irrelevant for the first four hundred, none of which was condemned. On Bishop Bonfrancesco of Reggio, see Intro., at n. 28.

13. *Apol.* p. 88, where Pico attributed these words to Augustine, perhaps reflecting something similar from *De gratia Christi et de peccato originali*,

2.26 (*MPL* 44:397); see Henri Crouzel, *Une Controverse sur Origène à la Renaissance: Jean Pic de la Mirandole et Pierre Garcia* (Paris: Vrin, 1977), pp. 142, 268; Edelheit, *Ficino, Pico and Savonrola*, pp. 338–41.

14. *Apol.* pp. 1, 110–11: in what follows, Gianfrancesco repeats phrases (italicized here) from the end of the *Apology*, including the comment about Averroes and Alexander. In the first sentence of the *Apology*, finished late in the spring of 1487, Pico wrote that he had gone to Rome "to follow custom and kiss the feet of the Supreme Pontiff, Innocent VIII," and at the end of the book he pledged fidelity again, noting that he had written the whole thing in less than three weeks. Once they saw the product, however, the pope and his advisers decided in June to open an inquisitorial investigation and order Pico's formal submission; then all the theses were condemned in August. If Gianfrancesco meant to imply that the papal ban on "reading the book" was broad and hence vague, he was wrong. Alexander VI issued his pardon on June 8, 1493. See Fornaciari, "Appendice III," in his edition of the *Apology: L'Autodifesa di Pico*, pp. 433–35.

15. *Apol.* pp. 110–11; Davidson, *Alfarabi, Avicenna and Averroes*, pp. 258–65, 282–83, 304, 310–14. The naturalism of Alexander of Aphrodisias, ca. 200 CE, contrasts with views of later commentators on Aristotle, especially Themistius and Simplicius, who were friendlier to Platonism. But Averroes developed his controversial account of the soul by rejecting Alexander and siding with Themistius. Opponents of naturalist psychology in Pico's Italy sometimes called its proponents—like Vernia—'Alexandrians.' See Intro. at nn. 18, 29–30 on debating in private or public.

16. Since Gianfrancesco reports Pico's awakening after citing the *Apology* in detail (*Vit.* 16–17) as evidence of orthodoxy, he may have placed the "illumination" just before the "twenty nights of intense labor" (*Vit.* 14) that produced the book, which was finished late in the spring of 1487. See Intro. at nn. 23, 25, 31, 44–45 for the conversion and "wiles of women."

17. *Vit.* 40; Cic. *Off.* 3.6; Pico, *Sonetti*, ed. G. Dilemmi (Torino: Einaudi, 1994); Kristeller, "The Latin Poems of Giovanni Pico della Mirandola: A Supplementary Note," in *Studies in Renaissance Thought and Letters*, vol. 3

(Rome: Storia e Letteratura, 1993), pp. 305–21; "Giovanni Pico della Mirandola and His Latin Poems, a New Manuscript," ibid., pp. 323–31: Of about sixty poems in Italian that survived the blaze, forty-five are sonnets edited by Dilemmi; Kristeller counted nineteen Latin poems, including the religious verse that attracted Thomas More. See also Copenhaver, "Studied as an Oration," pp. 157–68.

18. *Hept.* sigs. avi–b^r, g7^v; Quaquarelli and Zanardi, *Pichiana*, pp. 413–14; Black, *Pico's* Heptaplus, pp. 8–9: The British Library copy of the *Heptaplus* gives no date of publication; ISTC and other authorities have ca. 1490, which was Pico's "twenty-eighth year," but from external evidence Black opts for the fall of 1489. The "prophet" is Moses, especially as the author of Genesis, whose deepest mysteries are saved for the end of the book, with blank spaces left for Hebrew words. Near the end of the second proem, Pico advises those who want "a simpler explanation more suitable for them" that his intended readers are not beginners but have already "learned these things somewhere else." See *Vit.* 26 for Gianfrancesco's views on accessibility, and Intro., at n. 32, for Pico's "first fruits."

19. Plin. *Pan.* 31.2.

20. *Hept.* sigs. a2^v, a4, avi^r, b; *Orat.* 64, 68; Acts 7:22; Philo, *Opif.* 127–28; *Mos.* I, 5.21–24; Tert. *Apol.* 19.2–4; Orig. *Cels.* 1.15; Euseb. *Praep. evang.* 9.6.6–9, 8.1–2; 13 pr.; Aug. *Doct. chr.* 2.43; Cassiod. *Inst.* I pr. 1; Black, *Pico's* Heptaplus, pp. 70–77, 96–97: Instead of Augustine, Cassiodorus, Eusebius, and Tertullian, Pico — who liked to go his own way — referred to Acts and Philo to prove that "Moses was very learned in all that the Egyptians taught, and all the Greeks . . . had Egyptian teachers," then citing Numenius and Hermippus (from Origen and Eusebius) on Moses, the Pythagoreans, and Plato; and Paul's pedigree in the *Oration* is Mosaic — hence Egyptian. But here Gianfrancesco focuses on the Bible's "simple story" of faith, which he highlighted in the *Oration*.

21. Pico, *Dell'Ente* (2010), pp. 160–64, 268–70: the editors conclude that the book was written "between the last months of 1490 and the Spring of 1491"; if this was the "second year after finishing the *Heptaplus*," 1489 seems likelier than 1490 for that earlier work, as in *Vit.* 21. Gianfrancesco

repeats the title of the tenth chapter on *morum emendatio*. See Intro. at n. 91 on Antonio, Pico's opponent; also nn. 11, 84, 86, 90–91, 114 and *Vit.* 35–36, 43, and 92 on harmonizing Plato and Aristotle.

22. Pico, *Kommentar*, ed. Bürklin, p. 22: Gianfrancesco almost certainly means the *Commento*, not yet published when he wrote; its first words are *pongono e' Platonici per loro dogma principale ogni cosa creata avere l'essere suo in tre modi*; the eighth chapter adds *queste tre prime nature, cioè Dio, quella prima mente e l'anima del mondo, dagli antiqui teologi, che sotto velamenti poetici coprivano e' loro mysterii, sono denotate per questi tre nomi, Celio, Saturno e Giove*: see also Intro. at n. 33 on Gianfrancesco's wish not to vulgarize the mysteries.

23. *Orat.* 33, 58; Pico, *Expositiones in Psalmos* (1997), p. 32; Black, *Pico's Heptaplus*, pp. 84–94; Grafton, "Trials and Triumphs," pp. 115–32: Under the camouflage, Zoroaster's parable in the *Oration* supports a broadly traditional approach to biblical interpretation, moving from literal to moral, allegorical and anagogic readings—something like the four rabbinic senses, as in *Orat.* 33. The speech makes frequent use of the Psalms (*Orat.* 2, 11, 13, 25, 28, 34–35), which Pico was studying systematically by 1488—probably while working on the *Heptaplus*. In commentaries on nine of them, he applied the usual fourfold method, more or less, while handling not just the Greek Septuagint but also the Hebrew Bible and postbiblical Jewish material with remarkable skill. But the result was the same, to defend a traditional Latin text of the Psalms, while stretching the notion of allegory a bit. The version favored by Pico was Jerome's Latin translation of a Greek text. Hence, "disagreeing with our Latin texts," in Gianfrancesco's words, was a philological tool but not the purpose of the philology. In the *Heptaplus*, however, where philology all but vanished, an expansive conception of allegory—tested by the prince in this book—displaced the four senses. Still later, in the *Disputations*, a "computation of chronologies" (perhaps inspired by Poliziano) was crucial for refuting the ancient theology that structured the conception of tradition in the *Oration* and in the "poetic theology" of the *Commento*. For Pico's zealous originality, see *Vit.* 23 and Intro. at nn. 34, 40–41.

24. Intro. at nn. 35–36 on the seven enemies.

25. Hor. *Sat.* 2.3.132–36; Plin. *HN* 35.142–44; also *Orat.* 41 on trigon aspects. The *Disputations* have yet to be thoroughly studied, but the best place to start is Grafton, "Triumphs of an Omnivore," pp. 111–34.

26. *Disp.* 5.5, 8.6; Enrico Carrara, "Giovanni Pontano," *Enciclopedia Italiana* (1935; online at www.treccani.it); Garin, *Pico: Vita e dottrina*, pp. 49–50; John Monfasani, *Collectanea Trapezuntiana: Texts, Documents and Bibliographies of George of Trebizond* (Binghamton: MRTS, 1984), pp. 750–51; Copenhaver, *Book of Magic*, pp. 266, 277–78: The translation that Gianfrancesco saw was probably made not by Pico but by Giovanni Pontano in 1475; Pico may have corrected it from a Greek manuscript, and Gianfrancesco found his notes — perhaps. George of Trebizond had already made a Latin version from Greek by 1454. Pico had not seen George's translation but reported what he had heard — that George followed Haly Abenragel, another commentator, in a mistake that Albumasar could have saved him from. The medieval transmission in several languages of the pseudonymous *Centiloquium* (*Karpos*) left its text muddled: Pico complained about a "false understanding of ancient authors" as the problem.

27. *Apol.* pp. 12, 27–28; Aug. *Haer.*; Guido Terrena, *Summa de haeresibus et earum confutationibus* (Paris: Josse Bade of Asse, 1528): The work on heresies attributed to Augustine lists 88 offenses; Pico cited it in the *Apology* to show that "nothing is harder than defining something as heretical or not heretical," which undercuts Gianfrancesco's description of his uncle as a scourge of heretics. In the same part of the *Apology*, Pico relied on the handbook of heresies written by Guido Terrena of Perpignan in the early fourteenth century. In addition to early Christian heresies described by Augustine, Guido listed new unorthodoxies from the Middle Ages, thus increasing the count.

28. Jas. 2:26: Schmitt, *Gianfrancesco Pico*, pp. 8–9; Dougherty, "Three Precursors to Pico della Mirandola's Roman Disputation and the Question of Human Nature in the *Oratio*," in Dougherty, *New Essays*, pp. 140–41: The allusion, *fides sine operibus*, to the New Testament letter that Luther once called an "epistle of straw," might seem to resonate with criticisms of Pico's theology as Pelagian — accounts that see the *Oration* as a progressive celebration of human freedom. After his eventual turn to

skeptical fideism, however, Gianfrancesco may have had second thoughts about his uncle's view of faith and works.

29. *Vit.* 36–37, 43; Intro. at nn. 11, 86–91.

30. *Orat.* 8, 22, 24, 31, 52, 55, 57–58, 65, 68–69; *Concl.* pp. 22–23, 58–60; *App.* 1.18, 32, 33.10; also Cic. *Fin.* 2.15; *Off.* 3.39; *Sen.* 23; Vitr. *De arch.* 2.2.1; Apul. *Apol.* 27; Quint. *Inst.* 2.14.3: Orpheus, Pythagoras, and their disciples have leading roles both in the *Oration* and in the *Conclusions*. There is no sign of Democritus, Heraclitus, or Thales in the *Conclusions*, but the first two are named in the speech, where the single sentence about Heraclitus bears on the theme of peace or concord. Thales believed that nature's underlying material basis was water, Heraclitus fire, Democritus atoms.

31. Lact. *Inst.* 3.28.13, 30.6; Intro. at nn. 78–79, 90–91 on Averroes, Avicenna, Thomas, Scotus, and other medieval philosophers.

32. Wirszubski, "Giovanni Pico's Book of Job"; this pioneering article reproduces manuscript pages that confirm Gianfrancesco's description.

33. *Vit.* 29–30; Ov. *Tr.* 1.7.29–30; also Intro. at nn. 35–36 for the *Disputations* as the most finished part of this larger project.

34. *B*, sigs. VVvi, YYiv^v–vii, where Gianfrancesco published some of these "small pieces"; also *Vit.* 20 on the poems.

35. *Vit.* 28 on the Psalms commentary; Intro. at nn. 9, 18, 21, 36 on Gianfrancesco's response to the *Oration*; the letters are discussed in Copenhaver, "Studied as an Oration": Pico was "not yet twenty-four" until February 23, 1487.

36. Cic. *Att.* 2.1: Tac. *Or.* 18.6; ps.-Sall. *In Cic.* 2; Quint. *Inst.* 10.1.32; Apul. *Met.* 2.9, 11.9; Gell. 6.14; Macrob. *Sat.* 5.1.7: Gellius described plain, middle, and grand styles, and Macrobius made the list of four that Gianfrancesco copied; the words in italics closely reflect, without quoting exactly, phrases from these ancient authors. Brutus called Cicero's writing "flaccid," according to Tacitus, using the rare *elumbis* to say so, but the attack on the great orator's excess was by a pseudonymous Sallust. When Quintilian praised Livy for *lactea ubertas*, he meant that his rich prose was also pure (*lacteus*), not milky. The charge that Livy's Latin was provin-

cial — guilty of *Patavinitas* because of his Paduan origins — was made by C. Asinius Pollio and recorded by Quint. *Inst.* 1.5.56. With allusions to these belletristic squabbles, Gianfrancesco parades his knowledge of ancient norms of Latinity. But Bausi, *Nec rhetor neque philosophus*, pp. 190–98, concludes that *piagnone* concern for his uncle's piety caused the nephew to ignore a "rather clear line of development, leading from the *recherché* elegance, somewhat Apuleian, of the first letters and the *Oration* to the constantly cruder simplicity . . . of the *Heptaplus*, *De ente et uno* and *Disputationes*" — though the *Conclusions* and *Apology* were exceptional because of the latter's catastrophic circumstances and the subject matter of both.

37. *Vit.* 35–37, 43: The authorities on style just cited in *Vit.* 42 made their statements in the *Attic Nights* (Gellius) and *Saturnalia* (Macrobius), the latter commenting on Vergil; Livy was the premier authority on Roman history and Pliny on natural history. Gianfrancesco claims that Pico turned away from such works of worldly wisdom to write the *Heptaplus* and *Disputations* and work on his grand apologetic project (*Vit.* 29–39), with philosophical concord as its basis.

38. Claudio Mutini, "Matteo Bosso," *DBI* (1971); also *Vit.* 42, 46, and Intro. at n. 37 on Pico's affected style, especially in the *Oration*; and Intro. at n. 40 for Barbaro's exchange with Pico on philosophical language. Like Barbaro and Ficino, Matteo Bosso, a learned cleric, was Pico's friend; Battista Spagnoli of Mantua, who became General of the Carmelite Order after Pico died, was a renowned poet (traditionally 'the Mantuan' in English) who corresponded with him.

39. *Vit.* 42–44; *Concl.* pp. 1, 5, 31, 51; App. 1.2, 4.6, 24.17, 28.5; *Apol.* pp. 54–55; *B*, sigs, Ssii^v–iii^r; Breen, "Conflict of Philosophy and Rhetoric," p. 400; Bausi, *Nec rhetor neque philosophus*, pp. 165–67; Peter of Spain, *Summaries of Logic: Text, Translation, Introduction and Notes*, ed. and trans. Brian Copenhaver, Calvin Normore, and Terence Parsons (Oxford: Oxford University Press, 2014), pp. 16–19, 42–46: By "modern theologians" Gianfrancesco means scholastics (not his term) like Albertus, Aquinas, Scotus, and their followers down to his own time; see Intro. at nn. 27, 38–40. His uncle, knowing that such theologians were judging him in Rome, insulted their style in his *Apology*: after including part of his *Ora-*

tion in self-defense, he worried in print that the authorities could not grasp its elegant Latin "any better than barbarisms are understood by the learned." Hence, to teach them Kabbalah, he would resort to their own "Parisian style" (*Parisiensi stilo*) — which he had already used throughout the *Conclusions*. There — in his own words on the first page of the book — he described himself as "imitating not the splendid Roman tongue but the way the most famous disputants talk in Paris, since this is the custom of almost all philosophers in our day." Pico was right about the custom. Sometimes disputants used plain language to introduce technical issues, as when one of his theses proposed that "a tractate on suppositions does not belong to a logic": since the sixth chapter (*tractatus*) of the standard university logic (Peter of Spain's *Summaries*) was a presentation of supposition theory (a kind of semantics), Pico's proposal was out of the mainstream — just as he intended — yet clear to anyone with a university education. In other cases, however, the language of the medieval masters had meaning only for experts, as in a thesis *secundum Iohannem Scotum*: "any undivided (*individuum*) is an undivided through an individuating (*individualem*) difference of its own, called a just-this-ness (*hecheitas*)." The question was about individuation: what exactly makes a feline Sadie and a feline Sophie different cats — individuals of the same species? For answers, much turned on precise distinctions (like *individuus / individualis*) and invented terminology (like *haecceitas*, in the usual spelling) that were indispensable to philosophers but meaningless to others. A Latin adapted for such purposes left no room for the artful and evasive language of the *Oration*. Two years before the Roman debacle and in happier days, Pico defended the special linguistic needs of philosophers in his exchange with Barbaro. "What prevents the philosophers whom you call 'barbarian' from agreeing on a single norm of expression," he asked, and he objected to any "completely arbitrary name for it. If you think it doesn't deserve the name Roman, you can call it French, British, Spanish or Parisian — as the less cultured usually say."

40. *Orat.* 46–48; *Apol.* pp. 4–5: In the *Oration*, the orator "defends no one's dogma lest I seem bound to it while neglecting the rest." His descriptions of philosophers in the speech are repeated in the *Apology*; see Intro. at n. 27 and *Vit.* 48.

41. *Orat.* 45; *Vit.* 91; *Concl.* pp. 29–30, 33–34, 42; *Hept.* sig. b8ᵛ; App. 1.23.4; 24.45, 54; 26.8, 14; ps.-Dion. *CH* 208C–12B; Aquinas, *Sent.* 2.12.1.3, 13.1.3.7, 13.1.4.2; also Intro. at nn. 38–39 for Pico's view of Aquinas and Gianfrancesco's representation of it. Thomas is called *splendor nostrae theologiae* when the *Heptaplus* explains that the Bible's words in Genesis match "secrets of all worlds and Nature as a whole." What made the universe coherent and hence intelligible, as Gianfrancesco saw it, was a cognitive hierarchy, and he applied this cosmic psychology to support the reality of visionary experience in *Vit.* 91. Aquinas, with similar intent, cited the Areopagite to confirm that God's omnipresent light "flows into all bodies to be received differently in different bodies." The sorting that starts on high proceeds through descending levels of angelic cognition. Just as higher angels pass simple, nondiscursive intuitions down to lower ranks whose cognitions are complex and inferential, all sentient creatures have places in this graded framework, where humans can use reason to understand the Creator. Pico saw such patterns hidden in Genesis, where Moses used the same words, like 'water' and 'fire,' both for concrete things and for their abstract philosophical analogs. In the *Oration*, the orator contrasts himself with Gorgias, promising that he would *not* try to answer "all questions in all the arts." But his nephew seems not to have been convinced.

42. *Orat.* 47; *Vit.* 46, 49; Peter of Spain, *Summaries*, p. 256; Bacchelli, "Pico," *DBI* (2015); Russell Friedman, "Peter Auriol," *SEP* (2015): Disputation was a regular part of university life in Pico's time; he participated in or attended public and private debates as early as 1482, at twenty years of age. The two contestants in formal disputation were called *opponens* and *respondens* by Peter of Spain: Gianfrancesco describes his uncle in both roles—*in obiectando* and *in respondendo*—by comparing him to famous medieval masters and echoing similar descriptions in Pico's speech. Neither the *Oration* nor the *Conclusions* mentions Peter Auriol, a contemporary of Francis of Meyronnes (named in both works) and also a Franciscan. Like Pico, Auriol was a controversial innovator.

43. *Orat.* 65; Quint. *Inst.* 12.1.1, 2.6; cf. Gell. *NA* 20.5; Garin, *Pico: Vita e dottrina*, pp. 45–46: By *dialecticus*, Gianfrancesco means a debater, not a logician. Where Gellius reported Aristotle's comment, used in the *Ora-*

tion, about statements "published and not published," he also put philosophy and dialectic together on one side of a divide and rhetoric on the other, but he was not discussing maxims or adages. Nor was Quintilian when he asked how much philosophy an orator needs. A *vir bonus dicendi peritus* had to be educated though not "a philosopher since no other way of living has withdrawn farther from civic responsibilities and the orator's whole duty (*munus*). . . . I prefer an orator taught by me to be a Roman sage of sorts, showing himself to be a political person not in private disputations but in action and experience, yet those who have turned to speaking have abandoned philosophy." See Intro. at n. 46 for the debate in Ferrara. Dominicans who met there in the summer of 1492 may have known what Aquinas wrote about dialectic and philosophy in *Sent. metaph.* 4.4.3: "Dialecticians and sophists put on the same appearance as the philosopher, but dialecticians and sophists dispute about these matters, and then it's up to the philosopher to think about them"; also Intro. at n. 30 for Pico's efforts to "capture popular attention."

44. Apul. *Met.* 1.24: The pejorative *quisquiliae* (swill) is all the more pointed for being rare; the slops are called *suiseticus* (*sus*, swine) to insult the Swineshead brothers from Oxford's Merton College, on whom see Intro. at nn. 38–40.

45. *Apol.* pp. 54–55; Diog. Laert. 10.13; Cic. *Nat. D.* 1.72; Hier. *Epist.* 33.5: In the *Oration*, *Conclusions* and *Apology*, Pico mentioned Epicurus only once, when he quoted Jerome's repetition of the usual (and unfair) dismissal of Epicurean ethics as voluptuary hedonism.

46. Arist. *Eth. Eud.* 1248^{a}27–30; Jacopo Foresti, *Novissime hystoriarum omnium repercussiones noviter a reverendissimo patre Jacobo Philippo Bergomense Cordinis Heremitarum editae, quae supplementum supplementi cronicarum nuncupantur, incipiendo ab exordio mundi usque in annum salutis nostrae* MCCCCCII (Venice: Albertino de Lissona, 1503), fol. 436^r; *Cronaca della nobilissima famiglia Pico scritta da autore anonimo*, ed. Francesco Molinari, in *Memorie storiche della città e dell'antico ducato della Mirandola*, 2 (Mirandola: Cagarelli, 1874), p. 46, cf. 169; Francesco Calori Cesis, *Pico della Mirandola detto la Fenice degli ingegni* (Mirandola: Cagarelli, 1897), pp. 21–75; Kibre, *The Library of Pico della Mirandola*, pp. 3–22; Michael Engel, *Elijah del Medigo and Paduan Aristotelianism: Investigating the Human Intellect* (London: Blooms-

bury, 2017), pp. 7–8; Giuliano Tamani, "I Libri ebraici di Pico della Mirandola," in Garfagnini, *Giovanni Pico*, 2: 491–530. The two inventories of Pico's library transcribed by Calori Cesis and Kibre are roughly the same size—about 1,200 items—but they were made at different times for different purposes: the first was compiled in 1498 by Antonio Pizzomano when the books were sold to Cardinal Domenico Grimani; both Grimani and his agent studied with Elia del Medigo in Padua when Pico was there. The second inventory reproduces a sixteenth-century Vatican manuscript that may be copied from an earlier list—perhaps written during Pico's lifetime, but not before the end of 1489, since one item (Kibre 849) is the published *Heptaplus*. Although Pico made the books available in his will at low cost either to a religious institution (at 500 ducats) or to Gianfrancesco (1,000 ducats), there may have been no takers since the will's executor—Antonmaria, Pico's brother—sold them to Cardinal Grimani, presumably at a higher price. After the prince died, the books were held at San Marco until Grimani bought them, but they were never willed to the Dominicans: the evidence against this common mistake (as in Foresti's 1503 chronicle) is also explained on pp. 154–55, n. 92, of the *Cronaca della Mirandola dei figli di Manfredo*, as in *Vit*. 2, also in Molinari's edition of a later *Cronaca*, p. 169, n. 116. If Pico's spending on books was in the neighborhood of "seven thousand gold coins," he invested almost a quarter of what Gianfrancesco spent in 1491 to acquire his uncle's estates in Mirandola and Concordia. Any student of the *Oration* will recognize its sources—named and unnamed—in Kibre's list. More than a hundred items are Hebraica, and there is more Kabbalah than meets the eye, probably because the compiler found such books hard to identify. *Quidam liber sine titulo* (Kibre 1132) could be anything, but the list also leaves "33 books in Hebrew" untitled, along with more "small quires in Hebrew." A *Liber gubernationum* (429) is really a *Liber combinationum* on powers of the Hebrew alphabet; a *Secreta* by 'Aulphalachera' (532) is Abulafia's *Book of Secrets*, like another copy (599) of the same book ascribed to 'Abulafra'; a *Caldea expositio psalmorum* is a Psalms targum; and there is no doubt about a *Hebreus Cabalista* (880). Although Plato (*Laws*, 642D) called Epimenides an ἀνὴρ θεῖος, the term became widespread only in the period of the Second Sophistic, referring both to past sages like Pythagoras and Empedocles and to current celebrities like Apollonius of Tyana.

47. *Vit.* 2; *Cronaca della Mirandola dei figli di Manfredo,* ed. Ceretti, pp. 11, 17; Schmitt, *Gianfrancesco Pico,* pp. 21–22, 191: Maximilian I, elected king of the Romans in 1486, succeeded his father, Frederick III, as emperor in 1493. If Gianfrancesco's agreement with his uncle took place "three years before he [Giovanni] died," they made their deal before the winter of 1491, when Maximilian was not yet emperor, though he could have confirmed the transaction later. Gianfrancesco dedicated a book to Maximilian in 1501, and later they were allies in politics. The fourteenth-century chronicle that traces the Pico family's imperial connections to Constantine's granddaughter specifies that these "sons of Manfred were subject to no person except the Emperor alone."

48. Cesare Vasoli, "Girolamo Benivieni," *DBI* (1966); Ferdinando Calori Cesis, *Giovanni Pico della Mirandola, detto La Fenice degli ingegni: Cenni biografici* ([Mirandola]: G. Cagarelli, 1897), p. 29; Allen, "The Birth Day of Venus," in Dougherty, *New Essays,* pp. 83–86; Trevor Dean, *Land and Power in Late Medieval Ferrara: The Rule of the Este, 1350–1450* (Cambridge: Cambridge University Press, 2002), pp. 37, 99–102: Girolamo Benivieni (1453–1542), who lived to be eighty-nine, was a Florentine whose long friendship with Pico began around 1479: this pious and learned poet shared his friend's mystical Platonism and, eventually, his liking for Savonarola. By 1486 he had written the *Canzona on Heavenly and Divine Love* to which Pico responded in his *Commento;* in 1500 Benivieni dedicated a different *Commento* of his own to Gianfrancesco; and in 1519 his *Canzona* was published with Pico's *Commento* in a collection of his works. Corbola was an important Este holding, comprising a number of fiefs northeast of Ferrara on the Po. The distance from Mirandola is seventy-five miles, even farther from Florence, but the prince could have drawn income from Corbola without living there. However, since he acquired property there as early as 1483 — just after his stay in Padua — he may have been planning more trips to the Veneto with stops at Corbola. See Intro. at n. 42 on Pico's "former luxury."

49. See Intro. at n. 41 for "alms from his own body."

50. Sen. *Dial.* 10.5.3: this is the younger Seneca, and *supra fortunam* was a favorite Stoic phrase; see also Intro. at nn. 50 and 51 on "Chaldean," and n. 25 on the "handsome and graceful" Pico.

51. *Vit.* 82–84; Isa. 55:8; Paul. *Vit. Ambros.* 9; Possid. *Vit. Aug.* 4, 8; Sulp. Sev. *Vit. Mart.* 5, 9–10; Dante, *Inf.* 3.59–60; Petrarch, *Vit. sol.* 8.12–19; Eduardo Melfi, "Pandolfo Collenuccio," *DBI* (1982): Pandolfo Collenuccio (1444–1504) was a learned historian, diplomat, and poet who made and unmade alliances with various Italian powers, including the papacy, while maintaining cultural connections with Girolamo Benivieni, Poliziano, and other friends of Pico. In light of Savonarola's excoriation of Pico for refusing his vocation, Gianfrancesco may have been ambivalent about Celestine V as a model: he abdicated the papacy in 1294. But whether it was Celestine that Dante sent to Hell — *che fece per viltade il gran rifiuto* — is unclear, and Petrarch defended him as an exemplar of the solitary life.

52. *Orat.* 36–37: Pico, ranting about critics of his plan to dispute in Rome, denounced them as moneygrubbing sophists who pimped for Lady Philosophy to get "ill-gotten coin taken in cheap trade for her de-flowered virginity." Gianfrancesco, whose uncle's social outlook was also his, took Giovanni's disdain for riches and glory at face value.

53. *Orat.* 50–51; *Concl.* p. 1; *App.* 1.2; *Apol.* p. 1; *Hept.* sig. a2^r: "To worry little" about fame seems not to have been the prince's instinct at the time he wrote the *Oration* and published the *Conclusions*; he had his name and titles printed at the front of the *Conclusions* and the *Apology*, though only the name appeared in the *Heptaplus*. The orator, after promising to "put ideas of all sorts into play" in the *Oration*, was ashamed to "contribute nothing of one's own, nothing born of one's own talent."

54. Pico, *Dell'Ente*, ed. Bacchelli and Ebgi, pp. 242–44; Anon., *Compilatio assisiensis*, 103–5 (https://www.franciscantradition.org/francis-of-assisi-ea rly-documents); Eric Palazzo, *A History of Liturgical Books from the Beginning to the Thirteenth Century*, trans. M. Beaumont (Collegeville: Pueblo Books, 1998), p. 169: Pico made his exasperated statement about loving and knowing in *De ente* as his argument turned from metaphysics to mysticism and the hidden God of the Areopagite. The *Assisi Compilation* from the middle of the thirteenth century collected stories about Saint

Francis, reporting his remark in a slightly different form: *tantum scit homo de scientia quantum operatur*. He said this to a novice who asked him for a Psalter to practice reading. "After you get a Psalter, you'll want a breviary," Francis replied, "and after you get a breviary, you'll sit in a fine chair like a big bishop telling your brother 'bring me my breviary.'" To shame the novice, the saint poured ashes over his own head, scrubbed them in and said, "I am the breviary, I am the breviary!" Then he added that a brother should have only the simplest clothing, no other possessions at all. *Breviarium*, literally, 'something shortened,' is a joke about *fratres* <u>*minores*</u>, a name of the Franciscan order. The first 'breviary' so called was a Franciscan compilation of the thirteenth century.

55. *Orat.* 25; *B*, sigs. axii–VVvi^r; Ecclus. 3:19; Philostr. *VA* 4.16; Aquinas, *ST* II–I.27; Jules Dukas, *Recherches sur l'histoire littéraire du quinzième siècle: Laurent Maioli, Pic de la Mirandole, Elie del Medigo* (Paris: Techener, 1876), pp. 48–65; Léon Dorez, "Lettres inédites de Jean Pic de la Mirandole (1482–1492)," *Giornale Storico della Letteratura Italiana* 25: 352–61; Copenhaver, "Studied as an Oration," pp. 175–77, 185–91: Philostratus stressed the affinity among sages that Gianfrancesco observed among Pico's friends — *sophois gar pro sophous epitêdeia* — and Aquinas allowed that likeness (*similitudo*), not just knowledge of a good, causes love, especially among friends: "In that two persons are alike, as if they had a single form, they are somehow one in that form." Since a human's substantial form is her soul, one thinks of the *Oration* and the "friendship of the single-souled." But to philosophize about love, Thomas also considered unreasoning animals and physical similarities like whiteness (*albedo*) — a standard example of an accident or quality inhering in a substance. Morality rather than metaphysics was the issue for Philostratus, however, and the many friendships of Apollonius (a wizard as well as a wise man) matched Gianfrancesco's praise of his uncle's connections. The letters from Giovanni that he published were addressed to twenty of his uncle's friends — not to mention Gianfrancesco himself, who added testimonies and commendations by some of these recipients as well as praises from nine others: see Pico, *Lettere*, for the prince's correspondents. All in all, Gianfrancesco documented thirty cases of the "intellectual talent" admired by Giovanni — including important communications with Gi-

rolamo Benivieni, Ficino, and Elia del Medigo. In a collection introduced by Gianfrancesco's *piagnone* hagiography, some of this material would have confused his story because it promotes astrology, Kabbalah, and magic.

56. Hor. *Epod.* 4.2.1–8

57. *Vit.* 3; Bacchelli, "Pico," *DBI* (2015); Intro. at nn. 15, 24, 27, 46–47: Pico was in Florence briefly in 1479, the same year when he moved his studies from Bologna to Ferrara. He was there again for longer stays after 1483. The bantering about the Academy, more typical of Ficino than Pico, meant that Ficino's scholarship gave Pico access to later Platonic writings by Plotinus, Porphyry, Iamblichus, Proclus, and others: see James Hankins, "The Myth of the Platonic Academy of Florence," *Renaissance Quarterly* 44.3 (1991): 429–75.

58. *Vit.* 82–84, 88; Walter Pater, *The Renaissance: Studies in Art and Poetry, the 1893 Text*, ed. D. Hill (Berkeley: University of California Press), p. 34; Weinstein, *Savonarola and Florence*, p. 215; cf. James O'Neil, *Jerome Savonarola: A Sketch* (Boston: Marlier and Callanan, 1898), p. 166: Because Pico's first biographer was close to Savonarola, the prince's Dominican connections stand out in his legend. He lies buried in San Marco, where Savonarola presided, and burial in a Dominican habit is likely enough—as Pater, Weinstein, and many others have reported. But if Savonarola had actually clothed Pico like a friar on his deathbed, according to other stories, either the Prior or Gianfrancesco would surely have said so. The biography itself indicates that the prince had not firmly "decided to join the Order of Preachers" until he was dying. Otherwise, Savonarola would not have railed at him for not accepting his vocation.

59. *Vit.* 85–86; *Concl.* pp. 41–43; *App.* 1.3, 6, 8, 9, 10; 26.1–2, 10, 14, 18–19; *Apol.* pp. 37, 60, 99, 103, 165; Intro. at nn. 39, 47: Displaying a crucifix was part of the last rites, also giving communion and reviewing "customary points" of the creed like the Trinity, the Incarnation, and the Passion. But belief (*credere*) and constraints on it were problems in a condemned thesis from the *Conclusions*. Gianfrancesco, alert to such charges, describes Pico's death (which he did not witness, being "far away" at the time) by bringing up another topic—the eucharist—on which his uncle's

views had been denounced. He also reports a question asked at the deathbed — whether the dying man "believed the crucifix to be a true image of the true God" — that echoes yet another condemned thesis. Pico had put these troublesome propositions together in a group that he called "quite different from the usual way of talking about theology." Nonetheless, the desired effect of Gianfrancesco's narrative was to remove doubts about Giovanni's orthodoxy by showing "not only that he believed . . . but that he was sure."

60. *Vit.* 3, 17; *Concl.* 13; *App.* 1.12.1; *Themistii Peripatetici acutissimi paraphraseos libri . . . interprete Hermolao Barbaro* (Venice: Lucantonio Giunta, 1530), pp. 7, 14, 26–33; Fabio Forner, "Alberto Pio," *DBI* (2015); Eckhardt Kessler, "Alexander of Aphrodisias and His Doctrine of the Soul: 1400 Years of Lasting Significance," *Early Science and Medicine* 16 (2011): 9–10, 27, 30–33: Gianfrancesco (*Vit.* 17) has already labeled Alexander of Aphrodisias and Averroes "ungodly" philosophers disliked by his uncle. In Barbaro's translation of the paraphrase of Aristotle's *Physics* by Themistius, a preface introduces differences between Themistius and Alexander, who (incorrectly, according to Themistius) denies that "the soul is completely separated from all matter." If the soul is the body's *material* form, it cannot share the immortality of the divine and bodiless Agent Intellect. Nonetheless, in a proposition that he may have stated to refute it, Pico wrote that "the rational soul is immortal" as his first thesis on Alexander, though he may have been thinking of a different work by Alexander — *On the Intellect*, which is friendlier to Platonism. A few years later, by 1491, Alexander's *Explanation of Aristotle's Teaching on the Soul* was translated by Girolamo Donato, one of Pico's correspondents, whose Latin version made the text available to Vernia, Agostino Nifo, and others. The prince's nephew, Alberto Pio, was close to him, well educated, and friendly with Pomponazzi after Pico's death. Although Pio was a politician, not a philosopher, his excellent education and intellectual friendships could have introduced him to tangled debates among his philosophical contemporaries about Averroes and his Greek sources. Otherwise, why Gianfrancesco associated him with Averroism is unclear.

61. *Vit.* 74: Pico's final illness started with a "very nasty fever," and delirium could have been a symptom.

62. Calori Cesis, *Pico*, p. 22, for the will that leaves Pico's real property to the Hospital of Santa Maria Novella (not San Marco) and other property to Antonmaria.

63. Dorez and Louis Thuasne, *Pic de la Mirandole en France (1485–1488)* (Geneva: Slatkine, 1976), pp. 30–37, 73–76, 87–91, 102–3; Raymond Marcel, "Pic de la Mirandole et la France: De l'Université de Paris au donjon de Vincennes," in *L'Opera e il pensiero di Giovanni Pico*, 1.227–29: Charles VIII launched his invasion of Italy in August 1494, and by February of the next year his troops were in Naples, having passed through Florence in November. He had succeeded Louis XI in 1483, shortly before Pico came to Paris. Because of the prince's rank and the king's liking for the University of Paris, a meeting between them is plausible. When Pico left Italy because of the pope's actions and was arrested near Lyon in 1488, Charles and his agents were supportive.

64. *Apul. Met.* 1.3; Weinstein, *Savonarola and Florence*, pp. 74–77, 102–4, 126, 132: Santa Reparata was the old name for Florence's Duomo, renamed San Giovanni del Fiore in 1436. Since Gianfrancesco certainly knew what came after the "words from Apuleius" that he chose—bizarre tales of magic and sorcery—he may have been obtuse, but not ignorant.

65. The "maxim from John's Gospel" is unidentified, but see John 8:14: *Verum est testimonium meum quia scio unde veni et quo vado*; many such claims about truth, a major theme of John's Gospel, could have become proverbial by constant repetition. Or maybe Savonarola, not Florentine by birth, had heard members of his Tuscan congregation say *San Giovanni non vuole inganni*—"Saint John wants no tricks"—even though this John would have been the Baptist, not the Evangelist: see Intro. at nn. 22, 47–48 for Savonarola's sermon.

66. *Vit.* 84; Bacchelli, "Pico," *DBI* (2015): Pico met Savonarola by 1482 or perhaps earlier. He supported his return to Florence in 1490 and joined him at Lorenzo de' Medici's deathbed in 1492. In this context, "religion" means a religious order, like Savonarola's Dominicans: Pico sinned by not heeding this call to religion.

67. *Vit.* 90; Dante, *Purg.* 10.115–17: Savonarola's threats of the lash, if in retrospect he saw Pico's death as the outcome, would have started in

1492. Although the friar assured the Florentines that Pico would not burn in Hell forever, they knew that the temporal pains of Purgatory, even tempered by the certainty of salvation, were dreadful enough: *la grave condizione / di lor tormento a terra li rannichia*. Yet the friar's message, however harsh, could be helpful to Pico inasmuch as it prompted others to "help him with their support" by praying for his speedy release.

68. *Vit.* 75; *Ars moriendi, quamvis secundum philosophum* (1465–70; BNF xylo-21): Images in the *Art of Dying* pamphlets of Pico's era depicted demons swarming the bed of the *moriens* to battle angels for his soul. Savonarola's enemies, according to Gianfrancesco, said that evil spirits were tricking the friar with demonic phantasms, but the cross shown to Pico would have protected him.

69. Weinstein, *Savonarola and Florence*, pp. 24, 68–73, 154–55, 289–314; Eileen Gardiner, *Medieval Visions of Heaven and Hell: A Sourcebook* (London: Routledge, 1993): As a Dominican and therefore in the Thomist tradition, Savonarola had commitments to Aristotelian philosophy. The political part of his early (1484) *Compendium of All Philosophy* is Thomist but not doctrinaire. In his later *Compendium of Revelations* (1496), he took credit for predicting "the death of Innocent VIII and of Lorenzo de' Medici, also the revolution of the Florentine government at the time when the King of France would first approach Paris," which was also the time of Pico's death. Visions of the afterlife, including Purgatory, were common in medieval literature: the most famous is Dante's *Commedia*.

70. Vasoli, "Camilla Bartolini Rucellai," *DBI* (1964); Vanna Arrighi, "Cosimo Pazzi," *DBI* (2015): The prophetic nun was Camilla Rucellai (1465–1520), an ardent follower of Savonarola from a distinguished Florentine family. The *fleur de lys* had been a symbol of the French monarchy since the twelfth century. Members of the Pazzi family were exiled for conspiring to kill Giuliano and Lorenzo de' Medici in 1478. Lorenzo lived until 1492, and the surviving Pazzi were allowed to return to Florence in November 1494, the month of Pico's death. See *Vit.* 73 on the chronology of the prince's "commitment to religion."

71. *Vit.* 75, 83–84; *Concl.* p. 43; *App.* 1.1.2; 26.19–20; *Apol.* p. 33; Matt. 18:34–35; Aquinas, *ST* III suppl., app. 1.2: Jacques Le Goff, *The Birth of*

Purgatory, trans. A. Goldhammer (Chicago: University of Chicago Press, 1981), pp. 218–25: Defending his uncle's sentence to Purgatory, Gianfrancesco made no effort to use the careful terminology of sacramental theology. He certainly knew, despite the loose language, that only unforgiven mortal sins — not venial sins, even if unforgiven — were grave enough to deserve a place in Hell. Pico parsed the penalty for mortal sin in one of his condemned theses. Nonetheless, with all his theological learning, and even though he "knew God's will," he delayed submitting to it. In his nephew's view, this negligence justified "many lashes." However, we are not told whether the sin was venial or mortal, forgiven or unforgiven. The prince's last rites included communion, and he may also have been given the sacrament of penance. If he was absolved of "any other crimes" (*a noxis quibusque aliis . . . immunis*), this particular sin could have been still unforgiven yet venial: otherwise the guilt (*culpa*) for it, though not the temporal penalty (*poena*), would have been eliminated by confessing. Since no sufferers in Purgatory had died with mortal sins unforgiven, which would have sent them to Hell, all of them were already saved, though still in torment. Hence, Gianfrancesco was correct to say that the "just too are penalized." The Truth whom he calls to witness is Jesus speaking in the Gospel parable of the master and servant.

72. *Orat.* 20; *Vit.* 47; *Hept.* sig. b8ᵛ; Ps.-Dion. *CH* 165A–C, 196B–C: Pico appealed to the same principle of visionary hierarchy to support his novel exegesis in the *Heptaplus*.

73. *Vit.* 65; *Orat.* 11, 27–30; Num. 22–24, 31:16; Matt. 24:11; 1 John 4:1; 2Pet. 2:1, 13–16; cf. 1Thes. 5:19–22; Arist. *Div. somn.* 462ᵇ13–14; Anne Borelli et al., ed. and trans., *Selected Writings of Girolamo Savonarola: Religion and Politics, 1490–1498* (New Haven: Yale University Press, 2006), pp. 61–62, 280–82: Balaam made true prophecies — including one (Num. 24:17) that Christians applied to the birth of Jesus. But he was called a "false prophet" because of crimes against Israel. Biblical warnings against *pseudoprophetae* gave Savonarola's enemies an opening, which made the accuracy of his predictions all the more important. Defending his prophetic light in 1495, he was "more certain of this than you are that two and two make four," but "this light does not justify me; Balaam, who prophesied, was nonetheless a sinner." In the same year, he acknowledged

that the "predicting of future events that I do is much contradicted and many make mock of it, but . . . the Apostle Paul commanded us not to despise prophecies, . . . and the things I have predicted are continually seen to be proved true." Like his uncle's *Disputations*, Gianfrancesco's *De praenotione* attacked false divination, but not divination in general. Giovanni's *Oration* is enthusiastic about "Socratic frenzies" and various types of prophecy endorsed by Plato and other sages. Aristotle, in his little study of predictive dreams, wrote that "we cannot lightly either dismiss this with contempt or give credence to it." The "outside evidence" from pagan Aristotelians and Platonists, although Gianfrancesco called it "not serious" unless confirmed by sacred scripture, still had positive effects just because Savonarola's unrighteous critics relied on it, thus giving Gianfrancesco and his *piagnone* allies yet another reason to reprimand the friar's detractors.

74. Gen. 25:13; Isa. 21:16–17; Ps. 120:5–6 (Vulg. 119); Savonarola, *Sermones in primam Divi Ioannis Epistolam con il volgarizzamento toscano*, ed. Armando Verde (Rome: Belardetti, 1989), pp. 226, 438: The Psalm quoted in this sermon from 1490 on John's first Epistle is a prayer of distress and regret. "Woe is me that my sojourn there has been prolonged! I have dwelled with those who dwell in Kedar." Kedar, in the north of the Arabian peninsula, was the land of descendants of Ishmael: see Intro. at n. 47.

ORATION

1. Cic. *Orat.* 2.338; Cic. *De or.* 2.338; *Asclep.* 5–6, where the word order is different; Hier. *Epist.* 129.4; *Continuatio chronicorum beati Isidori sancto Hildefonso supposita*, MPL 96: 317, 321A. For Abdala, see Intro. at n. 64, and for Arabic gnomology, *Orat.* 55. Abdala is a "prophet" in F, where *homo* translates the Arabic *al-rajul*: see F 1 and the headnote to App. II. In a passage missing from B, F 46 also says that Arabic is a language needed for philosophy, while naming Flavius Mithridates as Pico's teacher. Jerome called "Arabs and Hagarites" *Sarraceni*, and Muhammad was the chief of the *Sarraceni* and *Arabes* in a chronicle that surfaced in the fourteenth century. What makes mankind miraculous in the Hermetic treatise is *medietas*, the middle status that links humans with gods and de-

mons as well as lower things: see *meditullium* in *Orat.* 5. Some people are
"contented" to be where and as they are in the cosmic order, but an enlightened person, according to the *Asclepius*, "despises the part of him that
is human nature, . . . in which he is earthly." For Pico's body-hating im-
materialism, see *Orat.* 4, 9, 26, 27, 33, and especially 18, where the *Asclepius* — confused like all the Hermetica about pessimism or optimism in
morals and metaphysics — underwrites the speech's relentless asceticism.
But *medietas* in the Hermetica is not the same as God's promise of "no
fixed seat" in *Orat.* 6, and even there Adam stands in the center of the
universe to survey it. Pico calls on the "Fathers" — the College of Cardinals — eleven more times at *Orat.* 3, 21, 28, 30, 34, 36, 38, 54, 57, 67, and
72, for a total of twelve, an "Apostolic" number, as in *Orat.* 39. For *scaena*
(stage) in Cicero, see *Orat.* 2.338. (On the words and phrases italicized,
see Intro. at n. 102. References to numbered paragraphs in the English
and Latin include these notes to the translation.)

2. Pico, *Comm.* 1.12 (Bürklin, p. 54); Ps. 8:6; Cic. *De or.* 1.1; *Orac. chal.* 6,
39, 42, 44 (Des Places); also Pl. *Ti.* 31C, 38E, 43A, 73B–D, 81D; Ti. Locr.
39 (98ᵉ–99ᵇ); Procl. *In Parm.* 2.768–69; *In Ti.* 2.53–55: Corresponding to
copula (bond) and *hymenaeum* (wedding knot) are *desmos* or *sundektikon*
and *humên* in the *Chaldean Oracles*; its authors are *Persae* in B, *Magi* in F 2.
In their theogony, "chaste Eros" is the first god to leap from the Paternal
Mind; Love is the "revered binder (*sundektikon*) of all," unifying the soul's
aetherial vehicle (*ochêma*). Like the vehicle, the *humên* is intermediate, an
immaterial membrane between intelligible and sensible states. Since a
cantus hymenaeus is a wedding song, *hymenaeum* — a substantive in apposi-
tion with *copula* and *interstitium* — may reflect nuptial language about
Hecate's "girdling" in the *Oracles*, where *desmos* (*copula*) is an erotic and
fertile principle. The context also seems sexual for Pico's only other use
of *interstitium* — at *Orat.* 30. Man is the *vinculo e nodo del mondo* in the
Commento as well, but only the prince's friends had seen this work when
Gianfrancesco decided to leave it out of his 1496 collection, and almost
no one could have detected allusions to the fragmentary *Oracles*. In Greek
they were "mutilated," according to Pico (*Orat.* 69), who said he had a
better text, "more complete in Chaldean," though it would have been intelligible only to his Jewish collaborators. His disdain for ordinary read-

ers is stunning, making it hard to see his litany of *admiror* and *admiratio* (eleven times within the first nine hundred words) as anything but teasing: see Intro. at n. 66. Throughout the speech, scraps of prose lifted from unnamed *auctores* — like *cogitanti mihi* here, and *scaena* in the previous paragraph — show off his erudition. The conceit is that identification is otiose: everyone knows that *cogitanti mihi* — placed here by the orator at the start of his *Oration* — are the first words of Cicero's work *On the Orator*. And everyone remembers Cicero saying in the same work that a *scaena* is where a speaker stands to deliver a speech of the "more embellished kind." The test for Pico's audience was to spot the embellishments, sometimes marked by signals like the *quasi* here; other decorations speak for themselves, like the triplet of *internuntius, interpres,* and *interstitium*. See *Orat.* 36, 38–39, 44 and *Bn*, pp. 3–4 on this and other features of Pico's style; also Intro. at n. 102 for similar practices, differently motivated, in rabbinical and Kabbalist texts.

3. Pico repeats his claim in *Orat.* 1 about the human miracle and promises to explain it. If the human animal is the "most fortunate" of all and "deserves all the astonishment," the orator's human listeners should have been flattered, and capturing their good will (*captatio benevolentiae*) belongs here at the beginning of the speech. Even if the *Oration* is not purely oratorical, it is constantly attentive to oratorical strategy.

4. Gen. 1:26–27; Isa. 29:14; Ps. 104:24; Wisd. 8:20, 9:15, 11:21–25, 18:16; 1 Cor. 1:17–27; Pl. *Ti.* 41 A–D; Ti. Locr. 7, 43 (94c, 99d); Apul. *De dog. Plat.* 1.11; *Corp. Herm.* 5.5–6, 6.4; *Asclep.* 8–9; *Orac. chald.* 88, 100, 113–14, 116, 129, 157 (Des Places); Macrob. *In somn.* 1.19.12; Julian. *Or.* 5.170C–D; Syn. *Hymn.* 3.321; Lact. *Ir.* 14.1; Psell. *Expos.* 1152[d]: Man was created to admire the Creator in the creation, according to Lactantius — "the Workman in the work," in Pico's words; see *Orat.* 13, also 59–60 on *Artifex* and *Opifex*. After making the same point, however, the *Asclepius* adds that humans laboring "under the body's bulk" never achieve the understanding that requires "looking up to heaven." Since Pico had just cited the *Asclepius*, Hermetic texts (see the translations in Copenhaver, *Hermetica*) were surely on his mind when he wrote *Orat.* 4. In some parts of this notoriously inconsistent collection, the universe is good and a "most happy sight to see." In others, "the cosmos is a plenitude of vice." Which per-

spective was Pico's? Did the "miracle" in *Orat*. 1 impress him less than the "noose" in *Orat*. 18 — both taken from the *Asclepius*? The asceticism — sometimes morbid — in the speech expresses a grim outlook, aggravated by the *Chaldean Oracles* and other authorities: see Lewy, pp. 264–68, 304–5, 385. The emperor Julian, who revered the *Oracles*, reviled the world of bodies and matter as dung (*faex, trux, hupostathmê*), like Macrobius and Synesius. Pico's showy diction (noted by *Bn*, p. 6) reflects this contempt for earthly existence: *excrementarius* is a coinage, and *faeculentus* is rare in classical Latin. Besides the Craftsman God, the only persons named in this passage are Moses, as the author of Genesis, and Timaeus of Locri, as Plato's Pythagorean interlocutor — unless Wisdom too is a person. Since Kabbalah has not yet been introduced, perhaps we are not to think of Wisdom as the second *Sefirah* (Intro. at n. 112). Then why is *Sapientia* — a secret kept by Paul in *Orat*. 64 — called *arcana* here? Although some Greek wisdom is also 'arcane' (*Orat*. 27, 57, 60), the speech highlights secrets of Kabbalah as "arcana of supreme divinity concealed beneath the bark of the Law" (*Orat*. 64, 66). But if Pico was thinking of a sefirotic *Sapientia*, his thoughts would have mystified a Christian audience, even though his Jewish tutors in Kabbalah, familiar with an androgyne God, would have known that the Creator consulted his own womanly Wisdom while creating. In the biblical book that bears her name, she comes to a "body undefiled," unless a "corruptible body is a load upon the soul." Likewise, God cherishes the universe ordered by him "in measure and number and weight," as Wisdom teaches, and yet to destroy his enemies he "filled it all with death." Wisdom's counsel is subtle, then, and according to Isaiah "the wisdom of the wise shall perish." Like Paul preaching folly to the Corinthians, perhaps Pico took the point. Because he disliked clarity, in any case, he kept his oratory unclear: see *Orat*. 35, 64, and Intro. at nn. 63–64. Sources silenced and allusions packed inside of allusions continue through the speech: secrecy prevails, making it hard to say which texts are in play at any moment.

5. 1 Cor. 1:24; Pl. *Phlb*. 23C; *Prtg*. 321 B–C; Lucr. 2.1150; Plin. *HN* pr. 1, 35.88; Apul. *De dog. Plat*. 2.5; *Met*. 3.27, 5.1, 7.19, 10.32, 11.24; Hier. *Pelag*. 1.12; Aug. *Trin*. 6.5; 15.3, 18; *Gen. litt*. 1.3, 14.52; *Civ*. 22.17; Chalc. *In Ti.*, after 32C; Ficino, *Pim.*, fols. 2–4: To extend the point of *Orat*. 4, that

God made humans to admire him, Pico now asks how the making happened, and his answer clashes with the orthodox doctrine of creation. Triplets (see *Orat.* 2) are prominent again, here and in the next paragraph: above/ethereal/below; archetypes/treasury/benches; seat/look/gift — all reflecting a Trinity of Power, Wisdom, and Love. *Potestas, Sapientia,* and *Voluntas* rather than *Amor* were the supreme Hermetic divinities, according to Ficino, but Augustine emphasized Love more than Will and Pico agreed. Either way, the theological crux is that Three acted as One to create Adam, a single human creature. Both triads sustain the mystery of trinitarian creation by dissolving it in grand abstractions. But Pico's *Opifex* — Plato's *Dêmiourgos* — is a Workman; there are *creaturae* in the speech (*Orat.* 2, 7, 10) but no *Creator.* Some found it hard to believe that "God is the maker of the world," according to Calcidius, "unless he has assembled it like some workman (*opifex*) with his hands." God *created* everything in the universe, however; he did not *assemble* Adam out of spare parts "reserved for every other being." Even assuming that Pico was speaking rhetorically, not as a theologian, the rhetoric suggests an odd sort of creation. Augustine was entirely clear: "All of creation . . . has been made by God out of nothing," including both Eve and Adam: the rib was just a symbol of unity between woman and man. *Meditullium* (midregion) is a rare term — but a favorite of Apuleius. In Jerome's attack on the Pelagians, the word indicates an unhappy place. A person stationed there falls "from the summit of virtue into vice or rises from vices to the heights, but at no time is he safe and must always fear shipwreck in the calm, and so a human cannot be without sin": see *Orat.* 1. When Pliny wrote that *imagines* made by Apelles were *similitudinis indiscretae,* he meant that likeness and reality were indiscernible in them. *Faetura* (breeding) and *effeta* (exhausted) are linked etymologically with *fetus;* see *Orat.* 51 and *Bn,* pp. 8–10, who identifies such rhetorical ornaments throughout the speech.

6. Gen. 1:26–27; Eccles. 15:14; Pl. *Symp.* 202E, 204D; Mart. Cap. 1.68; Plot. 1.6.9 (MacKenna); *Midr. Num.* 13:3; *Zohar* I, 2[b]–3[a], 20[a], 22[b], 63[a], 204[a], 209, 250[b]: "Never cease chiseling your statue" was advice given by Plotinus; good counsel for a *plastes* (molder) and *fictor* (maker) able to shape himself. But the original Creator — not Pico's stand-in — would not

have approved. "Let us make man in *our own* image and likeness," he/they declared. The divine image was perfect; nothing could improve on God's likeness. Since the pattern used to make Adam was faultless, nothing at all about his image could be indistinct, as in *Orat.* 5. What was Pico thinking about? Writing a new script for God was outrageous enough. Getting the theology wrong was worse, on two key points: creation *ex nihilo* in *Orat.* 5; and God's perfect simplicity here. For some risky ideas, however, like self-sculpture and man's authority to choose for himself, the prince could rely on classical or biblical authority. Inventing words for the Deity was more daring, but he had precedent in his Aramaic and Hebrew books, where storytelling of this type is common. See Intro. at n. 61; also *Orat.* 26 for another invented speech.

7. *Concl.* p. 56; App. 1.30.10; Exod. 19–20 (Vulg.), esp. 20:21; Ps. 97:2; Cic. *Off.* 1.20; Apul. *Apol.* 47; Lucil. 1.26.623; Iambl. *Protr.* 35.14–22; Asclep. 5; ps.-Dion. *MT* 997A–1001A; *Epist.* 1073A; *Zohar* I, 66ᵃ; Abulafia, *Sitre Tora*, fol. 61ᵃ, as cited by Idel, "Kabbalistic Backgrounds," pp. 29–32: With the same word, *contentus*, used by the *Asclepius* to describe humans who are satisfied with mere humanity (see *Orat.* 1), Pico now urges the others to act on their discontent. They must cease being human and become "one with God," first as the angel Metatron, to be named in *Orat.* 8. All humans, as sons of God, are already like angels. But Metatron, the Agent Intellect, is the unique Son of God, having once been the human Enoch—according to Abraham Abulafia and as suggested by Pico in a thesis from Zoroaster and the Chaldeans on the Intellect and the Boy: see Intro. at nn. 77–79. Unlike humans, good angels were never restless, having always been as they are and will be; it was the fallen angels who had become unhappy and were damned "a little later." (The "heavenly animal" in *B* is also a *demon* in *F* 7–8.) Pico marks a path for anxious humans with a silent borrowing from Iamblichus on plants, beasts, and divinities that sets the stage for the rest of the speech, especially the part through *Orat.* 35; see other progressions through four levels—sensual, rational, intellectual, and higher—at *Orat.* 8, 9, and 16, also Intro. at nn. 73–76 on the larger structure. The Areopagite's "truly mysterious darkness of unknowing" is "beyond everything" (*pantôn epekeina*) in his *Mystical Theology*: this classical statement of Christian mysticism is an exegesis

of Exod. 19–20, where "Moses approached the darkness (*caligo*) in which God was." Apuleius used *solitarius* in a similar way to describe "night vigils hidden in darkness and unwitnessed solitude (*arbitris solitaria*), as spells are murmured"; cf. *solitudo* in *Orat.* 26. Darkness in the *Zohar* protects Moses from God's overpowering light. When a mystic 'withdraws' from the body into the mind, as also in *Orat.* 9, the experience is psychological and intermediate; the final stage, when the mind drowns in God's bottomless lake, eliminates the subject's psychology.

8. *Concl.*, pp. 14–15, 49, 55, 62; *App.* 1.13.2, 15.4, 16.8, 27.51, 30.4, 33.10; Pico, *Comm.* str. 4 (= *Kommentar*, ed. Bürklin, p. 185); Gen. 4:17, 5:18–24; Lev. 11:30; Ecclus. 44:16, 49:16; *Tg. ps.-J. Gen.* 5:24; 3En. 4:2; *b. Sanh.* 108[b]; Pl. *Chrm.* 155B; *Phd.* 118A; Arist. *Hist. an.* 503[a]15–28; *Eth. Nic.* 1100[b]; *Mir. ausc.* 832[b]8–16; Plut. *Vit. Alc.* 23; *Quomodo adul.* 53[d]4–6; Plin. *HN* 8.120–22; 11.152, 188; 28.112–18; Diog. Laert. 8.14, 36; Chalc. *Comm. Tim.* after 42B–C; Greg. Naz. *Orat.* 4.62; *Koran* 2:65, 171; 7:166, 176, 179; *Zohar* I, 223b; II, 80[b]; Abulafia, *Secr.*, fols. 341[v]–42[r], 377[r]–78[v]; Ficino, *Op.* p. 1825: Without yet giving Kabbalah its name (see *Orat.* 34, 66), Pico alludes to it as a "more secret theology," having already dropped hints that a Christian audience would miss. For the chameleon, Empedocles, Mohammed, Proteus, Pythagoras, and metempsychosis, see Intro. at nn. 66–69. Enoch was a descendant of Cain and an ancestor of Methuselah and Noah: only biblical apocrypha tell his full story. According to the Bible, he "walked with God; then he was no more, for God took him." Extrabiblical texts treated this as an elevation to angelic rank: in a Targum, "Hanok served in the truth before the Lord; and, behold, he was not with the sojourners of the earth; for he was withdrawn, and he ascended to the firmament by the Word before the Lord, and his name was called Metatron." Where *B* leaves a blank space, *F* 8 supplies the angel's name, מטטרון, as in *Ba*, pp. 15–16; *Bn*, pp. 143, 171–72. In the *Conclusions*, a thesis on Themistius names *Matatron* in Latin, and Wirszubski fills a blank in another thesis with the same Hebrew name: "What Cabalists call מטטרון is beyond doubt what Orpheus names Pallas, Zoroaster the Mind of the Father, Mercury the Son of God, Pythagoras Wisdom, Parmenides the Intelligible Sphere." These are aspects of the Agent Intellect, identified by Abraham Abulafia with Enoch and Metatron: see Intro. at nn. 69, 77–79,

109. What about the Athenian Asclepius? The Hermetic Asclepius is Egyptian, not Athenian: perhaps this Asclepius is Socrates, a physician of the soul in the *Charmides* and a patient of Aesculapius in the *Phaedo* and in *Orat.* 32. The vegetable, animal, rational, and intellectual qualities at the end of this paragraph mirror the plants, beasts, angels, and unified spirits of *Orat.* 7, repeated in *Orat.* 9 along with "right reason." The "heavenly orb" is a *demon* in F 8.

9. Hom. *Il.* 2.140, 24.258; *Od.* 5.55–268; Arist. *Eth. Nic.* 1103^{b}32, 1114^{b}29, 1119^{a}20, 1138^{a}10, 1138^{b}20–34, 1144^{b}23–28, 1145^{a}15–28; Cic. *Leg.* 1.33; Luc. 5.97; Sen. *Epist.* 41.4–5; Diog. Laert. 7.128; Plot. 1.6.6–8; Mart. Cap. 1.7; Isid. *Etym.* 11.1.4: The nymph Calypso was not the witch Circe (see *Orat.* 58), but her magic was enough to delay Odysseus for seven years. Plotinus conflated the two women, warning against "sorceries of Circe or Calypso" which are "pleasures of the body" when the soul — in Pico's words — is still "cloaked in human flesh." "Right reason," mentioned in the previous paragraph and repeated here, is the Stoic *orthos logos* and Cicero's *recta ratio*, a providential rationality within nature. Aristotle's right reason ('correct prescription,' perhaps) is more abstract. Beings who rise to the level of reason, above nonsentient plants and unreasoning animals, may still be confined within nature. But with spiritual discipline, they can withdraw to the "mind's sanctuary," shed their material coverings and become angels — like Enoch becoming Metatron. Angels, at home beyond mutable nature, are not like the *numen* "held in a maiden breast" in Lucan's verses, where the words *virgineo* (maiden) and *conceptum* (held) resonate with Christian dogma. The *humus/homo* pun in the first sentence was very old when Pico used it: Isidore explained that "'humans' are so called because they were made from 'humus,' as it says in Genesis, 'God created man from the soil (*humo*) of the earth.'"

10. Gen. 1:21, 6:12–13, 7.21, 9:11; Acts 2:17; Rom. 8:22; 1Pet. 2:13; Apul. *Met.* 1.1; *Orac. chal.* 106 (Des Places), with Lewy, pp. 55, 254; *Zohar* I, 61^a–65^b: "All flesh" (*kol-bashar*) and "every creature" (*kol-nefesh*) are common biblical phrases, often pejorative and sometimes rendered literally by the Vulgate as *omnis caro* and *omnis creatura*. According to the *Zohar*, commenting on Gen. 6, the "end of all flesh" is the Angel of Death, who "desires nothing but flesh constantly. . . . He rules over body, not over soul.

Soul ascends to her site, while flesh is given to this site," like an animal
unfit for sacrifice. Evantes has not been identified. For the words in
'Chaldean'—actually Hebrew mixed with Aramaic in Ethiopic script—
see Intro. at nn. 50–51, *Orat.* 33, and the headnote to App. II. A translit-
eration is *barnash hu ḥay miteva meshtaneh venadad umaḥalephet garmah cho
vacho.* The first word, *barnash* (human being), alliterates with *bashar*
(flesh). *Barnash* is Hebrew, though not biblical, compounded from *bar*
(son) and Aramaic *nash* (man). If Pico also had the Greek *Oracles* in
mind, his thinking about "all flesh" was negative since man's "nature" (*phu-
sis*) there is "overweening" (*tolmêros*).

11. Pico, *Comm.* (stanzas 7–8, Bürklin, pp. 220–21); Ps. 8:6; 49:13–15, 21;
82:6–7; Pl. *Phdr.* 253B–C; Sen. *Epist.* 95.47; ps.-Dion. *CH* 164D–65C,
205B–D; *Expos. secr. punct.*, fol. 92ᵛ: Pico reviews his remarks and signals
a transition; for the structure of the speech, see Intro. at nn. 72–76. His
summary says that once Adam sinned and lost his original standing
(*honor*), humans became like animals. To recover, they must not only
scorn earthly things but also rise beyond heaven to surpass angels in rank
(*dignitas*)—a status they now lack, like barnyard cattle. Pico cites two
biblical verses and attributes them to Asaph, traditionally a prophet who
composed twelve Psalms, including Ps. 82 but not Ps. 49. A book of
Kabbalah known to Pico, an *Exposition of Secrets of Pointing,* reinforced this
confusion by reading two Psalms, 8 and 49, in light of one another. With
his own selection from Ps. 82, Pico seems to treat the message of Ps. 8 as
positive, that man's place in the universe is nearly divine. But in Ps. 82
God speaks to angels, not humans, and his words are harsh: "You sons of
the Most High shall die like men." The *Exposition* uses Ps. 49 to extract a
similar verdict from Ps. 8: although knowledge of the divine Name perfects the soul and makes her "mistress of the world," she still "differs not
at all from beasts." Never forget that God made man an animal and
therefore weak: this was a lesson learned from Kabbalah. But Pico's silent
Kabbalist exegesis also permits a remedy, a deliverance by the Areopagite's "sacred mysteries": abandon the bestial body and become an angel.
Joining the angels is a 'Junonian' goal because, while the ambition is regal,
the outlook is otherworldly and sees the gods as not at all bodily. Accordingly, Seneca forbade "lighting lamps on the sabbath since the gods need

no light. . . . The ambition (*ambitio*) taken with those duties is human; worship is *knowing* the god. Since God needs no attendants, let us forbid bringing towels and soap to Jupiter and holding a mirror for Juno (*Iunoni*)." Followers of Juno, or Hera, as Socrates explained, are royal by nature and look for a royal beloved to educate: "They emulate the god, leading the boy by persuasion and education to follow that god's practice and ideal," and then "mutual affection arises through the madness inspired by love"; on divine madness, see *Orat.* 27–29; also *Orat.* 13 on Seraphim, Cherubim, and Thrones; and *Orat.* 1 and 7 on contentment.

12. *Concl.* pp. 27, 68; *App.* 1.21.37–39, 33.67; Gen. 1:1–2; Ezek. 1:4, 26; 10:3–5; Ps. 18:11, 122:5, 148:4; Job 25:1–2, 38:6–7; John 10:30; 17:11, 21; 1 Cor. 12:11–13; Sen. *Dial.* 9.4.8; ps.-Dion. *MT* 1000C–1001A; *CH* 120B–21A, 165C, 205B–D, 272D; *Nom.* 637B–C; Greg. Magn. *Hom. in evang.* 34.10–14; *Zohar* I, 223b, 225b, 237; Axelrad, *Cor.*, fol. 177ʳ: Pico returns to the Psalms: in Ps. 18, the Lord sits "upon a Cherub"; in Ps. 122, "there sat thrones (Vulg. *sedes*, LXX *thronoi*) for judgment"; and in Ps. 148, "all the waters above the heavens" sang God's praises. The language about judging is closer to Gregory the Great's *Sermons* (see *Bn*, pp. 23–24) than to Gregory's source, the Areopagite, who saw the Thrones as "completely detached from any subjugation to the earthly." The "life full of action"—criticized by Seneca but not ruled out—is at best a distraction for the mystic. And the Areopagite's hierarchy of Thrones who purge, Cherubs who illuminate, and Seraphs who unify supports Pico's ranking of judgment below intelligence and love: see *Orat.* 16–17, 20, 34. He advises against standing firm (*soliditate firmare*) with the Thrones and staying attached to "lower things." Good Christians will disengage from activity and ascend to love through contemplation, following Cherubs up to the Seraphim. Seraphs blaze in the Creator's "devouring fire" while the divine Spirit broods over Cherubic waters. Ezekiel saw these angels in a vision of the Throne, and some Kabbalists called both the Shekinah (*S10*) and Metatron a Cherub. They also saw Cherubs in the opening of Genesis, where the heavens (*shamayim*) come first in the sequence of creation as both fire (*esh*) and water (*mayim*)—the *Sefirot* whose names are Water, South, Love, and Michael at *S4*; Fire, North, Judgment, and Gabriel at *S5*: see *Orat.* 16–17, 20, 34–35; also Intro. at n. 112 for a map of the *Sefirot*.

"That the heavens are made of fire and water," as Pico put it in the *Conclusions*, is a commonplace of Kabbalah whose biblical locus is Job 25, where "peace in his heights" ends a conflict between angels of Power and Terror: the passage is quoted in *Orat.* 20. Angels in Job 38 (cf. *Bn*, p. 25), joyous like those in Ps. 148, sing the Creator's praises in chorus with stars "of morning" — *matutinus*, like *antelucanus* for "daybreak hymns." Prayer at this hour, according to the *Conclusions*, belongs to the "Attribute of Piety," also a name of *S4*. Pico's closing allusions to John's Gospel repeat themes stated by the Areopagite.

13. Exod. 19–20, 24:15–18; ps.-Dion. *MT* 1000C–1001; Aug. *Trin.* 9.1.3, 10.1.3: Knowing or contemplating, a task for Cherubs, mediates between judgment below and love on high. The Areopagite established this pattern when he described Moses climbing Sinai in three stages, judging like a Throne (separating from the impure), then contemplating like a Cherub (hearing trumpets and seeing lights), and finally loving like a Seraph (within the darkness of God): see *Orat.* 7, 11, 13. When God's Seraphic lover has entered the Deity and the Deity is in him, as at the end of *Orat.* 13, "he and God are one," like Moses reaching the summit to "enter the truly mystical darkness of unknowing" and "belong wholly to the One beyond everything." For the theme of self-extinction, see *Orat.* 24 and Intro. at nn. 78–79, 109.

14. Rom. 8:5; Phil. 3:19; Pl. *Ti.* 24B–D; Plin. *HN* 17.38; *Orac. chal.* 72 (Des Places); *Hymn. Orph.* 32; Procl. *In Parm.* 1.692; *In Ti.* 1.141, 156–65: See the note on *Orat.* 8 for Pallas as Metatron, the Agent Intellect, and Wisdom — the *Sefirah* who mediates at *S2* between the Crown at *S1* and Intelligence at *S3*, just as Cherubs mediate between Seraphim and Thrones. Like judging and contemplating, Intelligence and Wisdom are mental acts, other-directed at *S3* but absolutely simple at *S2*. The Cherubs are a "knot of primary minds" because they bind these powers together. They are also an "order of Pallas" because they constitute Athena's wisdom. Proclus, reflecting on the *Timaeus*, wrote about an "Athena-given order (*taxis Athênaikê*)" in the *Chaldean Oracles*. Since there is no Pallas Athena in the Chaldean theology, he assimilated her to Hecate, another armed goddess, equipped to protect philosophy. The Orphic *Hymn to Pallas* praises her "thoughtfulness" (*phronêsis*) but says that her "mind is a

terror" (*phrikôdê thumon*). In *Orat.* 36 she is virginal. For the "ancient Fathers," see Intro. at nn. 70–72. In the Vulgate of Romans 8 and Philippians 3, *sapio* corresponds to *phroneô* in the Greek text: hence "mind the flesh" in KJV. The Latin verb also means 'smell of,' however, as in Pliny's remark: "Ointments that smell earthy (*terram . . . sapiunt*) are better than those like saffon."

15. Isa. 6:6; Acts 9:15, 17:34; 2 Cor. 12:2–4; Pl. *Soph.* 230B–D; ps.-Plut. *Plac.* 1.877A–B; *Orac. chal.* 135, 224 (Des Places); Procl. *Theol. Plat.* 1.2.10–11; ps.-Dion. CH 165C, 200C–201A, 300B; *Nom.* 977B–C: Pico's question for Paul is about "armies of Cherubim," but he already knew from books of Kabbalah that Michael commands these troops at *S4* against Gabriel and his Thrones at *S5*: see *Orat.* 13, 17, 20, 34–35. When Paul was "caught up to the third heaven," he had one of the "angelic visions seen by blessed theologians," in the words of the Areopagite, who also describes the Seraphim seen by Isaiah. For Paul's ascent, the Areopagite was the ideal interpreter: his apostolic pedigree came from the Dionysius converted by the "chosen vessel" in Athens. His mystagogy has three stages: cleansing by Thrones and enlightening by Cherubs before Seraphic completion (*teleiôsis*) — a rite of divinization. In the *Chaldean Oracles*, 'rites' are *teletê*, and the Areopagite taught that God's most lasting name is *Teleion kai Hen*, Complete Unity, which "already has all things in itself, . . . filling them up with its own completion": see *Orat.* 27. According to Proclus, however, such "blessed and divine teachings" were the last of four stages, not three: theology came after ethics, logic, and natural philosophy to complete the soul's faculties of "understanding, knowledge, opinion, and sensation." This progress — planned along the same lines by Iamblichus (see *Orat.* 7; also 17, 19, 26–27, 34–35) — was curricular and psychological, whereas the Areopagite's ascent was liturgical and experiential, and Pico recommends both in lines loaded with rhetorical devices: see *Bn*, pp. 29–30. Moral, dialectical, and natural philosophy at lower levels of the climb emulate a "Cherubic life" on earth even before mortals can "complete it with knowledge of divinity": see Intro. at nn. 73–76.

16. Gen. 28:11–15; Ezek. 1:10; *Tg. ps-Jon.* Gen. 28:12; Pl. *Phd.* 67B; Plut. *De Is. et Os.* 352D; Procl. *Theol. Plat.* 1.2.10; *Midr.* Gen. 68:12; *Bahir*, pp. 169, 196; Maimonides, *Guide*, 1.20ᵃ–21ᵃ; *Zohar* I, 19ᵃ; Abulafia, *Ve-zot*, fols.

120^v-32^v, esp. 120^v-21^v: The *Bahir*, a book of Kabbalah translated for Pico, asks "what is the earth that was carved" and answers with the same image: "It was carved by heaven, and it is the Throne of God." A Targum describes the Throne to interpret Jacob's dream of angels on a ladder — angels who saw Jacob's "likeness in the Throne of Glory," from where he "watches in the world above." In a Midrash, however, the same angels reproach the patriarch for sleeping: your "features are carved on high," they remind him. In Ezekiel's vision of the Throne, according to the *Zohar*, myriads of angels gaze eternally at images of an Ox, Eagle, Lion, and Man. Kabbalists located the Throne of Glory at *S6*, the central *Sefirah* called *Tiferet*, or Beauty, and also Jacob — well placed to make peace between warring angels at *S5* and *S4*: see *Orat.* 13, 16, 20, 34–35. These readings of Jacob's dream by Kabbalists were unknown to Christians when Pico alluded to them. But Jacob's ladder is a dominant image in a key work of Kabbalah put into Latin for him: Abulafia's *Ve-zot li-Yehuda*, on which see Intro. at nn. 73–74, 101. In a passage of the *Platonic Theology* where Proclus lays out a curriculum at four levels (*Orat.* 7, 16, 19, 26–27, 34–35), the lowest rung is ethics because "as Socrates said, 'it is not right for the impure to touch the pure,'" and moral philosophy is purgative. Pico could also have found this quotable line from the *Phaedo* in works by Plutarch and others who advised those who "aspire to the angelic life" — the "Cherubic life" of *Orat.* 16.

17. 2 Sam. 11:8; Job 40:10–19 (Vulg.); Ps. 9:16, 18:33–34 (17:34–35 Vulg.); Ruth 3:7; Matt. 22:13; Pl. *Resp.* 439–41; *Ti.* 69–71; Cic. *Leg.* 3.14; *Clu.* 59; *Tusc.* 1.20; Verg. *Aen.* 2.717–20; *Asclep.* 11–12; Aug. *Enarrat. Ps.*, ad 9:16; *Sefer yetz.* 3:6; *Bahir*, pp. 162, 195, 211, 226–27; *Zohar* I, 8^b: Pico's subject is the purging of lust and anger by moral philosophy. Hands and feet — mentioned three times in this and the preceding paragraph — are key symbols. Together they stand for the soul's "whole sensual part," but each has its own meaning. For Augustine, the soul's foot is love perverted into lust. For Pico, it is a "nutritive and feeding power," like the appetitive drive in Platonic psychology, and the hands are the "raging part," like the irascible drive. Plato's psychic anatomy in the *Timaeus* does not mention hands and feet. But in the *Asclepius*, "pairs of hands and feet . . . serve the lower or earthly world." Although humans use their physical and mental

faculties to "hunt in things" for their true causes, the "heavy and excessive vice of body" weighs them down and pleasure strangles them: cf. *Orat.* 1. Their lust is like the drowsy monster in the Book of Job, the Behemoth whose "strength is in his loins." When Kabbalists imagined the whole array of *Sefirot* as a cosmic human, they put the genitals at the bottom: the penis at S9, the female organs at S10, both euphemized as 'feet' by the rabbis. David ordered Uriah to "wash thy feet," but he was really telling him to have sex, according to the *Zohar*: see *hymenaeum* and *interstitium* in *Orat.* 2, and *cynnus* in *Orat.* 30. Bn, p. 32, notes Cicero's pairing of *sol* with *pulvus*, similar to Pico's.

18. *Concl.* p. 67; App. 1.33.59; Ezek. 1:27–28; Pl. *Symp.* 209E–10A, 211C; Plut. *De Is. et Os.* 354A, F; 357F–58E; 360E–F; 364E–F; *E Delph.* 388E–89A; *Orac. chald.* 164, 190 (Des Places); Orig. *Cels.* 6.21–22; Macrob. *In somn.* 1.12.1, 12; *Zohar* I, 80ᵃ, 129ᵃ; II, 30ᵇ; Abulafia, *Ve-zot*, fols. 120ᵛ–21ᵛ: Having shown the need for cleansing, Pico again describes the four levels of his curriculum: cleansing (ethics), reasoning (dialectic), and philosophizing (about nature) before being "consumed" by the joy of theology; see *Orat.* 7, 16–17, 26–27, 34–35. Things in nature, made of matter, are taken apart to be studied by philosophy, whose titanic powers of analysis break nature into pieces, like the limbs of Osiris. Like the god's scattered corpse, however, the parts can be reassembled with Apollo's help: in Neoplatonic terms (Intro. at n. 115), Remaining (rest) mediates between Procession (descent) and Reversion (ascent), to which a thesis on Kabbalah adds a fourth state of "blessed reunion," in order to put Osiris back together. Macrobius linked the Titans with Dionysus, not Apollo. But Plutarch interpreted both Dionysus and Phoebus as names of Apollo and symbols of that god's regenerative power — the unitive force at the theological level of Pico's curriculum. But Jacob's ladder (*Orat.* 16–18) is Pico's model for climbing "from rung to rung," as an initiate filled with a "Cherubic spirit" and taught Love's mysteries by the *Symposium*. For the Chaldeans, a "seven-wayed entrance (*bathmis*)" rather than a ladder (*klimax*) was the path of ascent (*anagôgê*), according to the *Oracles*. The spheres in Pico's cosmos had a single center, however, so passing through them "from center to center" would have been impossible. Maybe the cosmology was purely mental, hard for the body's eyes to see, like Abula-

fia's spherical cosmic ladder with 360 rungs: in the *Zohar*, rungs are levels of ascent through the *Sefirot* (see *Orat.* 34). Another possible inspiration is the *Book of Imaginary Circles* by Ibn al-Sid al-Batalyawsi, a twelfth-century text known to Italian Jews in Pico's day, or maybe a comment by Origen about "Persian mysteries" and the soul's voyage through "two circuits (*periodôn*) in the heavens." According to Macrobius, souls start falling to earth through two solar gates, marked by Capricorn and Cancer, on the great circle (*circulus*) of the ecliptic. In the sense of "charge off," *deorbitare* displays Pico's gaudy diction again: *Bn*, p. 34.

19. *Vit.* 69; *Concl.* pp. 26–27, 41, 55; *App.* 1.21.6, 14, 24, 41; 25.71; 30.4; Gen. 11: 27–32; Isa. 43:5; Job 1:1, 8; 5:7; 12:2; 14:1; 15:14; 25:1–4; 31:1; 33:27–30; Dan. 7:10; Emped. fr. 8(17), 107(115); Plut. *De Is. et Os.* 369B–71A; ps.-Dion. *CH* 209A; *Bahir*, pp. 185–86, 200–201, 221–23, 231–32; *Zohar* I, 48^a, 131^a, 186^b–88^a, 239^a; II, 75^a, 99^b; III, 7^a, 88^b, 182^b; Gersonides, *Comm. on Job*, in Wirszubski, *Pico's Encounter*, p. 183; Scholem, *Godhead*, pp. 197–228, 304, citing *Ra'aya Mehemnah* III, 216^b: After a Christian saint (Paul) and a Jewish patriarch (Jacob), Pico turns to a biblical figure who was not a Jew: Job is the third of the "ancient Fathers" to be consulted (*Orat.* 15). He was from the "land of Uz," or Edom, and his story is precovenantal: the word *foedus* (covenant) occurs only once in the book named for him. In an authoritative commentary used by Pico, Levi ben Gershom (Gersonides) said that Job did not have the Torah—reason enough to call on another gentile, Empedocles, to interpret this part of the Bible. Empedocles studied the titanic forces that drive the cosmos, as in *Orat.* 19. His philosophy of nature rose to a "middle order" between theology above and ethics and dialectic below, teaching that nature's basic processes are strife (*neikos*) and friendship (*philia*), which are also sefirotic in the *Conclusions*: on middle, lower, and higher orders, see *Vit.* 69. If conflict prevails, warfare banishes the soul from divinity, but Pico found a remedy, partly revealed by a thesis on Kabbalah: "When Job said *who makes peace on high*, he understood the Southern Water, the Northern Fire, and their Commanders, of whom nothing more should be said." The secret is that the Almighty settles a conflict among the *Sefirot*—Michael and Love at *S4* fighting against Gabriel and Power (or Judgment) at *S5*, as in *Orat.* 13, 16–17, 34–35. Their angelic armies are the "hundreds of

thousands" in Pico's question to Job, these fantastic numbers perhaps reflecting a vision seen by Daniel: *Bn*, pp. 36–37. Although the Bible introduces Job as "simple and upright" (*simplex et rectus*), Pico pointedly calls him "just" (*iustus*). And yet two of Job's comforters doubt that any man "born of a woman" can be just. Later, to deflect a charge of *iniustitia* (iniquity), Job connects this problem with sexuality: "I have made a covenant (*foedus*) with my eyes not to gaze on a young girl." But if the comforters were right, Job must have made this promise before he was "born of a woman." In that state, as a disembodied soul, he was still fit for transmigration through the line of Terah—which was Abraham's line as well—not yet corrupted by the flesh. "Every good soul is a new soul coming from the East": in the *Conclusions* this is Pico's summary of Kabbalist teachings on metempsychosis, for which he cites Empedocles there and in *Orat.* 8.

20. Luc. 1.1–4: Pico alludes to the opening of Lucan's epic of civil strife, "Wars worse than civil on Thessaly's plains I sing, and crime made right." Philosophy's task is to quell the discord that would spoil the peace of theology—the "peace on high" of *Orat.* 20.

21. 2 Cor. 4:16; Hom. *Il.* 18.107, cited by Plut. *De Is. et Os.* 370 C–D; Heracl. fr. 53; Pl. *Ti.* 70E; Verg. *Aen.* 8.641; Ov. *Met.* 6.465: As in *Orat.* 16, Pico divides the philosophical prelude to theology into ethics, dialectic, and natural science. But the first moral lessons call a truce only in the strife feared by Empedocles (*Orat.* 19). Bestial lust and anger (*Orat.* 18) must be checked by ethics, like Hercules slaying the Hydra and the Nemean lion. When such monsters ravage *noster homo* (our man) from the outside, the person within can still be saved, as Paul promised. Romans killed pigs to seal peace treaties, but the ascent to theological peace rises above morality only when dialectic—if it is neither sophistry nor empty rhetoric—reaches inside to "calm the turmoils of reason." Then the tranquil soul, no longer agitated by disputes, can study nature without distraction—even though nature originated in strife. When natural philosophy ignores mere opinion (*doxa*) and attains real knowledge (*epistêmê*), the initial insight is that strife is natural and innate in the cosmos. Thus, when Homer prayed for strife to vanish—according to Heraclitus—his wish would have eliminated everything right at the start.

22. Matt. 11:28; John 14:27: The Gospels confirm that the peace which philosophy can produce is transitory—like everything in nature or relying on it—and therefore insufficient. The only reliable and authentic peace is theological.

23. *Concl.* pp. 7, 14; *App.* 1.7.3, 14.7; Ps. 55:7; Job 25:1–4; Luke 2:13–14; Pl. *Phdr.* 249C; Verg. *Aen.* 4.239, 7.335; Ov. *Fast.* 5.663–66; Iambl. *VP* 33.229, 240: Theology is the mother who brings the peace promised in *Orat.* 20, but lying beyond the reach of philosophy. This real peace arrives when souls become "absolutely one," when they "and God are one," as in *Orat.* 13–14—individual humans no longer. Melding with the divine Mind is the "supreme human happiness," according to two of Pico's theses: see also *Orat.* 14 and Intro. at nn. 78–79, 109 on self-extinction and the Agent Intellect. On their way to the bliss of annihilation, humans turn into angels—not metaphorically but really, as surely as Enoch was transformed into Metatron (*Orat.* 8): also Intro. at nn. 69, 76–77. In the *Aeneid*, by contrast, the *unanimi* (single-souled) were subject to dissent when Juno sent Allecto, one of the Furies, to keep the Trojans fighting against the Latins. But on the Ides of March, according to Ovid, Mercury comes *alato pede* (on winged foot) as "arbiter of war and peace": for more wings, see *Orat.* 26 and 29.

24. *Concl.* pp. 55, 62; *App.* 1.30.7, 33.11; Ps. 24:3–10; 45:13–16 (44:9–12 Vulg.); 116:15 (115:6 Vulg.); SS 1:2, 4:8–5:1; Matt. 10: 12–13; John 14:23; Acts 14:12–14; Pl. *Phd.* 64A, 67D–E; Cic. *Tusc.* 1.74; Suet. *Dom.* 4.1–2; Plot. 1.6.6–9; Macrob. *In somn.* 1.13.5–11; Maimonides, *Guide*, 3.129; *Zohar* II, 195^b–96^a; III, 260^b; Recanati, *Comm.*, fols. 77^v–78^v; Gersonides, *SS*, fols. 15^v, 19^r (Andreatta): Jacob had his vision of the ladder in Bethel, the "house of God and heaven's gate," thus also theology's house, open to the soul after her philosophical education. The garlands on the gates are theological and blessed—unlike the "wreaths above the gates" of the pagan city where Paul and Barnabas were mistaken for gods, according to the Book of Acts. But the gates that open for the King of Glory in Ps. 24 are truly sacred. God's Dwelling is also the Shekinah at S10, and like her the human soul is God's spouse, as in the Song of Songs. The imagery—nuptial and erotic—is standard in books of Kabbalah like the *Bahir*, a key source for Pico that relates intricate parables about a King's royal

women. Their finery comes from a Psalm about a "royal daughter fringed in gold." (Pico borrowed the Latin for "courtly splendor" from Suetonius: *Bn*, p. 43.) If the King is theology, the "manifold variety" of natural philosophy is the woman's magnificent clothing. But a Psalm advises her to "forget your people and your father's house," and she must "die in herself that she might live in her spouse." Instructed by another Psalm, she knows that the "death of his saints is truly precious" in God's eyes. This was the "death of the kiss" understood by Maimonides as conjunction with the Agent Intellect: see Intro. at n. 109. In Pico's *Conclusions* it is "the soul's parting from the body, not the body's parting from the soul." The *Zohar* assigns the three evening watches to three camps of chanting angels: "Who is the King of Glory," they ask, and "who may ascend the mountain of the Lord?" The second question concerns sleepers who "experience a taste of death" as "their souls depart to ascend," and the angels decide which souls may go up. A person who prays disrespectfully "brings the Angel of Death on to himself before his time, and when his soul leaves him he will not behold the face of the Shekinah, nor will he die by a kiss." But if the parting is blessed and joyous, as Plotinus suggested, it comes after "practicing death," the *meletê* or *meditatio* taught by Socrates in the *Phaedo*.

25. *Concl.* p. 55; App. 1.30.9; *Hept.* sigs. avi^r–aviii; Gen. 3:21; Exod. 24:17; 25–27; 29:43; 35–40; Num. 1–10; Deut. 4:16, 22:11; Ezek. 16:13–18; 1 Chron. 28:11; Hebr. 7:5, 11, 24; 10:1; Rev. 5:12; Plut. *E Delph.* 393B–C; *Zohar* II, 76^a, 135^a, 139^a, 147^b: After learning from Job how God makes peace on high, Pico asks Moses — the fourth of the "ancient Fathers" — to show him how to scale those heights. The new path goes through a sanctuary, however, not up a ladder. Souls wandering in the wilderness of sin seek shelter in the Tabernacle, God's house as in *Orat.* 25. The architecture is another model for Pico's curriculum, and the imagery is cosmological as well: but not even philosophers can look through the starry curtain of the heavens to see the Deity. The first supplicants — kept outside the sacred precincts like priests of Thessaly described by Plutarch — remain in the Tabernacle's court, still to be purified by moral philosophy: they honor their god by not defiling his temple. Entering the sanctuary

as Levites, the second group touches nothing sacred until rites of dialectic have prepared them. While still under instruction in natural philosophy, the third group contemplates three barriers — the curtain, candelabra, and coverings of skin — that bar them from the Holy of Holies. Only the fourth group that has learned theology can get a clear view of divinity. Pico had already put words in God's mouth at *Orat.* 8: now it was less daring to write this speech about the Tabernacle for Moses — a mosaic of snippets from the Bible. Speculation on the same material is abundant in Kabbalah. Every detail of the Tabernacle is a symbol — like the exotic animal skins seen by the *Zohar* as layers of the human creature or of creation as a whole or even of the Creator. In the *Conclusions*, Pico compares the "skins that were in the Tabernacle" with Chaldean teachings on the soul's "earthly" covering outside its two immaterial layers — in all a "three-layered wrapping." In the *Heptaplus*, he also divided the sacred edifice into three areas: the court, outside the veil, and inside the veil. But here, to match his curriculum, he attributes a four-part plan to Moses: see *Orat.* 7, 16–17, 19, 27, 34–35. The great lawgiver built the Tabernacle and carried it through the wilderness but never reached the Promised Land. After opening the forty-nine gates of the seven lower *Sefirot*, he could not pass through the fiftieth Gate of Understanding at S3, where mighty angels guard the Throne above. The nectar that they drink confers immortality in *Orat.* 27; see also the ambrosia in *Orat.* 32.

26. 1 John 5:19; Rev. 21:2; *Tg. Ps.* 122:3–4; *Midr. Ps.* 122:3–4; *b. Ta'an.* 5ª; Pl. *Ep.* 7.333E; *Phd.* 69B–D; *Phdr.* 244A–45C, 246C, 247E, 249C–51B, 265B; *Symp.* 203B, 209E–10A; *Soph.* 230B–D; Cic. *Div.* 1.80; Verg. *Aen.* 1.301, 6.19; Plut. *De Is. et Os.* 382C–E; Plot. 3.5.7–9; ps.-Dion. *CH* 121A; Boet. *Cons.* 4.1; Procl. *Theol. Plat.* 1.10.44; 4.9.27–30, 26.77; Syn. *Dion*, 8.6, citing Arist. fr. 15 (Rose); Damasc. *In Phd.* 167; *Zohar* I, 183ᵇ, 209ᵇ: After taking advice from Paul, Jacob, Job, and Moses, Pico turns for his fifth consultation to ancient pagan sages without biblical standing, starting with Socrates and Plato. Their philosophy is an initiation, which, like climbing the ladder and processing through the Tabernacle, leads to theological mysteries: on the "theology of the ancients," see *Orat.* 52 and 55. When Socrates bantered about Love with Diotima in the *Symposium*,

she wondered if he could attain "complete seeings" (*telea kai epoptika*) even if "initiated" (*muêtheiês*) into the mysteries of Eros. In the *Parmenides* — Plato's "most epoptic" work according to Proclus — "completing (*teletê*) precedes initiating (*muêseôs*), which itself precedes seeing (*epopteias*)": see *Orat.* 16. But Proclus also finds "full seeing of the complete mysteries" in the *Phaedrus* where Socrates explicates the "fourth sort of madness." This divine frenzy makes lovers grow wings and fly beyond physical beauty to real immaterial splendor, "caring nothing for the world beneath." Before being chained to the body, their souls had tasted the nectar (see *Orat.* 26, 32) and ambrosia of eternity. Initiates who can soar beyond the skies "have moved by reasoning beyond all confusions of opinion," according to Plutarch, which is "why Plato and Aristotle call this part of philosophy 'epoptic.'" But at preliminary stages, the philosophy in Pico's curriculum has started with purging and cleansing by ethics and dialectic, as in *Orat.* 7, 16–17, 19, 26, 34–35. And in Book 1 of the *Aeneid*, Mercury has foretold the soul's ascent by flying with an "oarage (*remigium*) of wings" to help the fleeing Trojans — gear of the same type that Daedalus dedicates to Apollo in Book 6: see also "winged feet" and "winged lovers" in *Orat.* 24 and 29. The heavenly Jerusalem of the Book of Revelation also appears in rabbinical writings and Kabbalah, as well as in *Orat.* 68: the Shekinah (S10) dwells in peace in the holy city.

27. *Concl.* pp. 55, 60, 63; *App.* 1.31.3, 6; 33.24; 34.17; *Num.* 12:7; *Ps.* 36:8–9 (35:9–10 Vulg.); *Isa.* 63:3; *Jer.* 2:21; *Rom.* 1:20; *Hebr.* 3:2–6; *Rev.* 14:18–20; *Midr. Gen.* 1:11, citing *Num.* 12:7; Pl. *Resp.* 363C–D; *Leg.* 653C–D; Plut. *E Delph.* 389A–B; *De Pyth. or.* 396C–D; *Orac. chal.* 1.10 (Des Places), as in Ficino, *Plat. theol.* 1.6.5; Euseb. *Praep. evan.* 9.26–27; ps.-Dion. *Nom.* 712A; Peter Lombard, *Sent.* 1.3.1.1, 3; *Lib. rad.*, fol. 243^r; *Zohar* I, 36^b, 73, 76^a, 238; Ficino, *Op.*, p. 1361: At the fourth rung of his ladder, Pico's ascent reaches "outside the mind," taking the path of the Chaldeans — beyond the theory in his curriculum toward experience and regimen. The theological and Socratic frenzies already introduced (*Orat.* 27) are now inspired by the Muses, whose "leader" (*mousagetês*) is Apollo, according to Plato. But one of the god's many names (*Orat.* 30) is Bacchus, who also leads the nine sisters in song. Bacchus drives the initiate mad in

a "double" drunkenness that comes from "God's house," in the words of Ps. 36: see also *Orat.* 25. Pico's exegesis of this Psalm in the *Conclusions* refers to Kabbalah and the Chaldeans. Their *Oracles* describe immortality as being drunk on God, but Kabbalists discussed two types of wine described by prophets: one, for *S10* and the righteous Israel, is good wine still in the grape; the other, the bad wine sacrificed to idols, is for *S5* and the wicked Sodom. Initiates as faithful as Moses—who was also called Musaeus (a son, student, or teacher of Orpheus) and who handed down the wisdom of Kabbalah—will honor these secrets: see *Orat.* 66. The duality in Pico's "double frenzy" is higher or lower, however, not good or bad. Bacchus, leading the nine Muses through the spheres in a cosmic dance, teaches his initiates how to look at Nature's beauty. But the god's madness also drives them to see beyond visible splendor to "God's invisible things." Pico took these words from a passage of Paul's Epistle to the Romans that supplied the primary proof text for medieval natural theology: like the scholastics, Pico thought that studying the world of nature (including natural magic, as in *Orat.* 61) was a step toward understanding the divine.

28. *Concl.* p. 7; App. 1.1.3; Isa. 21:8; Jer. 31:21; Gal. 2:20; Hom. *Il.* 1.70, 3.277, as in Plut. *E Delph.* 387B–C; also Boet. *Cons.* 5.m2.11; Averroes, *Beat.*: Experience on the ladder's theological rungs becomes frenzied and Seraphic, beyond the Cherubic life of the mind; see *Orat.* 13–14. Isaiah and Jeremiah, two prophets of Israel, direct the faithful to theology, the Lord's lofty watchtower, where the visions seem to be gentile as well as Jewish because they resemble Apollo's prophecies: but see *Orat.* 30 on Christ as the "true Apollo." Phoebus Apollo inspired Homer's heathen diviners: the god's priest in the *Iliad* "saw what is, might be, and would be"—*quae sint, quae fuerint veniantque* in a verse by Boethius. This vatic madness—the lowest of Plato's four frenzies—covers past, present, and future time, all of it transcended when Aphrodite's beauty excites Eros in the soul, causing its wings (no longer earthly, as in *Orat.* 24) to grow again in the supreme erotic madness that finally eliminates the time-bound self, dissolving it in God's eternity, as in *Orat.* 14, 24, and Intro. at nn. 78–79, 109. A thesis on Averroes identifies this "supreme human hap-

piness" as conjunction with the Agent Intellect—"at the peak of the ascent," as Averroes wrote, when the soul "conjoins with the separated Intellect and is unified with it to become one with it."

29. *Concl.* pp. 58, 68; App. 1.31.23, 25; 33.65; John 1:9; Pl. *Alcib.* 121B–22A, 131A–33C; *Chrm.* 164D–65A; *Prt.* 343A–B; Catull. 97.8; Hor. *Sat.* 1.3.107; Plut. *E Delph.* 385B–F, 387C–D, 388E–89A, 392A, 393A–C, 394A–C; *Pyth. Orac.* 408E; *Orac. chal.* 112 (Des Places), with Klutstein, *Orph.*, p. 117: Apollo must be honored for prophecy and for philosophy; Plutarch learned this from Ammonius, the sage who also taught him that Zoroaster was a prophet, Socrates was a philosopher, and Apollo was both. Plutarch cited Ammonius in his essay *On the E*, while discussing the god's many names: see *Orat.* 28. He also analyzed the three Delphic maxims interpreted by Pico, who connected them with the "true Apollo"—Christ as the light of the world in John's Gospel, brighter than Apollo's Sun. Seen in this light, the sayings illuminate a philosophy with three parts: ethics, dialectic, and natural science; the same maxims, according to Plutarch, teach virtues of temperance, wisdom, and justice. The moral lesson of the first saying, *mêden agan,* is plain enough, and moderation is also a dialectical rule. But in the first *Alcibiades,* cited here, Socrates described self-control as self-knowledge—not by stating the *gnôthi seauton* maxim but by alluding to it. Pico's language, by contrast, is more strange than subtle. His *prima facie* message is that human self-understanding must start with man's position in Nature. But why is human nature an *interstitium* and a *cynnus*? The renderings in *Bn,* pp. 56–57, are 'nexus' and 'mixture,' which may be correct. However, after the "bond" and "wedding-knot" in *Orat.* 2, the issue is *linking* two unlike items—the matter and spirit in man—not *blending* them. *Cynnus* as the female genitals (*cunnus* in Catullus and Horace) would have shocked some Christian readers, of course, more than the euphemistic 'feet' in *Orat.* 17. But the Shekinah's sexual anatomy was well known to Kabbalists. Just below her at *S*10, past the bottom of the *Sefirot,* between the Creator and his creatures, came a seam or interval (*interstitium*) in reality. This exposition of *gnôthi seauton* is hazier than Pico's account of the third maxim. He evokes the scene in the *Alcibiades* where Socrates told his arrogant student that Persians learned self-knowledge from the "magic of Zoroaster": see *Orat.*

57. Zoroaster was thus the first to teach self-seeing, insisting that the soul must emerge from the depths to ascend on high and "open all your eyes upward," according to the *Chaldean Oracles*. Looking within precedes looking above where the final maxim — the utterly gnomic *ei* — greets the real Apollo by affirming his unconditioned existence beyond time. Zoroaster's entrance here prepares us to understand natural philosophy as Chaldean natural magic in *Orat.* 56–62. Likewise, the arithmetic in Plutarch's study of Apollo's names anticipates the numerology in Kabbalah. "Just as characters belong to an act of magic," according to Pico, "so numbers belong to an act of Kabbalah." But he revealed this secret only in the *Conclusions*, never in the *Oration*: see *Orat.* 4, 35, 64; Intro. at nn. 106–9.

30. Jer. 3:4 (Vulg.); Ps. 84:12; Cic. *Tusc.* 5.8–10; Plin. *HN* 28.69; Val. Max. 8.7 ext. 2; Diog. Laert. 1.12, 8.8, 17; ps.-Plut. *Lib. ed.* 12E; Porph. *VP* 2, 42; Iambl. *Protr.* 21.105–8, 115–17, 121–22; *VP* 8.44, 12.58, 23.103–5, 28.151, 154, 29.159: In Ps. 84 "God is the Sun," in *Orat.* 30 the "true Apollo," and "my father and the guide (*dux*) of my virginity" according to Jeremiah, where the prophet rails against whoring with false gods. (See also *Orat.* 28 for Bacchus as *dux Musarum*.) Another preacher of morals was Pythagoras — sixth on Pico's list of ancient sages and by tradition a student of Zoroaster, the Chaldeans, and Orphic priests. He left 'instructions' (*akousmata*), preserved by Iamblichus and others, as terse as Apollo's Delphic sayings. Three precepts, like the maxims in *Orat.* 30, regulate morals, reasoning, and thinking about the natural world. When wrathful and lazy people, unschooled in ethics, "sit on the bushel," vices block their rational faculties, and they cannot master the rules of dialectic. Getting rid of the body's wastes by urinating and clipping the nails will purge their vices — but only if they act at the right moment, never during a sacrifice or while facing the blessed Sun. If times and rites have been duly observed, these purgations open the way to liturgies of Bacchus, which in *Orat.* 28 are "nature's visible signs" pointing up to "God's invisible things," the truths of theology.

31. Job 4:11, 38:7, 36, 39 (Vulg.); Prov. 30:30–31 (Vulg.); Matt. 26:34, 69–75; Hebr. 5:12–14; *Midr. Lev.* 25:5; Hom. *Od.* 5.92–94; Pl. *Alcib.* 133C; *Phd.* 118A; *Phdr.* 247E; Lucr. 4.712–17; Plin. *HN* 8.52, 10.47; *Corp. Herm.*

1.29; Porph. *VP* 2; Iambl. *Protr.* 21, 107, 116; *VP* 28.147; Plut. *De Pyth. or.* 400C; Procl. *Theol. Plat.* 4.46–47; *De sacr.* 149–50; *Zohar* I, 63^b: After philosophy has nourished the soul's "rational part" (*Orat.* 31), theology will feed her "divine part"—about which Socrates questioned Alcibiades—by offering her the ambrosia already provided after her flight beyond the heavens. This was the dietary rule enforced by Pythagoras when he gave his order to "feed the cock"—the fourth of his instructions examined by Pico. Ambrosia is liquid in the *Hermetica* but "solid food" (*sterea trophē*) according to Homer and Proclus, a nourishment that is stable on high, unlike the providential nectar (see *Orat.* 26–27) that flows down to the world below; also unlike the "strong meat" (KJV; *solidus cibus*, Vulg.) in the Epistle to the Hebrews that beginners in righteousness must avoid. Just as ambrosia is steadier than nectar, the puny cock is mightier than the lion, just as intelligence rules the soul's lower faculties—irascible and appetitive like a ravening beast: see *Orat.* 18. Sacred to the Moon, Sun, and Apollo, the cock is no ordinary animal. Lucretius and Pliny reported folklore about lions fearing cocks, and Proclus theorized about it: since the bird is aerial and the lion is earthy, the cock is higher in the metaphysical order that gives natural magic its ontological framework: see *Orat.* 59–60. Nonetheless, when a lion meets a cock in the Latin Book of Proverbs, *gallus* is just an artifact of the Vulgate, and the lion fears nothing at all. The cock credited with *intelligentia* (understanding) as the Lord rebukes Job—in the chapter where "morning stars sang together"—is also missing in the Hebrew. The *Zohar*, commenting on Proverbs and Job, is ambivalent about the lion's strength, but not because of the cock, whose roles are clearer in the Gospel passion story and at the end of the *Phaedo*. Like the rooster that called Peter back to his senses, the cock that Socrates—cured by hemlock of all bodily ills—asked Crito to pay brought the philosopher closer to the gods. He owed the bird to Aesculapius, a divine healer of souls. Setting an example for Plotinus, who would "strive to give back the divine in myself to the divine in the All," Socrates repudiated the body and desired death, which is why he called philosophy "practicing for death," as in *Orat.* 25.

32. *Concl.*, pp. 25, 55–56; *App.* 1.21.11; 30.1–3, 6–7; *Apol.* pp. 54–55; B, sigs. TTi–ii^r; *Gen.* 2:10–14; *Ezek.* 1:4–10; *Phdr.* 246A–50C; *Orac. chal.*

67, 128, 217.6 (Des Places), with Klutstein, *Orph.*, p. 117; *b. Ḥag.* 14^b; *Midr. Lev.* 13:5; *Zohar* I, 26^a, 85^a, 208^a; III, 290^b; Recanati, *Comm.*, fol. 18; Flavius, *Sermo*, pp. 116–17: Zoroaster, the prophet of the Chaldean Magi, is the seventh and last of Pico's ancient witnesses. He taught a therapy for the soul, the "same arts" blessed for the dying Socrates by Aesculapius, now summed up by the prophet in two sayings and a parable. The first saying is familiar from Plato's *Phaedrus*, that the "soul has wings," as in *Orat.* 24, 27, and 29. But Pico said that his text was Chaldean, not Greek, and he told Ficino while writing the *Oration* that he had others like it in that exotic language. One of the *Oracles* mentions the "soul's light wings," but the only source known for this fragment is a commentary by Proclus which, as it seems, was not read in Italy until 1492. To strengthen the wings and tend their feathers, Zoroaster advised his disciples to water them well, on which point the surviving Greek fragments give no help. In one of the Kabbalist *Conclusions*, however, water flows from four streams: "Out of Eden comes a river that divides into four headwaters, meaning that out of the second Numeration comes the third that divides into the fourth, fifth, sixth and tenth." Eden is *S2*, the river running out of it is *S3*, and the four lower streams are *S4*, *S5*, *S6*, and *S10*: see the sefirotic geography in *Orat.* 34 and Intro. at n. 112. These waters are also angels — Michael, Gabriel, Uriel, and Raphael — as in *Orat.* 35. Other sacred fours, according to the *Apology*, are the faces of the creatures in Ezekiel's vision and the Evangelists symbolized by them. In the Vulgate, Eden's rivers are *Phison*, *Geon*, *Tigris*, and *Eufrates*, but in Zoroaster's parable they have different names in Aramaic and Hebrew — like the sentence about "Chaldean theology" in *Orat.* 10 that Pico linked with Euanthes. Also like that sentence, the four Chaldean words in the parable, written in Ethiopic script in F 33, were reconstructed by Wirszubski to fill blanks in the Latin text with *qeshot*, *kafron*, *nehora*, and *raḥamanut*, transliterating Hebrew and Aramaic words. Since the statement in *Orat.* 10 was supplied to Pico in Ethiopic script, and since his chief translator of Hebrew and Aramaic — Flavius Mithridates (see *Orat.* 67) — used Ethiopic elsewhere to write 'Chaldean' words, the likelihood is that Flavius was also responsible for the Chaldean parable and sayings: see Intro. at nn. 50–51, 82, and the headnote to App. II. Pico cited "Chaldean translators" repeatedly in the *Conclusions:* what he thought the originals were is unknown. When Flavius translated comments by Abulafia (see *Orat.* 17 and Intro. at n. 83) on the parable's locus in Genesis, where Abulafia had copied the Bible and wrote *gan* in Hebrew for 'garden,' Flavius followed the Vulgate and used *paradisus* — *pardes* in Aramaic. The parable here has the same word — in Aramaic a famous acronym for four levels of biblical interpretation: *peshat* (literal), *remez* (philosophical), *derash* (homiletic), and *sod* (secret). Used only here in the *Oration, paradisus* is an undeclared declaration — "published and not published," as in *Orat.* 65 — of Pico's mastery of secrets, including those of the four rivers, explicated in *Orat.* 34. But his confidence in this material was conditional: *si illis creditur.* Who or what made him think twice? Was it Flavius or Zoroaster or the Chaldeans or all of them? See *Orat.* 69 on the "mutilated" state of the *Oracles;* cf. *Vit.* 27 on the revision of the traditional four senses by the *Heptaplus.*

33. *Concl.* pp. 25, 27, 62, 65–66; App. 1.21.14, 37–39; 33.13, 37, 39, 47; Gen. 12:4–9, with Rashi; also 11:27–31, 12:4–10, 13:1, 15:7, 16:16, 18:11, 20:1, 21:5, 25:9–10; Deut. 33:2; Ps. 55:18 (54 Vulg.); John 8:56; Koran 2:124–27, 3:96–97, 14:35, 22:26, 26:92–95; Aug. *Gen. litt.* 4.46–47; cf. *Enarrat. Ps.* 54:18; *Zohar* I, 79^b–81^b, 83^a, 85^a, 111^a, 140^b; Recanati, *Comm.*, fol. 44^r; Gikatilla, *Port.*, fols. 121^v–22^r: Zoroaster's parable, despite the exotic names of the rivers, is straightforward in curricular terms (see *Orat.* 7, 16–17, 19, 26–27, 35): western waters of *ethics* first wash our eyes before *dialectic* comes from the north to align our sight, so that we can glimpse the faint light of *natural truth* dawning in the east, which prepares us for the full midday vision of *theology* blazing in the south. Pico thought of the Psalmist's morning, noon, and evening prayer, a meditation on time interpreted by Augustine as angelic knowledge breaking through temporal barriers. Such knowledge is "direct" and nondiscursive, a timeless illumination like the divine splendor that shines on the Cherubs and makes the Seraphs burn. Since North and South are names of S_5 and S_4, a sefirotic map (see Intro. at n. 112) of the curriculum is implied — oriented like the rivers in *Orat.* 33. S_4 is also Abraham, Michael, and Love (or Piety), struggling against Isaac, Gabriel, and Justice (or Power) at S_5: see *Orat.* 13, 16–17, 20, 35. As peacemaker at S_6, Jacob stands between them with his phallic lad-

der, and as the male *Tiferet* he stands above the female Shekinah at *S10*. She is the West and brings morality for cleansing. Isaac at *S5*, with strict justice, enforces rules of dialectic in the North. At *S6* in the East, Jacob's ladder will transport those who philosophize "along the rungs" above Nature's confusion, as in *Orat.* 19. Above them all in the South at *S4*, Abraham presides over theology in its full glory. The Hebrew patriarch belongs in a story about Zoroaster because his family came from "Ur of the Chaldees." If Ur was somewhere east of the Dead Sea, he traveled west from his birthplace to die near Hebron on the other side of the water. He also went as far north as Harran in Assyria and at least as far south as Kadesh in Egypt. But according to the *Oration*, he *always* headed south, and a thesis about Kabbalah (mentioned here for the first time in the speech) claims that "the southern Attribute in the group on the right" explains "why *every* journey of Abraham always goes to the South." The "group on the right" is the gentler side of the *Sefirot* (see Intro. at n. 112), and the "Attribute" is *S4*, called the South, Love, and Piety. Besides 'Attribute,' another term for a *Sefirah* is 'Day' — crucial information for Pico's account of Abraham's journeys. In another thesis, the patriarch "did everything out of Love through the Attribute of Piety," and in a third thesis "the subordination of Piety to Wisdom in the group on the right" shows how he "saw the day of Christ through a straight line and rejoiced," affirming what Jesus said in the Gospel, that Abraham rejoiced — because "in his Day (*S4*) he saw the Day (*S2*) of Christ." Piety at *S4* comes below Wisdom at *S2*, both on the right of the *Sefirot*. And if the highest triad is Christianized as a Trinity, *S2* is also Christ, the second person, whom Abraham saw by looking straight up from *S4*. On a map — theosophical, not geographical — where *S4* is the South, Abraham always traveled in the same southerly direction. His southward ascent to *S4*, keeping *S10* on his West and *S6* on his East, was continuous: see App. III. Muslims revered a different locus of *S4*, the Kaaba, which Abraham built on yet another voyage — with Ishmael to Mecca. Evil spirits may not enter because *S4* is also Michael, who ejected Satan and his legions from heaven.

34. *Concl.* p. 25; App. 1.21.1; Jer. 9:20 (21 Vulg.); Ps. 21:4 (20 Vulg.); Tob. 3:8, 4:4, 6:1–8, 8:2; 1 Cor. 13:12; Pl. *Ti.* 69B–72D; Hier. *Epist.* 76.2; Aug. *Serm.* 126.2; *Midr. Gen.* 1:3, *Num.* 2:10; Recanati, *Comm.*, fols. 127^r, 129^v–

30^r, 131^v; *Expos. decem num.*, fol. 78^v; *Zohar* I, 18^b, 26^b, 46^b; II, 67^b, 147^a, 153^a, 159^a, 231^a: Pico, underlining his own rule about secrecy with a question, piles up more riddles; see *Orat.* 4 and 64. Once again, his revelation is a four-stage curriculum, now angelic and anatomized: see *Orat.* 7, 16–17, 19, 26–27, 34. As in *Orat.* 22, "our man" is more inner than outer. Having lost its wings, his inward soul fell into an outward body, dizzying the highest of three major organs—brain (head), heart, and liver. The two-lobed brain is S2–3, whence blessings flow to the heart at S6 and down to the liver at S10, in the lower places where Plato puts appetitive and irascible passions. These troubled emotions follow when fatal perceptions enter through the windows of the senses, as Jerome taught in a comment on Jeremiah: vice invades the soul "through the five senses, as if they were windows of some sort; . . . if a person delights in . . . shapely women and splendid jewelry, . . . the soul's freedom is taken captive through the windows of the eyes, fulfilling the prophet's words, *death has entered.*" Divine protection comes from Raphael, however, whose theophoric name is 'God's healing.' He protected Tobias by having him gut a fish and save the gall, heart, and liver. The gall cured a malady of the head: the blindness of Tobit, the father of Tobias. The smoke of the fish's heart and liver expelled "every kind of demon." Asmodeus is the demon in the Book of Tobit, but the *Zohar* connects the sin of murder with the liver and Mashith the Detroyer, a demon who lurks there. Raphael's place among the *Sefirot* is the lowest, at S10, where he dispenses medicines of ethics and dialectic. Gabriel, 'God's strength,' teaches natural philosophy at S5; opposite Gabriel—like the merciful Abraham correcting the just Isaac—is Michael's theology at S4: see *Orat.* 13, 16–17, 20, 34. A transfer from Gabriel's battalions to Michael's would be a promotion, but Pico's advice in *Orat.* 20–25 is to escape the conflict between archangels by rising above it. A military honor—like the *corona* awarded to Roman soldiers—would commend the effort, like the "crown of precious stones" from a Psalm. The good death of the kiss (see *Orat.* 25) is the ultimate reward from Michael, according to Pico's first thesis about Kabbalah. Just as Aaron and other priests sacrificed unreasoning animals in the Tabernacle, "Michael, a higher priest, sacrifices souls of animals that reason," which then leave the body in ecstasy.

35. Dan. 2:28; Matt. 13:11; Acts 20:27; Cic. *Fin.* 1.1; *Tusc.* 1.1; Hor. *Carm.*
1.7.5, 3.3.23; Lucr. 1.146–48, 402–9; Prop. 3.20.7; Verg. G. 2.490; Gell.
NA 5.15.9: Here at the midpoint of his speech, Pico turns from describing what he means to defend — his philosophical curriculum and its purpose — to the defense itself. For a wealthy aristocrat to disdain profit was an easy pose: see Intro. at nn. 28, 41–42, 44, 83. Tags from biblical and pagan authorities include echoes of *De finibus* that continue in the next paragraphs: see *Bn*, p. 68, also *Orat.* 38–39, 44; cf. *De oratore* in *Orat.* 2. Opening his essay on moral ends, Cicero defended philosophy against critics whose attitudes varied, including those who rejected the whole enterprise. Pallas — proverbially virginal — also protects philosophy in *Orat.* 15.

36. 1 Cor. 9:18; Rev. 18:12–17; Pl. *Apol.* 30A–B, 31B–C; *Dig.* 50.13.1.1–6: After his brief try at studying law, perhaps Pico remembered where philosophers stood legally in ancient Rome. Although the state set salaries for physicians, lawyers, and other educated experts, the *Digest* excludes philosophers "not because the subject is not revered but because the first thing they should profess is to despise working for pay (*mercennariam operam*)." Note the repetition of *merces*, recalling Paul in Corinthians: "What then is my profit (*merces*)? That I may offer the gospel free of charge (*sumptus*) when I preach." But when he wrote the *Oration*, the orator's claim to have "put aside all concern for private or public affairs" was exaggerated: see Intro. at nn. 41–44.

37. Cic. *Fin.* 1.1, as in *Orat.* 36: "I have been far from unaware"; Plaut. *Mil.* 681; cf. *Orat.* 62, 70.

38. Cic. *Fin.* 1.1, as in *Orat.* 36: "this type." An orator uncomfortable with a "display" might not have made his speech an oratorical exhibition: see *Bn*, p. 74; *Vit.* 12. According to the *Conclusions*, Pico planned to defend his nine hundred theses "after Epiphany" — twelve days after Christmas — in 1487: see App. 1.34; Intro. at n. 30. For him to be "barely" twenty-four at the time, since his birthday was February 24, he would have been planning for the end of February or shortly afterward. According to Gianfrancesco, however, "he could never manage to get a date scheduled." Epiphany is the Feast of Kings — the Magi, who from Pico's point of view were

descendants of Zoroaster and the Chaldeans: see *Orat.* 10, 30, 33–34. The "Apostolic Senate" is the College of Cardinals: see *Orat.* 1.

39. Acts 8:9, 19–23; Pl. *Phdr.* 247A; ps.-Dion. *Nom.* 857A: Arguing that humans can achieve immortality, the Areopagite insists that the "contradictory words of the deranged Simon on this point are therefore banished from God's choir (*theou chorou*)," alluding to the *Phaedrus* and also to Acts, where Peter accuses Simon Magus of being "in the gall of bitterness."

40. Prov. 27:17; Eccles. 10:10; *b. Ta'an.* 7ᵃ–8ᵃ; *Midr. Eccles.* 10:11; Plat. *Chrm.* 153a; *Lys.* 204A, 206C–E; Arist. *Pr.* 916ᵇ19–24; Verg. *Aen.* 8.435; Firm. Mat. 3.7.1–2, 6.5.4: Socrates goes to the gymnasium (*palaestra*) to "give a demonstration of how to carry on a conversation," and Aristotle asks "why contentious discussions are good exercise." Ecclesiastes answers that "if the iron (*barzel*) is blunt, it will be sharpened with much labor, and wisdom (*ḥokhmah*) will follow effort." Proverbs adds that "as iron sharpens iron, so a man sharpens the wit of his friend," meaning—according to the Talmud—that "just as in the case of one iron sharpening another, so do two scholars sharpen each other." Talmudists are *ḥakhmim* or 'sages,' equipped with the arms of Pallas, like the breastplate that Vergil mentions: see *Orat.* 15, 36. (The particle *shel* prefixed to *ḥakhmim* means 'of.') Chaldeans here are astrologers, not necessarily Zoroastrians: see *Orat.* 10, 30, 33–34. A planetary aspect is the angle formed by rays from two planets with the earth at their vertex; the angle separating planets in trine (trigon) aspect is a third of the celestial circle, or 120 degrees. The hard iron of Mars is a mismatch for Mercury's quicksilver, but Pico regards the contradiction as beneficial in a philosopher's horoscope, agreeing with Firmicus Maternus: "If Mars is in trine aspect with Mercury, . . . and both are situated in favorable parts of the geniture, . . . they produce sages . . . able to explain themselves, . . . sharp, good at reasoning and calculating."

41. Job 32:6–8; 1 Tim. 4:12–14; *Zohar* II, 166: Elihu, one of Job's comforters, stays silent out of respect for Job and his other friends, who are older, until he concludes that "it is not the aged who are wise" since understanding comes from the spirit that God breathes into all humans. The *Zohar* cites Elihu's speech to argue that a young man can be wise in

Torah. Encouraging Timothy not to be timid about his youth, Paul urges him "to be an example to the faithful in word and conversation, . . . to attend to reading, to exhortation, to teaching, nor neglect the grace that is in you, which was given you through prophecy."

42. Eccles. 9:11; Matt. 23:4; Luke 15:5; Phil. 13.40–41; *Midr. Num.* 22:7; Caes. *B. civ.* 1.64.4; Cic. *Div.* 2.105; Plin. *Ep.* 3.9.11; Quint. *Inst.* 5.12.22, 12.3.5–6; Hor. *Ars P.* 38–40; Smaragd. *Prolog. reg. S. Ben.* = *MPL* 102: 696B: The wicked shift their burdens to others, according to the Gospel, while the Good Shepherd gladly shoulders the load. Wisdom, strength, and wealth are everything, says a Midrash on Exodus, "when they are gifts of heaven, . . . but the strength and wealth of mortals are naught, as proved by what Solomon says" — in Ecclesiastes about winning the race or the battle. A prologue to the Rule of St. Benedict distinguishes "soldiers of Christ" from "soldiers of the world" who "take up weak (*infirma*) and unreliable arms"; see also Caesar's *Civil War* and Pliny's *Letters* on weak soldiers; and *Orat.* 31 for Pythagoras and disclaiming wisdom.

43. *Orat.* 43; Cic. *Fin.* 1.2–3, as in *Orat.* 36; Prop. 2.10.5–6.

44. *Vit.* 47; Cic. *De or.* 3.129: Pico needs hundreds of theses from scores of authorities because his method, described in *Orat.* 46, requires them all: the underlying motive is the peace advocated by *Orat.* 20–25, which is not fully achieved by the philosophizing that precedes it. Although Pico claims to be more restrained than the pandering sophist described by Cicero in *De Oratore*, Gianfrancesco conceded that when his uncle was "young and lusting for glory, . . . he chased after fame like Gorgias . . . by defending any and all sides": see Intro. at nn. 30–31.

45. *Concl.* p. 1; *App.* 1.2; *B*, fol. [1ʳ]; Pl. *Ep.* 7.341; Cic. *Orat.* 47; *Fam.* 8.11.4; Hor. *Epist.* 1.1.14–15; Quint. *Inst.* 1.8.19, 5.7.7; *Vit. Arist.* 5.1–2 (Düring): Horace's words about not pledging allegiance later became a motto for eclectics who despised Pico as a syncretist: on 'picking out' (*seligire*), eclecticism, syncretism, and concord, see Intro. at nn. 85–87. Pico denies being sectarian — in contrast to philosophers and theologians in the universities of his time — and yet he organized the *Conclusions* by "nations and heads of schools," meaning Albert, Scotus, Thomas, and others. Ancient philosophy was also sectarian. Nonetheless, suggesting

that Aristotle was too inquisitive to be partisan, an anonymous Greek biographer—whom Pico thought to be Philoponus, as in *Orat.* 53—reported "that Plato calls Aristotle's house the *house of the reader*": see *Bn*, pp. 85, 97–98. Between the last two sentences in this paragraph, F 46 adds Plato's remark in the seventh letter that philosophy cannot be mastered by any one thinker or school: "There never was nor will be after us anyone to whom truth might give itself to be fully grasped; greater its immensity than what mankind's capacity can equal"; see *Orat.* 50 on the same text. The Stoics got their name from a Porch near the Agora where Zeno taught, as Plato and his successors taught in the Academy, Aristotle and his followers in the Lyceum. *Commentationes* (books, writings, works) was the title used by Gianfrancesco for his 1496 collection: see Intro. nn. 17–18.

46. *Concl.* pp. 1, 7, 12; *App.* 1.2, 6, 10; Cic. *De or.* 3.28: Pico lists names taken from the first (roughly four hundred) of two groups of theses in his *900 Conclusions*, described as 'regarding' (*secundum*) the views of those thinkers. (The two groups are T1 and T2 in these notes; see App. I.) "Our people" are Christians, and "finally" indicates the state of philosophy after 1328, the year when the last philosopher named by Pico died. He assigned his first 115 theses to six "Latin philosophers and theologians" who disagreed on major issues: Albert, Scotus, Thomas, Francis of Meyronnes (d. 1328), Giles of Rome (d. 1316), and Henry of Ghent (d. 1293). He linked the next 82 theses with eight "Arabs who generally declare themselves to be Peripatetics," but the speech mentions only Alfarabi, Avempace, Averroes, and Avicenna: Alfarabi is al-Farabi (d. 951), Avempace is Ibn Bajjah (d. 1138), Averroes is Ibn Rushd (d. 1198), and Avicenna is Ibn Sina (d. 1037). Then come 29 theses for "Greeks who declare the Peripatetic view." Theophrastus (d. 287 BCE) was Aristotle's student and successor. The other four commented on Aristotle in late antiquity: Alexander of Aphrodisias (fl. 200 CE), Ammonius (d. 526), Simplicius (d. 560), and Themistius (d. 390). All but Alexander were Platonists or friendly to Platonism, and this Ammonius was not the Ammonius of *Orat.* 30, who taught Plutarch five centuries earlier, though whether Pico noticed the difference is unknown—several philosophers were called Ammonius. For language assigning qualities to such thinkers,

Cicero showed the way: see *Bn*, p. 87. The custom was also medieval: traditional designations were *acutus* for Francis, *angelicus* for Thomas, *fundatissimus* for Giles, *magnus* for Albertus, *solemnis* for Henry, and *subtilis* for Scotus, but Pico had his own opinions (*ut mihi visum est*); see also Intro. at nn. 38, 90–91.

47. *Concl.* pp. 14–22, esp. 21; App. 1.14; 15; 27.36; Iambl. *VP* 23.103–5, 28.156; *Myst.* 1.15; Procl. *Theol. Plat.* 1.7–8; Hier. *Jov.* 1.1.238: Of the five "philosophers called Platonists" in the first four hundred theses, Pico omitted "the Arab Adelandus"—perhaps Adelard of Bath, a twelfth-century Englishman with experience in the Muslim world. The others are Plotinus (d. 270) and his greatest sucessors: Porphyry (d. 305), Iamblichus (d. 325), and Proclus (d. 485). Hermias (d. 450), Damascius (d. 538), and Olympiodorus (d. 570) were also in the Neoplatonic succession, and Hermias appears once in a thesis that lists some of them. But Proclus, despite the statement about skipping him, gets more attention than anyone else in T1: fifty-five of ninety-nine Platonic theses come under his name. His theology of triads was irresistible (see Intro. at n. 114), and his philosophical curriculum was formative for the *Oration*: *Orat.* 16–17, 27. However, since the speech mentions him only this once, the version used by Gianfrancesco in 1496 may have been prepared before the theses assigned to him were ready. On the other hand, works by Proclus were important for preserving the *Chaldean Oracles*, which are prominent in the speech, so Pico had good reason to study him. Pico's curriculum also reflects earlier Neoplatonic plans like the one described in the *Protrepticus* by Iamblichus, who is named again in the speech: see *Orat.* 7, 16, 69. Later, in Ficino's Latin translation, his *Mysteries of Egypt* would introduce the theurgical side of Neoplatonism. For a Kabbalist *symbolum*, see *Orat.* 41; followers of Pythagoras called the maxims in *Orat.* 31–32 'passwords,' or *sumbola*. The remark about sweating comes from Jerome.

48. Isa. 42:3; Acts 5:17; 15:5; 24:5, 14; 26:5; 28:22; Cic. *Parad.* 2; Diog. Laert. 1:19; Lact. *Inst.* 4.30; Iambl. *VP* 34.241: Diogenes Laertius cites a work *Peri haireseôn* that divides Greek philosophy into nine "sects or schools (*haireseis kai agôgas*)," including Stoics, Academics, and Peripatetics. The Latin *haeresis*, used instead of *secta* in F 49 and by Cicero to

mean 'school of thought,' became 'heresy' for Lactantius, the Christian Cicero. Already in the Book of Acts, *hairesis* is pejorative, suggesting something deviant. See *Orat.* 43 for strength in apparent weakness, and *Orat.* 46 for Pico's opposition to sectarian philosophy.

49. Pl. *Ep.* 7.341; Sen. *Epist.* 33.10–11; Diog. Laert. 1.1–11; cf. Euseb. *Praep. evan.* 10.3.26; Aug. *Conf.* 7.26, 8.3; *Ver. rel.* 2–3; *Civ.* 8.12, 9.1: Plato's Letter 7, where Pico read about the scope of philosophy (*Orat.* 46), also insists that the deepest truth comes "like light flashing forth"—an intuition that eludes all speech and can never be learned from written words, certainly not words written by others nor, as a practical matter, by Plato himself since even his insights would help "only a few." Pico's different observation that medieval philosophers relied on non-Christian strangers (and their books) may reflect the letter by Seneca cited next in *Orat.* 51: see *Bn*, p. 92. A barbarian origin for Greek philosophy was Christian propaganda aimed by apologists like Eusebius at the nativism upheld by pagan Hellenes or Hellenizers like Diogenes Laertius. Eusebius wrote that "all the vaunted learning and philosophy of the Greeks . . . has been collected by them from barbarians." Starting with Porphyry, Neoplatonists treated Aristotle's expertise on nature (physics) as preparatory for Platonic theology (the Academy): see *Orat.* 53. Had Ficino seen the *Oration* before 1496, when Gianfrancesco first published it, he might well have objected—as *Bn*, p. 93 notes—to Pico's claim for priority, though the prince may just have meant that he was the first—or the first in his place and time—to *debate* Platonism publicly and in grand style. Ficino lectured publicly on Plato and Plotinus but did not hold disputations. For "Albert, Thomas, Scotus, Giles, Francis, and Henry," see "our own people" in *Orat.* 47.

50. *Concl.* p. 27; *App.* 1.21.36; Pl. *Symp.* 208E–9E; Lucr. 2.1147–52; Sen. *Epist.* 33.7, 94.15; Gell. *NA* 7.13.2; Val. Max. 2.1.4–5; *Orac. chal.* 39, 108–9 (Des Places), with Klutstein, *Orph.*, p. 117; *Corp. Herm.* 2.14–17, 9.3; Serv. ad Verg. *G.* 2.51; *Dig.* 19.2.15.4: A *sumbolon* can be 'what one brings to a party,' but *asymbolus* also recalls the philosophical 'passwords' in *Orat.* 48. In the *Chaldean Oracles*, the "Father's Mind has sown symbols (*sumbola*) across the cosmos" and "inseminates everything with a bond which is heavy with the Fire of love." A divine Fire above two levels of Mind was the supreme Chaldean triad. How much of this dogma Pico understood

is unclear, but a Latin version of the *Oracles* then in circulation translates the salient line faithfully: *symbola patria mens seminavit in animabus*. See also *Orat.* 2 on 'bond,' and *Orat.* 7, where the "Father has planted seeds of every kind," and man's duty is to cultivate them correctly. The contrary failure would neglect the seeds and 'cut the plants off' — an offense against God's fecundity that Pico called the sin of Sodom in a Kabbalist thesis. The first Roman to divorce his wife charged her with *sterilitas*, according to Valerius Maximus, and Servius attributes *infecunditas* to trees whose nature (*animus*) is wild. The Creator's name is "Father," according to one Hermetic discourse, and childlessness is punished in human creatures by the soul's migration into a eunuch's body. Like the *Oracles*, however, the same discourse specifies — more clearly, in fact — that "God is not mind," though another discourse describes human minds as impregnated by seeds that can be divine or demonic, good or evil. See also *Orat.* 5 and Lucretius on *effetus* and cosmic exhaustion along with *Bn*, pp. 92–95 on all these points, as the *Oration* moves from harmonizing past authority to proclaiming the orator's own creativity.

51. *Concl.* pp. 22–28, 30, 36, 41, 54–56; *App.* 1.18–21, 25–26, 30–31; *Corp. Herm.* 12.2, 11, 13–15, 18–19, 21; 13.6–7, 12; Ficino, *Pim.*, fols. 42ʳ–53ᵛ: The last seventy-seven theses in *T1* are assigned to Pythagoras (14), Chaldean theologians (6), Hermes Trismegistus (10), and the "secret teaching of Hebrew Kabbalist sages" (47). Hence, the *T1* theses might be rising to the "theology of the ancients" mentioned in *Orat.* 27 and again in 55. The order is not a reverse chronology, however: Pico's list starts with Albert the Great (d. 1280), for example, next moves forward in time to Francis of Meyronnes (d. 1328), but then back to Averroes (d. 1198): the twenty-four individuals named in headings before the Pythagorean theses are grouped by ethnicity, language, and school. Of all the figures in *T1*, only Proclus gets more notice than the Kabbalists: see *Orat.* 48. The "ancient mysteries of the Jews," yet to be described in *Orat.* 63, are not just Jewish but also Pico's Christian interpretation of them, stated in the final seventy-two theses. All ten Hermetic theses, almost exactly in sequence, come from just two discourses (12 and 13) of the Latin version available to Pico — Ficino's *Pimander*. Zoroaster and the Magi support "theorems about magic" introduced in *Orat.* 56, but the six Chaldean theses men-

tioned here are distinct from the fifteen on Zoroaster and the Chaldeans that precede the twenty-six on magic in T2. T2 also presents novel claims by Pico about natural philosophy and theology.

52. *Concl.* pp. 28–30; App. 1.23; Aug. *Acad.* 3.19.42; Simpl. *In Cat.* 8.7.23–32 (Kalbfleisch); *Vit. Arist.* 8–9 (Düring); Boet. 2 *Interp.* 2.80: See Intro. at nn. 11, 86–92 for Pico on concord: his first thesis in T2 declares that "there is no problem, natural or theological, about which Plato and Aristotle do not agree in meaning and substance, though they may seem to differ in words." Of the next sixteen theses, twelve deny disagreements between Thomas and Scotus, Avicenna and Averroes, and other medieval teachers. That Plato and Aristotle converge on fundamentals was also the view of Greek commentators on Aristotle starting with Porphyry, most of whom were Platonists (see *Orat.* 50): Augustine cites them as "most acute and skilled," Boethius says that Plato and Aristotle "agree in most things," and Simplicius concurs. John the Grammarian is Philoponus, thought by Pico to be the author of the *Life of Aristotle* where Plato calls Aristotle a 'reader,' as in *Orat.* 46. Just after that passage, the same *Life* says that Aristotle "does not, in any simple sense, oppose Plato, only those who have not understood what Plato says. Yet even if he opposes Plato himself, this is nothing strange since even then he minds what Plato says."

53. *Concl.* pp. 28, 30, 36, 41, 44, 50, 51, 54, 56, 58, 60; App. 1.22–27, 32–33: In the headnote to T2, Pico promises 500 theses in ten sets, but the number printed in 1486 was 498 (depending on how corollaries are counted) in eleven sets whose sequence does not match the headnote. The headings of two sets in T2, the third and eleventh, mention 71, but the count of the eleventh set on Kabbalah is 72: see *Bn*, pp. 99–100 on the numbers, and Intro. at nn. 99, 108–9, 111, 113 on the bookkeeping and the numerology of 72; also *Orat.* 66. In this part of his speech, however, Pico's point is originality—not numerology. He called two of the first three sets of theses in T2 "unusual" (*paradoxae*): the first set (17 theses) aims to "reconcile" by eliminating discord where it is merely apparent; the second set (80) "disagrees with the usual philosophy" but is not "unusual" and does not reject ordinary methods; the third (71) is "unusual" and introduces "new teachings in philosophy." The fourth set (29, but 31 mis-

printed in the headnote by transposing XXIX to XXXI) is "quite different from the usual way of talking about theology" but is not called "unusual," though that term is applied by the headnote of the fifth set (62) on Platonic doctrine to the first thesis of the first set, which states Pico's doctrine of concord. Of the six other sets, only the tenth on the *Orphic Hymns* explicitly claims originality (see *Orat.* 56), but Pico labels all eleven sets as following his own view (*secundum propriam opinionem*).

54. *Concl.* pp. 11, 51–54; *App.* 1.28.1, 11; 29.12–14; Pl. *Resp.* 525; *Epin.* 976D–78C; Arist. *Cael.* 271^{b}1–4; *Mete.* 353^{a}35–53^{b}2; *Pr.* 956^{a}11–14; Cic. *Acad.* 2.72; *Fin.* 4.17; *Nat. d.* 1.79; *Off.* 2.8; *Tusc.* 3.40, 69; 5.10, 34; Apul. *Apol.* 38; Plut. *Cons. Ad Apoll.* 104C, 111F; Iamb. *VP* pr. 23, 38.146–48, 162; Procl. *Theol. Plat.* 1.25–26; *In Ti.* 5.174.9–13; Orig. *Cels.* 1.25; Ficino, *Op.*, p. 25: Aristotle discussed "ancients (*archaioi*) who worked on theology" as well as "ancient philosophers," but in classical Latin texts there are no *prisci theologi* or *philosophi*, as in *Orat.* 27 and 52; cf. *poetica theologia* in *Orat.* 58. Cicero, Apuleius, and other Romans talked about *antiqui* and *veteres philosophi*, however. *Archaios theologos, philosophos*, and related phrases are common in Greek, especially in later authors, including four of Pico's favorites: Iamblichus, Origen, Plutarch, and Proclus. Ficino's conception would also have been familiar to him: an "ancient pagan theology (*prisca gentilium theologia*) about which Zoroaster, Mercury, Orpheus, Aglaophemus, and Pythagoras agreed, all of it contained in books by our Plato. . . . To interpret Plato, Platonists received divine illumination from Christians . . . , and the chief mysteries in Numenius, Philo, Plotinus, Iamblichus and Proclus were taken from John, Paul, Hierotheus and Dionysius the Areopagite." Both Iamblichus and Proclus also supplied a genealogy like Pico's for "mystical traditions of the theologians" that "harmonize with Platonic principles." Iamblichus omits Philolaos but includes Damo, the daughter of Pythagoras mentioned in *Orat.* 65. Abu Ma'shar, the renowned astrologer of the ninth century, could not, strictly speaking, have reported anything from the person usually known as Avenzoar, the physician Abu Marwan Ibn Zuhr who died in 1161—perhaps also the Abumaron of Babylon in the *Conclusions*. Abu Ma'shar was famous not only for astrology, however, but also for chronography and chronicles, where fragments of his were cited out of context. In its form,

the utterance about numbers is like the lapidary 'man is a miracle' in *Orat.*
1 and, like that saying, may come from an Arabic gnomology, perhaps in
Latin translation. The seventh set of theses on mathematics starts with
eleven axioms like "mathematical sciences are not real," on the one hand,
or on other, "there is a way through numbers to investigate and understand everything knowable." Next come "74 questions that I will answer
through the method of numbers," like "whether there is a God," "whether
God is infinite," "whether God is the cause of everything," and so on.
Most of the questions are theological, though some involve physics and
psychology.

55. *Concl.* pp. 54–58; App. 1.30.1–2; 31.15; 32; Gorg. *Hel.* 11; Pl. *Alcib.*
122A; *Grg.* 483E; *Leg.* 909B; *Meno* 80A; *Resp.* 584A; *Soph.* 234E–35B;
Symp. 203A; Apul. *Apol.* 25; Diog. Laert. 1.8; Plot. 4.4.40; Porph. *Abst.*
4.16.1; Aug. *Civ.* 10.9; *Schol. in proleg. Hermog.* 14.284 (Rabe); *Suda,* Γ 365:
The twenty-six theses in the ninth set of T2 are "about magic." "Natural
magic" is also a topic in the previous set of fifteen on Zoroaster and the
Chaldean Magi and, in the next set of thirty-one, the Orphic *Hymns* are
interpreted as "magic, a secret wisdom of divine and natural things that I
was the first to discover in them." None of the theses labeled as Kabbalist
in T1 or T2 mentions magic, and yet "no magical action can have any effect unless it has an act of Kabbalah . . . linked with it," according to
a thesis in the ninth set of T2: see also *Orat.* 61. For Pico's conception
of the difference between natural and demonic magic, see Intro. at nn.
92–94; and for the background, Copenhaver, *Magic in Western Culture,*
pp. 231–91; and *The Book of Magic,* pp. 347–409. As for *goêteia* and *mageia,*
Plato and other authorities used both words but with no such clarity: see
Orat. 59. A strong and consistent distinction between criminal *goêteia* and
innocent *mageia* came late in Greek usage and even then was rarely as
explicit as this scholium on Hermogenes: "Drugs (*pharmakeia*) are one
thing, sorcery (*goêteia*) another and magic (*mageia*) yet another. We use
drugs . . . through the mouth or as a salve. But sorcery is called up from
matter-bound and unclean spirits (*daimonôn*) that do evil. . . . Magic does
its work through middle angelic spirits, however, as well as the matter-
bound." Diogenes Laertius, citing Aristotle, claimed that Persian *Magoi*
had no use for "goetic magic." But Apuleius said that a *magus* in Persian

was a *sacerdos*, and Porphyry—thinking of Persian teachers in the first *Alcibiades*, as in *Orat.* 58—wrote that *magoi* are "experts on the gods and serve (*therapontes*) them." Both *mageia* and *goêteia* call on spirits (*daimones*), according to the *Suda*, but the spirits do good with magic, whereas *goêteia* sins by raising the dead. Augustine was more rigid, condemning all magic as demonic.

56. Pl. *Alcib.* 121E–22A; *Chrm.* 156D–57B, 158B; Cic. *Fin.* 5.50; *Tusc.* 4.44; Plin. *HN* 30.1, 3–4, 8–11, 14; Apul. *Apol.* 25–26; Diog. Laert. 1.1–2, 8; Iambl. *Myst.* 1.1; *VP* 19.90–94, 28.135–38, 30.173; Aug. *Epist.* 120.12: Here and through *Orat.* 62, Pico develops the distinction introduced in *Orat.* 56. Magic is Pliny's topic in Book 30 of his encyclopedia, a collection of recipes introduced by a hostile history—used twice in this paragraph. Pliny, like Cicero and other authorities, named Greek philosophers who brought magic home from faraway places. Plato appealed to exotic authority in a subtler way: in the *Charmides*, Socrates discusses a charm learned from Thracian healers who got it from Zalmoxis, their divine king, or from Abaris the Hyperborean. Iamblichus called Zalmoxis "a servant of Pythagoras" and told a long tale about Abaris, a priest of Apollo from the far north, who flew south on his magic arrow to be instructed by Pythagoras. Pliny indicates confusion in his sources about Zoroaster's chronology and identity—how many Zoroasters there were, for example—but the teacher of wisdom named by Plato in the first *Alcibiades* was "the son of Horomazes (*Hôromazou*)." The pious wisdom taught by this royal tutor—see *Orat.* 30—was "magic (*mageia*)" and the "service of the gods (*theôn therapeia*)." The phrase *disparilitas et dissimilitudo* comes from a letter by Augustine, who used it to emphasize a distinction between the spiritual and the bodily: see *Bn*, p. 106.

57. *Vit.* 26; *Concl.* p. 48; *App.* 1.27.45; *Apol.* p. 49; Pico, *Comm.* str. 4 (Bürklin, pp. 188–90); Hom. *Od.* 13.102–12; Pl. *Alcib.* 121E–22A; *Chrm.* 156D–57B, 158B; *Leg.* 898E–99B; *Phd.* 113D; *Phdr.* 247B; *Ti.* 41E, 44E, 69C; Cic. *Div.* 1.91; *Leg.* 1.57, 2.14, 3.5; Plin. *HN* 30.5–6, 8, 11, 14; Sen. *Epist.* 90.6; Apul. *Apol.* 27, 90; *Orac. chal.* 120, 201 (Des Places); Porph. *De antr. nymph.* 31; Procl. *Inst.* 207–10; *Theol Plat.* 3.21; ps.-Dion. *CH* 177B: For Zalmoxis and Zoroaster, see *Orat.* 57. Defending himself against a charge of magic, Apuleius repudiated a whole coven of wizards:

"The famous Carmendas or Damigeron or their Moses or Jannes or Apollobex"—not Apollonius—"or Dardanus himself or any other celebrated magus since Zoroaster and Ostanes." Elsewhere he excused "Epimenides, Orpheus, Pythagoras and Ostanes," believing that they were defamed as sorcerers. In Pliny's narrative, the Persian Ostanes traveled to Greece with Xerxes, writing the first book on magic that still survived (in Pliny's day) and starting a magic craze in the West. Pliny identified Dardanus as Phoenician, and Apollobex as Coptic, linking both with Democritus. Pico may have confused Apollonius, the holy man of Tyana, with this Apollobex, and the ancient lawgiver named by Cicero was not Carmendas but Charondas—a Pythagorean, according to Seneca, bound by the silence of that sect. Homer "concealed" *mageia* and *goêteia* by never using those words. But the Poet got credit or blame not only for Odysseus and Circe (see *Orat.* 9) but also for Proteus, the Sirens, and calling up the dead, according to Pliny, who also cited Eudoxus and Hermippus on Zoroaster's chronology and the documentary remains of his religion. The astronomer Eudoxus worked in the fourth century BCE; Hermippus wrote biographies in the third. The "poetic theology" promised by Pico and mentioned by Gianfrancesco had Homeric roots in the *Cave of the Nymphs*, where Porphyry detected teachings of "ancient philosophers and theologians" in eleven lines of the *Odyssey*—a hermeneutic method validated by the Areopagite: see also *Orat.* 27, 52, and 55 on the ancient theology. Pico's *Apology* singled out William of Paris (or Auvergne, d. 1249) to corroborate the distinction between licit and illicit magic. But William, Alkindi, and Roger Bacon come up only once in the *Conclusions*, where a thesis identifies the "feeling in nature" described by them and the Magi with the vehicle of the soul (*ochêma*: see *Orat.* 2) studied by Proclus and others in the *Chaldaean Oracles*: the vehicle, a vital and physical force, accounted for magical phenomena naturally. Al-Kindi (d. 870), as much a Platonist in philosophy as an Aristotelian, is not mentioned in the *Conclusions* with the "Arabs who talk mainly like Peripatetics": see *Orat.* 47. Since he was best known for *De radiis*, however, a book on astrological physics, Pico could have seen him as a naturalist; likewise Roger Bacon (d. 1292), who was aggressively naturalist and opposed non-natural magic: Intro. at n. 93.

58. *Concl.* p. 57; App. 1.31.10; Plot. *Enn.* 4.4.40–45 (MacKenna); Porph. *Vita Plot.* 10 (MacKenna); Intro. at n. 93: Plotinus claims that "magic spells" (*goêteia*) work by "sympathy (*sumpatheia*). . . . The true magic (*mageia*) is internal to the All.... Here is the primal mage (*goês*) and sorcerer (*pharmakeus*) — discovered by men who thenceforth turn these same ensorcellations (*pharmakois*) and magic arts (*goêteumasi*) upon one another." The terminology blurs the distinction between *goêteia* and *mageia*, as in *Orat.* 56. But Plotinus supports Pico's main point, that magic is always already there in the physical world, supplying power that a magus cannot produce independently yet may exploit, as in a magical thesis of T2: "What a magus who is human does artificially, Nature has done naturally by making the human." But since Pico, unlike Plotinus, believed that Christian Kabbalah could sanctify magic (see *Orat.* 56), he did not need to confine it entirely to the world of nature — where magic was "Nature's minister" and nothing more. In *Orat.* 60, a more expansive *magia* acts *quasi ipsa sit Artifex* — "as if it were" the supreme Artificer and Workman of *Orat.* 4–5, who, as Nature's Creator, can look inside, see her wonders, and reveal them to human creatures. For Plotinus, however, magical power was a distraction just because it was merely natural. Nonetheless, although a sage is "immune from magic (*goêteusin*)" because "his reasoning part cannot be touched by it," his body and lower soul are left exposed. Accordingly, even Plotinus once defended himself with countermagic. He also attended a séance to call up his guardian angel, who turned out to be a god (*theos*). But on another occasion, explaining why he refused to go to a religious festival, he made the famous remark about who should come to whom — probably objecting to the rank of the deities involved but not calling them evil.

59. *Concl.* pp. 56–57; App. 1.31.5, 13; Pl. *Symp.* 188A–D, 202E–3D, 209E–10A, 211C; Arist. *Hist. an.* 504^{a}10–19; Varro *Ling.* 5.76; Verg. G. 1.2, 2.221; Hor. *Epod.* 2.9–10; Ov. *Met.* 14.623–97; cf. Columella *Rust.* 11.2.79; Plin. *HN* 11. 107, 20.1, 37.156; Apul. *Apol.* 40; Plot. 4.4.40–45, as in *Orat.* 59, esp. 40.9–19 (MacKenna); *Orac. chal.* 77, 206, 223 (Des Places), with Klutstein, *Orph.*, p. 118; Procl. *De sacr.* 148–49; Syn. *Insomn.* 2, 8, 14; *Calv.* 6; Psell. *In Orac.* 1133^a: On sympathy in Plotinus and on Nature see *Orat.* 59. "Love is given in Nature," Plotinus explained, remembering the magic

in the *Symposium* (*Orat.* 19, 27): "Qualities inducing love induce mutual approach, . . . an art of magical love-drawing (*dia goêteias technê*) whose practitioners apply by contact certain substances . . . so informed with love as to effect a bond of union, . . . as they might train two separate trees toward one another." With help from Vergil, Horace, and Ovid, Pico nuptialized the trees, while invoking a thesis from T2: "Doing magic is nothing but marrying the world." Horace has *maritare* where Vergil has *adiungere*, but Ovid gives the fullest description of elms supporting grape vines: when Vertumnus, a shapeshifting harvest god, courts Pomona, who presides over orchards, he carries a ladder to climb the elms and pick fruit, just as Pico imagined a magus ascending to the heavens in order to bring a harvest of cosmic power back down to earth, where natural forces operate in plants and animals. In the *Chaldean Oracles*, cosmic sympathies are energized by love spells called *iunges*, or jynxes

> that are thought from the Father as they themselves think,
> moved to thinking by his unutterable counsels.

These supernal ideas are also charms, spoken or sung, or even physical objects — a child's toy, a musical instrument, or a bird — that activate magic by motion or sound or both. The bird is either the wagtail (*Motacilla alba*) — small, sparrow-like, constantly wagging its long tail (hence the name) — or the wryneck (*Iynx torquilla*), a woodpecker that hisses while twisting its head. The toy is a perforated disk sliding on a loop of string to make noise. Commenting on *Oracle* 206, Michael Psellus describes a different device for adult rituals now called a 'bull-roarer' — a *rhombos* in Greek. Where the Greek *Oracles* have *iunges nooumenai*, the Quattrocento Latin verses have *intellectae motacillae* — birds mentioned by Varro and Pliny. Synesius, rejecting *goêteia*, echoes Plotinus in explaining that the "jynxes of the Magi . . . are spells cast as if signing to one another, and the sage, recognizing kinship among parts of the cosmos, draws the one through the other." Noting Pico's unusual choice of words — *intersparsas* reflecting *interseminatas* — *Bn*, p. 113, cites Apuleius; see also a thesis in the *Conclusions* on powers "separated seedwise" until unified by magic. Accused of sorcery, Apuleius defended his extensive knowledge of fish (see *Orat.* 35 on Tobias) as legitimate information — innocent data collected by a student of nature. But see *Orat.* 58 on magic and the Artificer.

60. *Concl.* pp. 57–58; App. 1.1.6, 9, 10; 31.15, 26; *Apol.* pp. 8, 60, 103, 165; Isa. 6:3, as in *Miss. rom., Ordo miss.* 31; Hab. 3:3; Rom. 1:20; 1 Cor. 13:13; Rev. 4:8; ps.-Dion. CH 209D, 212A–B; Peter Lombard, *Sent.* 1.3.1.1, 3: In *Orat.* 28, Pico quoted Paul's letter to the Romans for the fundamental theorem of natural theology, that God's "invisible things . . . are clearly seen, being understood by the things that are made" — or in Peter Lombard's formulation, that "the Creator could be known through created things." Since natural magic comes with natural philosophy, which supports natural theology, knowledge of licit magic confirms Christian faith, and magic rituals put faith into practice. Pico went even farther, however, hinting that Christian sacraments themselves are somehow (not naturally but supernaturally) magical. *Plena est omnis terra gloria eius* are Isaiah's words — but not the preceding phrase, *pleni sunt caeli*, which comes from the *Sanctus*, the eucharistic prayer in the Mass that repeats Isaiah's triple benediction, "holy, holy, holy." In this context, alluding to the blessed sacrament — bread and wine changed into Christ's body and blood — would have provoked the prince's critics, had they taken the hint: in the *Apology*, which includes this part of the *Oration*, Pico was forced to defend three theses about the Eucharist. The Areopagite also quoted the Seraphic blessing heard by Isaiah, explaining that what the Seraphs "complete" (*teleiousa*, see *Orat.* 11, 16, 27) is "knowledge of the most resplendent initiations." In this part of the speech, approaching the finale, earlier stages of discursive cognition in Pico's curriculum have passed. Fiery angels are the last creatures encountered before initiates vanish within the Creator. Just as natural philosophy comes before divine theology at lower levels (*Orat.* 16, 19, 22, 26, 28, 30, 34–35), rituals of "divine and helpful" magic now precede ecstatic Kabbalah and even loftier visions. Suited to such heights are the theological virtues — faith, hope, and love — that "abide" in Paul's Epistle to the Corinthians and surpass the cardinal virtues (wisdom, temperance, courage, and justice) practiced by good pagans, as in *Orat.* 30. Theology's supernatural powers are beyond the reach of purely natural magic — though not of a magic empowered by Kabbalah. Although no magic works without Kabbalah, according

to one thesis on that topic (see *Orat.* 56), another stipulates that "if the Kabbalah is pure and unmediated, something happens that no magic touches": magic needs Kabbalah more than Kabbalah needs magic. The power of S_1 — the "First Agent" of this same thesis — which reaches down through S_{10} to reinforce magic in the created universe, acts first in higher sefirotic realms, as in the angel magic of *Orat.* 8, 13–19, 24–25.

61. Hier. *Comm. Ezech.* 6.pr.1; Plaut. *Poen.* 1234; Ov. *Pont.* 4.10.25: Dogs are parts of the monster Scylla's body, rotting around her waist but still yelping — *latrare non cessant*, according to Jerome, like the heretics who opposed him. Jerome's metaphor was classical, and Pico unleashed the dogs again in *Orat.* 70; cf, *oblatratores* in *Orat.* 38.

62. *Concl.* pp. 24–28, 60–69; *App.* 1.21, 33; *Apol.* pp. 55, 57; Tert. *Marc.* 1.19.1: Since Pico's task was to convince "people who know nothing" about Kabbalah that, far from being useless nonsense, it could defend Christianity against Jewish slander — a goal restated and stressed by the *Apology* — he goes on through *Orat.* 68 to describe Kabbalah's divine and esoteric nature, to cite testimony supporting it, and to trace its ancient origins. See Intro. at nn. 100–111 on this relatively restrained presentation — compared to the 119 theses on Kabbalah in the *Conclusions*. Speaking positively of Christ, Tertullian used the rare *circumlator* to mean 'messenger' or 'transmitter,' but *Bn*, pp. 116–17, prefers a medieval sense of the word: 'illusionist' or 'faker.'

63. *Concl.* p. 68; *App.* 1.33.63; *Apol.* pp. 55–57; Ecclus. 24:24–33, 46:1; 4 Ezra 14:1–7, 21–26, 42–48; Matt. 7:6, 13:44–45; Rom. 3:2; 1 Cor. 2:6–7; 2 Cor. 3:6; Stat. *Theb.* 1.584–86; Hilar. *Tract. Ps.* 2.2; Orig. *Comm. Rom.* 2.14.1–12, 5.2.12, 5.5; *Comm. Matt.* 10.6–8; *Comm. Jo.* 5.4, 6.2; Abulafia, *Secr.*, fol. 449^v: The five books of the Law (Torah) written down by Moses were made public, but the Law's interpretation and its secrets — eventually transmitted as Talmud, Midrash, and Kabbalah — were propagated orally. God told the priest Ezra in a vision that when he revealed the Law to Moses, he also gave this order: "These words you shall make public and these you shall conceal." Moses passed the secrets on through Joshua — called *Jesus Nave* (cf. *nabi*, 'prophet') in Ecclesiasticus — under a rule of silence that allowed access to the Law needed for everyday life. Later, at the time of Ezra's vision, after the Temple and the written Torah

had been destroyed, God gave the priest instructions like those he had given to Moses: Ezra was to appoint five scribes to write new books, "making some public, giving some to the wise for concealment." The five (not seventy) scribes produced ninety-four books, and God again told Ezra to make some of them public — the twenty-four parts of the Hebrew Bible — but not the other seventy: see *Orat.* 66. (In the Vulgate, 4 Esdras, *nongenti quattuor*, or 904, is a mistake for *nonaginta quattuor*, 94.) In the passage from Ezra's vision quoted in *Orat.* 67, everything is written yet still divided into public and secret teachings, the latter thought by Pico to be books of Kabbalah. Describing "certain more secret mysteries of the Law from hidden sources," Hilary implied that Moses left the secrets unwritten but "made them known separately to the seventy elders." Commenting on Romans 3:2 and the "oracles" entrusted to Jews, Origen made a distinction between spoken secrets (*eloquia* in Pico's *Apology*) and what had been written down. Commenting on Matthew's parable of hidden treasure, Origen explained that Scripture contains "both the manifest and the hidden." A wise man hides his treasure, "thinking it not without danger to reveal to everybody the secret meanings," and then he "goes away, . . . receiving from the people of God the oracles of God with which the Jews were first entrusted." Origen turned next to the parable of the pearl and the Savior's warning not to throw such treasures to pigs, a statement seen by Pico as a divine command to keep the holiest things secret. In a Kabbalist thesis, he also claimed that Maimonides "embraces mysteries of Kabbalah through hidden interpretations of deep meaning while seeming through the outer bark of words to proceed philosophically." For Wisdom (*S*2) as an arcane power, see *Orat.* 4, also Intro. at nn. 63, 104–110 on secrecy.

64. B, sig. RRii^v; Pl. *Ep.* 2.312D–E; Gell. *NA* 20.5; Plut. *De Is. et Os.* 354C; Diog. Laert. 8.42; Iambl. *VP* 28.146, 34.245–46; Orig. *Comm. Matt.* 14.11–12; *Cels.* 6.6; Syn. *Insomn.* pr.; ps.-Dion. *EH* 376B–C: Pythagoras forbade his daughter Damo to give his "notes" (*hupomnêmata*) to any one "outside the house." In Pico's view, a rule that Plato gave to his successors preserved this Pythagorean silence along with the secrecy of ancient Egypt, thus keeping the most important teachings hidden by speaking "in enigmas." Aristotle divided his writings, according to Gel-

lius, into *exoterika* for rhetorical and political use and *akroatika* for students admitted to the "deeper and subtler philosophy" — the metaphysical theology that relied on dialectic and natural science. When Aristotle eventually released the *akroatika*, Alexander of Macedon — once a student of those mysteries — got this answer when he complained: "Know that those books, with their secrets not then hidden, are published and not published," the master explained, "since they will be intelligible only to those who have heard us." According to Origen, Jesus too conveyed secrets to his disciples, leading the Evangelists to state them in parables with "secret and mystical import." Discussing divinization, the Areopagite called it God's gift given through Scripture, "the oracles transmitted by our divine initiators": this apostolic "knowledge (*gnôsis*) is not for everyone" and must only be spoken, not written, "from mind to mind, . . . by means of speech — even the bodily, yet more immaterial just the same, as being outside of writing." The Greek words — discussed by *Bn*, p. 165 — are not printed in the 1496 text, and Pico does not translate them all.

65. *Apol.* pp. 52–54; Num. 11:16–17; 1 Ezr. 3–4, 7 (Vulg.); 4 Ezr. 14:21–26 (Charlesworth); Hilar. *Tract. Ps.* 2.2; *b. Sanh.* 2ª, 3ᵇ; *Midr. Num.* 13:20, 15:19–20; *Zohar* II, 6ª, 86ᵇ, III, 161ᵇ, 260ᵇ; Abulafia, *Ve-zot*, fol. 122ʳ: Here Pico explains why his own access to Kabbalah was mainly through *written* texts, even though the original tradition was *oral*. The word קבלה can mean 'reception' of any kind, but Abraham Abulafia (see Intro. at nn. 73–74, 100–101, 109) used it for "secrets of the Law received from the mouth of one person to the mouth of another," adding that "this way of receiving does not exist in other nations." Zerubbabel, a Jew who governed Judah for Persia, began to rebuild the Temple in the early sixth century after Cyrus released the Jews from Babylon: this was the setting for biblical and extra-biblical stories of the priest Esdras (Ezra) and the preservation and transmission of the Law. However, neither the Vulgate nor the pseudepigrapha mentions "correcting" the Law — perhaps marking (pointing) the unvocalized text to clarify its meaning, like the Masoretes, whose work Pico could have learned about from Flavius. In Pico's remark about seventy sages, the number matches only one detail in the chapter from 4 Ezra cited in *Orat.* 67 (see also *Orat.* 64): seventy newer

books were kept secret when twenty-four older items of an original ninety-four were made public, and Hilary reported that one secret was made known to each of seventy ancients. The number seventy can be found in or derived from any number of biblical texts, but, since the topic is Kabbalah, Numbers 11 stands out as a channel to Midrash and the *Zohar*. On the march away from Sinai, God directed Moses to appoint helpers to share his burden of revelation, ordering him to "gather unto me seventy men of the ancients of Israel . . . and bring them to the door of the Tabernacle . . . that I may come down and speak. . . . And the Lord came down in a cloud and spoke to him, taking away of the spirit that was in Moses and giving to the seventy men, . . . and they prophesied." Citing this passage, the *Zohar* bewails "words of the Torah that are concealed" because of Rabbi Shim'on ben Yohai's ascent to heaven—that rabbi being the *Zohar's* legendary author. Another rabbi responds by way of the Numbers text, comparing Rabbi Shim'on to Moses: "*He held back some of the spirit that was upon him and put it upon the seventy men, the elders*—like a lamp from which many lamps are lit." Like a new Moses, the great Kabbalist passed his illumination on, undiminished, to many others. The Talmud defined its supreme court, the Great Sanhedrin, as seventy-one members, though the *Zohar* has seventy or seventy-two—probably not by mistake. Pico will also have been thinking of the seventy or seventy-two translators of the Septuagint: see *Orat.* 54 and Intro. at nn. 108–11 on the number seventy-two.

66. *Concl.* pp. 60–61; *App.* 1.33.1–2; 4 Ezra 14:44–48 (Charlesworth): Ezra's three channels, as Pico navigates them, are secrets of theology, metaphysics, and natural philosophy. The first two conclusions of his final seventy-two divide all of Kabbalah in some such schematic way, including a "threefold particularizing philosophy about divine, middle and sensible natures." The outline is vague, however. Having named three topics, did Pico connect them with the three Latin books commissioned by Sixtus IV (1471–84)? From the current evidence, one cannot say. But Sixtus had been pope for about ten years when Flavius Mithridates, called Guglielmo Raimondo Moncada after conversion, came to Rome from Sicily and worked as a translator for Cardinal Giovanni Battista Cibò, who followed Sixtus as Innocent VIII (1484–92). As pope, Inno-

cent condemned thirteen of Pico's theses, including one about Kabbalah. As a cardinal he had already broken with Moncada (before he became Flavius): dislike for the obstreperous convert may have helped sour the pope-to-be on Pico, who praised Flavius in a draft of the *Oration* (F 46) but not in the version published in B. See Intro. at nn. 82, 98, 106, and *Orat.* 32 on Flavius and Sixtus.

67. *Apol.* pp. 7, 52–53, 58; Exod. 34:28; Deut. 29:5; Matt. 4:2; Ter. *An.* 161, 676; ps.-Quint. *Decl.* 12.6; *b. Sotah* 22[b]; *b. 'Abod. Zar.* 19[b]; *Pirkei Avot* 5:22; Aug. *Conf.* 7.13, 26; 8.3; *Ver. rel.* 2–3; *Civ.* 8.12, 9.1, as in *Orat.* 50; *Zohar* I, 4[a]; Flavius, *Sermo*, p. 89: Ancient Talmudic rules set minimum ages for various purposes. In the *Ethics of the Fathers*, forty is the age "for understanding," and Pico's translator, Flavius, applied "forty for understanding" to Kabbalah. Moses fasted at Sinai for forty days and wandered in the wilderness for forty years—preparing for enlightenment. Jesus also fasted for forty days. As the *Zohar* opens, Rabbi H̲iyya must fast twice as long before seeing a vision of Rabbi Shim'on (see *Orat.* 66) studying in the Celestial Academy. Pico's *Apology* confirms the high cost of his books about Kabbalah—many translated into Latin by Flavius, who sometimes added Trinitarian and Christological clues to the originals. Some Christian doctrines on Pico's list—the Trinity, the Incarnation, Jesus as a divine Messiah—divided Christians from Jews, but others connected them: atonement, orders of angels, and a heavenly Jerusalem; see *Orat.* 27. Antonio Cronico, or Vinciguerra, was a powerful Venetian, described by the *Apology* as an authority on magic: for the incident with Dattilo at his house and Pico's Trinitarian Kabbalah, see Intro. at n. 110. 'Hand and foot' would render *pedibus manibusque* more literally than 'top to toe': see *Bn*, pp. 130–32, citing Terence for the Latin idiom.

68. *Concl.* pp. 54–69; App. 1.30–33; *Apol.* 52–54; Iambl. *VP* 23.105, 28.145–47: Theses on Zoroaster, the *Chaldean Oracles*, and the *Orphic Hymns* come before Kabbalah in the eighth and tenth parts of *T2*, with propositions on magic in between. Why the order in the speech is different is unclear, though Pico says in *Orat.* 70 that his analysis of the *Hymns* would demonstrate the importance of his project to his critics—a good point to emphasize when closing a speech. The *Oracles* were "mutilated" in Greek because only fragments survived (see *Orat.* 33), though Pico

NOTES TO THE TRANSLATIONS ·

claimed to have seen better versions in 'Chaldean' — most likely Aramaic or Syriac, perhaps concocted by Flavius. Proclus and other Platonists after Porphyry revered the *Oracles*. Iamblichus said that the *Hymns* were the basis for the theological arithmetic of Pythagoras, but the *Oration* — unlike the *Apology* — says nothing about the numerology in Kabbalah or, in fact, about any of its distinctive teachings, even sefirotic theosophy: see Intro. at nn. 106–9, 112–13 for this material.

69. Plaut. *Poen.* 1234; Cic. *Sen.* 23; *Tusc.* 4.44, 5.47; Gell. *NA* 12.6.1: Pico now charms his critics — who will not have missed the sarcastic (and Ciceronian) "princes among philosophers" — by claiming sole credit for unveiling three types of mystery, Chaldaean, Orphic, and Kabbalist, and for succeeding at this original task despite envious opposition, as in *Orat.* 62. For criticisms about quantity, see *Orat.* 39–40, 44–45, 71. According to Gellius, *scirpi* or *scyrpi* are *aenigmata*, though not in this case, as *Bn*, pp. 134–35 points out. The dogs that barked earlier in *Orat.* 62 were Jerome's, but here the words are a near quotation from the *Poenulus: Etiam me meae latrant canes?*

70. Cic. *Ver.* 2.2.24; Suet. *Prat.* 176.83–84; Sen. *Ep.* 71.4; Aug. *Solil.* 1.4.9: On concord between Plato and Aristotle, see *Orat.* 53 and Intro. at nn. 11, 86–91.

71. Stat. *Theb.* 3.610.

Bibliography

❧❦❧

EDITIONS OF GIOVANNI PICO CITED

Conclusiones DCCCC publice disputandae. Rome: Eucharius Silber, December 7, 1486. ISTC ip00639200.

Conclusiones DCCCC publice disputandae. [Ingolstadt: Printer of Lescherius, 'Rhetorica' (Bartholomeus Golsch?), about 1487]. ISTC ip00639300.

Apologia conclusionum suarum. Naples: Francesco del Tuppo, after May 31, 1487. ISTC ip00635000.

Heptaplus de septiformi sex dierum Geneseos enarratione ad Laurentium Medicem. Edited by Roberto Salviati. Florence: Bartolomeo de' Libri, not after November 2, 1489. ISTC ip00641000.

Commentationes Ioannis Pici Mirandulae in hoc volumine contenta, quibus anteponitur vita per Iohannem Franciscum illustris principis Galeotti Pici filium conscripta . . . Bologna: Benedictus Hectoris, 1496. ISTC ip00632000. Reprinted in 1498. ISTC ip00633000. Works of Giovanni Pico, including *Orat.*, edited by Gianfrancesco Pico, with his *Life.*

Opera Joannis Pici Mirandulae Comitis Concordiae litterarum principis novissime accurate revisa (addito generali super omnibus memoratu dignis regesto), quarumcunque facultatum professoribus tam iucunda quam proficua. Strasbourg: Johann Prüs, 1504.

De hominis dignitate, Heptaplus, De ente et uno e scritti vari. Edited by Eugenio Garin. Florence: Valecchi, 1942. Latin text with an Italian translation.

Disputationes adversus astrologiam divinatricem. Edited by Eugenio Garin. 2 vols. Florence: Vallechi, 1946–52. Latin text with an Italian translation.

Expositiones in Psalmos. Edited by Antonino Raspanti. Translated by Antonino and Giacomo Raspanti. Florence: Olschki, 1997. Latin text with an Italian translation.

Farmer, Stephen Allen. *Syncretism in the West: Pico's 900 Theses (1486): The Evolution of Traditional Religious and Philosophical Systems.* Tempe: MRTS, 1998. With an edition and translation of the *Conclusiones.*

Kommentar zu einem Lied der Liebe, italienisch-deutsch. Edited and translated by Thorsten Bürklin. Hamburg: Meiner, 2001. Pico's commentary on a love poem by Girolamo Benivieni.

Discorso sulla dignità dell'uomo. Edited and translated by Francesco Bausi. 2nd ed. Parma: Guanda, 2007.

Dell'Ente e dell'uno con le obiezioni di Giovanni Pico della Mirandola. Edited and translated by Franco Bacchelli and Raphael Ebgi. Milan: Bompiani, 2010. Edition with Italian translation of *De ente et uno.*

L'Autodifesa di Pico di fronte al tribunale dell'Inquisizione. Edited by Paolo Fornaciari. Florence: Galluzzo, 2010. Edition of the Latin text of the *Apologia* with Italian translation.

Oration on the Dignity of Man: A New Translation and Commentary. Edited and translated by Francesco Borghesi, Michael Papio, and Massimo Riva. Cambridge: Cambridge University Press, 2012.

Lettere: Edizione critica. Edited by Francesco Borghesi. Florence: Olschki, 2018.

EDITIONS OF GIANFRANCESCO PICO CITED

Commentationes Ioannis Pici Mirandulae in hoc volumine contenta, quibus anteponitur vita per Iohannem Franciscum illustris principis Galeotti Pici filium conscripta . . . Bologna: Benedictus Hectoris, 1496. ISTC ip00632000. Reprinted in 1498. ISTC ip00633000. Works of Giovanni Pico edited by Gianfrancesco Pico, with his *Life* of his uncle.

Liber de imaginatione. Venice: Aldus, 1501.

De rerum praenotione libri novem pro veritate religionis contra superstitiosas vanitates. Strasbourg: Knobloch, 1507.

Liber de veris calamitatum causis nostrorum temporum ad Leonem X Pontificem Maximum. Mirandola: Mazochius, 1519.

Examen vanitatis doctrinae gentium et veritatis Christianae disciplinae distinctum in libros sex. Mirandola: Mazochius, 1520.

Vita R.P. fratris Hieronymi Savonarolae Ferrariensis ordinis praedicatorum. Paris: Billaine, 1674.

Compendio delle cose mirabili della venerabile serva di Dio, Catterina da Raconisio. Bologna, ca. 1681.

Giovanni Pico della Mirandola: His Life by His Nephew Giovanni Francesco Pico, . . . translated from the Latin by Sir Thomas More. London: David Nutt, 1890.

Life of Pico. Translated by Thomas More. In *The Complete Works of St. Thomas More*, 1: *English Poems, Life of Pico, The Last Things*, edited by A. S. G. Edwards, Katherine Gardner Rodgers, and Clarence H. Miller. New Haven: Yale University Press, 1997. Latin text of Gianfrancesco's *Life* with More's translation.

Vita Hieronymi Savonarolae. Edited by Elisabetta Schisto. Florence: Olschki, 1999.

SECONDARY LITERATURE

Allen, Michael J. B. "The Birth Day of Venus: Pico as Platonic Exegete in the *Commento* and the *Heptaplus*." In *Pico della Mirandola: New Essays*, edited by Michael Dougherty, 81–117. Cambridge: Cambridge University Press, 2008.

——. "The Second Ficino-Pico Controversy: Parmenidean Poetry, Eristic and the One." In Allen, *Plato's Third Eye: Studies in Marsilio Ficino's Metaphysics and Its Sources*, 417–55. Aldershot: Variorum, 1995.

Anagnine, Eugenio. *Giovanni Pico della Mirandola: Sincretismo religioso-filosofico*. Bari: Laterza, 1937.

Azzolini, Monica. *The Duke and the Stars: Astrology and Politics in Renaissance Milan*. Cambridge, MA: Harvard University Press, 2013.

Bacchelli, Franco. "Giovanni Pico, conte di Concordia e Mirandola." *Dizionario biografico degli italiani* (treccani.it, 2015).

——. *Giovanni Pico e Pier Leone da Spoleto: Tra filosofia dell'amore e tradizione cabalistica*. Florence: Olschki, 2001.

——. "Pico della Mirandola traduttore di Ibn Tufayl." *Giornale critico della filosofia italiana* 72 (1993): 1–25.

Bausi, Francesco. *Nec rhetor neque philosophus: Fonti, lingua e stile nelle prime opere latine di Giovanni Pico della Mirandola, 1484–87*. Florence: Olschki, 1996.

Black, Crofton. *Pico's* Heptaplus *and Biblical Hermeneutics*. Leiden: Brill, 2006.

Bori, Pier Cesare, and Saverio Marchignoli. *Pluralità delle vie: Alle origini del Discorso sulla dignità umana di Pico della Mirandola*. Milan: Feltrinelli, 2000.

Breen, Quirinus. "Giovanni Pico della Mirandola on the Conflict of Philosophy and Rhetoric." *Journal of the History of Ideas* 13 (1952): 384–426.

Brucker, Jacob. *Historia critica philosophiae a mundi incunabulis ad nostram usque aetatem deducta*. Leipzig: Breitkopf, 1742–44.

Busi, Giulio. "'Who Does Not Wonder at this Chameleon': The Kabbalistic Library of Giovanni Pico della Mirandola." In *Hebrew to Latin, Latin to Hebrew: The Mirroring of Two Cultures in the Age of Humanism: Colloquium Held at the Warburg Instituite, London, October 18–19, 2004*, edited by Giulio Busi, 167–96. Berlin: Institut für Judaistik, 2006.

Busi, Giulio, and Raphael Ebgi. *Giovanni Pico della Mirandola: Mito, Magia, Qabbalah*. Torino: Einaudi, 2014.

Campanini, Saverio. "Guglielmo Raimondo Moncada (*alias* Flavio Mitridate), tradutorre di opere cabbalistiche." In *Guglielmo Raimondo Moncada alias Flavio Mitridat*, edited by Perani and Pepi, *Guglielmo Raimondo Moncada alias Flavio Mitridate*, 49–88.

Copenhaver, Brian. *The Book of Magic: From Antiquity to the Enlightenment*. London: Penguin, 2015.

——, ed. *Hermetica: The Greek Corpus Hermeticum and the Latin Asclepius in a New English Translation, with Notes and Introduction*. Cambridge: Cambridge University Press, 1992.

——. *Magic and the Dignity of Man: Pico della Mirandola and His Oration in Modern Memory*. Cambridge, MA: Harvard University Press, 2019.

——. *Magic in Western Culture from Antiquity to the Enlightenment*. Cambridge: Cambridge University Press, 2015.

——. "Number, Shape, and Meaning in Pico's Christian Cabala: The Upright *Tsade*, The Closed *Mem*, and the Gaping Jaws of *Azazel*." In *Natural Particulars: Nature and the Disciplines in Renaissance Europe*, edited by Anthony Grafton and Nancy Siraisi, 25–76. Cambridge, MA: MIT Press, 1999.

——. "Studied as an Oration: Readers of Pico's Letters, Ancient and Modern." In *Laus platonici philosophi: Marsilio Ficino and His Influence*, edited by Stephen Clucas, Peter J. Forshaw, and Valery Rees, 151–98. Leiden: E. J. Brill, 2011.

Copenhaver, Brian, and Daniel Kokin. "Egidio da Viterbo's Book on Hebrew Letters: Christian Kabbalah in Papal Rome." *Renaissance Quarterly* 67 (2014): 1–42.

Craven, William. *Giovanni Pico Della Mirandola, Symbol of His Age: Modern Interpretations of a Renaissance Philosopher*. Geneva: Droz, 1981.

Davidson, Herbert. *Alfarabi, Avicenna and Averroes on the Intellect: Their Cosmologies, Theories of the Active Intellect and Theories of the Human Intellect*. Oxford: Oxford University Press, 1992.

Dougherty, Michael, ed. *Pico della Mirandola: New Essays*. Cambridge: Cambridge University Press, 2008.

Dulles, Avery. *Princeps Concordiae: Pico della Mirandola and the Scholastic Tradition: The Harvard Phi Beta Kappa Prize Essay for 1940*. Cambridge, MA: Harvard University Press, 1941.

Edelheit, Amos. *Ficino, Pico and Savonarola: The Evolution of Humanist Theology, 1461/2–1498*. Leiden: Brill, 2008.

Garfagnini, Giancarlo, ed. *Giovanni Pico della Mirandola: Convegno internazionale di studi nel cinquecentesimo anniversario della morte (1494–1994), Mirandola, 4–8 ottobre 1994*. 2 vols. Florence: Olschki, 1997.

Garin, Eugenio. *Giovanni Pico della Mirandola: Vita e dottrina*. Florence: Le Monnier, 1937.

——. "Le Interpretazioni del pensiero di Giovanni Pico." In *L'Opera e il pensiero di Giovanni Pico*, 1: 3–33.

Grafton, Anthony. "Giovanni Pico della Mirandola: Trials and Triumphs of an Omnivore." In *Commerce with the Classics: Ancient Books and Renaissance Readers*, 115–32. Ann Arbor: University of Michigan Press, 1997.

Grendler, Paul. *The Universities of the Italian Renaissance*. Baltimore: Johns Hopkins University Press, 2002.

Idel, Moshe. *Kabbalah in Italy, 1280–1510: A Survey*. New Haven: Yale University Press, 2011.

——. "The Kabbalistic Backgrounds of the 'Son of God' in Giovanni Pico della Mirandola's Thought." In Lelli, *Giovanni Pico e la cabbalà*, 19–45.

Kibre, Pearl. *The Library of Pico della Mirandola*. New York: AMS Press, 1966.

Kristeller, Paul Oskar. *Eight Philosophers of the Italian Renaissance*. Stanford: Stanford University Press, 1964.

———. "Giovanni Pico della Mirandola and His Sources." In *L'Opera e il pensiero di Giovanni Pico*, 1: 35–142.

Lelli, Fabrizio, ed. *Giovanni Pico e la cabbalà*. Florence: Olschki, 2014.

L'Opera e il pensiero di Giovanni Pico della Mirandola nella storia dell'umanesimo. Convegno internazionale (Mirandola: 15–18 settembre 1963). 2 vols. Florence: Istituto Nazionale di Studi sul Rinascimento, 1965.

Manetti, Giannozzo. *On Human Worth and Excellence*. Edited and translated by Brian Copenhaver. Cambridge, MA: Harvard University Press, 2019.

Martines, Lauro. *Scourge and Fire: Savonarola and Renaissance Florence*. London: Jonathan Cape, 2006.

Perani, Mauro, and Luciana Pepi, eds. *Guglielmo Raimondo Moncada alias Flavio Mitridate: Un ebreo converso siciliano; Atti del Convegno Internazionale, Caltabelotta (Agrigento), 23–24 ottobre 2004*. Palermo: Officina di Studi Medievali, 2008.

Quaquarelli, Leonardo, and Zita Zanardi. *Pichiana: Bibliografia delle edizioni e degli studi*. Florence: Olschki, 2005.

Scapparone, Elisabetta. "Pico della Mirandola, Gianfrancesco." *Dizionario biographico degli italiani* (treccani.it, 2015).

Schmitt, Charles. *Gianfrancesco Pico della Mirandola (1469–1533) and His Critique of Aristotle*. The Hague: Nijhoff, 1967.

Scholem, Gershom. *Kabbalah*. Jerusalem: Keter, 1974.

———. *On the Mystical Shape of the Godhead*. Translated by J. Neugroschel. Edited by J. Chipman. New York: Schocken, 1991.

Weinstein, Donald. *Savonarola and Florence: Prophecy and Patriotism in the Renaissance*. Princeton: Princeton University Press, 1970.

Wirszubski, Chaim. "Giovanni Pico's Book of Job." *Journal of the Warburg and Courtauld Institutes* 32 (1967): 171–99.

———. *Pico della Mirandola's Encounter with Jewish Mysticism*. Cambridge, MA: Harvard University Press, 1989.

Index

Julius Caesar, Gaius, *Civil War*,
 281n42
Julius II (pope), xxxviii
Juno/Hera, 89, 259–60n11, 267n23
Jupiter, 149, 260n11
Just, 164
Justice, 276n33

Kaaba, 277n33
Kabbalah, viii–x, xxiv, xxx, xxxv,
 xl, xli, xliii, xliv, xlv, xlvi, xlvii,
 l, li, lvii, lix, lx, lxi, lxii, lxiii,
 lxiv, lxv, lxvi, lxvii, lxix, lxxi,
 lxxii, lxxiii, 15, 133, 135, 143, 147,
 150, 160, 161, 162, 163, 164, 165,
 166, 167, 170, 232n10, 239n39,
 242n46, 246n55, 254n4, 257n8,
 259n11, 261n12, 262–63nn15–16,
 264–65nn18–19, 267n24, 269–
 71nn25–27, 273n29, 277–
 78nn33–34, 293–94n60,
 294nn62–63, 295n63, 296–
 99nn65–68
Kabbalist(s), viii, xxxv, xlv, liii, lx,
 lxi, lxvii, lxix, lxxi, 107, 135, 151,
 159, 161, 162, 163, 164, 165, 167,
 260n12, 263–64nn16–17, 271n27,
 272n29, 275n32, 285nn50–51,
 288n55, 297n65, 299n69
Kabbalist: teachings, lxviii, 145,
 153, 266n19, 295n63; texts,
 253n2
Kadesh (in Egypt), 277n33
Kant, Immanuel, xviii, xxxvi,
 xxxix, xli, xlii; post-Kantian,
 xviii
Kedar, xxxii, 77, 251n74

King (title), 47
Kingdom, 151, 166
King of Glory, 97, 267–68n24
Knowledge, lxx
Koran, xliii, 29, 257n8, 276n33
Kristeller, Paul Oskar, xviii

Lactantius (Lucius Caelius Firmi-
 anus), 253n4, 284n48; *Divine
 Institutes*, 237n31, 283n48; *On the
 Wrath of God*, 253n4
Lady Philosophy, 244n52
Last Plant, 152
Latin: language, ix, xxv, xxvi, xxxii,
 xxxv, lxiv, 27, 33, 47, 51, 59, 135,
 171, 237n36, 239n39; letters,
 lxvii; texts, xxiv, xxxiii, xxxiv,
 xxxix, xlii, 15, 27, 41, 146, 171,
 235n23, 287n54, 297n66; think-
 ers, li, lv, 41, 145; translations,
 xlv, lix, lxii, 31, 232n9, 235n23,
 236n26, 247n60, 263n16,
 283n47, 285n51, 288n54, 298n67
Latinity, xxvii, 39, 238n36
Latinizing, xxiv
Latins, 119, 121, 144, 267n23
Law, the, xxxix, xl, lix, lxix, lxx,
 25, 131, 133, 161, 166, 167, 254n4,
 294–95n63, 296n65
Leonardo da Vinci, xi
Leo X (pope), ix, xxxviii
Levites, 99, 269n25
Liber de radicibus, 270n27
Life of Aristotle, 281n45, 286n52
Light, 75
Lion, 263n16
Living, the, xlix

Proclus (*continued*)
  On Sacrifice, 274n31, 291n59; *Platonic Theology*, lxxiii, 148, 262–63nn15–16, 269n26, 274n31, 283n47, 287n54, 289n57
Promised Land, xxxii, 269n25
Propertius, Sextus, 279n35, 281n43
Proteus, xlii, xliv, 85, 257n8, 290n57; Old Man of the Sea, xliii
Protogonus, 161
Prüs, Johann, xxxvi, xxxviii
Psalter, 245n54
Psellus, Michael, 292n59; *Expositio brevis*, 253n4; *In Oracula chaldaica*, 291n59
Ptolemy, 31
Puglia, 231n5
Purgatory, xix, xxxii, 69, 73, 249n67, 249n69, 250n71
Pythagoras, xliv, l, 15, 35, 103, 121, 123, 125, 131, 135, 137, 150, 163, 237n30, 243n46, 257n8, 273–74nn30–31, 283n47, 285n51, 287n54, 289–90nn56–57, 295n64, 299n68
Pythagorean/Pythagoreans, xliii, liii, lx, lxvi, lxviii, 85, 87, 97, 127, 161, 169, 234n20, 254n4, 285n51, 290n57, 295n64

Quintilian (Marcus Fabius Quintilianus), 237n36, 241n43; *Training in Oratory*, 237n30, 237–38n36, 240n43, 281n42, 281n45
Quintilian, pseudo, *Declamations*, 298n67

Raphael, xxi, xlvii, 107, 275n32, 278n34; God's healing, 278n34
Recanati, Menahem, lx; *Commentary on the Torah*, lxii, 267n24, 275–77nn32–34
Redeemer, 164
Reformation, the, xiv
Reformers, xxxvii
Reggio, 230n5
Remaining, lxxii, 264n18
Reuchlin, Johann, lxix; *Art of Kabbalah*, ix
Reversion, lxxii, 264n18
Rhea, 161
Rigg, James, lxxvi n19
Right Reason, 258n9
Rinuccini, Alamanno, 232n9
Ritter, August, lxxiv n2
Roman: history, 39, 238n37; letters, xxxv, 172
Rome/Roman/Romans, xxi, xxii, xxiii, xxv, xxvii, xxxvii, xxxix, l, lxiv, lxvii, 15, 17, 37, 47, 61, 65, 145, 167, 172, 232nn10–11, 233n14, 238–39n39, 241n43, 244n52, 266n21, 278n34, 279n36, 285n50, 287n54, 297n66
Rucellai, Camilla, 249n70
Rule of St. Benedict, 281n42

Sabbath, 164, 166
Sabellians, 162
Sallust (Gaius Sallustius Crispus), 39, 237n36
Sallust, pseudo, *Invective against Cicero*, 237n36

Publication of this volume has been made possible by

The Myron and Sheila Gilmore Publication Fund at I Tatti
The Robert Lehman Endowment Fund
The Jean-François Malle Scholarly Programs and Publications Fund
The Andrew W. Mellon Scholarly Publications Fund
The Craig and Barbara Smyth Fund
for Scholarly Programs and Publications
The Lila Wallace–Reader's Digest Endowment Fund
The Malcolm Wiener Fund for Scholarly Programs and Publications